The
AMERICANS
in their Moral, Social, and Political Relations

SERIES IN AMERICAN STUDIES

Editor-in-Chief: Joseph J. Kwiat
PROGRAM IN AMERICAN STUDIES
UNIVERSITY OF MINNESOTA

The

AMERICANS

in their

Moral, Social, and Political

Relations

By Francis J. Grund

TWO VOLUMES IN ONE

With a New Introduction by
ROBERT F. BERKHOFER, JR.

DEPARTMENT OF HISTORY
UNIVERSITY OF MINNESOTA

Johnson Reprint Corporation

New York and London

1968

The edition reproduced here was originally
published in 1837

INTRODUCTION

The avowed purpose of Francis Joseph Grund's *The Americans, in Their Moral, Social, and Political Relations*, published in London and New York in 1837, was to correct the incomplete, and often jaundiced, impressions of American society and politics conveyed by the many travel accounts then in print. Grund hoped particularly to offset in English minds the many prejudicial tourist observations written by their fellow countrymen. More specifically, he aimed to controvert the views of Frances Trollope, Basil Hall, and Thomas Hamilton. The "grotesque sketches" of Mrs. Trollope's *Domestic Manners of the Americans* (1832) he brushed aside as the animadversions of a woman who never saw or traveled among the better parts of American society and hence never had a chance to observe refined people. Far more serious to Grund were the aspersions of Basil Hall's *Travels in North America in the Years 1827–'28* (1829), and Captain Thomas Hamilton's *Men and Manners in America* (1833). Neither author was particularly unfair to American life in the manner of Mrs. Trollope, but for that reason their work needed refutation.

Hall and Hamilton viewed the United States with "Tory condescension," as Allan Nevins terms it, because they, like so many other English travelers of the period, used their American observations to argue against the liberal political and social reforms urged at home. As Hamilton admitted candidly in his preface:

But when I found the institutions and experience of

the United States deliberately quoted in the reformed Parliament, as affording safe precedent for
British legislation, and learned that the drivelers who
uttered such nonsense, instead of encountering merited derision, were listened to with patience and approbation, by men as ignorant as themselves, I
certainly did feel that another work on America was
yet wanted, and at once determined to undertake a
task which inferior considerations would probably
have induced one to decline.

Whether his actual motives or even his observations
really support this statement is entirely beside the
point. Englishmen of all shades of political opinion
looked upon Jacksonian United States as an example
of democracy in action, and to be judged accordingly.
Would the political and social customs of Americans
become those of all peoples, especially Englishmen?
Ought the future of England and the world to be the
same as the United States of the 1830's? These two
questions were the battleground of ideology in contemporary travel accounts, including the great work of
de Tocqueville. Furthermore, these two questions were
inseparably fused in the minds of both those who
praised and those who condemned American society
in the age of Jackson. Actual observation was inevitably shaped and subordinated to the ultimate moral
judgments upon the question of the desirability of
democracy and the implications of it.

Grund's book forms no exception to the battle of
ideology as manifested in the observations on American character and institutions. Although born near
Vienna in 1798 and educated there, Grund was a committed democrat after ten years residence in the
United States. Other authors, native-born and foreign,

had praised American customs and activities, but none had been so thoroughgoing in their compliments as this German converted to Americanism. He believed American ideals and practices ought to be and were to be the ideals and practices of all peoples.

History proved to him what was to be as well as what had been, and his view of history clearly reveals his commitments. Although the discovery of America coincided with the birth of liberal ideals in Europe, the Old World, even England, had not actualized the dreams of democrats as had the United States.

> The seed of liberty found in Europe no soil favorable to its germination; but it flourished luxuriantly in America; and has since so multiplied that there is no fear of its ever becoming extinct. The United States have assumed a rank amongst the most powerful nations on the globe; but their strength lies in the moral justice of their government. America possesses not only the elements of power, but her onward march is hailed by the sympathies of increasing civilization. Her cause is adopted by the people of all countries; and instead of exciting jealousies, her progress is identified with the success of liberal principles throughout the world. America has become the representative of freedom, and as such is destined to act as the animating principle on the rest of mankind.

If America was the forerunner of what must occur elsewhere, then "all she has done to this moment is but a feeble prelude to the gigantic part which she is destined to perform in the universal drama of the world." The critics of America worried that Grund might be right and sought to find the defects in the United States that would prove the future he envisaged was impossible.

With this image of and faith in America, Grund's job becomes one of justifying the United States against those who sought to delay the "animating principles" of American liberty and justice by finding Jacksonian America defective in ideals or in practice of those ideals. His book therefore is a panegyric on all aspects of American society of his time. His outright criticisms are few, and they concern such seemingly minor, and perhaps personal, matters as teachers' salaries, wooden church buildings, and Unitarianism. From this book, the reader would conclude that Jacksonian Americans practiced their ideals and that all practices were part of their ideals. Even discrepancies so evidently wide as those between the ideal of social democracy and the practices of Negro slavery and Indian removal are explained, if not justified, according to higher American ideals in this best of all possible worlds, to borrow another phrase from the same Doctor Pangloss Grund quotes so often. Grund's hopes demanded nothing less than his total commitment to all contemporary American practices as the fulfillment of the highest universal ideals. Therefore, he had to refute all adverse criticism no matter how just or how picayune. If such criticism could not be denied, then the criticized activities must be justified as subordinate to higher ideals than they appeared to represent upon superficial viewing.

The list of criticisms of Americans was long and ranged from relatively minor attributes to fundamental attacks upon their basic integrity and intellect. Foreign observers had noted the rapid decline of female beauty, the widespread practice of living in boarding houses, the shoddy craftsmanship, the reck-

lessness of American sailors, the never-ending consumption of hard liquor, the lack of manners and
hospitality, as well as the tendency to lawlessness,
the lack of literature and arts, poor education, want
of patriotism, regional distrust, and a host of other
defects large and small in American life. Above all,
they condemned the radical democracy and base materialism so often seen as typical of the United States
at that time.

Grund did offer specific replies to these criticisms.
Sometimes he merely denied the truth of the charge;
thus for example, he denied American ships were un-
safe. Other times, he affirmed the correctness of the
observation, but asked that the observer note other
comparable merits. For example, American women did
blossom earlier and fade faster than European women,
but they had far more delicate feet and ankles. Another favorite device of defense was to cite statistics
to prove how industrious, how educated, or how
benevolent Americans were in comparison to Europeans. If the statistics proved superiority in absolute
terms, such as canal and railroad mileage, then Grund
offered little interpretation other than a summary:

> When we reflect on the multitude and extent of
> these improvements, the incredibly short time in
> which they were executed, the high price of labor,
> and the comparatively small and thinly scattered
> population of the United States, we shall irresistibly
> arrive at the conclusion, that in this particular branch
> of national industry, the Americans have done more
> than all other nations taken together.

The statistics on benevolence and education were
not so clear in their implications as those on transpor-

tation and business, but they were more crucial to his defense of the United States. Thus, Grund interpreted them for his readers to be sure everyone understood the United States was still superior, although not in absolute terms. Therefore he moved to a per capita basis of relativity to prove continued superiority. After his statistics on benevolent societies, he concluded, for example:

> All these societies are formed for the promotion of morality, religion, and education; and impose a tax of 3s. sterling *per annum* on every white inhabitant of the United States. When to this are added the ordinary taxes for the support of common schools, it will be found that the Americans pay more for the moral and religious improvement of society, than any other nation, England herself, in proportion to her population, not excepted.

Why is this fact as derived so important? Because Americans were too frequently pictured as crass and materialistic:

> And yet they have been reproached with selfishness; with a sordid attachment to pecuniary gain and profit, and a total neglect of the nobler qualities of the mind! "Money," it has been added, "is the sole talisman of the Americans;" but not a word has been said of the manner in which they disburse it. Europeans could see no other causes of prosperity in the United States, than the mercantile habits of their inhabitants, and the immense natural resources of the country. But the time will come when they will be convinced of their error — when the moral progress of America will keep pace with her physical developments, and her influence on mankind, in general, be hailed with joyful gratitude.

So things were not what they first had seemed to be.

If the relative basis for judgment was insufficient, then he resorted to placing the blame on England's colonial tyranny and the infant state of America; this was particularly true in the realm of the arts, literature, and college education. When all else failed, Grund argued that the qualities English tourists found obnoxious in Americans were the very same qualities other travelers found objectionable in Englishmen.

> Thus, it has been remarked that Americans are much given to extolling the excellence of their own institutions, whether civil or political, and to undervalue those of foreign countries. This is precisely the complaint about the English, by their continental neighbors, the French and Germans. If we were to investigate the matter, we should find the cause to be perfectly analogous in both countries: a certain satisfaction that they are themselves belonging to that glorious community whose achievements, in the field and at home, have "astonished the world."

In the end, then, Grund hoped by praising the Americans inordinately to flatter the English also, for many American qualities had been transferred from the British homeland. As Grund often reminded the critics of the United States:

> The progress of America reflects but the glory of England; all the power she acquires, extends the moral empire of England: every page of American history is a valuable supplement to that of England.

Therefore:

> It is the duty of the patriots of both countries, to support and uphold each other, to the utmost extent

compatible with national justice; and it is a humiliating task, either for private individuals or public men, to make foibles of the one the subjects of ridicule in the other.

Grund apparently expected to parry English critics of the United States by burying them beneath love and laudation of things English as well as American.

A reader could compile a long list of the American customs and institutions that Grund defended in one of these preceding ways against the censures of other commentators, but to look at his book in such a fashion distorts his approach to American society. His defense of the United States was not only a systematic one, but also formed a system, like that of de Tocqueville whose first volume of *de la Démocratie en Amérique* was cited by Grund. (Perhaps it even inspired him to this specific approach.) While Grund did refute individual criticisms specifically, he really tried to incorporate most of his defenses into a general and systematic exposition of American character and institutions. Thus he hoped to show that Americans talked only business, lacked refined manners, disdained fine craftsmanship, traveled rapidly, lacked great literature, and did countless other things because they were democrats, or as he would say, republicans, who believed in certain ideals. In short, he tried to explain Americans' actions in terms of their national character or culture.

Grund's explicit conception of "national character" seems narrower than our own, but the organization of chapters and exposition of topics in his book indicates that he meant nothing less than to place American practices within the context of the basic values or premises of the culture. Thus he notes:

> Though the Americans, in general, have fewer prejudices, than other nations in Europe, and possess, therefore, less of a national character; though they have no community of religious feeling; yet there exists amongst them an uniformity of thought and sentiment, which is sufficient to mark them as a distinct people. These sentiments are principally *political,* or have reference to *their habits of industry.*

The basic values, or principal "sentiments," he lists are really fundamental orientations to life. Thus by political values he means such attitudes as independence and equality in addition to a belief in liberty and representative government. Industry includes not only constant activity and an abomination of idleness but also a spirit of enterprise and entrepreneurial daring. From these two clusters of basic values, Grund evolved a complex analysis of American customs and institutions that is both systematic and consistent, yet always sympathetic.

The emphasis on basic value-orientations determined a topical analysis, but the small number of values he saw as fundamental meant that each value could not be the subject of a separate chapter. Therefore he had to include a seemingly diverse collection of topics in each chapter, and the same topics were often covered in more than one chapter. A prime example of his logic of analysis and organization is Chapter Seven. This central chapter of his book covers such a seeming miscellany of topics as patriotism, morality, belief in property, religion, status of women, an attitude of independence, riots, lynchings, temperance, and missionary societies. By following the argument of this chapter, we see his logic of organization and his view of basic values as a key to understanding American society.

This chapter begins by defining the national character and the two underlying value-orientations that I quoted above. Then he defends Americans against the charge of lacking patriotism by arguing that their love of country is not a concrete attachment to land or place as with Europeans but to a spirit of liberty and a "love of principles." Therefore the American Commonwealth consists of a community of reason and sentiment, not a specific locale. Furthermore, Americans are never content with their country as it is but prefer it as it will be. They love not the land of their fathers so much as the land they will build for their children. Their belief in the future and their devotion to liberty and independence urges them westward to develop their physical resources; this development is encouraged and protected by the just laws of property enacted by republican legislators. Grund argues that Americans owe their ideals of liberty and property to England, for these principles were English in origin and were brought to the New World by Englishmen.

From this explication of liberty, Grund moves suddenly to morality and religion. He argues that the stability of republican principles depends upon morality, and morality in turn is based upon religion. Although Americans were tolerant of different creeds, they were intolerant of those people who had no religious persuasion at all. He maintains Americans saw religion as the basis of morality and morality as the foundation of civil and political liberty in the

Republic. Therefore to lack religion, it is implied, is unpatriotic. Americans read their Declaration of Independence from pulpits and treated their liberties religiously. This mutual reinforcement of political and religious aspects of life was necessary because the American government lacked force to coerce the citizens. Thus private morality was crucial to the maintenance of civil order, but since Americans were so moral anyway, no coercive force was needed. Respect for morality was inculcated in the home, and the family was the hostage to, as well as the evidence of, good morality. Men busied themselves in acquiring property to support their families and reputations, and thus they were too busy to do wrong. This high morality of American men uplifted the status of women. He continues his analysis of morality with a denial of the exaggerated reports of riots and lawlessness in the United States. Certainly, the Irish were not to blame as so many editors and foreign travelers argued. He then explains lynch law and justifies it as a popular supplement to legal authority. At the end of the chapter, he cites benevolent societies and temperance work as evidence that Americans associated religious feeling with morality. They backed their idealism by voluntarily supporting great national organizations devoted to these causes.

From this brief and incomplete summary of Chapter Seven, the reader can glimpse how Grund pieced together his analysis of American institutions from the basic values of the people. Many of the subjects treated in this chapter are treated elsewhere in the book, just as many other aspects of American life are said to manifest the values he discusses in the chapter. In short, he has woven an elaborate tapestry of the American character from the warp of fundamental values and the woof of institutional practices.

To ground his defense of American life upon basic cultural values was a superior ploy in refuting his critics for many reasons. First, he could present even the most criticized aspects of American life as manifestations of positive liberal ideals. Then, too, he could concentrate on ideals more than practices. Thus he could avoid, when he chose, the problem of discrepancy between high ideals and actual practice. Third, he could defend certain practices as representing quite different ideals than they seemed on the surface. Last, he could ally less noble ideals with nobler ones if he treated them as a whole system. Whether or not he realized all these advantages in such a mode of analysis is not certain, but surely his exposition makes use of all these ploys in defense of one of the most criticized aspects of American life.

The tendency of Americans to talk, think, and conduct business all the time was always noted and nearly always condemned by those Grund sought to controvert. Even the way he admitted this criticism cast new light upon it:

> There is, probably, no people on earth with whom business constitutes pleasure, and industry amusement, in an equal degree with the inhabitants of America. Active occupation is not only the principal source of their happiness, and the foundation of their national greatness, but they are absolutely wretched without it. . . . Business is the very soul of an American: he pursues it, not as a means of procuring for himself and his family the necessary comforts of life, but as the fountain of all human felicity; and shows

as much enthusiastic ardor in his application to it as any crusader ever evinced for the conquest of the Holy Land, or the followers of Mohammed for the spreading of the Koran.

Grund over and over urged his readers to look beyond mere materialism as an explanation for this behavior. Actually, American business was based upon the higher ideals of morality, enterprise, daring, inventiveness, and independence rather than the petty characteristics of crass selfishness and base materialism. In the United States, business credit was founded upon trust in fellow human beings, and business success was determined by character and intellect:

> Thus the amount of floating capital in the United States is not merely based upon the gross value of real and personal estate, but also on the moral qualifications of the merchants, and the resources of the country which *it is the genius of the people* to develope. The figures on 'change denote not merely money and merchandise; but represent also the intelligence, enterprise, economy and probity of the people: they are the index to the mind as well as to the property of the merchants.

This same high-minded spirit settled the west and constructed the internal transportation network. Not a mere desire for profit but the joy of labor and provision for future generations peopled the frontier and financed the factories. If foreign tourists resented the reckless speed of travel, the everlasting talk of "trade and traffic," or the omnipresent hustle and bustle, let them remember Americans were on the move in the finest sense. What they lacked in art, music, literature, or the other elements of high culture would follow this phenomenal physical growth, for the spirit was already there. What few things they now lacked, they more than compensated for in the other aspects of life and would soon have anyway.

In the end, Grund's defense and therefore his method of analysis rested upon the belief that a nation should be judged by the bulk of its people, not by its highest or lowest classes. If Mrs. Trollope harped upon the manners of the latter, Messrs. Hall and Hamilton viewed things too often through the eyes of the former. In Grund's view, Americans were *"mediocre par excellence,"* thereby having neither the vices of the European nobility nor the viciousness of the European lower classes. Therefore, observers should:

> turn their attention to the thousands with whom they hardly come in contact on their tours; let them observe and watch the elevated character of the merchants, the skillful industry of the mechanic, the sober regularity of the workman, and they will find ample room for a more charitable exercise of their judgment: they will then find the true strength and superiority of the American *people* over all nations on the globe.

The best way to present the United States was surely in this manner, but Grund could not convince his opponents of his view any more than they did him of theirs. Basically, the matter was a dispute over ideology and not the scientific observation of actual behavior. His description of social reality like those he criticizes is as much determined by what he believes ought to be as it is guided by what he thinks he actually sees.

The success of Grund's entire endeavor depended

to some extent upon whether he could establish his credentials as an objective, impartial observer. By reference and implication he wanted to persuade his readers that he was both foreign-born and raised but yet a long-time resident of the United States. He implied moreover that he had traveled widely in Europe, in South America, and in the United States. Thus, he could compare the various regions of the United States with each other. Moreover, he could compare the United States with France, Germany, and England, and, in regard to slavery, with Brazil.

Does his biography really support such a stance? Most of his ten years in the United States prior to the book's publication were spent teaching mathematics and French at Chauncy Hall School in Boston. He authored some school textbooks in mathematics and the sciences during this period and wrote a campaign biography of Martin Van Buren for German readers. Whether he traveled farther south than New York or perhaps Philadelphia during this time is doubtful. How much touring he did in Europe after studying mathematics and philosophy at the University of Vienna is also uncertain, for he came to the United States as a young man in his twenties. Whether he ever taught school in Rio de Janeiro before emigrating to the United States, as one usually incorrect authority claims, is also unknown. Even the year of his entrance into the United States, 1827, is not certain. Most authorities claim he lived in the United States for a decade before the publication of *The Americans,* but in the book itself he claims fourteen years. In any case, Grund presumes to have cosmopolitan experiences of this kind as a basis for his judgments upon the comparative worth of American customs and institutions. Contemporary reviewers accepted these credentials. Today's reader, however, notices that his concrete references are more often to New England ways and to German experiences than to customs in the Southern or Western states or to life in England or France.

In his zeal to defend the status quo in the United States, Grund lapsed into party politics. From praising the democracy of Jacksonian America, he slipped into extolling the Democracy of Jackson. As Charles Sumner, an opponent of Jackson and his followers, pointed out in a contemporary review, Grund sounded like a "counsel of defense" and his book possessed an "air of advocacy" not only because it exaggerated American idealism but because it was a party tract too. According to Sumner, de Tocqueville viewed American democracy from the height of unprejudiced philosophy, but Grund chose the "humbler elevations" of political party for his perspective. Thus his comments on President Jackson may be viewed as more than a defense of the man who gave his name to the age. His exposition of political parties in the last chapter is clearly slanted toward the Democrats and their standard-bearer. His defense of the Irish and their politics and American lawfulness are also in line with his party views, as are his strictures on Henry Clay's program for internal improvements. His views on Indian removal were precisely those of the Jacksonians as Sumner pointed out at length in his review. Grund's long justification of slavery, so strangely partisan for a foreign observer, also followed current politics. Grund was a Democrat as well as a democrat, and his defense of American society reflected both positions, as Sumner saw very well.

In fact, publication of *The Americans* marked a turn in Grund's life from a teaching to a journalistic and political career. He supported the election of Martin Van Buren by pen and voice and even gave the impression of controlling the German vote. As a reward he received a consulship abroad. Disillusioned with his service abroad and with Van Buren, he returned to the United States as a Whig and became editor of a party paper. His change in mind about Van Buren and his United States can be seen in *Aristocracy in America, from the Sketch-book of a German Nobleman* (London, 1839). In this work Grund adopted the more conventional travel format and focused on the discrepancy between ideal and practice when desired. The book also illustrated the new journalistic style, supposedly invented by Grund, by which behind-the-scenes information presumably received from creditable sources was displayed for the edification of the reader.

After another disappointing consulship, Grund returned to the Democratic Party, and, except for his defection in 1848, remained loyal until shortly before his death in 1863. By retaining a pro-slavery attitude in the 1850's, he lost leadership of the German vote, as his fellow countrymen moved into the anti-slavery camp and the Republican Party. Even during the initial years of the Civil War, he stayed in the party of Buchanan and Douglas. Only in 1863 did he finally switch to the Republican Party. A Democratic Party rally outside his home shortly after this conversion literally frightened him to death. Thus he died as he had lived, in the midst of politics.

To point out the personal background and prejudices of Grund is not to impugn the utility of his attempt to construct the cultural system of Jacksonian America. Though his politics and his love of the United States influenced both what he omitted from and included in the book, still his work offers an extremely useful portrait of American character at that time. By the very fact of neglecting practices in favor of ideals, his book provides a valuable insight into the basic values espoused by American citizens in the 1830's. What seems a deficiency at first glance constitutes in reality a strength. His systematic attempt to delineate the totality of American culture in terms of its fundamental values ranks second only in importance to that done by de Tocqueville as a guide to the foundation of Americans' actions in the "Age of the Common Man." No where else can the reader find, except in de Tocqueville's work, such an over-all view of American thinking at the time as Grund's *The Americans, in Their Moral, Social, and Political Relations.*

Robert F. Berkhofer, Jr.

SELECTED BIBLIOGRAPHY

The most satisfactory biography of Grund is the brief one by Albert B. Faust in *Supplement One* (New York, 1944), to the *Dictionary of American Biography*. Faust also provides references to other sources on Grund's life and a list of his publications. His *Aristocracy in America* was republished (New York, 1949), with an introduction by George E. Probst, an ardent proponent of Grund's worth as an analyst of Jacksonian America. Charles Sumner's review of *The Americans* appeared in the January, 1838, issue of the *North American Review* (volume XLVI, pages 106–26).

Examples of the type of English observations Grund sought to refute may be found most easily in Allan Nevins' anthology, *America through British Eyes* (New York, 1948), Part Two. Grund's chief target, Thomas Hamilton's *Men and Manners in America*, will be reprinted by the publisher of this edition of *The Americans*. Recent analyses of English travel literature, besides Nevins' excellent introduction in the work previously mentioned, are Jane L. Mesick, *The English Traveller in America, 1785–1835* (New York, 1922), and Max Berger, *The British Traveller in America, 1836–1860* (New York, 1943). An extended review of all American travel literature from the perspective of Grund's time is Henry T. Tuckerman, *America and Her Commentators* (New York, 1864).

Modern scholars have also attempted to construct

the cultural values of Jacksonian America. Two of the most complete are John W. Ward, *Andrew Jackson: Symbol for an Age* (New York, 1955), and Marvin Meyers, *The Jacksonian Persuasion: Politics and Belief* (Stanford, 1957). Other recent works that bear upon this topic are: Arthur A. Ekrich, *The Idea of Progress in America, 1815–1860* (New York, 1944); Henry N. Smith, *Virgin Land: The American West as Symbol and Myth* (Cambridge, 1950); Perry Miller, *The Life of the Mind in America from the Revolution to the Civil War* (New York, 1965); Rush Welter, *Popular Education and American Democratic Thought in America* (New York, 1962). Still other volumes among many that illuminate some of the ideological values covered by Grund are: Albert K. Weinberg, *Manifest Destiny: A Study of Nationalist Expansion in American History* (Baltimore, 1935); Paul C. Nagel, *One Nation Indivisible: the Union in American Thought, 1776–1861* (New York, 1964); Sidney E. Mead, *The Lively Experiment: the Shaping of Christianity in America* (New York, 1963); William S. Jenkins, *Pro-Slavery Thought in the Old South* (Chapel Hill, 1935); Roy H. Pearce, *The Savages of America: A Study of the Indian and the Idea of Civilization* (Baltimore, 1953); Leo Marx, *The Machine in the Garden: Technology and the Pastoral Ideal in America* (New York, 1964).

Some recent scholarly works that discuss the practices as well as the ideals of the period in a way particularly relevant to Grund's observations are: George R. Taylor, *The Transportation Revolution, 1815–1860* (New York, 1951); Lee Benson, *The Concept of Jacksonian Democracy: New York as a Test*

Case (Princeton, 1961); Alice Felt Tyler, *Freedom's Ferment: Phases of American Social History to 1860* (Minneapolis, 1944); Robert E. Riegel, *Young America, 1830–1840* (Norman, 1949). A standard, detailed history of the period is provided by Glyndon Van Deusen, *The Jacksonian Era, 1828–1848* (New York, 1959). Another frequently cited social history of the era, Carl R. Fish, *The Rise of the Common Man, 1830–1850* (New York, 1927), confuses ideology and social reality as much as any of the people did who lived in Jacksonian America. Michael McGiffert, ed., *The Character of Americans* (Homewood, Illinois, 1964), provides both readings on the subject of its title and a lengthy bibliography on that topic as well as on the theory and practice of national character studies in general.

THE

AMERICANS,

IN THEIR

MORAL, SOCIAL, AND POLITICAL RELATIONS.

BY FRANCIS J. GRUND.

FROM THE LONDON EDITION OF LONGMAN, REES, ORME, BROWN, GREEN AND LONGMAN.

TWO VOLUMES IN ONE.

BOSTON:
MARSH, CAPEN AND LYON.
1837.

PREFACE.

I RESPECTFULLY submit the following work to the English public, not as the observations of a tourist, but as the result of the experience of one who has resided in America many years.

I have anxiously endeavored to give an impartial account of the present condition of the United States, and faithfully to delineate those characteristic features which distinguish the Americans from the different nations of Europe. Whether I have succeeded, the public must decide; of whom I claim no other indulgence than that to which I may be entitled from the rectitude of my intentions, and an honest desire to correct prejudices — American or English — and not to furnish them with fresh aliment.

The Americans have been grossly misrep-
esented; and this not so much by ascribing
to them spurious qualities, as by omitting all
mention of those which entitle them to hon-
or and respect, and representing the foibles
of certain classes as weaknesses belonging
to the nation.

The object of this publication will be attained, if it serve to inspire the English with
more just conceptions of American worth, and
increase the respect and friendship of America for England.

Regent Street, London, Dec. 24, 1836.

ERRATUM.—Page 80, line 16 from top, for "gratify," read *mortify.*

CONTENTS.

THE AMERICANS

IN

THEIR SOCIAL, MORAL, AND POLITICAL RELATIONS.

CHAPTER I.

AMERICAN MANNERS AND SOCIETY.—FASHIONABLE COTE-
RIES.—DANDIES.—ARISTOCRACY.—ITS COMPOSITION AND
PECULIARITIES.

THERE is scarcely a theme with which English readers
are more familiar than that of American manners. From
the grotesque sketches of Mrs. Trollope to the lofty and
elegant conceptions of Hamilton and Basil Hall, the British
public have been entertained with the portentous matter of
an American drawing-room. I may, perhaps, disappoint
my readers by not following the beaten track, so fertile in
amusement and rare sports; for I shall neither repeat
the silly prating of boys and misses, (which one may hear
in every country,) nor shall I make those who entertained
me the subject of scorn and ridicule.—Neither shall I
write an eulogy; for, the truth being told, there is enough
in the moral and social condition of Americans to interest the general reader.

By American manners I do not mean those of the fashionable coteries, nor the peculiar customs of certain districts, to which the refinements of society have, as yet,
hardly penetrated; but the general terms on which Americans associate with each other, and with strangers.

2

Society, in America, is composed of a great number of heterogeneous elements, and the conventional standard, therefore, is less fixed than in any part of Europe. In the large towns it consists of persons from all parts of the world, with a valuable admixture of "Western," "Southern," and "Eastern people;" which names denote almost as many distinct varieties of the human race. Under these circumstances, an American drawing-room must often present anomalies, which, at first, will strike an educated Englishman; but which are hardly ever offensive, and may always be explained by the moral and political condition of the country.

In the absence of a court, or a powerful aristocracy, elegant accomplishments are seldom cultivated with a view to ornament society; and are rather the property of a few, whose good fortune it has been to move in the higher circles of Europe, than a general characteristic of a polite education in America. The Americans have, with very few exceptions, no time to cultivate fashionable elegance, which they consider a mere appendage to civilization; but they are, notwithstanding, a highly sociable people, and, in their own way, both pleasing and instructive.

It has always been the fault of European writers to compare American manners, and especially those of the coteries styled "aristocratic," to the polished ease of the higher classes of Europe. Occasionally they have, indeed, condescended to speak of merchants and manufacturers, whom they have ever found equal to those of Liverpool and Manchester; but, with a forbearance which does credit to their ingenuity, they have not pushed the inquiry further, lest the superiority of the laboring classes might have compensated for the inferior accomplishments of the fashionable circles, and a certain nameless class in Europe altogether lacked its term of comparison in the United States. They seem to have been aware of the fact, that America is really what Hamilton calls the city of Philadelphia—*médiocre par excellence;* her political institutions depriving her of the splendor of a throne—the focus of polite society in Europe; but, at the same time, saving her from the pernicious influence of an idle and turbulent mob—the destruction of public morality and virtue. The manners of Americans, therefore, are as far removed from the elegance of courts, as they are from the boorishness of the lower classes in Europe ; and, perhaps, equally free from the vices of both. The true manners of a people do not show themselves in the drawing-room—*les hommes du salon se ressemblent partout ;* but in the common transactions of public and private life ; and it is, therefore, neither good sense nor justice to select a particular class, and in a peculiar situation, for the term of comparison with Europe.

In order to understand the customs and manners of Americans, we must trace them to their origin ; when we shall find that most of what is valuable and substantial in their character is inherited from the English ; but that, at the same time, many of their foibles may be traced to the same source, and especially those for which they are most censured by the English.

I shall not here stop to apologise for my belief that the manners and morals of the English (and there is an intimate connection between them,) are essentially superior to those of the people on the Continent. There may be less pliableness in the address and carriage of an Englishman ; but there is something in the composition of his character which is sure to command respect ; there is that dignity which is incompatible with low cunning or conceit, and least capable of stooping to a wilful falsehood. This character, in all its severity, and enforced by the most solemn injunctions of religion, has been transplanted to the shores of the new world, to lay the foundation of what are now called American manners and morals. New England, of all the colonies, has had the greatest influence on the establishment of national customs, as a part of her sturdy population has been always emigrating westward, to renew and perpetuate the principles which gave rise to the settlement of Plymouth. But the people of New England were English, and are so now, in their feelings and sentiments : to the English, therefore, must be attributed most of the peculiarities for which they are condemned, as, indeed, most of the virtues for which they are celebrated.

This does not seem to have been taken sufficiently into consideration by any English traveller whose work has gone forth to enlighten the public. It is truly surprising how certain pictures of American manners could have contributed so much to the diversion of English readers, when we reflect on the fact that they were drawn from a class of society which has no particular claim to refinement in any country, and which, in Europe, presents the same mixture of vice and folly as in America, without, perhaps, some of its redeeming virtues. It remains to be explained why the fair author should have exposed herself to the expense and inconvenience of a long voyage, when she might have found sufficient matter for her book at home. What absurd caricatures of English manners and customs are not daily drawn by French and German satirists, without derogating one iota from the dignity of English society, of which most of them have nearly as correct a knowledge, from personal observation, as the author of " Domestic Manners " has of the better circles in the United States. Peculiarities and anomalies will always exist in every country; but their number must naturally be greater in one whose boundless territory is divided into almost as many different states as there are counties in England. The peculiar features of a country, the physical distinction of its soil and climate, the principal occupation of its inhabitants, &c., imprint each a distinct character on the people, which it is difficult to efface, even by the means of education. What difference does not, in this respect, exist between a North-Briton and an inhabitant of the Isle of Wight ; or between the latter and a native of Yorkshire? And how preposterous would not be the idea of publishing either of these characters as correct specimens of the English ?

Another remarkable trait of English travellers in the United States consists in their proneness to find the same faults with Americans which the people on the continent of Europe are apt to find with themselves. Thus, it has been remarked that Americans are much given to extolling the excellence of their own institutions, whether civil or political, and to undervalue those of foreign countries. This is precisely the complaint about the English, by their continental neighbors, the French and the Germans. If we were to investigate the matter, we should find the cause to be perfectly analogous in both countries : a certain satisfaction that they are themselves belonging to that glorious community whose achievements, in the field and at home, have "astonished the world."

Some apology may, indeed, be offered for this patriotic weakness, when we reflect on the actual superiority of British institutions, and especially on the immense influence they have had on the civilization and happiness of the human race. But all the causes of British pride are equally operating on Americans. They are of the same origin; all the glory attached to the British name is that of their ancestors; and they have themselves had an honorable share in its acquisition. Their fathers were the bold settlers who first transplanted British laws and British genius to a new world, to perpetuate them to the end of time. But they have improved upon them; they have opened God's temples to all his worshippers; and, perhaps, for the first time on earth, raised the standard of equal liberty and justice. They have rallied round this standard to wage war against the most powerful nation in Europe—and they were not conquered. A second time they were arrayed in battle against England, and a second time they proved themselves not inferior to their proud progenitors. Are these no causes for national vanity? And is this vanity not the highest encomium which they can possibly bestow on the English? Do not the English furnish the standard of American pride—the character to which they will not acknowledge themselves inferior? When did any one hear the Americans draw envious comparisons between themselves and other nations, save the English? And what, after all, is this pride or conceit but English, strengthened and improved by the republican institutions of America? Is it not natural for men to be proud of belonging to a nation in proportion as they have a share in its government? Is there, in this respect, no difference between a British peer and a commoner! Is it, then, a wonder that the Americans should esteem others in proportion to the franchise they have acquired; and that as born legislators they should carry their heads sometimes higher than is consonant with the English idea of politeness?

A second not less striking characteristic of American manners is a degree of seriousness, which, at first, might

2*

almost be taken for want of sociability. An American is,
almost from his cradle, brought up to reflect on his condition, and, from the time he is able to act, employed with
the means of improving it. If he be rich, and have consequently a larger stake in the public weal, then every
new law, every change of election (and there are many
in the course of a year,) will make him reflect on the future: if he be poor, every change may offer him an opportunity to improve his circumstances. He is ever
watchful, ever on the alert, not as most Europeans, as a
mere spectator, but as one of the actors, engaged in maintaining or reforming the existing state of affairs. Something like it may, at times, be felt in England, and perhaps even in France; but this cannot be compared to the
effects of universal suffrage in America.

The whole mass of the population is constantly agitated; an expression of public opinion is constantly demanded, constantly hoped for, constantly dreaded. There
is no man so rich or powerful but can be made to quail
under its influence; nor any one so humble, in whom it
may not raise hopes of success and preferment. It is an
all-powerful organ of public justice, sparing none, from
the president down to the most obscure citizen; elevating, humbling, or annihilating whatever it meets in its
progress, if justly the object of its reproach.

This state of incessant excitement gives to the Americans an air of busy inquietude, for which they have often
been pitied by Europeans; but which, in fact, constitutes
their principal happiness. The Americans have no time
to be unhappy—and this is saying much in favor of their
government. The duties of republicans are more arduous than those of men living under any other form of
government; but then their performance is pleasing and
satisfactory; because it is connected with consciousness
of power. No American would exchange his task for
the comparative peace and quiet of Europe; because, in
the words of Franklin, "he would be unwilling to pay
too dear for the whistle." He finds his solace and quietude at home; abroad he is "up and doing." Peace
there would be death to him. He would not, for the world,
exchange his political activity for the speculative inertness
of the Germans; the glorious privilege of having himself

a share in the government of his country, for the "*dolce far niente*" of the Italians; the busy stir of an election, for the idiot noise of a Vienna prado. Let those, who are so prodigal of their compassion for the melancholy restlessness of Americans, but remember the painful stupor which befel the Romans after the overthrow of the republic, when, all at once, released from their active duties of citizens, they found in "tranquillity" the principal punishment of their abandonment of virtue.

In proportion as the liberties of a people are enlarged, and their franchise extended, they must necessarily become more active and serious. For an illustration we need only compare the character of the French, since the revolution of July, with that which they possessed under the old Bourbon dynasty, previous to the revolution of 1789. How much gaiety and outward politeness is there not missing; but how much understanding and rational liberty gained? What difference is there not between the buffoonery of "merry England," under the reign of Queen Elizabeth, and the sober, demure composition of John Bull since the acquisition of the *habeas corpus*, and the revolution? And yet what unbiassed individual, in either country, would wish back "the good old times," or deny that the condition of the people has been materially improved by the change? Well, then, the Americans are, in common with the English, a more sober, calm, and reflecting people than, perhaps, any other in the world; and, for this very reason, able to bear a larger proportion of rational liberty.

The influence of this character on the sociable circles of America is undoubtedly felt; but not in the manner generally described by Europeans. Thus, for instance, it does not destroy the spirit of hospitality, for which the Americans were always distinguished, although it has but too often been ill requited; it does not prevent them from receiving their friends in a cordial manner, or enjoying their own domestic fireside: but, being always accustomed to thought and reflection, their minds are, perhaps, too fraught with the events of the day and the apprehensions of the future, to preserve throughout that fashionable indifference on all topics, which can neither affect nor cheer any of the company present, and which, for that very reason, is considered essential to good manners in Europe. Their sentiments are often expressed with warmth bordering on enthusiasm, and require, therefore, a greater degree of attention and sympathy on the part of their audience, than Europeans of rank are willing to bestow on ordinary subjects of conversation. On this account, American society is sometimes fatiguing; and the complaint has often been made by foreigners, that it requires a certain preparation in order to understand or enjoy it. Its demands on a stranger are more numerous than is always agreeable; and if he be a man of talent or reputation, he is expected to show off and entertain the company. The Americans, on such occasions, are always willing to listen, to learn, and, perhaps, to question; but Europeans are not always ready to teach or to answer, and still less disposed to receive instruction from their entertainers. In this manner, society proves often a task to men of consideration and learning, instead of offering them a convenient respite, as in Europe.

The most bitter reproach, however, which has ever been heaped upon American manners, is their unhallowed custom of talking about trade and traffic. This, during a period of more than fourteen years, I confess not to have remarked half as often as Hamilton, and never, except from one man of business to another. I rather think an honorable exception was made in his favor, in order to acquaint him the better with American affairs, on which they knew he was about to write a book; little suspecting that subjects so intrinsically mean, as mere trade and commerce, must necessarily be beneath the notice of an author. The Americans, I admit, show, on all such occasions, a morbid solicitude to forestall the good opinions of their guests; and would, perhaps, succeed better if they were more careless and reserved. Notwithstanding all this, we have his own acknowledgment as to the new ideas he acquired in this manner, which is at least a proof that American society was not without the means of improving his stock of information.*

---

* "Since my arrival," says Mr. Hamilton, "I have received much involuntary instruction in the prices of corn, cotton, and tobacco. My stock of information as to bankruptcies is very respectable; and if the manufacturers of Glasgow and Paisley knew only half as well as I do

The Americans have also been reproached with an almost slavish imitation of European manners; which, amongst the wealthier classes at least, is said to exist in a degree bordering on the ludicrous, This is decidedly the greatest and most merited charge that can be brought against them and that noble spirit of independence for which they are, in other respects, remarkable.

Every nation has an indisputable right to fix its own conventional standard, which must be based on its history and the general habits of the people, resulting from the climate, soil, and the political institutions of the country. No native of Russia would judge a West Indian by the conventional standard of Petersburg; nor would an Englishman govern his conduct by the rules of etiquette of Rome or Naples. What, in a mercantile community, might be perfectly just and proper, would, under a military government, be considered in a very different light; and the ceremony of a Turkish divan would ill suit the council chamber of the King of England. The Americans alone seem to have given up the privilege of establishing conventional rules of their own; and thus, with a singular complaisance, judge the manners of every foreigner, and suffer their own to be judged, by the standard of another country. The consequence of this want of independence is felt in the arrogance and presumption with which even the meanest and most ignorant of Europeans passes sentence on American manners, whenever they disagree with his own; and in his unrestrained contempt for those whom he sees anxiously striving to imitate what a European valet or a footman is infinitely more successful in accomplishing; whilst their laws, their political institutions, and the industrious habits of the people, are in open contradiction with the frivolities of mere fashionable life. How often have I not, myself, seen Europeans curl their lips at the apparent plainness of Americans, who were, in every respect, their superiors, save in the cut of the coat and the felicitous adaptation

how thoroughly the new market is glutted with their goods, they assuredly would send out no more on speculation."

If the learned author had gathered more such "respectable" information, he would, at least, have made his work more useful to his country.

of a coxcomb's bow; and, what is worse, beheld these sentiments approved by some American exquisite, who had just returned home, fraught with the follies of all countries, but seemingly light of the good sense of his own.

The attempt to create fashionable and aristocratic distinctions, will, in America, never be crowned with success. The reason is apparent.   Every species of aristocracy must be based on wealth and power, and contain, within itself, the principle of perpetuity.   Without these requisites their superiority will never be acknowledged, nor will they have the means of enforcing it.   There exists, in the large cities of America, certain coteries, composed principally of wealthy families ; but their wealth is not permanent, and they are perfectly powerless when opposed to the great mass of the people.   Not more than one fourth of all the men who possess property in the United States have inherited it ; the rest have acquired it by their own industry.   Scarcely one fourth, therefore, could have been brought up in the elegancies of fashionable life ; the remainder are recruits and stragglers.   But, in the total absence of monopolies, and with the immense resources of the country, the road to fortune is open to all ; while those who possess property may lose it, and must, at any rate, ultimately divide it equally amongst their children.   The elements of American coteries are, therefore, constantly varying ; but every new change brings them nearer to a level with the people.

The abrogation of primogeniture, in America, has done more towards equalizing conditions than the spirit of exclusiveness will ever be able to overcome ; aristocratic pretensions may exist ; but they will always remain impotent, and die with the respective pretenders.   The absence of primogeniture acts as a constant moderator in society, humbling the rich and elevating the poor.   It obliges the sons of the wealthy to join personal application to an honest inheritance, and elevates the hopes of the lower classes with the expectance of future prosperity. It is thus the strongest pillar of democracy in the constitution of nearly every State of the Union.

No aristocracy can exist or maintain itself without property.   The nobility of France had virtually ceased to exist long before the hereditary peerage was abolished ;

while the patronage of the English would alone be sufficient to establish a power which would make itself felt,
even if the House of Lords were reformed.   There are
even those * who believe that in the latter case its power,
instead of being confined to its usual channel, would extend itself over every department of state, and absorb, for
a time at least, the main interests of the country.   The
American aristocracy, on the contrary, possess neither
hereditary wealth nor privileges, nor the power of directing the lower classes,   The prosperity of the country is
too general to reduce any portion of the people to the abject condition of ministers to the passions and appetites
of the rich.   It is even gold which destroys the worship
of the golden calf.

   But how can it be possible for the American aristocracy to lay claims to superior distinctions, when the people
are constantly reminded, by words and actions, that *they*
are the legislators, that the *fee-simple* is in *them*, and that
they possess the invaluable privilege of calling to office
men of their own choice and principles ?   Are not the
American people called upon to pass sentence on every
individual whose ambition may prompt him to seek distinction and honor at their hands ?   And what is not
done to conciliate the good will and favor of the people ?
Are they not constantly flattered, courted, and caressed
by that very aristocracy which, if it truly existed, would
spurn equality with the people ?   Is the judgment of the
people, expressed by the ballot-box, not appealed to as
the ultimate decision of every argument and contest ?
Aristocracy, if it shall deserve that name, must not only
be based on the vain pretensions of certain classes, but
on its public acknowledgment by law, and the common
consent of others.   This, however, is not the work of a
generation, and requires an *historical* connexion with the
origin and progress of a country.

   Why, then, should the Americans recognise a superior
class of society, if that class be neither acknowledged by
law nor possessed of power ?   How shall they be brought
to worship those from whom they are accustomed to
receive homage ? — who are either men of their own election, and consequently of their own making, or the de-

* Heine.

feated and unhappy victims of their displeasure ? The
aristocracy of America may claim genius, and talent, and
superiority, and they may be ambitious ; but it is an
" ambition of so airy and light a quality that it is but a
shadow's shadow " — a sort of *fata morgana* reflected from
beyond the waters, whose baseless fabric can neither excite apprehension, nor arrest the progress of democracy.
Coteries there always were, and always will be, in large
cities ; but they need not necessarily be connected with
power. In America, moreover, they exist, principally,
among the ladies ; there being, as yet, but few gentlemen
to be called " of leisure," or exclusively devoted to society. The country is yet too young, and offers too large a
field for the spirit of enterprise and business, to leave to
the fashionable drawing-rooms other devotees than young
misses and *elegants* of from fourteen to twenty years of
age. That such companies may, nevertheless, have their
attractions, no one can reasonably doubt; but they are not
composed of elements capable of changing the manners
and customs of the country ; and, as long as their composition does not materially alter, must remain deprived of
that influence which the higher circles in Europe are wont
to exercise over all classes of society.

The manners of republicans must necessarily be more
nearly on a level with each other than those of a people
living under a monarchical government. There are no
nobles to vie with the splendor of the throne ; no com-
moners to outdo the nobility. The dignified simplicity of
the American President and all high functionaries of state
is little calculated to furnish patterns of expensive fashions ; and, were all Americans, in this respect, exact imitators of the amiable plainness of General Jackson, their
manners would soon cease to be an object of satire to
English tourists. They would then present dignity without ornament, candor without loquacity, loftiness of mind
unmingled with contempt for others. Europeans would
then visit the United States, not to ridicule American
manners, but for the purpose of studying them ; and, perhaps, carry home the useful conviction, that though
republics are no fit schools for courtiers, they may, nevertheless, abound in good sense, agreeable address, and
genuine cordiality of manners.

When I said that the manners of republicans must be more nearly on a level with each other than those of a people living under a different form of government, I was far from conceiving it in the sordid sense in which it has often been applied to Americans. The tendency of American democracy is not to debase the wealthy in mind or fortune, but to raise the inferior classes to a moral elevation, where they need no longer be degraded and despised. It is not a drawback on individual distinction or merit,—which, on the contrary, it encourages more than any other government—but it is a great safeguard against the total abjectedness of the lower classes. The seeming equality of conditions in America is not effected by withholding certain privileges from the educated and wealthy, but by extending them to the middle, and even inferior orders of society.

The man of education, or of fortune, is respected in America as in Europe ; but the deference paid to his person is untinged with the humiliating consciousness of being incapable ever to attain to the same distinctions. There is nothing in the institutions of America to derogate from the dignity of gentlemen ; they simply prevent a certain class from enjoying that title to the prejudice and exclusion of all the rest. They are not unjust to the rich and the learned because they are more just to the poor ; they do not prevent good breeding or good manners, but, on the contrary, spread them amongst a larger number of people. But there are men who cannot enjoy wealth unless they know that others are poor ; who value knowledge only in proportion as it gives them power over their fellow-creatures; who could not relish venison unless they knew a half-starved population was dying for the want of bread. Such men have repeatedly visited the United States, and were, of course, much annoyed with the vulgar plenty of the land, and the desire of every American to be considered " a gentleman." It was this feature of democracy which they described as begetting low breeding, because it is apt to make Americans wanting in that outward respect, which a certain class of men is always sure to meet with in Europe. But deference for the just claims of others need not necessarily be accompanied by marks of humiliating self-denial ;

3

and it is, perhaps, better that the whole distinction should be dropped, than that the inferiority should exist in the degree indicated by the outward forms of civility.

But to judge of the manners of a people, one must have been a resident amonst them, and not a mere tourist. From the writings of Basil Hall and Hamilton, it is evident that neither of these gentlemen became acquainted with any but the fashionable coteries of the great cities; and that the manners of the *people*, and especially those of the respectable middle classes, escaped altogether their immediate attention. What they say of them in their respective works is not the result of personal observation, but rather the stale reiteration of some evening's conversation, colored by the partisan spirit of politics and religion. Mrs. Trollope, on the contrary, was hardly known in fashionable society, and only saw the western part of the country, yet; notwithstanding all this, her book is clever, and has that superiority over the productions of her masculine competitors which a caricature, ever so badly drawn, has over a portrait destitute of resemblance.

The most remarkable characteristic of Americans is the uncommon degree of intelligence which pervades all classes. I do not here speak of the higher branches of learning which, in the language of Europe, constitute scholarship; but of the great mass of useful knowledge calculated to benefit and improve the condition of mankind. It is this latter knowledge for which the Americans are distinguished, and for the attainment of which they have, perhaps, made better provision than any other nation in the world. This is as it should be. No democracy can exist for any length of time without the means of education being widely diffused throughout the country; but it is certainly not to be expected that republicans should tax themselves, in order to gratify certain elegant tastes which are of no immediate benefit to the public. The study of the higher branches of science, and the cultivation of the fine arts, find their principal reward in the pleasure arising from the pursuit, and require seldom the assistance of the law to be called into active existence. Wherever this is done, the people have to bear the expense of it, without receiving the gratification. The Americans are yet occupied with what is necessary and useful, and are, therefore, obliged to leave the higher accomplishments to the protection of individual munificence. But let any one cast his eye on the sums annually expended for the establishment and support of common schools and colleges, and he will, at once, be convinced of the liberality of Americans in the cause of education ; although no allowances are, as yet, made for professorships of heraldry, or the discovery of a north-west passage. I shall not, here, discuss the matter any further, as I intend to recur to it in another place ; but I would ask what influence the higher branches of learning have on the social intercourse of a people, or the manners of society in general ? What fashionable company in England was ever graced or edified by the conversation of Sir Isaac Newton ? What select circle in Germany ever enjoyed and delighted in the philosophical researches of Kant and Leibnitz ? Men of letters, and more especially, *proficients in science*, are rarely welcome guests at a party ; and, in Germany, they have been uniformly banished to the universities. Neither the arts nor the sciences have, till lately, received particular encouragement from the German courts ; and it was with great justice Schiller could say of Frederic the Great that the German muse was banished from his court ; * and yet, at that very period, the most effectual measures were taken, by men of letters themselves, to ensure the progress and independence of German literature.

But the remark that men of letters do not hold a distinguished rank in American society is totally false and unfounded. There is, perhaps, no society to which learn-

---

* Von dem grössten Deutschen Sohne,
Von des grossen Friedrichs Throne
  Gieng sie schutzlos ungeehrt.
Rühmlich darfs der Deutsche sagen,
Höher darf das Herz ihm schlagen :
  Selbst erschuf er sich den Werth.
                    SCHILLER'S *German Muse.*

From the greatest German son,
From great Fred'rick's noble throne,
  Unprotected went she forth.
Proudly may the German speak it ;
Loudly may his heart repeat it :
  He himself achieved his worth.

ing furnishes a better introduction ; and I am quite certain that some of the gentlemen who have lately visited the United States " for the laudable purpose of information," owe their friendly reception there more to their high reputation as *scholars*, than to any rank they may hold in the army or navy. Scholarship, in America, is, indeed, not so common as it is in Europe ; but the individuals who are able to lay claims to it, are sure of meeting with the acknowledgment due to their merits, and a certain acquaintance with the elements of science is an almost indispensable requisite for admission into good company. The conversation of Americans turns, generally, more on scientific subjects than would be believed by Europeans, and differs, in this respect, widely, from the insipid common-place of the fashionable circles of Europe.* There is hardly a branch of learning which, at some time or other, is not introduced into their colloquies, and there are few scholars in America who would be denied the privilege of expressing their opinions on a favorite topic, or whose conversation would not be listened to with increased interest and pleasure. To this may be added the proneness of Americans to argue, which, though it may not always correspond to the European idea of good manners, lends, nevertheless, to conversation a zest of which it would otherwise be deprived.

Society, in all countries, gains more from the amount of floating intellect, and the capacity of all its members to join in conversation, than from the amount of knowledge treasured up in the minds of individuals. This principle applies most happily to the social condition of the United States ; for it would be difficult to find a country where information is more generally diffused, or the peo-

---

* I write this at Munich, a city which has been much and justly extolled on account of its liberal institutions, and whose progress in the sciences and the fine arts has occupied a large space in the "Foreign Quarterly." The King of Bavaria is himself a poet and an artist; and possesses the most perfect judgment of every thing relating to the arts. But, notwithstanding this noble example of the king himself, and his liberal and munificent encouragement of learning, there are but two scientific gentlemen—Mr. T * * and Mr. S * *—who can boast of being freely admitted into the highest circles: but as the usual topics of conversation do not often allow them to display their acquirements, they are merely pointed out to strangers somewhat in the same manner as the giraffe or the elephant in the zoological gardens.

ple of all classes more capable of expressing their ideas with clearness and precision. A certain directness of thought and expression may, indeed, be considered a national peculiarity of Americans, and contributes certainly much to their apparent plainness of manners. Mere fashionable elegance passes with them for little or nothing; but in no country are power of reasoning, force of argument, and acuteness of observation at a greater premium. Good sense is the ruling element of society, as it is the main-spring of all their public actions; and the country at large is much a gainer in the result. Mannerism is hardly ever cultivated to the prejudice of the more substantial acquirements, as the conventions of society offer but little or no protection to the ignorance or pretensions of impostors; and I cannot imagine any circumstances more capable of exhibiting an idiot in trouble than an empty-headed coxcomb in company with rational Americans. Fashionables and exquisites there are in the large cities of the United States as in Europe; but they are certainly less the object of envy or admiration, and are almost exclusively in favor with the young misses of the boarding-schools. Their bright career commences and finishes with the lights of the drawing-rooms, and their only chance of distinction is at a waltz or a quadrille. But, once entrapped by some fair enchantress, they quickly turn their attention to objects more useful and profitable. The prospect of supporting a wife and family becomes then the all-engrossing object of their thoughts and reflections; and it is by no means unfrequent, to see an American, at the age of twenty-one, settle down into a sober husband and father of a family. I have hardly ever known an American fashionable, who was not a minor; but I have never seen one at the bar, or on change.

With all the misfortunes which the abolition of primogeniture may have entailed on America,* it certainly has done much towards establishing permanent habits of industry; and as long as these last, buffoons and coxcombs must certainly despair of success.

To sum up the argument. — Whatever advantages, with

* The learned author of "Men and Manners" ascribes the *total* absence of the higher elegancies of life in America to the abolition of primogeniture.

3*

regard to elegance and external accomplishments, Europeans of rank and fashion may possess over the great majority of Americans, the balance of common sense, general information, and high moral rectitude, may, nevertheless, incline in favor of the latter.   American society offers, as yet, but few attractions to the man of the world; but it has wherewith to satisfy the heart and the understanding of the follower of nature: it does not command the luxuries of the aristocratic coteries of Europe; but it abounds in comforts and rational enjoyments: its general ton and etiquette may fall short of the expectations of a courtier; but it is inferior to none — and perhaps unrivalled — in simplicity and cordiality of manners,

CHAPTER II.

HAVING thus far expressed my opinion of American
society in general, I may, perhaps, be permitted to offer
a few remarks on the women. I am fully aware of the
delicacy of the subject, and the difficulty of the task ; but,
having once undertaken it, I shall offer the result of my
observations, notwithstanding the failures in comparison,
and the errors in judgment, of which I may have been
guilty.

The forms of American ladies are generally distinguished by great symmetry and fineness of proportion ;
but their frames and constitutions seem to be less vigorous
than those of the ladies of almost any country in Europe.
Their complexions, which, to the South, incline towards
the Spanish, are, to the North, remarkably fair and bloom-
ing, and, while young, by far the greater portion of them
are decidedly handsome. A marked expression of intelligence, and a certain indescribable air of languor —
probably the result of the climate — lend to their countenances a peculiar charm, to which it would be difficult to
find a parallel in Europe. An American lady, in her
teens, is, perhaps, the most sylph-like creature on earth.
Her limbs are exquisitely wrought, her motions light and
graceful, and her whole carriage at once easy and dignified. But these beauties, it is painful to say, are doomed
to an early decay. At the period of twenty-four a certain
want of fulness in her proportions is already perceptible ;

and, once passed the age of thirty, the whole fabric goes seemingly into decay. As the principal cause of this sudden decline, some allege the climate; but I ascribe it more willingly to the great assiduity with which American ladies discharge their duties as mothers. No sooner are they married than they begin to lead a life of comparative seclusion; and once mothers, they are actually buried to the world. At the period of ushering their children into society they appear, indeed, once more as respectable matrons; but they are then only the silent witnesses of the triumph of their daughters. An American mother is the nurse, tutor, friend and counsellor of her children. Nearly the whole business of education devolves upon her, and the task is, in many instances, beyond her physical ability. Thus it is customary with many ladies in New England not only to hear their children recite the lessons assigned to them at school, but actually to expound them, and to assist them in the solution of arithmetical and algebraic problems. There are married ladies who apply themselves seriously to the study of mathematics and the classics, for no other purpose than forwarding the education of their children; and I have known young men who have entered college with no other instruction, in any of the preparatory departments, than what they received from their mothers. But this continued application to the most arduous duties, the increasing care and anxiety for the progress and welfare of their children, and the consequent unreasonable confinement to the house and the nursery, undermine constitutions, already by nature sufficiently delicate; and it is thus, by the sacrifice of health and beauty, that American ladies pay to their offspring the sacred tribute of maternal affection. No human being can ever requite the tender cares of a mother; but it appears to me that the Americans have, in this respect, obligations immeasurably greater than those of the inhabitants of any other country.

But there is one perfection in ladies — sometimes the first to attract our notice, and the last to vanish when every other beauty has faded and departed — which consists in delicate feet and ankles. The idea is taken from Goethe's celebrated novel " Die Wahlverwandtschaften," and would have hardly found its introduction here, were

I not backed by the all-powerful authority of the immortal poet, who, at the same time, was the most accomplished artist. Well then, this perfection is one, of which American ladies can certainly boast, and which they possess even in a higher degree than the French, though they take infinitely less pains to obtrude it on the notice of strangers. I would recommend this to the attention of certain tourists who have much expatiated on the forms and features of American ladies, and profess to be " competent judges of female beauty."

With regard to education, American ladies resemble the English, which is, probably, the highest encomium which can be bestowed on their good sense and manners. If I judge right, there is, in this respect, less distinction between an English and American lady than between an English and American gentleman. Differences in politics, occupation, &c., must necessarily draw stronger lines of demarcation between men than the more limited sphere of action can possibly create between woman ; but the distinction must become small, indeed, where the education of the latter rests upon one and the same basis. The principles of revealed religion and a sound moral philosophy constitute, in America as in England, the foundation of all female instruction ; and it is (with the exception of the fashionable circles) a rare case, in either country, to see the mere *agréments de société* preferred to the more substantial acquirements which qualify ladies for their future stations as wives and mothers. Female dignity is ever more the result of character and principle than of mere outward grace and refinement ; and I cannot, in this respect, imagine the women of any country superior to the English or American. In the United States, where there are no classes of society debased in the estimation of the people, and, consequently, none degraded in their own, this distinction extends even to persons in the humblest walks of life, and is there productive of a species of pride, which Europeans have often mistaken for presumption ; but which, in fact, arises from a consciousness of moral worth and unexceptionable behavior, which can lay a just claim to our consideration wherever we find it. I have seen nothing among the lower classes of Europe at all to be compared to it ; and it has certainly given me the highest opinion of the general morality of female republicans.

In point of fashionable accomplishment, American ladies are, perhaps, inferior to those of Europe ; but the elements of an English, and even classical, education are in no country more widely diffused.   In addition to Latin and Greek, a young miss of respectable parents is expected to become versed in the elements of chemistry, mineralogy, botany, natural philosophy, algebra, geometry, and astronomy, to which the more gifted add even Hebrew and the higher branches of mathematics.   In the pursuit of these studies, they are generally allowed to spend quite as much time, and even more, than the young men at college ; and it cannot, therefore, be surprising if the balance of general information should, in the United States, incline in favor of the women.   There are few scientific topics of conversation on which an American lady would not be ready to join ; and there are certainly less of English reading which are not more or less familiar to the wives and daughters of respectable tradespeople.   Music and drawing are, in America, less cultivated than they are in France or Germany ; but there is quite as much parlor-amusements as in England, and certainly no lack of the graceful accomplishment of dancing.   One deficiency, however, I cannot refrain from mentioning, which consists in the imperfect acquirement of modern languages.   This, I think, must be the fault of the instructors, who are in the habit of teaching French or Italian in the same manner as the classics, troubling themselves little about accent or emphasis, and still less about the familiar idioms of the language.   The consequence is, that many American ladies are well able to read French, Italian, and German, and to understand and appreciate even the literature of these languages ; but there are comparatively few who can speak either of them with purity or elegance.   Great improvements, however, are daily making in the American system of instruction ; and it is, therefore, to be hoped that this defect will soon yield to the efforts of more experienced teachers.

What I have above remarked in reference to scientific acquirements, applies more particularly to the ladies of

New England, of whom it is said that they are always infused "with a slight tinge of the blue." Whether this be true or not, I am unable to judge; but I am quite certain that there are few ladies, in any country, whose company and conversation are more agreeable and encouraging to men of letters. The society of Boston, especially, is distinguished for its unusual number of clever women, and a certain literary taste is perhaps on this account diffused even amongst the merchants. The influence of this intellectual refinement is strikingly visible in the manners of the Bostonians, and has created an honorable distinction in favor of their city, which, by the common consent of Americans, is called the Athens of the United States.

The ladies of Philadelphia, and the south generally, possess other advantages not less conspicuous and attractive. Theirs is the province of the graces and the fine arts. I can safely affirm that I have heard as good *amateur* concerts in Charleston and Philadelphia as in any part of France or Germany; and I am, certainly, not disposed to undervalue, in this respect, the claims of my native country. Drawing and painting are also much more cultivated than they are to the north; and foreign languages, especially French and Spanish, are spoken with greater fluency. Their manners are more distinguished for grace and elegance, and their personal attractions are in England known by the appellation of "American beauty." But all these accomplishments do not prevent them from discharging their duties as wives and mothers; and it is quite an erroneous notion, though sufficiently prevalent in the Northern States, that the ladies of the south are deficient in their domestic arrangements, or negligent in the education of their children. The case is indeed quite the reverse. The household of a southern planter is generally quite as well arranged as that of a farmer to the north; though it is infinitely more complicate, on account of the slaves. In case of sickness, even among the negroes, or any other domestic calamity, the energy and patience of the southern ladies are severely taxed; and, as for the instruction of children, the task devolves almost entirely on them; few good schools or seminaries of learning being comparatively at the command of the parents, and among these, hardly any for the education of daughters.

It has, sometimes, been remarked that American ladies, though usually fine and agreeable, are not always replete with imagination. It is not long since I heard his Royal Highness the duke of * * , remark that he had seen many American ladies at his mother's court ; but that, to *him*, they were like a gallery of statues. The prince made some other very witty remarks on America, the precise meaning of which I was unable to comprehend, and concluded by comparing the western world to a woman, (he propably meant a young and a bearing one,) while Europe was to him the strong and lordly *man* of creation. I took the liberty to reply that *young women* were frequently more vigorous and powerful than *old men*, especially when the limbs of the latter afforded already specimens of morbid anatomy, which, of course, I could not be supposed to apply to the duke's own dominions. There could be nothing offensive in his sarcasm on American ladies, as it was generally whispered in society *that the duke's indiscretions had rendered his admiration of women somewhat more than suspicious.*

There is, in the great majority of American ladies, that calm subjection of passion and temper, which they deem indispensable to female dignity or grace ; but it does not follow that, on this account, they must be devoid of imagination and feeling. Their eyes are, perhaps, less expressive of what, in Italy, would be called *passion ;* but they are beaming with intelligence and kindness ; and the great number of Europeans annually married in the United States, proves at least, that they are capable of kindling love and permanent attachment. But the strongest argument in favor of their sentiments is the almost universal practice of marrying "for love," to which only few of the fashionable coteries in the large cities seem to make an exception. The influence of this moral habit, based, as it is, on the salutary principle of a free choice, manifests itself powerfully in the rapid progress of population, and perhaps also in the substance and composition of the American people.

As regards the morality and virtue of American ladies, it will suffice to say that they are not inferior to the

English, who are universally acknowledged to be the
best wives and mothers in Europe. The slightest suspicion against the character of a lady, is, in America, as
in England, sufficient to exclude her from society; but,
in America, public opinion is equally severe on men,
and this is certainly a considerable improvement. Accordingly, there is no country in which scandal, even
amongst the most fashionable circles, is so rare as in the
United States, or where the term " *intrigue* " is less known
and understood. I shall always remember the observation of a French gentleman, who could find nothing to
interest him in American society, because " it precluded
the very idea of a *liaison.*" " *Ah,*" exclaimed he, " *c'est
le paradis des maris!* "

Thus far, I have spoken of the manners of Americans
in general; much, however, remains yet to be said of
their peculiar domestic habits.

The houses of the wealthier classes resemble those of
the gentry in England, and are wanting in nothing which
can materially contribute to comfort. Some of the higher
elegancies of life, are, indeed, confined to a few imitators
of European fashions; but there is a sufficiency of all
that is essential and needful. No ostentatious attempt is
ever made to display either fortune or riches; but, on
the contrary, every thing avoided, which, being contrary
to republican plainness, might offend, or unnecessarily
attract the attention of the people. Furniture, dress,
carriages, &c. are all of the simplest construction; and
the oldest and most aristocratic families set, in this respect, the example to the more recently promoted fashionables. Whatever political reason there may exist for the
prevalence of this taste, it is, nevertheless, a good one,
and being shared by the great majority of the nation,
impresses a peculiar character of simplicity on the domestic life of Americans. It is impossible for an European to live for any length of time in the United States,
without being constantly reminded, in town or in the
country, at home or abroad, that he is living in a republic,
and that the sovereign power of that republic is solely
vested in the majority; for, whatever is capable of exciting envy or jealousy by too glaring a distinction from
the inferior classes, is condemned by public opinion, and,

4

on that account, studiously avoided by persons of all
ranks of society.   But then the great prosperity of the
country enables even the laboring classes to enjoy comforts much beyond the reach of superior orders in Europe ;
and prevents the scale from becoming too low.

On entering the house of a respectable mechanic, in
any of the large cities of the United States, one cannot
but be astonished at the apparent neatness and comfort of
the apartments. the large airy parlors, the nice carpets
and mahogany furniture, and the tolerable good library,
showing the inmates' acquaintance with the standard
works of English literature.   These are advantages
which but few individuals of the same class enjoy, by
way of distinction, in Europe ; but which, in America,
are within the reasonable hopes and expectations of
almost all the inferior classes.   What powerful stimulus
is not this to industry ? What premium on sobriety and
unexceptionable conduct ?   A certain degree of respectability is, in all countries, attached to property, and is,
perhaps, one of the principal reasons why riches are coveted.   A poor man has certainly more temptations, and
requires more virtue to withstand them, than one who is
in tolerable circumstances.   The motives of the rich are
hardly ever questioned, while the poor are but too often
objects of distrust and suspicion. *Pauper ubique jacet.*

The laboring classes in America are really less removed from the wealthy merchants and professional men than
they are in any part of Europe ; and the term " mob,"
with which the lower classes in England are honored,
does not apply to any portion of the American community.   With greater ease and comfort in his domestic
arrangements, the laboring American acquires also the
necessary leisure and disposition for reading ; his circle
of ideas becomes enlarged, and he is rendered more capable of appreciating the advantages of the political
institutions of his country. Both thought and reflection
may be crushed by excessive labor, and the lofty aspir-
ings of the mind enslaved by the cravings of the body.
Liberty, without promoting the material interests of man,
is a thing altogether beyond the comprehension of the
multitude ; and there are many who, had they attained
it, would, like the Israelites of old, wish themselves back

to their flesh-pots. I know not whether it is quest of liberty or property which causes Europeans to emigrate to America, but I am satisfied that there is an intimate connection between the two, and a constant reaction of one upon the other.

An excellent habit of the Americans, which is an incalculable promoter of domestic happiness, consists in their passing all the time which is not required for active business at home or in the circle of their acquaintance. To this custom must be ascribed the unusual number o happy marriages in the United States, which is the corner-stoneof the high morality of the country. Public houses, in America, are almost wholly frequented by travellers; and the practice has recently been introduced into many of them not to sell wine or liquor of any description, except to boarders.

But there is one deficiency in the general routine of pleasure in the United States, which is particularly oppressive to the laboring classes, and consists in the almost total absence of public gardens or pleasure-grounds in the large cities. There is nothing more favorable to a community of feeling, and a certain momentary oblivion of all ranks and distinctions, which attaches us more warmly to our kind, than public places of rendezvous, frequented by all classes of society, and enjoyed alike by all. In Europe, nearly every large city is adorned with them; and in Germany, every hamlet; but in America, they seem to be opposed to the domestic habits of the people. New York has something in the shape of a public garden, in the establishment of Niblo's, and the battery. But there is, generally, an admission fee to both; and neither one nor the other is large enough to contain a considerable portion of the whole population of the city. The battery, especially, can only be frequented in the evening, there being neither trees nor shrubs to afford the least shelter against the sun, though the place itself, from its elevation, commands a most beautiful view of the harbor. Boston, alone, of all the cities in the United States, has a large public mall; but even this (the munificent gift of an individual) is but little frequented, though the scenery around it is highly picturesque, and the walks themselves shaded by a most superb double row of chestnuts. There seems to be no want of disposition, on the part of the Bostonians generally, to profit by these advantages; but unfortunately the taste of the fashionable society has pronounced a verdict against it, and avoids most carefully being mixed and confounded with the multitude.

This morbid sensitiveness, on the part of the higher classes, arises, unquestionably, from the total absence of any exterior distinction between themselves and the lower orders, which could point them out as objects of particular respect and reverence; but I must greatly mistake the general character of Americans if I am not right in the conjecture, that a greater degree of condescension in the learned and wealthy could hardly fail of meeting with a proper acknowledgment on the part of the people; while, on the contrary, too great a reserve in the former must necessarily deprive them of a portion of that power and influence which they would, otherwise, be sure to possess. If the American people are guilty of any fault, it is certainly not ingratitude. Whoever has observed their conduct at public meetings, in presence of their favorite speakers and representatives, can testify to the unfeigned respect and uncommon propriety of manner with which they are wont to meet those whose stations and acquirements are really superior to their own. Nothing can be more pusillanimous than the fear of being confounded with the vulgar; and it is certainly the worst argument, in favor of real or assumed superiority, to dread the contact of those whom we affect to despise. May a more Christian and charitable feeling soon take the place of this mawkish resuscitation of aristocratic pride, which would befit certain orders in Europe infinitely better than the even-born citizens of a republic.

The style of buildings in America is chiefly English, with some slight variation in New York and Philadelphia; but, to the south, the houses are adapted to the climate, and of an architecture somewhat resembling the Spanish. The parlors are usually on the ground-floor, (in all the new houses they are on the first floor,) and communicate with each other by folding-doors: the story immediately above contains the chambers and the nursery, and the third and fourth floors are occupied by

the remainder of the family and the servants. **Nearly**
all the houses of the wealthier citizens contain a number
of spare rooms, reserved for the accommodation of guests
from the country; and the same kind hospitality is frequently tendered to strangers. Most of the modern houses are of brick or stone, and generally from three to four
stories high; the Americans showing great fondness for
large and spacious dwellings, and the ground in the cities
being already too dear to allow them to expatiate much
in area. The exterior of the buildings is less marked by
style or elegance than the interior is clean and comfortable; and the custom prevails, as in England, for each
family to occupy a house of its own. The principal ornament consists in a sort of portico of various dimensions and orders, and a flight of steps leading up to the
entrance. In Boston and New York, these steps are
commonly of sandstone or granite (a species of sienite;)
but, in Philadelphia, they are of beautiful white marble,
which, by daily ablution, is kept as clean as the floor of
the parlors, and contributes much to the neat appearance
of the streets.

The residence of a planter, in the southern states, is
altogether adapted to the climate; the rooms having as
many windows as practicable, and a large covered piazza,
resting on wooden or stone pillars, extending the whole
front of the building. This piazza is sometimes carried
all round the house, and composed of as many stories as
the building itself. Its effect on the eye is far from disagreeable, and its practical advantage in affording shelter
against the sun and the dew of those climates, makes it a
pleasant retreat for all the members of the family.

The streets of the large cities are well paved or macadamised, and the side-walks, commonly of brick or of
flag-stone, elevated, as in England, to protect the people
against horses and vehicles. In Boston and Philadelphia,
they are kept exceedingly clean; but in New York, with
the exception of Broadway, the principal street, they oft-
en contain wherewithal to feed multitudes of those gentle creatures "that plow not, nor obey thy call." The
continued bustle and stir of business in New York seems
to preclude the possibility of sweeping and cleansing
them; and it may, therefore, be considered a happy cir-
4*

cumstance, that a, set of scavengers should have been
found willing to do the needful from sheer inclination ;
and ready, at any time, to pay with their own flesh and
blood for whatever advantages they may thus be suffered
to enjoy.

It must not be inferred, however, that the part inhabited
by the more wealthy inhabitants (which is now the West
end of the town, and bids fair to rival, at some future day,
the most fashionable parts of London,) are in the same
filthy state. There all is neatness and cleanliness. The
streets are daily swept and sprinkled with water ; the side-
walks are kept clean ; the porticos of the houses are of
marble or sienite; in short, that part is superior in style
and elegance to anything exhibited in other cities of the
United States.

Neither is the vicinity of the dwellings of the lowest
classes more disgusting and mean than some of the dirty
lanes of London or Southwark, and certainly far superi-
or to the wretched hovels of the poor in Dublin. Whenever the Americans speak of the poor, the term is used
merely in contradistinction to the rich, but never denotes
that abject order of human beings, who, in the larger capitals of Europe, offend and disgust the eye with scenes of
the most abandoned wretchedness. How long this state
of prosperity is to last, it is difficult at present to foretell,
but as long as any portion of the Western territory remains to be settled, no period can be assigned to its duration.

At the beginning of this work I proposed to myself not
to give descriptions of inanimate objects, further than
might be necessary to illustrate the manners of the people. Whether works of architecture come under this
head or not, I am unable to decide ; but I think it not in-
consistent with the general plan of this work to offer a
few remarks on American churches. The greater number of these, when compared to the wealth of their respective congregations, are decidedly mean, both in their
exterior and interior appearance ; and there exists, in
this respect, an infinitely greater disparity between them
and the houses of worship in Europe, than between the
dwellings of the rich and the palaces of European princes. If republicans are at all permitted to display splen-

dor and magnificence, without offending the pride of their fellow-citizens, it is certainly in the edifices of public worship, and in the halls of their legislative assemblies. With regard to the latter, the Americans possess, already, a proud monument of national grandeur. The capitol at Washington, situated on an eminence commanding an unobstructed view of many miles in circumference, is an edifice of the most imposing structure and proportions; and, from its very position, incredibly superior to any of the public palaces in Europe. The interior, too, corresponds well with the dignity of the design; but the most sublime effect is produced by its standing high, free, and alone, as the institutions it guards in its bosom; overshadowing hills and valleys, and rivers of the mighty land over which it exerts the benign influence of law and justice.

But, proud as the Americans may be of their halls of congress, they have not, as yet, a single place of worship at all to be compared to the finer churches in Europe, where they might render thanks to the Omnipotent Being for the unexampled happiness and prosperity with which he has blessed their country. Some not altogether unsuccessful attempts have been made in Boston and Baltimore, at what might be called a cathedral; but neither the size nor the order, nor even the materials, are resembling those of the nobler specimens of Gothic architecture in Europe.*

Our feelings and emotions are always tinged with the reflections from the objects around us; and I cannot, therefore, divest myself of the opinion that a superior style of architecture in an edifice of public worship may materially assist the imagination, and enable the mind to turn from mere wordly objects to the contemplation of heaven and the adoration of God. I have known persons who could never pray so fervently as when encompassed by the sombre vaults of a gothic cathedral, and I have, myself, experienced the same feelings on similar occasions.

But, in addition to the deficiency in style and ornament

* Trinity Church, in Boston, is a building of pure taste and uniform architecture; and the cathedral at Baltimore enjoys the reputation of being the finest church in the country.

there exists, in America, an almost universal practice of
building churches, or at least the steeples, of wood, to
which are frequently given the most grotesque figures,
partaking of all orders of architecture, from the time of
Noah to the present day.   There is scarce an excuse for
this corruption of taste, except the cheapness of the material, which may recommend the custom in practice.   A
church ought to be the symbol of immutability and eternity, the attributes of the Infinite Being; but nothing
can be more averse to either, than its construction of so
frail a material as wood.   An *imitation* of stone-work is
still more objectionable, as it appears like an attempt at
deceit—a sort of architectural counterfeiting, least pardonable in a house of prayer.   Such an edifice seems to
be unworthy of its noble purpose—a sordid mockery of
grandeur, which, without elevating the mind, represents
to it only the melancholy picture of human frailties.

Yet the Americans are not deficient in liberality towards their clergymen, whose pecuniary compensation
is certainly generous, when compared with the moderate
salaries of the first officers of state, and enables them,
generally, to live in houses much more tastefully built,
and better furnished within, than those in which they deliver their sermons.

This is again republican, and shows the Americans to
be much more attached to substance than to forms.   The
most essential part of divine service is assuredly performed by the clergyman, whose example and admonitions
have a more salutary influence on the general morals of
his congregation, than the most gorgeous cathedral, or
the most moving *cantabile* of Haydn.   Yet the latter have
their advantages too, which, no doubt, will, at some future
day, be duly appreciated in America as in Europe.   In
the Western States, where new settlements are daily forming, it would be absurd to erect buildings, the use of
which would be reserved for the third or fourth generation.   The principal object, there, must necessarily be
immediate usefulness; and it is certainly better for the
people to worship in a wooden church than to have no
church at all.

Another cause, operating against the erecting of costly
churches in the United States, is the absence of a power-

ful hierarchy. Churches in America are built when they are wanted, or whenever a congregation is sufficiently numerous and able to pay a preacher. With them the clergyman must be of more importance than the church, in the building of which they voluntarily tax themselves, without having recourse to the pecuniary assistance of others. This will always keep the church poor; but I doubt whether the practice, while it lasts, does not actually benefit the people. I am convinced there is as good preaching in the United States, and quite as fervent too, as in any country with a church establishment.

Setting aside the injustice (of which Americans at least are fully persuaded) of taxing people of a different belief with the support of an establishment in which they have no stake or interest, there is, in an hierarchy, that which makes its members indolent and lazy. A person provided for, cannot, by the rules of common sense, be supposed to work as hard as one who has to exert himself for a living, or whose services are remunerated in proportion to their merit and usefulness. An hierarchy, from its superior organization and discipline, may have its *political* advantages under peculiar forms of government; but I cannot see any spiritual benefit accruing from it to the people. Every member of a hierarchy is necessarily more interested in *the continuance of the establishment*, than in the discharge of his duties *toward the people*. He is paid by the establishment, of which he is either a functionary or a pensioner, and is as much concerned in its welfare as a British mariner in the safety and endurance of Greenwich Hospital, or a clerk in the solvency of his employers. In America, every clergyman may be said to do business on his own account, and under his own firm. He, alone, is responsible for any deficiency in the discharge of his office, as he is alone entitled to all the credit due to his exertions. He always acts as principal, and is, therefore, more anxious, and will make greater efforts to obtain popularity, than one who serves for wages. The actual stock in any one of those firms is, of course, less than the immense capital of the Church of England; but the aggregate amount of business transacted by them jointly, may, nevertheless, be greater in the United States. The subordinate member of a hierarchy does not act on

his own responsibility; he merely discharges the obligations enjoined by his superiors. It is to them he must
look for advancement, as a soldier looks for promotion
to his commanding officers; and a fault of discipline is
more severely reprimanded than an actual injustice towards a different order. Like the soldier, he has frequently an interest different from that of the people; and,
like him, he is ready to turn his weapons against them
whenever the establishment itself is in danger. A church
establishment resembles always, more or less, a standing
army. It is strong, endurable, and disciplined, but a severe tax upon the people, and nearly as dangerous an instrument for their subjugation.

The situation of an American clergyman is usually
comfortable; but there are no church-livings as in England; no rich prelates, or other high dignitaries, sufficiently wealthy to employ large sums in the building of churches. Every preacher is paid by his congregation; and
there is, consequently, no accumulation of wealth on the
part of the clergymen, nor proportionate poverty on the
part of those who employ them. The conditions of the
different members of the clergy are, as nearly as possible,
on a level with each other and those of the private citizens—no distinction being claimed, save that which is
based on superior talent and application. Hence the
American churches resemble each other as the dwelling-
houses. They are built for use, not for ornament; and
are neither calculated to attract particular attention, nor
to embellish or adorn the cities.

But what they lack in quality is more than compensated by increase of numbers; and in this consists the advantage of the system. There is no village in the United
States without its church, no denomination of Christians
in any city without its house of prayer, no congregation
in any of the new settlements without the spiritual consolation of a pastor. Religious instruction is obtained
every where, at a comparatively cheap rate, without directly taxing the people; and the enormous sums which
would be required for the maintenance of an established
church circulate freely in commerce and manufactures,
and contribute to the general prosperity of the country.

Before I leave this subject, I ought, perhaps, to say a

few words on the observation of the sabbath. No universal practice exists, in this respect, in the United States; the Northern and Western States following the example of England, or rather of Scotland, whilst the extreme south are yet adhering to their original French manner of considering Sunday as a day of amusement.* A sabbath in New England is peculiarly impressive and solemn, but at the same time, so cheering, that I do not remember having spent, in Europe, a day half so satisfactorily. It is only by contrast that the real merit of religious institutions may be duly appreciated; and especially those of the Americans.

The sabbath was instituted for the poor. As the gospel was preached to them in order to direct their hearts to heaven, as the period of their sufferings and the reward of their toils, so the keeping of the sabbath was to alleviate their bodily hardships below; once a week, at least, the rich are to render thanks to the Almighty for the kind dispensation of His providence; but, on that day, the poor also are to rejoice in a partial exemption from labor, and even the beasts of the field are to be reclaimed from the yoke of their owners. It is the day on which all nature is to sanctify the Lord by the universal happiness of His creatures. I have always looked upon the sabbath as the most *democratic* feature in the whole Christian religion. On the sabbath all aristocratic distinctions of rank and fortune are to be forgotten. The powerful are to be humbled before the Lord, and the meanest of mankind exalted to a momentary equality with the highest of their fellow beings, by worshipping the Father of all, in the common capacity of His children.

" The sabbath was made for man, and not man for the sabbath." Mark ii. 27.

As a religious and political institution, it is alike unequalled in church or state; and, on this account, the Americans, and especially the people of New England, have, at an early period, directed to it the whole wisdom of their legislation.

---

* A notion is sufficiently prevalent in England that the Catholics alone indulge in amusements on the sabbath; but the Protestant parts of Germany, and many of Switzerland, have adopted the same practice.

It has been the established maxim of the "Pilgrim fathers" that the principles and doctrines of revealed religion constitute the broadest and safest basis of every rational system of liberty. No sooner, therefore, had they
organised themselves into a political community than they
enacted a series of laws for the strict observation of the
sabbath; and although many of them were not marked
by the spirit of liberality of the present age, they were,
nevertheless, of incalculable advantage in practice; and
did more for the preservation of the infant colony than
any other provision which, at that time, they could have
made for that purpose.* The religious principles inculcated at the solemn meetings of the people on that day,
created a unity of faith and sentiment, which gave their
deliberations and actions that singleness of purpose, which
alone enabled them to triumph over all obstacles which
the soil and the climate had placed in the way of their
progress.

It cannot be objected that other religious institutions,
besides the sabbath, might have been capable of producing the same salutary effect; or that religion might have
been taught and practised at all times, without appoint-
ing a particular day for that purpose. An observance
generally enjoined is more apt to be neglected and forgot
ten than one commanded at specified periods. A duty
which we are required to perform at a certain time is always
more impressive than one to which we are rendered familiar

---

* Amongst the earliest laws for the observation of the sabbath were
these :

" Whoever profaneth the sabbath after admonition, pays, for the first
offence, 5s.; for the second, 10s.; and to be bound over to the County
Court for the third. Governors of youth under seven years, to suffer
for them.

" Drinking and sporting on *Saturdays*, after sunset, pays 5s.; persons
refusing to pay, must suffer corporeal punishment as the Court deter-
mines.

" No work to be done on the sabbath, on penalty of 10s. for the first offence, to be doubled for every following one.

" To travel to a meeting, not allowed by law, is a profanation of the
sabbath.

" Whoever sells drink to a person, except to a stranger, in time of a
lecture, pays 5s.

" Constables may *search* for offenders on the Lord's day; they forfeit
10s. for any neglect."

NEAL's *History of New England, London,* 1720.

by daily usage. No legislator would entrust the safety of a state to the *habit* of its representatives to assemble for the purpose of enacting laws ; but would specify the period on which they are to discharge their duty without fail. Besides, it is impossible to make laws capable of embracing generalities, or of binding men to certain *universal* principles of morality and religion. If a law be not enacted for a specific purpose, which it is distinctly to state, with all its bearings on those whom it is to guide, no true obedience to it can be enforced ; and it can only serve to bring the Legislator into contempt. A law, recommending, in general terms, the principles of the Christian religion, would be of little more force than one enjoining all men to be good, or to abstain from evil. We are to know in what religion consists, and by what external evidence we are to judge of its being practised. No testimony can, in this respect, be more solemn and universal than an act of public worship ; and nothing more satisfactory than a repetition of it at stated periods. For this reason, it has been the practice of all nations to fix upon certain times for the exercise of their religious rites, which were considered as national distinctions, and as so many means of instilling patriotism and virtue. The history of every country is intimately connected with that of its religious progress ; and it is a fact not less remarkable than instructive, that the period of the greatest religious devotion of a people is always coëval with its heroic age. The sabbath of the Jews was long the rallying point of their religion, under the banners of which they accomplished all their victories, and which, while they kept it unsullied, protected them against every assailing power. With the early Christians, the observation of the Lord's day was scarcely of less moment, and became subsequently one of the characterising distinctions of the different sects. Each denomination of Christians celebrated it according to their peculiar form of worship, and availed itself of its recurrence as a means of propagating their doctrines and principles. The observation of the sabbath became associated and identified with the religion to which it gave support, and contributed powerfully to the formation of the Christian character.

When the dissenters became the object of the most unrelenting persecution in England, the sabbath became the day of their spiritual comfort. On that day they gathered strength to bear the sufferings to which they were exposed, and fortified themselves against the trials which awaited them in the future. This is the reason why, immediately after having effected a settlement in America, for the free exercise of their religious worship, they turned their attention to the strict observation of the sabbath. On the Lord's day the whole of their little community was assembled to implore the blessings of Providence on their infant state, alike struggling against famine and the cruelty of the Indians. With them, it was, at once, a religious, political, and social institution, creative of a kind of patriarchal feeling for which their descendants are yet remarkable. It is to this feeling I would allude, in speaking of a New England sabbath.

Much of the original severity of religious discipline has, indeed, yielded to sentiments of greater liberality and forbearance ; enough, however, is yet remaining to reflect the customs and habits of the first settlers. The sabbath is no longer a day of mere " humiliation and prayer, " but also of " thanksgiving and rejoicing ;" yet partaking of all the gravity which distinguishes the character of the New Englander. Whatever change the feelings of the people may have undergone, the external forms of worship are still preserved, and give to the whole a solemn dignity, which cannot but increase their respect for public worship.

Sunday is ushered in by a universal stillness on the evening of Saturday. The theatres are closed ; the sound of music and of revel is alike hushed ; and the members of the different families assemble and fill up the period of cessation from labor with cheerful and friendly conversation. Strangers are not usually admitted to those circles ; but those who are, will leave them with feelings of reverence. I was neither born in New England, nor lived there at a very early period of my life ; but I can easily conceive them to beget a strong attachment to home, and to fill the mind with reminiscences which, wherever a New Englander may wander, will associate the idea of the sabbath with the happiest dreams of his childhood. On Sunday itself, the quiet and stillness of the eve continue till after the evening lecture, when a certain portion of the people relax from the severity of religious performances, by joining a small party of friends and relatives, similar to that in which other families indulge on the evening of Saturday. These *réunions* are far from being marked by noise and merriment. No music or song is heard, save the sacred composition of the German masters, and the ruling character of the whole is happiness and peace.

In the other cities of the United States, the Lord's day is observed as in England. The shops are closed ; the chiming of bells invites to fore and afternoon service; the people are moving to church to worship God, each according to the dictates of his own conscience ; in short, every thing indicates the worship of pious Christians : but the pecular spirit of peace of a New England sabbath is wanting, and, I feel sure, is not to be found in any other part of the world. In some parts of the Southern states, I have seen the sabbath kept in a manner still more rigorous than in any town of New England; yet I could not catch the inspiration, which, though a stranger, educated under different influences, and in a different religion, I often felt during my long residence in Boston.

16 2666

CHAPTER III.

RECEPTION OF FOREIGNERS IN THE UNITED STATES.—THE ENGLISH, SCOTCH, IRISH, GERMANS, FRENCH, ITALIANS, AND SPANIARDS.—AMERICAN PREJUDICES.—THEIR ORIGIN.

When thousands of emigrants, of all nations, are annually embarking for America, with the determined purpose of making it their home, the question would naturally arise, whether, on their arrival thither, they may all expect the same welcome ; and, if there exist any prejudices with regard to the inhabitants of the different countries of Europe, in whose favor, or to whose detriment they are established. It might also be proper to inquire whether these prejudices are purely of a national character, in which case they would refer to the moral habits of the people ; or, whether they relate more to certain professions more exclusively practised by some of them, and repugnant to the feelings of Americans. In either case, the inquiry would be interesting and useful ; as it might not only serve to put foreigners in America on their guard, but explain also a number of peculiarities in the intercourse of Americans with strangers, which, by most travellers, have been traced to a wrong source.

That the Americans have prejudices, I do not pretend to deny ; what nation is entirely free from them ?—though a great number of these must be put to the account of their ancestors ; and the remainder is proportionably small, as their intercourse with foreign nations is great, and the means of information extensively diffused throughout their country. A large portion of these consist, however, in retaliations on the prejudices of others, and especially on those of the English.

The Americans are proud of having achieved their independence, proud of the moral and political progress of their country since that period, proud of the wealth and power they have acquired, and exceedingly jealous lest other nations, and particularly those whose opinions they value most, should not give them sufficient credit for wisdom, perseverance, and patriotism. The Americans cannot persuade themselves that the English will ever do them justice, (and it must be confessed that hitherto little justice has been done to them,) and are, therefore, more frequently guilty of solecisms of deportment with regard to them than towards any other nation with whom they come in contact. A German or a Frenchman might reside for years in the United States without being struck with those traits of Americans, which prove, sometimes, annoying to the English. He might, perhaps, complain of their national prejudices in other respects; but the complaint would arise from a different source, and would be similar to that which might be caused by a residence in England. I will explain.

There exists, in America, as, perhaps, in every other civilized country, a strong prejudice in favor of the *English nation*. The Americans love and admire British thoughts and conceptions, which they have chosen for their permanent models; they entertain a high respect for British customs and laws, on which they have established their own, and cherish a proud remembrance of the achievements of that glorious people from whom they are themselves descended. They allow, in many instances, the superiority of the English over themselves; but they are too well informed to apply the same distinction indiscriminately to *individuals*.

An American, in his private capacity, will receive any stranger with politeness, and is always willing to distinguish individuals in proportion to their reputation and acquirements. In the words of Mr. Hamilton, " he is quite aware of high breeding, *when he sees it;* " but he is the last ready to pay homage to any man, merely " because England has produced him." This, however, is precisely what most Englishmen expect; and they are,

5*

therefore, often bitterly disappointed. Few English gentlemen of reputation, however, will visit America without meeting with a cordial reception, bearing witness of the prejudice which is there established *in their favor*. The Americans are, on all such occasions, anxious to make the most favorable impressions; but are, perhaps, inclined to praise and even exaggerate the advantages of their country, from the known propensity of their guests to make the most liberal discount.

Many anomalies of conduct of which they are found guilty towards the English, arise from the conviction that their usual simplicity of manners would be apt to be misconstrued; and that the English, accustomed to judge all people by their own conventional standard, will not make allowances for those changes which the difference of the climate, the political institutions of their country, and the early habits of the people may have rendered necessary. In such cases, therefore, they endeavor to copy Europeans *au pied de la lettre*, and thereby furnish, themselves, the standard by which they are but too often condemned. The Americans are not often guilty of a similar error with regard to Europeans from the Continent. To them they show themselves as they are, and are even *proud* of their national peculiarities. The consequence is a greater freedom of manners, and a degree of cordiality which is seldom experienced by Englishmen. Few distinguished Germans or Frenchmen would bestow so much philosophical criticism and analysis on the manners of those who receive them with kindness and hospitality: they would find in the civil and political institutions of America enough to arrest their attention; and enjoy at least this advantage over the English, that they might converse with Americans without being taken for spies.

Amongst the number of works which have been published in England, on the United States of America, it is really surprising to see the quantity of space devoted to the subject of "manners;" and this not to the manners of the people *in general*, but (with the exception of Mrs. Trollope) to those of the fashionable coteries. Is this not sufficient to justify the belief of Americans that the English are abusive critics, whose severity increases even with the obligation conferred upon them to win their

good will? The Americans, in return, are guilty of another injustice; they ascribe the abusive character to the
British NATION, when, in fact, it is the peculiar gift of
individuals, who, dissatisfied with their own country, are
travelling over the Continents of Europe and America in
order to annoy themselves at leisure, and occasionally
publish a book to defray a part of their expenses. Censure to them is as natural as the sting to the scorpion,
and it is even dangerous to approach them by way of rendering them a service. On their way they abuse every
thing that is *not* English; on their return to England,
every thing that *is* English; and when they think of the
future, every thing that *will* be English in less than a
century. We must look to the political doctrines of these
gentlemen for an interpretation of their sentiments as
regards society. We shall find that their attachment to
every thing claimed by age is perfectly legitimate; that
they are themselves travelling antiquities, belonging to
an age that is past; and that, consequently, America is
much too young to merit their serious attention. Her
achievements require no *herald*, though they may be sufficient for a *chronicle*.

Nothing, indeed, can be more gratuitous than the extraordinary pains which the Americans take to please
foreigners, who are to give an account of their country.
Tourists, especially from England, are literally loaded
with civilities; and, perhaps, the more kindly received
by the fashionable coteries of the large cities, as their stay
is expected to be short, and their grateful returns as everlasting as paper and ink can render them. In this manner a number of individuals may hope to be introduced to
the English public, whose fame, were it confined to
America, could hardly be wrested from oblivion, and
whose wise sayings would never be known to the world,
were they not quoted as valuable specimens of American
sapience.

No sooner is the arrival of some English literati gazett-
ed in America than all is bustle and confusion; and the
question is seriously debated in what manner they must
be received, and what sacrifices ought to be made in
order to win their good opinion. Invitations and visits
crowd upon them, and they can actually find no time to

observe what is truly interesting. From the time of their landing to the hour of their departure, they are never left alone, and have, therefore, no opportunity of seeing America *as it is*, but as it is *shown to them*. The Americans are then *sitting for their portraits*, and, as is usual on such occasions, contort their features either in an unnatural frown, or disfigure them by an insignificant simper, ill suited to their habits of business and reflection. Under such circumstances an accurate likeness can hardly be expected from the most accomplished artists, much less from the *pseudo dilettanti* who have lately travelled to those regions.

But the task of an English tourist is rendered doubly difficult by the inordinate adulation with which his vanity is pampered. He must imagine himself really a great man, when he sees the *élite* of a nation willing to pay him homage, in order to be entitled to a portion of his favor. He is made the arbiter of their political and religious dissensions, and is expected either to become the apostle of their fame, or the rigid censor of their public and private morals. Both, the Americans and the tourist, are put in a false position ; and if the former are disappointed in seeing themselves caricatured, the mortification of the latter must be equally great, when, on his return to England, he finds himself divested of his imaginary power, and his *opus magnum* levelled to an equality with the ephemeral productions of the day. The incurable wounds which he thought to inflict on the Americans are scarcely felt, except by a few of those who see their hospitality so ill requited ; and the great bulk of the nation is quietly progressing onward, in their happy simplicity hardly suspecting that any one has been aiming a blow at them.

That some of the writers on American society thought it in their power to injure the United States past all recovery, is sufficiently evident from the dedication of the learned author of " Men and Manners," to William Wolryche Whitmore, Esq., M. P.

" But," says our author, " when I found the institutions and experience of the United States deliberately quoted in the reformed parliament, as affording safe precedent for British legislation, and learning that the drivellers who uttered such nonsense, instead of encountering

merited derision, were listened to with patience and approbation, by men as ignorant as themselves, I certainly
did feel that another work on America was yet wanted,
and at once determined to undertake a task *which inferior
considerations would probably have induced me to decline.*"

Would one not be led to infer, from this dedicatory epis-
tle, that he thought it as easy to make the quietus of a nation
as to despatch a novel ? The event, however, must have
convinced him of his error; as it may, perhaps, persuade
the Americans that justice would sooner be done to them
if they were to show themselves more indifferent on trial,
and less anxious to win the good opinion of their judges.

But the prejudices in favor or against Englishmen
which exist amongst the fashionable coteries of the United
States are not the same as those which belong to the laboring classes ; and the civilities with which an English
gentleman is loaded, on his first arrival in America, undergo a material change, from the time he intends to
become a resident, or to enter into competition with the
natives. He will then find, that in proportion as the *élite*
recede from him, the middle classes are ready to receive
him. He will find no difficulty in procuring patrons and
friends, and no prejudices to debar his success, provided
it be based on *individual* exertion, and not upon *national*
preference.

The Americans are always ready to associate with
Englishmen on terms of *equality ;* they are willing to
consider English as part of their own family ; but they
will not pardon overweening conceit, and are most uncompromising on questions of a national complexion.
The Americans, of all people in the world, are the
readiest to take and resent an insult ; but they are more
particularly sensitive with regard to the offences of the
English. If any such be given by a person of notoriety,
it will be prudent for him to avoid the popular revenge.
His best friends will not be able to protect him from injury, and the wisest plan for him to adopt will be to make
a speedy reparation. I write this particularly for the
benefit of certain actors who may visit the United States
for the purpose of paying their debts. Let them not
abuse the popular favor which their talents are sure to
receive ; let them be guarded in their language, not only

on the stage, but also in their private intercourse with
Americans; let them not consider the condition of any
man so low as to be unable to injure them; in one word,
let them keep out of the debt of the people; for the people will make themselves paid.

Nor is it always popular violence which, in such cases,
is most to be dreaded. Whenever a national insult is
given, the Americans of all classes unite to punish the
offender. His career in the United States is blasted forever, and he is, at once, banished from society, to which
neither fortune nor cleverness will be able to procure him
a second introduction. But if the Americans are thus
severe in their punishment, they are equally generous in
their reward of forbearance. Their favor is easily won,
and still more easily preserved. They claim of the
English but that which the English claim of every other
nation in the world — a compliance with their rules and
customs, and a *total* abstinence from censure; for which,
in return, they are willing to make every honest conces-
sion, and even those public acknowledgments which it
would be impossible to extort from them by derision and
scorn.

The customs and peculiarities of the English are not
generally liked in the United States; and a settlement of
several hundreds of them in one place would excite considerably more jealousy than one of so many thousand
Germans. The reason is this. The Germans have their
peculiar habits, which, however, they are careful not to
obtrude upon others. They persevere in them, not because they think them superior to those of other nations,
but merely because they are accustomed to them, and do
not like to quit the early companions of their childhood.
This is perfectly well understood in America, and, therefore, no fears entertained of their ever attempting to make
proselytes. The French, too, have their peculiarities;
but their notion of good breeding forbids their exhibiting
them wherever they might give private or public offence.
Not so with the English. They *glory* in the most trifling
difference between themselves and other nations; because
they are accustomed to consider that difference *in their
favor*. They obtrude it, therefore, constantly, on the
notice of others, or, at least, take no pains to soften its

appearance. They heed not the feelings of others, or are so much in the habit of considering every other people inferior to themselves, that they care not, if, by chance, they give offence. In Europe they pay for this arrogance with money ; in America with the loss of personal consideration.

It is true, there are ample apologies for the conduct of the English. They are really, in most respects, superior to other nations, and especially to their neighbors on the Continent. They enjoy, in the first place, a greater degree of political freedom than any other people, save the Americans, in the world. They have produced the ablest statesmen, the wisest legislators, and (with few exceptions) the bravest and most skilful commanders of armies and navies. Their philosophers have been the glory of the human mind, and have wrested more truths from nature than all other sages combined together. They can boast of the most manly and classical literature of the moderns, and may, perhaps, add that there is not a valuable thought which the human mind is capable of conceiving which is not already, and most happily, expressed in the English languages. They have surpassed all other nations in the mechanic arts, and have become equally superior in every thing relating to manufactures. They have increased the facilities of commerce by the establishment of powerful colonies, and have (with probably but one exception) distinguished themselves for the humanity and justice with which they have governed them. They have carried the blessings of civilization and religion wherever they went, and established, in every clime, the glory of the British name.

But in their intercourse with Americans, they ought to remember that the latter are of the same origin ; that they have not only the means, but also the disposition to imitate them in all that is great, and enough prudence and experience to avoid falling into the same errors. They ought to reflect, that if the Americans have as yet a comparatively small catalogue of great men, these men were, nevertheless, distinguished by the most exalted virtues, and that, on the other hand, there is no black list of names to detract from their national honor. They ought to consider that America is the country, which, eventually must rival even England, and that the Americans, conscious of their physical and political advantages, are, perhaps, a little prone to anticipate the future.

They have already entered upon a fair competition with the English in almost every branch of human industry; and, by the universal consent of all nations, become their peers in navigation and commerce. A people, progressing with such rapid strides, is not apt to bear taunts with good nature, or allow others to constitute themselves masters of ceremonies. Their progress has been one of uninterrupted prosperity, and as long as this lasts, they will consider their policy and their customs, if not superior, at least equal, to those of any other nation. As republicans, they love their country with an enthusiastic ardor, which can only be understood and appreciated by those who have, themselves, a share in the government of their country. It is, therefore, neither wise nor expedient to treat their peculiarities with contempt, or to wound their national pride by a too rigid adherence to a set of manners, which, from peculiar associations, have become irritating and offensive to the people. I do not mean to say that an Englishman in America must necessarily be a radical ; but if he means to become a citizen, (especially in the Western States,) toryism will be less pardoned in him than in a native of America. He will create enemies without making himself friends ; while those who are his friends will not show their friendship in public. If he should undertake any thing, the success of which depends on the favor of the public, he will hardly be able to succeed ; and even in his social relations he will find himself deserted and alone.

What I have said of the English will equally apply to the Scotch, though in such matters the latter seldom need admonition — their manners and customs being already similar to those of the New Englanders. They usually succeed in whatever they undertake, and hardly ever fail to make America their home. Most of them, on their arrival in the United States, are poor but industrious ; and having been emigrants before, have had sufficient instruction, in the school of adversity, to bear success or ill-fortune with equanimity and patience. They do not easily offend the prejudices of the people among whom they hope to prosper, and, in general, understand their own interests too well to require advice from others. To the acquisitiveness of the New Englanders they join the great art of saving, which is the cause of their accumulating wealth with even greater facility than native Americans ; and it insures to them its quiet possession. Their sentiments are generally in accordance with those of the majority of the people, and they are, therefore, doubly certain of meeting with that sympathy and hospitality which the Americans are always ready to extend to the natives of Britain.

To sum up the argument, English and Scotch are received in America as relatives. Their younger brethren are willing to share with them the paternal estate. They love them, befriend them, assist them ; in short, do everything for them which one brother can for another; but they burst into indignation at the very mention of *primogeniture*, or the least attempt to claim, by right, what they are willing to concede from kindness.

The Irish are, by the great majority of Americans, considered as an oppressed and injured people, which is sufficient to entitle them to the sympathies of freemen. It is true, the greater number of Irish who arrive in the United States are poor, and some of them tainted by the vices of poverty, which, in some of the states, have created a prejudice against them. But, considered collectively, they constitute a highly useful part of the American community, and contribute, by their honest industry, to increase the wealth of the country. They perform the hardest labors at the lowest wages given in the United States, and are satisfied and happy to provide for themselves and their children the bare necessaries of life. But it is even their being contented with little, and their less heeding the future, which render their actions and motives less acceptable to the Americans. The Americans (as I shall prove hereafter) are living altogether for their children. They are ready to make any sacrifice for the advancement of future generations, and love their country not *as it is ;* but *as it will be made* by their enterprise and industry. The Irish, on the contrary, are by habit, inclination, and the vivacity of their temperaments,

6

inclined to enjoy the present. Their previous lives contain but the sordid catalogues of privations and distresses, and, on their emerging from the most cruel misery which ever extorted groans from a nation, they are apt — as all human creatures would be — to draw the first free breath with joy and exultation. Like Lazarus, they were accustomed to feed upon the crumbs that fell from the rich man's table ; and now that they are invited to sit down, and partake themselves of the banquet, those rigid censors stand by and scoff at their greedy appetites. A man whose morning meal consisted of capon can certainly await dinner with better grace, than he who went hungry to bed and awoke to breakfast on sorrow. Cheer to him is manna distilled from heaven, to support him on his way through the desert ; and he is eager to snatch at a gift of which he knows not when it will again be within his grasp. Excess is the companion of poverty, and its consequences perpetuate its direful existence. Misery they drown in stupefying potions ; for oblivion alone is the happiness of the damned.

These are the vices of some of those wretches who are annually thrown upon the hospitality of the Americans. And shall America, the land of political and religious freedom, cast them from her * and let them perish, while a bounteous Providence has put in her possession the most fertile regions on earth, capable of supporting thousands and millions of human beings ? And shall the supplications and prayers of these emigrants ascend up to heaven without invoking a blessing on the children of liberty ? Are their habits and their vices not to be corrected by improving their wretched condition ? All human experience speaks loudly in the affirmative. Set before them the prospect of steady employment, the hope of not only earning a subsistence, but something more ; give their children an opportunity of education ; and you will breathe into them a new vivifying principle. Occupation will prevent the commission of crimes ; the influence of religion and good example will abolish the vice of intemperance, and the facilities of instruction will make

* In some of the States provisions have lately been made against the importation of foreign (Irish) paupers.

respectable citizens of their children.   This is not declamation.   I speak of facts which I know, and to which I
shall have occasion to allude hereafter.

The Irish in Boston are a remarkably orderly people.
They are *not* usually given to intemperance ; but on the
contrary, willing to aid in its suppression.   If the annals
of prisons and houses of correction furnish a larger number of Irish than American names, it must be remembered that, in all countries, the greatest number of culprits
is furnished by the poorer and the least educated classes,
and that as strangers, unacquainted with the peculiar
police regulations of the towns, they are more apt to
trespass against the laws, and make themselves liable to
punishment, than those who have been brought up under
its influence, and with whom obedience to it has become
a habit.

Abstract numbers are no criterion of public morals.
Hundreds of crimes against God and against man are not
amenable to the law, while others, arising sometimes
from innocent motives, are visited by its severest penalties.   During the space of nearly ten years I have lived
in Boston, but very few capital crimes were committed,
and certainly not more than three or four considerable
robberies and forgeries ; but not one of them, so far as
my remembrance goes, has been perpetrated or abetted
by an Irishman.   Their offences consisted, principally,
in disorderly conduct, and in infringing on the police
regulations of the city.   Theft they were rarely charged
with ; and I am fully persuaded that were it not for the
still too pernicious influence of ardent spirits, not one
half of these acts would have been committed, and no
stain left on the honest reputation of even the lowest of
the Irish laborers.   But, when we reflect upon the number of crimes committed by the poor, we ought not to
forget their exposed situation ; and when we praise the
moral rectitude of the rich, we ought to consider the high
premium which is paid to their virtue.   It does not belong to man to condemn a whole nation as vicious, or to
pray,—

" Lord, we thank Thee that we are not as these men
are ; " for they too will pray, and " the prayer of the

poor shall be heard," as it is more likely to come from the heart.

> Who never ate his bread with tears,
>   Who ne'er, through nights of bitter sorrow,
> Sat weeping on his wretched bed;
> He knows ye not, ye heavenly powers! *

But it is not so much the vices of the Irish, as their political principles, which prove sometimes offensive to Americans. Some disturbances which of late arose in New York, at the election of the Governor, and in which the Irish unfortunately participated, furnished a certain party with a convenient pretext to ascribe their want of success to the destructive influence of the Irish. In consequence of this, a series of resolutions were adopted to prevent their occurrence in future. The subsequent election, however, proved the insufficiency of the ground they had taken; for, not only did it pass without the public peace being, for one moment, disturbed, but the majority *for* the government was nearly doubled. But I shall not expatiate on this subject now, and will only remark that the Irish are naturally supposed to be in favor of democracy, having been, for centuries, the victims of the opposite doctrine.

But, whatever be the character of some of the Irish emigrants, on their landing in the United States, they all improve with their circumstances, and their children are found amongst the most peaceful and respectable citizens. There are Irish names in the History of America of which she must ever be proud, and which will act as mediators between the angry feelings of a party, and the hospitable inclinations of a whole nation.

Let the Irish, on their arrival in the United States, be, above all things, careful not to disturb the peace of the citizens, by revels of any kind; let them remember that the Americans are proud of their voluntary submission to the law, and that they cannot respect those who habitual-

---

* Wer nie sein Brot mit Thränen ass,
Wer nie durch kummervolle Nächte
  Auf seinem Bette weinend sass
Der kennt Euch nicht, Ihr himmlischen Mächte!
  GÖTHE'S *William Meister.*

ly infringe on them, or are given to excess of any kind. Let them abstain from all participation in political quarrels, before they are able to form a correct opinion or to obtain sufficient information on the subject. Let them refrain from violence of any kind, even if they should be provoked; and let them not fight or break the peace with each other. If they should happen to be wronged, let them appeal to the law ; and the Americans will assuredly procure them justice; for the Americans love peace, and liberty, and justice, more than any people in the world.

If there exist prejudices against the Irish, they are principally founded on their readiness to avenge their own wrongs. Let them remember that there is no occasion for it in the United States ; for America never assumed more jurisdiction over them than over her own citizens; but, on the contrary, received them with generous hospitality, and entitled them to all the privileges of her own children. They must be aware that they remain *guests* till the period prescribed by the law shall have entitled them to the honor of citizens, and that they are, consequently, bound not to abuse the hospitality of their entertainers by disregarding their rules of society, or meddling with their family dissensions.

If a dispute should arise amongst the Americans themselves, let them remain neutral, until, as naturalized citizens, they shall have become members of the same family ; and even then let them imitate the forbearance and moderation of Americans. In this manner they will win golden opinions from all parties, and establish a reputation which will recross the Atlantic, and combat prejudices, which, in Europe itself, are detrimental to the progress and final emancipation of their country. They have already made a noble beginning in Boston. Let it be imitated throughout the United States—nay, let it be imitated in Ireland itself; and their worst enemies will be obliged to render them "*justice.*"

Few words need be said about the French in the United States. Not only is emigration from France exceedingly limited, but those who do emigrate are so seldom inclined to interfere with the policy of the country that, *as a political party*, (with the exception of the French Creoles

6*

in Louisiana,) they are hardly forcing themselves on the notice of Americans. The French do not take an active part in politics, at least nothing to compare with the English or the Germans, and, where they cannot conform to the customs of the country, follow their own with so much modesty and so little intrusion on the established rules of society, that their conduct is approved and commended in every part of the country.

In Philadelphia, Baltimore, Charleston, and New Orleans, French society is not only numerous, but of the highest respectability; and as much may be said of the French society of New York. But in all these places, except New Orleans, they have exchanged the fashions of France for the more substantial customs of America; or, at least, blended them with the English, and thereby produced a mixture which I cannot but think an improvement on social intercourse in general.

As to the French poor, who resort to America as a means of improving their condition, they are known to be remarkably peaceful and industrious. They possess the art of being contented with less than almost any other people, and their whole lives offer, sometimes, instances of the utmost frugality and continued self-denial. This applies also to the French emigrants who have seen better days in Europe. It has been my good fortune to become acquainted with some of these gentlemen, who, during the empire, had held distinguished ranks in Buonaparte's army. They were all distinguished by a peculiar meekness of demeanor, and a total absence of that acidity of temper which is but too frequently engendered by sudden reverses of fortune. When addressed on the subject of their exile, they would answer with the utmost patience, and accompany their explanations with some of those smiles of which it was difficult to determine whether they were produced by the irony of their fate or the unsuspecting simplicity of the inquirer. They evinced an entire resignation to their lot, which enabled them to enjoy life in a new form, and under different auspices, though the affections of their hearts were still fastened to the beautiful land of their nativity.

Yet, with all these amiable qualities of the French, the English are generally preferred to them in almost every employment, except the teaching of their native language and other fashionable accomplishments in which they are known to excel. A Frenchman, on his arrival in the United States, must depend more on the patronage of his own countrymen, or such Americans as have visited, or resided in France, than on a popular feeling in his favor. The Americans have inherited the prejudice from their ancestors that gravity of deportment is inseparable from solidity of character; and they cannot, therefore, persuade themselves that the French, with their fondness for public amusements, can combine those essential domestic virtues with the continuance of which they associate the welfare of their country, and the stability of their political institutions. Neither are the Americans converts to the philosophy of Rousseau and Voltaire; but are, unfortunately, in the habit of beholding in every Frenchman a true disciple of these masters.

French reasoning and French doctrines are not in vogue in the United States; neither is the political experience of France in very high repute with American Statesmen. If the French revolution has advanced the cause of liberty in Europe, it has had a chilling influence on the ardor of its votaries in America. It has made a portion of the Americans doubt their own sentiments, and filled even the mind of Washington with anxious apprehensions of the future. The murdered victims of the French revolution were nigh acting on the Americans as Cæsar's wounds on the Romans, and their spirits are, to this moment, haunting the Senate Chamber of the Capitol. Were it not for the awful warning of the Modern History of France, democracy in America would have met with less opposition, and would have been established quietly, without the assistance of a party.

The French, then, are looked upon with suspicion, though, in a national point of view, they are much admired and caressed. The Americans are too honest and just, not to bow to their genius; but they are slow of imitation while having the example of the British. They prefer English routine to French philosophy, and are more willing to follow a precedent than to establish a new doctrine. I do not think that the French will ever make proselytes in America; though the agreeableness of their manners, and the peculiar charm of their conversation will always insure them the most favorable reception at the drawing-rooms.

The Germans and Dutch are old settlers in the United States, and have, in a measure, acquired a legitimate right to the soil. The Dutch, as is well known, settled New York and a considerable portion of New Jersey, before the colony was conquered by the English, and became the property of the Duke of York. The Germans, also, were amongst the earliest settlers of Pennsylvania, and amongst the most pious and virtuous quakers who had been converted by the preaching of William Penn.* They introduced the manufacture of paper, linen and woollen cloth,† and were, from the earliest period of the colony, amongst those who contributed most to its wealth and prosperity. Germantown was entirely founded by Germans, previous to the establishment of Philadelphia, and descendants of those settlers, or new emigrants from Germany, are now conducting the principal manufacturing establishments in that city.

The Germans fought with the Americans in the early wars against the Indians,‡ and assisted them in their struggle for independence. They raised amongst themselves several regiments of militia, and shared the fatigues of Washington's army in the long war of the revolution.§ The question with regard to them, therefore, is no longer whether they shall be tolerated, or what hopes they may have of success?—they are citizens, who have already succeeded. They, are, moreover, possessed of political power; for, having, at an early period of their settlement, adopted the plan of remaining together, they have brought whole districts under their influence; and there are now villages in the states of Pennsylvania and Ohio, and even in the new state of Illinois, where no other language is spoken but their own.

Their power is derived from the possession of the soil, and the remarkable union which prevails in their sentiments. It is, indeed, a gratifying spectacle to see those Germans, who from the time of Tacitus to the present

---

* Proud's History of Pennsylvania.
† Ibid.   ‡ Ibid.
§ Botta. *Storia della guerra dell' independenza.*

day, could not unite on any uniform government of their own, rally cheerfully round the banner of the American republic, and uphold it as their guide and their law. I know that they love that republic with all the fervor with which their brethren in Europe are attached to their ideal Germany, which, as yet, exists only in song.* Neither do the Americans themselves doubt the sincerity of their attachment to their adopted country, though some may differ from them as to the manner in which it ought to be manifested. I shall give, hereafter, my views on the political character of the Germans, and their influence on the government of the United States, from which it will appear, that, much as it may be deprecated by one party, it is gratefully hailed by the other.

Neither is the power of the Germans stationary, but, on the contrary, increasing constantly in numbers and possessions. Thousands of Germans are annually emigrating to the United States; and thousands of them purchase real estates, or acquire them by persevering industry. They do not disperse and become mixed with the Americans, but increase the settlements which are already established by their countrymen, or settle in their immediate neighborhood. They are, therefore, in the very outset less dependent on the Americans than on their own brethren, from whom they derive the principal means of support. Their own countrymen undertake their instruction in the rules and regulations of the country, and, being for the most part, sturdy democrats, teach them to refrain from all measures not in strict accordance with that doctrine.

Their sentiments are easily explained. The Germans, even in Europe, are more fit for a republican government than any other nation on the continent. Their habits, inclinations, morals, and, above all, their superior educa-

---

* The English know the patriotic song of Arndt,

" Where is the German fatherland?
Wherever the German tongue is spoken,
And sings songs to God in heaven, &c.

Was ist des Deutschen Vaterland?
So weit die Deutsche Zunge klingt,
Und Gott im Himmel Lieder singt," &c.

tion, render them fit for a democratic republic. For nearly twenty-five years their efforts were directed towards a
gradual improvement of their social and political institutions; and amongst the most ardent partisans for improvement were three-fourths of the talent, enterprise and
learning of all Germany. Were the Germans united under one government, the largest standing army could not
have withstood their movement; for it has communicated
itself to all classes, and, in part, even to the army itself.
There is no opposition to it, except from the ignorant and
vulgar; because even those whose interest it is to prevent
the spreading of liberal doctrines are convinced of their
moral and philosophical justice, and differ from the rest
only as to the manner in which they are to be applied in
practice.

Even the rulers of Germany are tacitly admitting their
truth, and relent in the persecution of those who have sin-
ned against sacred majesty. Many German princes have,
at least, given a semblance of a constitution to their subjects. They have surrendered the right of arbitrary taxation, and would, perhaps, have done more, if Austria
and Prussia had allowed it. But, whatever the form of
government in Germany may be, the abstract rights of
the governed, and the sacred obligations of the rulers,
were always implicitly admitted. I do not remember
having read an imperial decree of Austria, in which the
emperor did not undertake to justify his motives to his
people, in order to convince them that he is taxing them
for their own good.

There is, in truth, this peculiarity in the character of
Germans, that they can neither act against, nor ever act,
except from conviction. They are most intrepid when
convinced of the rectitude of their intentions; but they
are totally incapable of motion before the principle itself
is established. Their strength is derived from their consciences, and not from the degree of exaltation of which
their passions are capable. Hence, reform in Germany
has not begun with an appeal to national glory or cupidity; but with the establishment of truths in the minds of
the people. It has altogether been of an intellectual nature; but, in that sense, it has, perhaps, progressed further than in any other country. Its action has, indeed,

been too much confined to education and literature; but
by these means it will not less find its way to all classes;
and what shall once have become the unanimous will of
the nation, will be with difficulty withheld by their rulers.
But the Germans will, for a long time yet, abstain from
positive violence, in which they have as little faith as their
Saxon kindred the English. They will not pull down one
edifice before they have erected another; but, like the
British, prefer a " coat with many patches " to one which
does not fit.

With these characteristics of the Germans we shall
find no difficulty in comprehending the position they have
taken in the United States. The democratic principles
of the American government agreed perfectly with their
notions of right, justice and humanity; and they have,
therefore, embraced them with the same holy faith with
which their ancestors clung to the principles of the reformation. They are morally convinced of their excellence;
and instead of ratiocinating and subtilizing about them,
believe in them as they do in their Bible, and transmit
their faith to their children. Every new comer is initi-
ated into their creed, and soon becomes a convert to it;
for if he should not, they would shun him as given to idol-
atry. In this manner the doctrine spreads with the extent of the territory they occupy; but they never over-
step their boundary, or obtrude their faith on the Americans. So far from preaching their doctrines to the inhabitants of other states, they are satisfied with enjoying
liberty at home; and, instead of acting as a *moving principle* in the political councils of the nation, their influence
is only felt by the *masses* which they oppose to, or employ
in favor of, a particular measure.

Yet, with all their quietude and forbearance, they have
not been able to escape from sarcasm and ridicule, and
the terms "high" and "low Dutch" are applied to them
in all the various significations of which they are capable.
The feelings of an educated German are not very nicely
touched by certain figurative expressions from the lips of
ladies; such as "a regular *Dutch* figure," (meaning the
reverse of Mdlle. Taglioni;) "a *Dutch* face," (somewhat quadrangular and full of listless simplicity;) "a
Dutch head," (not one of Raffaello da Urbino's; but

square at the top with large bumps behind the ears, indicative of gentle resistance ;) "a *Dutch* mouth," (capable of holding a common-sized orange without injuring the skin ;) "a *Dutch* foot," (the highest American conception of magnitude and expansion ;) "Dutch manners," (any thing but good breeding,) &c. These epithets are sometimes inadvertently used in the presence of Germans from Europe, when the mistake will be instantly repaired by assuring them that they do not apply to *them*, but to their awkward *countrymen* in Pennsylvania. The Germans, however, are far from taking these sallies in dudgeon, but, on the contrary, concede to the fair satirists the most unrivalled superiority in wit, beauty and accomplishments.

With regard to the American prejudices for, or against Germans, I can only say that some are highly favorable ; but others decidedly *against* my countrymen. I shall begin with those in their favor. These exist principally in the Northern States, and especially in New England. To a more limited extent they are also to be found to the south, and more particularly in South Carolina. The New Englanders and the southern planters are acquainted with German literature, and transfer a portion of their regard for that imaginary world of beauty, harmony and grandeur, the creation of German genius, to every well-educated individual from that country. But while they look upon Germany as a fairy land, in which one cannot wake, sleep or move, without being charmed or tormented by some spirit, they are apt to consider its inhabitants as dreamers, and its philosophers as so many weavers of moonshine. A very similar opinion is sufficiently prevalent in England, even among the lierati, though the conceptions of the German mind are there more highly prized and better understood than in any other country.

The cause is apparent. Few German authors, especially on metaphysics, have, as yet, been ably translated into English ; and if the public are to rely on the judgment of critics, they will always be told that those works contain "moonshine," rather than "that their light is incapable of illumining the dark;" though it may be sufficient to "make darkness visible." The Americans, entertaining on most subjects of taste and learning the same feelings as the English, or, taking the English for their standard, do not consider German thought and reasoning as very safe guides to "*practical truths,*" and bestow, therefore, but a limited confidence to professional men of that school. They are willing to give the Germans credit for general scholarship and great grasp of mind ; but they will not easily trust them in a particular branch, except, perhaps, in the elementary departments of education, which they think sufficiently removed from the "practical business of life " to be safely confided to their care. German theology, medicine, and jurisprudence are at a considerable discount ; but philosophy is an absolute drug. If a poor emigrant from Germany, on his arrival in the United States, should possess no other marketable commodity, he may prepare to die at the alms-house ; for private charity might at last become weary of supporting him. If he be not " hanged," he will at least be buriėd " at the State's expense," though during his life-time he may enjoy the sympathy of scholars and friends. The Americans will treat him with kindness, and show the greatest consideration for his mind and character. There will be those who will offer him pecuniary assistance ; but by far the majority will be ready to confine him to a mad-house. The most prudent course for him to pursue will be to hire himself out on a farm, to make himself, in some way or other, " useful to the community." In no other country could he be so forcibly convinced of the truth of Mephistopheles' comparison,—

> I tell thee, friend, a man who speculates,
> Is like a beast upon a barren heath,
> Forever led in circles by the devil;
> While all around full fresh the meadows bloom.*

With regard to the mechanical arts, the Germans are hardly better. If they are not employed by one of their own countrymen, their chance of success is but small, and by no means equal to the English. Not only will

---

* Ich sag es dir ; ein Kerl, der speculirt,
  Ist wie ein Thier, auf dürrer Heide
Von einem bösen Geist im Kreis herum geführt,
  Und rings, umher liegt schöne grüne Weide.
Göthe's Faust.

7

they find their language an impediment, but most of their work either done better than what they are accustomed to do in Germany, (because the American master mechanics give and obtain higher prices for labor,) or forestalled by the British who excel in it, and are, therefore, certain of having the preference over all other competitors. Agriculture is the proper resort of Germans emigrating to the United States; and there are few instances in which they have not been successful. But any honest trade will succeed amongst their own countrymen, who will sooner patronize them than Americans themselves.

My advice to the German emigrants, therefore, is, not to remain an instant longer in any of the large sea-port towns than is absolutely necessary to make provisions for their journey westward; for, every moment they tarry in the cities is a loss of time and money, and, consequently, an impediment to their ultimate success.

As cultivators of the soil, they have the finest prospect before them; for no other country offers the same resources, or will so richly reward their industry. As farmers, the German emigrants have a decided advantage over all other settlers; for they find friends, relatives, and a home in three or four of the largest and most fertile states of the Union. There the German language is no obstacle to their progress; because thousands around them speak no other. They will find German papers, German churches, and German schools. Their officers of justice will be Germans; their physicians, and—if they should be so unfortunate as to need them—their lawyers. It will appear to them as if a portion of the land of their fathers had, by some magic, been transplanted to the New World. They will find the same dwellings, the same corn-fields, the same orchards, and, of late, the same vines. Every object which may strike their eyes will revive some dream of their childhood, and increase their affection for the country of their adoption. The peace, quietude, and happiness of Germany will be unfolded to their delighted senses; only the fore and back ground will be indistinct—they will discover neither princes nor beggars.

It remains for me yet to say something of the reception of Italians, Spaniards, and Portuguese. Practically there can be no prejudices against gentlemen from any country; but theoretically there exists, in the United States, as in England and all the North of Europe, a peculiar dislike to Southerners in general, which must always be more or less injurious to individuals. The Texian war is not apt to soften these prejudices with regard to the Spaniards; nor has the late history of Italy very materially increased the respect which the English entertain for the Italians. There is something in the manners, habits and inclinations of these nations which appears to be repugnant to the feelings of the North, and there is something even in their love of liberty, which will fill an American with horror.

The number of Spaniards and Portuguese in the United States is comparatively small, and is not likely to increase; as they are generally as little satisfied with the country as the people with them, and seldom resort to America, except when every other enterprise has failed. Yet there are some highly respectable Spanish families in all the sea-port towns, and a considerable number of them in the State of Louisiana. They, there, imitate the manners of the Americans; and, acquiring property by honest industry, become sincerely attached to the customs and institutions of the country.

CHAPTER IV.

THE Americans, as a nation, cannot be said to be very
fond of theatrical performances; though nearly all the
large cities of the Union are provided with one, or several good play-houses. In the fitting up of these there is
often displayed considerable elegance; and in New York
and Philadelphia they may be said to be decorated
with taste. Boston has two theatres; New York three,
and an Italian Opera ; Philadelphia three ; Baltimore
one ; Washington one ; Cincinnati one ; and the city of
New Orleans, besides the English house, a very good
French *Vaudeville* and *Opéra Comique.* The company
of the latter quit New Orleans in the summer, and perform in all the large towns of the North ; which, therefore,
in addition to the English plays, may be said to possess,
(for a season, at least,) a French Comedy.

All these establishments seem to prove that the Americans take an interest in theatres; but when we inquire
into the financial operations of the managers, we must
either conclude that the taste of the people is not sufficiently understood and gratified, or that the Americans
have not, as yet, contracted that particular habit of amusement. Of all the theatres in the United States there is
but one (in New York) which is known to have carried
on a profitable business ; and most of the enterprises of
individuals have entirely failed.

For my own part, I do not think the fault lies so much
with the managers, as with the public itself. The Americans are not fond of any kind of public amusement ; and
are best pleased with an abundance of business. Their

pleasure consists in being constantly occupied; and their evenings are either spent at home, or with a few of their friends, in a manner as private as possible. The continued public excitement, occasioned by their political proceedings, the extent and magnitude of national enterprise, and the constant activity which pervades all classes of society, render rest and quietude much more desirable than an additional stimulus, were it but to pleasure. The Americans are too young a people; they are yet themselves too active performers in the historical drama of their country, to take delight in contemplating the world as it is reflected from the stage. There is not yet any thing " foul in the state " to create a taste for tragedy.

Theatrical performances, moreover, are opposed to the religious doctrines of the majority of Americans, and they always interfere with their domestic arrangements and habits. Few ladies, therefore, are ever seen at the theatres ; and the frequenting of them, even by gentlemen, is not considered a recommendation to their character. In several places where theatres had been established, they have again been abolished by the religious influence of the clergy ; and there are Christian churches in America who will not allow any of their members to be seen at a play-house.

Under these circumstances, the only harvest of an American theatre (with a few honorable exceptions at home) is the arrival of some stars from England, who have so much found their account in the journey, that of late whole constellations have travelled out of their orbits to afford brother Jonathan an opportunity of improving his taste. Some of these have even published their *bright* career in the New World, and have not a little contributed, on and off the boards, to the general diversion of the public.

But this apparent success of English actors in America must not be ascribed to a taste for dramatical performances. It is, then, curiosity, and not a particular interest in the play, which acts as a stimulant on the Americans ; they rather go to see what pleases the English, than in order to be pleased themselves. But their curiosity being once satisfied, they soon relax into their domestic habits, and abandon the drama to the actors. The exhi-

7*

bition of a sagacieus elephant, or a learned dog, would have afforded them a similar attraction ; and of all the public exhibitions of any kind, none succeeded so completely, or drew, for so long a period, full and fashionable audiences, as that of the automaton chess-player and the "conflagration of Moscow." But, then, Mr. Maelzel, who exhibited these wonders, was a very agreeable man, who, with a good-natured German smile always reserved the first benches for the children, and regularly pampered them with sugar-plums. There was, besides, *mechanical* ingenuity in the performance ; and a *problem* to solve, which is always interesting to Americans.* Of all the English actors and actresses who have visited America at different periods, none have so completely succeeded as Miss Kemble ; but even *her* talents and accomplishments had a fearful rival in the powerful attractions of the automaton Turk.

It appears, then, that the Americans, in some instances at least, are willing to pay for the privilege of being *spectators*, but that few of them only are ever desirous of becoming *actors ;* that they are sometimes willing to be amused, but not disposed to divert others.—This might be expected from a young enterprising people, whose talents and labors are turned to a better account in agriculture or commerce ; and whose early habits and education are repugnant to the comparatively inactive lives of performers. Yet the Americans have produced some very good tragedians, and have amply supplied the comic department, for which they seem to have a prevalent taste.

But Jonathan's wit is essentially different from the English, and is, with very few exceptions, deficient in humor. I never saw an American attempt the broad humor of John Bull without his appearing *outré*, and unnatural ; but I have hardly ever known him to fail in

* The automaton chess-player was but a short time in the United States, when an American rival appeared, in every respect equal to that which was exhibited by Mr. Maelzel. The mechanism was the same, and it was exhibited in the same manner, by opening but one door of the box at a time. But Mr. Maelzel had the triumph of beating him, or rather of making him decline his challenge ; the person concealed in the American automaton being a weaker player than Mr. Schlumberger (employed by Mr. Maelzel) whose skill in the game had for many years been tested by the players of the *Café de Regence.*

satire and sarcasm. Neither did I ever hear those shouts of laughter, in America, which an English comic actor is wont to draw forth from his audience at home.

The Americans do not laugh at honest bluntness, or good-natured simplicity, and are, of all people in the world, the least capable of appreciating *la bagatelle.* If Jonathan is to laugh he must have a point given him, or, in other words, he must laugh to some purpose. One resemblance, however, there is between him and his brother, which consists in both being very fond of laughing at the expense of their neighbors. English, French, Dutch and Germans are in turn made to suffer the stings of American wit, and the respective descendants of these nations in the United States furnish a fund of anecdote for that purpose. Accordingly the Germans of Pennsylvania, the Dutch of New York, the Creoles of New Orleans, &c., have each, their caricaturists, and are successively represented on the American stage. The western people, especially, are the objects of peculiar merriment, and among them the Kentuckians, on account of their natural boldness and simplicity, are the most prominent. The latter are, perhaps, the only people in the United States, who, with great natural wit combine also a fund of humor and good nature. They are the Irish of America, at whose expense every body laughs, and who, in return, make sport of every body. The best anecdotes are told of them, and the keenest repartees are ascribed to their shrewdness. They are represented as reckless of enterprise, intrepid in danger, chivalrous of conduct, and as jolly in company as any son of the Emerald Isle. But they have this advantage over the Irish, which is manifest in their whole carriage—that their merits are acknowledged, and their peculiarities (the offsprings of many manly virtues) readily excused by the more charitable feelings of their countrymen.

But the most salient point of American wit consists in their political caricatures, which have all the poignancy of the French, with the weight and substance of the English. I remember many of them which were exceedingly ingenious, and as readily seized by the people, as those of France are by the Parisians. I shall only mention one of these, illustrative of Jonathan's capacity to take off characters. Before the late amicable adjustment of the difficulties with France, a caricature was published in America, representing General Jackson shaking his cane at the King of the French, while in the left hand he was holding a bag of money, bearing the inscription " 25,000,000 francs; " with the words to his mouth, " 'Tis well that you paid me, or by the Eternal —— " to which the king was represented bowing and waving his hands with the words " Not another word of *apology*, my dear General, I beg you." It would, perhaps, be difficult to make a better comment on the conduct of either of these distinguished individuals than is contained in that print.

Yet with all this wit the Americans do not laugh as much as either the English or the French, and indulge in sarcasm only for their private gratification, or to gratify an enemy. Owing to this peculiarity of character, few English actors, in the comical department, have ever satisfied an American public, *for any length of time*, and their own countrymen, however popular, must equally despair of success.

I know no object more deserving of pity, than a comic actor on an American stage. He is always expected to say something witty ; and yet, he is to give no offence to any part of his audience. His doings and sayings are to be pointed ; yet, in whatever direction he turns, he is sure to give offence, and to have his transgressions *visited on his head*. He is to be a politician, and yet offend no party ; he is to ridicule the whims and follies of women, but not offend any of the ladies present ; he is obliged to please the taste of the rich, who are best capable of rewarding his merits ; but he must take care lest, by offending the poor, he may be hissed off the stage, and when too late be made to repent of his folly.

For this reason there are but few characters well represented on the American stage, among which that of " a tar," is always sure to give satisfaction. The Irish, of late, has also become very popular. But since Power's representation of that character, few Americans can hope to succeed in it. Punning, therefore, is the usual resort of a comic actor in trouble. But this is a kind of wit, which, in time, is sure to produce surfeit, and requires such a variety of objects for its exercise, that it is with difficulty replenished when it is once spent upon one. The efforts, too, which a punster is contantly obliged to make to conceal the ebbs and flows of his wit, are disagreeable, and deprive it of the best part of its effect. Besides, it is impossible to be always new and successful; and the disappointment produced by a bad pun, or one with which we are already familiar, is more than sufficient to overbalance the pleasure which we receive from one that is pointed and original. We can see a good character represented an hundred times, and still be pleased by the performance; but it would be difficult to listen to a repetition of puns without feelings of perfect disgust.

In music the Americans seem to succeed better than in tragedy or comedy; and the establishment of an Italian Opera in New York, on a scale which would do credit to any capital in Europe, shows, at least, the willingness of a certain portion of the people to contribute largely to the cultivation of that taste. The Italian Opera-house in the city of New York, was built in a very costly style; singers were procured from Italy at a great expense, and the orchestra filled with skilful performers from France and Germany. The company left nothing undone which could gratify the public; but unfortunately the prices of boxes and the pit were very high, (just double of what they were in the other theatres,) and the entertainments not sufficiently varied to please the American palate. The undertaking, therefore, proved a failure, and involved its projectors in considerable loss. The principal cause of this ill success must have been the language, to which the by far greater part of the audience were total strangers; and which, to brother Jonathan, is, after all, not half as sonorous as the King's English.

But of whatever depravity of taste the lower classes of Americans and English may be judged guilty, (for I believe John Bull is, in this respect, not a whit better than his brother,) I maintain that their relish of what they are able to *understand* is far from being discreditable to their good sense, and is at least as valuable as the spurious refinement of those distinguished admirers of the opera, who frequent it only because it is a fashionable entertainment. Music, it is true, does not address itself directly to the understanding; but affects it indirectly through the feelings; yet I do not see how the understanding can be made judge of it at all, without the medium of language. I am aware there are those who believe that the understanding has nothing to do with it, and that harmony and melody are productive of a sort of agreeable sensation in the ear, similar to that which a cat may feel when its ears are scratched.

But there are others who opine — and probably with more justice — that music has the power of indicating the particular tone of our feelings, and of causing them to sympathise with those of the composer. They maintain that an opera is but a musical drama, in which melody and harmony take the place of declamation, and that its excellency, therefore, must be judged by the perfect agreement between the music and the text. On this account they are apt to admire the compositions of Mozart and Beethoven, and prefer them by far to the brilliant works of Rossini and Bellini. They claim of an overture that it shall be a proper *introduction* to an opera, by preparing the feelings of the audience for the dramatic action which is to follow, and to which it ought to be the index. For this reason they extol the overtures to " Don Juan " and " Fidelio," and criticise those of the " Gazza ladra " and " Tancredi " as being little adapted to their respective subjects. They can see no miracle in Mozart's composing the overture to " Don Juan " within an hour of the time of its first performance; because it was merely the index to a work, which, as the author, he must have known by heart. Neither do they wonder at the musicians' performing it *prima vista;* because, having rehearsed the opera, they must have been familiar with the theme. Our modern composers and performers, they pretend, would be reduced to a greater stress were they ever placed in similar circumstances.

These doctrines, it must be allowed, contain a tolerable apology for the simple taste of Americans in not patronising the Italian opera. If the perfection of an opera consists in the mutual agreement between the text and the music, the good people of New York lost, at least, one half of the entertainment by not understanding the language, and were obliged to pay for the remaining half double of what they were accustomed to pay for a whole night's amusement at another theatre. The ratio was as one to four when compared to the other plays, and was, consequently, too unreasonable to satisfy such nice calculators as the Americans.

A beautiful song, of which we understand neither the words nor the meaning, can, after all, produce little more satisfaction than original iambics to a person unacquainted with Greek. He might be pleased with the measures and the harmony; but he could not appreciate their adaptation to the subject of the poem. Whatever opinions men of fashion may entertain on this subject, I shall always believe that there is no more charity in condemning a man's taste for music, because he does not join in the common-place admiration of Italian operas, than in denying his taste for literature, because he is not delighted with the original text of an author of whom he does not understand the language.

But it must not be inferred that, because the Americans have not patronised the Italian opera, they are utterly insensible to music. They are, on the contrary, passionately fond of it; but gratify their taste in a manner much more substantial and profitable. They like to become musicians themselves, and prefer paying for tuition to a master, to encouraging the art in others.

Most of the Italian and German performers, who, at first, gave concerts in the United States, were finally induced to become teachers, and, in the latter capacity, have not only been able to maintain themselves, but have laid up something for the future. The success of the instructers can only be ascribed to the readiness of the pupils to improve; which, in turn, bespeaks a prevalent taste for the accomplishment.

Neither are the Americans behindhand in supporting operas performed in English; and the names of the best German, Italian and French composers have, in this manner, become as familiar to American ears as they are to any *dilettanti* of Europe. "Der Freischütz," "The Barber of Seville," "The White Lady," "Fra Diavolo," and "Gustavus," have all had their run on the American stage; and it may even be observed that MadameMalibran was first brought into notice by the encouraging plaudits of an American audience.*

The general predilection, however, is in favor of sacred music; and there exist, in most of the large cities of the United States, societies for its cultivation and encouragement. Among these the "Händel and Haydn Society" of Boston, and the "Musical Fund Society" of Philadelphia, are most deserving of notice, as they are both extremely well organised, and directed by able and scientific leaders. The latter, especially, ranks amongst its members not only a great number of German and French *amâteurs*, but also a very respectable body of professors, whose talents are called into active exercise by frequent concerts and oratorios, and by the liberal prizes which the society annually offers for the best compositions in the various departments of the art.

One fact, however, is most remarkable in the "Händel and Haydn Society" of Boston, which consists in most of its members being mechanics, cultivating music for no other purpose than because they are really fond of it, and wish to introduce it into their churches. Vocal music, therefore, is their principal object, and the choruses the best part of their oratorios. The taste is certainly laudable, and the more so as it is peculiar to a class of men which are unjustly supposed to be incapable of refinement.

It is quite a curious spectacle to see the sacred compositions of the old German masters revived and studied by a company of unassuming workmen in the New World, while, in Germany, it would be difficult to procure a fashionable audience for either, as long as Lanner and Strauss set the whole population on waltzing. The much admired sensibility of the Germans seems, by some sad perversion, to have betaken itself to their heels, where it is now productive of such vehement revolutions as are scarcely equalled by the wheels of a locomotive. Even the classical operas of Mozart are gradually withdrawing from the German stage, to go begging in England; and I am certainly not exaggerating the case when I state it as my

---

* I am aware that Madame Malibran first sung in England; but she was then not so much applauded as subsequently in America.

candid opinion that the best compositions of Mozart and Beethoven are becoming more familiar to English and American ears, than to the greater portion of their own countrymen.

I have already alluded to the parlor amusement in the United States, which consists principally in vocal and instrumental music. The performers, on such occasions, are usually ladies; the gentlemen's accomplishments in the arts being commonly confined to the flute. I do not remember having heard a single amateur performer on the violin during my whole residence in the United States. The ladies who are able to devote a much longer time to their education, are, in this repect, vastly superior to the gentlemen, and perform often exceedingly well on the piano, the guitar, and the harpsichord. Those of Philadelphia and Baltimore are most accomplished in the art, as they are not only more assiduous in its cultivation, but enjoy the advantage of the best German instructers. Their being, in part, descended from Germans, may also contribute to their predilection in favor of "concord of sweet sounds," which taste is any thing but diminished by a southern latitude.

On the whole, I should judge the musical talents of Americans superior to those of the English, especially in the middle and southern States, where they have been constantly improving by emigrants from the continent of Europe. The English will *hear* the best music as long as they are willing to *pay for it ;* but the Americans will soon be able *to make it themselves.* The English will always remain great consumers of musical talent, but the Americans will produce it.

No transition seems to be more natural than that from music to painting; and it will be proper, therefore, to offer a few remarks also on that subject. As far as I am able to ascertain, there is, in America, no deficiency of talent either for drawing or painting; but there is little or nothing done for their encouragement. The education of an American artist, with the only exception of a few, not very competent drawing-masters, is altogether left to himself, and to the chance he may have of visiting Europe and studying the old masters. There exists, as yet, no public gallery in any of the large cities of the United

8

States, to which a young painter could have free access,
or where his taste might be formed. There is not even
a school for painting, or any other public institution of a
more elevated nature, to foster or develop talents of this
kind; and yet the Americans have produced some very
eminent painters, amongst whom it will suffice to mention
the names of Stuart and West. The former was one of
the best portrait painters of the age, and the latter is too
well known in England to need further comment. Mr.
Alston, of Cambridge, New England, has, by dint of genius, become an historical painter of vast poetic conceptions; and Mr. Harding has, from a soldier and a chair-
painter, with no other assistance than that of his own energetic mind, become one of the most successful portrait
painters of America. He went to England to learn and
improve his native talents, but met with such encouragement that he was not only able to pursue his main design,
but also to lay the foundation to his subsequent independence.

Where talent forces its way through such obstacles, and
triumphs at last over all difficulties in the way of its progress, it must be genuine, and warrant the conclusion that,
with a little more encouragement on the part of the people, and some appropriate institutions for the education
of artists, the Americans might be made to compete with
Europe also in this department. It has been observed,
frequently, by French and German writers, that the United States of America, could, with difficulty, be made the
successful sphere of an historical painter. This may be
true for at least the next fifty years, but then, I would
ask in what part of *Europe* his talents would now meet
with adequate acknowledgment ? Where are the historical painters in Europe, who, in this age of political and
mechanical improvement, could be sure of not dying the
death of starvation ?

With the exception of the court of Bavaria, there is
no royal favor extended to these victims of a more sanctified taste—though their works and their fame might live
to eternity. The encouragement, which, by persons of
rank and distinction, is given to this branch of the art, is
almost wholly confined to purchasing a few works of the
old masters for a gallery. This is a kind of gratification

in which a patron of the arts will always more readily indulge, than in encouraging a *growing* talent. A fine gallery is constantly admired, and reflects on the good taste
of the owner ; but the money laid out on an artist is not
always sure of bearing interest or of pampering the patron's vanity.

Neither are the performances of the present schools
more than a feeble reflection of the glory of former days.
Neither the feelings, nor the imagination, nor the taste of
our modern artists resemble those of the old masters, inspired by a holy faith and fraught with religious devotion.
They are no longer personations of the Divinity itself;
but, at best, but tolerable copies of prosaic originals, or
of the world as it appears to our senses, unadorned by
what Goëthe would call "the glorification of the Italian
painters." The mysticism of catholic worship, as it existed in the middle ages, and the spiritualism of those
ages gave to the genius of the artist a noble direction,
and imprinted on his works a peculiar dignity of character, for which they will ever be distinguished.

This applies equally to the specimens of architecture
which remain of that period. They all bear the historical characteristics of their age, and represent to us,—if
I am permitted the expression,—*ideas* rather than *objects*
to delight our senses : the conception is in all of them superior to the form by which it is expressed, and the peculiarities of the artist's mind lost in the grandeur of his subject. In this, I believe, consists the true superiority of
the ancient over the modern schools; but it is a superiority which belongs to their age more than to the individuals who flourished in it, and cannot, therefore, be re-pro-
duced by the most strenuous efforts of our contemporaries.

Our present artists move in a narrower sphere. Their
province does not extend beyond the borders of humanity ;
and their conceptions, therefore, must be of a lower cast.
They may picture to us man in his most perfect form ;
but beyond this, their imagination will not easily soar,
and in beholding their works we are irresistibly chained
to the earth. They may still have the power of gratifying the senses, but they lack the nobility of conception
and the divine spirit which presides over the works of the
old masters.

Neither are our modern worshippers of the art any longer imbued with the same spirit which characterised the people of the middle ages. Ours is the age of demonstrative philosophy, the most totally opposed to the gentle sympathies of a believing mind. Our understandings have become accustomed to seize abstract forms and ideas, established by a process of reasoning, rather than to be led to a generous belief by the beauty and harmony of nature. In proportion as we have trusted our understanding, our feelings have lost the power of guiding us, and our imagination has become dull and obscure.

Hence, instead of representing angels, genii, and saints to our turbid imaginations, our modern artists entertain us with subjects more on a level with ourselves; and what can be more so than the *portrait* of a friend, or of our own perfections. Portrait painting has become the chief branch of the art to which all others are not only accessory and subordinate, but without which no other can now please or succeed.

The artist, therefore, has no longer the choice of his subject; but exhausts his talent, as he may be employed and directed ; and, instead of following his own imagination and genius, is obliged to conform to the peculiar taste of his patrons. The art, it is true, has become more popular, but, with the greater number of its votaries, its former sanctity is lost. It gives more universal pleasure, but is less capable of affecting individuals ; and instead of entertaining them with subjects above them, is obliged to descend to their level.

This is the reason why portrait painting has become so universally popular. We hardly become tired to look at ourselves in a glass, which, moreover, reflects our image without flattery, and exhibits to us daily the visible marks of time and decay ; how much more, then, must we be pleased with a portrait, which is not subject to decrepitude, and represents us always under the most favorable combination of light and attitude ? The foible is pardonable, and flatters our vanity. What, after all, can be more satisfactory to a man of *taste* than to leave to the world some traces of his ephemeral existence ?—to be immortalized by a favorite of the muses, and hung up in a gallery amongst a whole heaven of gods and goddesses ?

—to carry the sweet consolation to the grave that his picture, after generations shall have past, may yet be more
valuable than the original? If he wear an uniform, a
mitre, or some other decoration to distinguish himself
from the rest of mankind, nothing but a *touch of the brush*
will be required to transmit his merits, *in the brightest
colors*, to an admiring posterity; and if his name be not
inscribed on *marble*, he may at least cherish a hope that
some of his friends will have it engraved on *steel*, " from
an original picture of Sir Thomas Lawrence."

Our feelings have grown too egotistical even to *understand* the works of the old masters; much less to imitate
them. Amongst the hundreds who annually visit Rome
and Florence for the laudable purpose of improving their
tastes, there is scarcely one whose mind is tuned in unison
with their spirit, to comprehend the vastness of their designs, or to perceive the divine attributes of truth and
eternity which are every where imprinted on their poetic
personages. But without sympathising with the masters
of the old school, we shall in vain attempt to catch the
inspiration of their works. Let us analyze them as we
may, let us descend to the minutest details; the soul will
not be found in any particular part of the body, but will
forever escape our anatomical investigation. It is of too
sublime a nature to cling to so rude an instrument as the
knife of a modern dissector. The old painters are doomed to the fate of the classics, an acquaintance with which
is indispensable to erudition; but whose works are no
longer understood without a commentary. They may
still be the object of universal admiration, but inspire no
longer those electric feelings which prompted the ancients
to deeds of heroic valor.

If this is the fate of the masters exalted in the opinions
of mankind, what can be the prospects of a beginner?
Which way is a young artist to turn, to keep his heart and
his mind uninfluenced by the growing egotism of the
world? Where are the awful mysteries of religion, and
the enchantments of a spiritual world to fecundate his
imagination, and to preserve it pure in an age of unbelief
and material philosophy? Cause and effect of real greatness in the arts are alike vanishing from the present gen-
S*

eration ; and the lofty pupil of the divine masters degenerates into a sordid copyist of his patron's pimples.

The great advantage, then, which Europe possesses
over America, with regard to the fine arts, are the numerous collections of paintings and statuary treasured up
in her churches and galleries. These will probably remain forever unequalled, not only by Americans, but also
by European artists of all times. They are now more
the objects of pride and vanity in their owners than of real veneration for the genius of their author.

Ours is an age of science, and not of the arts. The
eternal truths " of nature and of nature's God," which it
is the province of the fine arts to reveal *in forms*, are no
longer the objects of pious mysticism, but of philosophical
discussion and mathematical demonstration. The present age cannot be affected by what they are unable to
understand, and not convinced, except by a process of
reasoning. Hence the progress of the exact sciences and
their accessories,—and the visible decline of poetry and
the arts. The aggregate of human knowledge is increased, and the condition of man improved beyond all comparison ; but the more delicate feelings of our hearts
have become blunted, and the sacred awe of the spiritual
world changed into a self-sufficient complacency at the
subjugation of inanimate nature.

In proportion as the understanding and the judgment
are cultivated, the imagination must suffer or be checked
in its progress, and, with it, the arts to which it gives life.
The more accurately a thing is defined, the less room is
left to the imagination to enlarge upon it ; and the mind
once accustomed to the rigor of mathematical demonstration, is not apt to lose itself in the boundless regions of
fancy. Judgment, too, partakes always of the nature of
criticism. It is an analytical process of the mind, which
consists rather in dissecting and destroying, than in uniting different objects to an harmonious whole. In every
work of art, on the contrary, the unity of all the parts—
the totality of the impression—is the principal object to
which all others must be subordinate. The genius of the
artist is creative, and his conceptions are at once a complete and perfect whole ; the province of science is the
universe, and the means of exploring it a finite intelli-

gence. The man of science, therefore, can only combine what exists; but in no instance is he able to add, create, or improve on a single object in nature. Step by step is nature to be conquered; each new idea must give birth to another, and it is only by their painful combination that the truth is finally revealed. But the characteristic of science is certainty, and its reward consciousness of power. Its applications are universal, and contribute everywhere to the amelioration of conditions. The arts may flourish in a despotic country; but the light of science cannot be diffused amongst a people without raising them above the condition of slaves. The arts may be employed for mean and sordid purposes, but science always ennobles human nature, and is, of all pursuits, the most calculated to secure permanent happiness. Monarchs may patronise the arts—republics must encourage the sciences.

In proportion as the sciences advanced, the arts deteriorated; but it was not until the decline of the latter, that America rose into an independent existence. The period in the history of Europe, advantageous to the cultivation of the arts, was passed: the very settlement of the United States was owing to protestantism in religion and politics. There were no monuments of Rome and Greece to awaken a taste for the arts; and the wild dramas of the Indian wars called for energies and talents different from those which play in the lap of the Muses.

Hardly had America escaped from destruction at home, and oppression from abroad, before the French revolution began to convulse the whole world with its doctrines and victories. America was again forced into a war, and it is scarcely twenty years since she has enjoyed unmolested tranquillity. But what period is this for a nation in its history of the fine arts? And what has been the *progress* of the arts during that period in Europe! Let the question be presented in this light, and its inevitable answer must be, that, compared to former times, they have, in Europe, deteriorated, while in America they have certainly progressed, notwithstanding the almost total want of encouragement of artists in the United States.

CHAPTER V.

AMERICAN LITERATURE.—ITS RELATION TO THE ENGLISH.
—PERIODICALS.—DAILY PRESS.—CITY AND COUNTRY PA-
PERS.—THEIR INFLUENCE ON THE POLITICAL PROSPECTS
OF THE NATION.

" THE termination of the Revolutionary War," says the
learned author of " Men and Manners," " left the United
States with a population graduating in civilization from
slaves to planters. The scale went low enough, but unfortunately, not very high. The great mass of the white
population, especially in the Northern States, were by no
means deficient in such education, *as was suited to their*
circumstances. In a country in which abject poverty was
happily a stranger, there existed few obstacles to the general diffusion of elementary instruction. But between the
amount of acquirement of the richer and poorer classes
little disparity existed. Where the necessity of labor was
imposed on all, it was not probable that any demand
should exist for learning, not immediately connected with
the business of life. *To the grower of indigo and tobacco, to the feller of timber, or the retailer of cutlery and dry
goods, the refinements of literature were necessarily unknown.*
In her whole population America did not number a *single*
scholar in the higher acceptation of the term, and had
every book in her whole territory been contributed to
form a national library, it would not have afforded the
materials from which a scholar could be framed."

     *   *   *

"In short, the state of American society is such as to
afford no leisure for any thing so unmarketable as abstract

knowledge. For the pursuit of such studies, it is necessary that the proficient 'should fit audience find, though few.' He must be able to calculate on sympathy, at least, if not encouragement; and assuredly he would find neither in the United States."

*   *   *

"I am aware, it will be urged that the state of things I have described is merely transient, and that when population shall have become more dense, and increased competition shall have rendered commerce and agriculture less lucrative, the pursuits of science and literature will engross their due proportion of the national talent. I hope it may be so; but, yet it cannot be disguised that hitherto there has been no visible approximation towards such a condition of society. *In the present generation of Americans I can detect no symptoms of improving taste, or increasing elevation of intellect.* On the contrary, the fact has been irresistibly forced on my conviction that they are altogether inferior to those, whose place, in the course of nature, they are soon destined to occupy. Compared with their fathers, I have no hesitation in pronouncing the younger portion of the higher classes to be less liberal, less enlightened, less observant of the proprieties of life, and certainly far less pleasing in manners and deportment."

Thus ends his discussion on American literature and education, in which not a single author or work is named, to corroborate his statements, and which it would be impossible to recognize as bearing on literature at all, if the reader were not good-naturedly informed of it by the running title of the book. Every assertion it contains is purely gratuitous,* and but the echo of his own feelings

---

* Except, perhaps, his observation on the *manners* of the young men of the "*higher classes.*" But in America the offspring of the higher classes are usually not only inferior to their progenitors, but, in the greater number of instances, also to the children of the inferior orders. The most active and enterprising merchants of Boston and New York are not sons of rich men. Neither were the names of the most distinguished American statesmen known in the *fashionable* circles, before their fame had connected them with the history of their country. Genius is seldom hereditary; and in a country where every man advances by his own talents and energies, we need be as little astonished to see the son of a rich man inferior to his father, as to behold the offspring of poor parents rise to consideration and dignity.

and prejudices. Surely the learned author furnishes a powerful illustration of the quantity of philosophy a man may gather from travelling, and how the inmost thoughts and springs of action of a nation may be discovered from the top of a stage coach. There is nothing so easy as for a man who has, either from disposition or habit, taken a strong dislike to republican institutions, to declaim, *in general terms*, on their pernicious influence on science and literature ; but if he attempt to state facts with which he is only acquainted from hearsay, he will assuredly betray the particular tone of his sentiments, or be guilty of misrepresentations.

America, at the close of the revolutionary war, *did* number amongst its population, not only scholars, but men of the purest and loftiest genius. — Franklin and Thomas Jefferson would have immortalized themselves by their writings and reasonings, even if neither of them had ever risen above the political horizon of his country. The theory of electricity of the former would, alone, have sufficed to mark him as one of the most logical intellects which ever graced science, and would have transmitted his fame to the latest posterity. America could boast of orators like James Otis and Patrick Henry,* and exhibited the virtues of her legislators in the framing of her constitution. John Edwards, William Douglas, and William Bartram had distinguished themselves by their writings ; and the latter, a quaker of Pennsylvania, was pronounced by Linnæus to be "the greatest natural botanist in the world." Thomas Godfray, of Philadelphia, was the inventor of the invaluable instrument to navigators which, afterwards, by a misnomer, was called "Hadley's Quadrant ; " David Rittenhouse invented a new method of fluxions ; and Timothy Cutler, Elisha Williams, and Timothy Clap, of Yale College, were celebrated for their knowledge of classical literature.† In 1761 the transit of Venus was observed from the coast of Newfoundland (the most westerly part of the world from which the conclusion could be seen,) by Professor Winthrop, of Harvard

---

* "Henry, the forest-born Demosthenes,
    Whose thunder shook the Philip of the seas."
                                                    BYRON.
† Grahame's History of the United States.

College; who acquitted himself of the task in the most able manner; and had his expenses defrayed by the general court of Massachusetts.* This undoubtedly proves that " to the grower of indigo and tobacco, to the feller of timber, and the retailer of cutlery and dry goods, the refinements of literature were necessarily unknown."

Mr. Hamilton attributes the infant state of literature in the United States to the state of society, and especially to their republican form of government. Let us see how far his conclusions are borne out by history ? Let us inquire how much England has done for the mental emancipation of her colonies; and whether the arts and sciences have received a check or an impulse, by the declaration of independence ?

We find Britain, in the earliest stage of her American colonies, desirous of governing them not only by superior physical power, but also by a preponderance of intellect. Commerce and literature were alike monopolised by England, whose interest it was to keep America dependent on British manufacture and science. This state of servitude, the most degrading which ever existed in any country, was enforced by the most rigorous laws; and the privilege of printing and publishing books was, by the very charter, refused to some of the colonies.

The encouragement which American gentlemen of science and literature had to expect from England, was most happily illustrated by the conduct of William Pitt, afterwards Earl of Chatham, who refused to commune personally with Dr. Franklin, but sent him word, through one of his under secretaries, " that he thought him a *respectable* man." † Franklin was then at the zenith of his scientific and political renown; and if he received such flattering testimonies of his " respectability " from men, favorable to the cause of America, what could he and his colleagues hope for from the jealousy of their political opponents.

The only literary institution aided by royalty, in America, during the space of two centuries, was the college of "William and Mary," in Virginia, to which a donation

---

* Grahame's History of the United States.
  Ibid.

was made by the King and Queen, more for political and religious purposes, however, than for the actual promotion of learning. When Dean Berkeley (afterwards Bishop of Cloyne) went to America to establish a seminary of learning, the House of Commons voted the sum of 20,000*l.* for that purpose ; but this sum was never paid—and afterwards voted in aid of the colony of Georgia, a kind of military establishment, for the protection of the frontiers of South Carolina. Gibson, bishop of London, after repeatedly pressing the subject on Walpole, obtained finally the following unceremonious answer : " If you put this question to me as a Minister, I must and can assure you that the money shall undoubtedly be paid, *as soon as the public convenience will allow ;* but if you ask me as a friend whether Dean Berkeley should continue in America, expecting the payment of the 20,000*l.,* I advise him, by all means, to return to Europe, and to give up his present expectations."

The attorney-general expressed himself in still plainer terms; for, when the agent of the colonies applied to him for his sanction to have a patent sealed confirming the grant of the 20,000*l.* under the religious plea, that it was for the benefit of the souls of the colonists, he merely replied, laconically, " Never mind their souls " — " let them plant tobacco."

Governor Johnston, of North Carolina, (the first royal governor after the surrender of the proprietary Charter,) levied, it is true, taxes for the purpose of founding schools ; but unfortunately employed the money so raised for other purposes. No sooner, however, was the declaration of independence acknowledged by Great Britain, than the Assembly of North Carolina, " *aware of the bonds which connect knowledge with liberty, and ignorance with despotism,*" founded a seminary of learning in that province. Yale, and Princeton colleges were established by the munificence of the people, without the assistance of the British government, or of royal bounty. Harvard College was established by the Puritan fathers only ten years after their settlement in America ; but never enjoyed the academical privileges of similar institutions in England ; though many laws were enacted, for that purpose, by the provincial legislature of Massachusetts, which were all

disallowed by the British parliament, bent upon protract-
ing the period of America's mental and national pupillarity.   The editors and authors of periodicals were thrown
into prison, and until 1730 a strict censorship established
in New England, the most literary of all the colonies.

" No encouragement," says Grahame, "seems ever to
have been given by the English government to the cultivation of science and literature in the American provinces, except in the solitary instance of a donation of
William and Mary in aid of the college which. took its
name from them in Virginia.   The policy adopted by the
parent state in this respect is very directly indicated by
one of the royal governors in the beginning of the
eighteenth century.

' As to the college erected in Virginia,' says the officer,
' and other designs of the like nature, which have been
proposed for the encouragement of learning, it is only to
be observed in general, that *although great advantages
may accrue to the mother state both from the labors and
luxuries of its plantations*, yet *they will probably be mistaken who imagine that the advancement of literature, and the
improvement of arts and sciences in our American colonies,
can be of any service to the British state.*'

" We have already seen the instructions," continues
Grahame, " that were given to the royal governors by
the English court, both prior and subsequent to the revolution of 1688, *to restrain the exercise of printing* within
their jurisdiction.   Many laws were enacted in New
England after that event, for enlarging the literary privileges and honors of Harvard university, which were all
disallowed by the British government."

With what justice, therefore, does our modern tourist,
after expounding on venison and Madeira — for the
learned author of " Men and Manners " treats very fully
on these subjects — obtrude his remarks on American
literature and science at that period ? — and this to prove
that liberal governments are necessarily opposed to their
progress ?

Again, Mr. Hamilton assures his readers that in the
present generation of Americans " he can discover *no
symptoms of improving taste*, or increasing elevation of in
tellect."   On the contrary, the fact has been irresistibly
9

forced on his conviction " that they are altogether inferior to those whose place, in the course of nature, they are soon destined to occupy." By what *facts* does he establish this gratuitous assertion ? Have the Americans, since the revolutionary war, produced no men of science known in Europe ? no writer of note whose works have been republished in England and on the Continent ? One single fact will answer these questions better than all speculations on the subject.

The "American Booksellers' Advertiser" notices the following different publications, during the year 1835, exclusive of pamphlets, periodicals, and new editions. (The first column contains the number of original American publications; the second, the number of republications of foreign works; and the third, the sum total of both.)

Subjects.	American.	Foreign.	Total.
Biographies - - -	19	11	30
History - - - -	4	8	12
Travels by Sea and Land -	12	11	23
Statistics and Commerce -	9	2	11
Theology - - -	20	22	42
Religious and Domestic Duties -	15	15	30
Miscellaneous - - -	24	10	34
Almanacks - - -	10	—	10
Ethics and Politics - -	5	3	8
Law - - - -	9	3	12
Medicine and Surgery - -	6	5	11
Arts and Sciences - -	15	8	23
Novels and Tales - -	31	33	64
Poetry - - - -	7	12	19
Education - - -	60	15	75
Juvenile - - - -	22	17	39
	268	175	443

Making in all 443 works, or 547 vols. Allowing each edition to consist only of 1000 copies, the number of volumes printed amounted last year (1835) to 547,000 ; exclusive of pamphlets, periodicals, and new editions.

We remark here the great increase of original publications, instead of the diminution which struck the learned author of "Men and Manners."

In 1833, there were published, in the United States, one third more foreign than original works; but, in 1835 the ratio had already increased in favor of the former. A German writer * observes that this is a strong proof that the United States are about to form their own literature, especially as regards the solid and useful branches of education. These publications show better than all reasoning that in America an author may at least " fit audience find," and that he may calculate on the sympathy and encouragement of the public ; else the enterprising spirit of the Americans would not be engaged in publishing and republishing books.

But Mr. Hamilton says, in another part of his work, that literature in the United States is a *disgrace*, and that he heard the term "literary gentleman," applied, in Washington, in the most taunting manner, to one of the representatives. This was a gross misunderstanding on his part. All parties in the United States—those *in* and those *out* of power—are proud of the literary achievements of their champions; but they are alike averse to mere *rhetorical flourishes*. The term "literary " is sometimes applied ironically to a politician, in contradistinction to *practical good sense*, which, indeed, was the case when Mr. Hamilton heard it pronounced on the floor of Congress; but then the distinction is not so absurd as he imagines, there being more than one "literary gentleman " to whom it will happily apply.

Once more I would ask whether the writings of Hillhouse, of Bryant, Percival, Paulding, and, above all, of Washington Irving and Fennimore Cooper are so little known in England and Europe generally, as to entitle the learned author of " Men and Manners " to the conclusion that America will never enjoy a state of society favorable to literature ?

What was the literary and scientific condition of America at the time of her emancipation ?—and what is it now ? Have no improvements been made in the system of education ? Is there any branch of literature in which the Americans do not, at least, enter into competition with Europe, from the most abstruse science of mathematical

* In the journal entitled " Das Ausland."

analysis down to the "woful ballad" and the "flower-garden of epigrams and sonnets?"

It may, perhaps, be observed, that in all these branches the Americans are as yet the imitators of Europe. Granted. But what are fifty years in the history of a nation's literature, or in the scientific development of a people yet combating against nature and the savages? Only a small portion of the inhabitants of the United States are as yet permanently settled; the rest are no-mades, or lead the lives of conquerors. Yet these wandering tribes know the value of literature and science, and, wherever they go, establish schools and seminaries of learning. All other nations have conquered by the sword, and their traces were marked by ruin and desolation: America, alone, vanquishes her foes by civilization, and marks her course by moral and religious improvements. There is poetry in her national development, and the settlements of her early colonists. Poetry is so much diffused throughout nature, and so intimately connected with man, that there is hardly an object, or an historical fact, incapable of inspiring its sentiments. There is poetry in light, color, sound, form, and even in numbers. The creation and redemption of man is the most sublime and Godlike poetry recorded in the Bible. Newton, by his optics, has become the philosopher and poet of light; Mozart and Chladni sang, the one from inspiration, the other by philosophical combination, the praises of music; and the Greeks have given us the most perfect models of the poetry of forms. The gigantic antediluvian drama, with its volcanos, and earthquakes, and floods, involving all creation in a general wreck, has found its poet in Cuvier; but the sublimity of his conceptions consists in numbers.* The spiritualism of the middle ages, and the holy inspiration of the followers of Christ, are the subject of Walter Scott's poetry; and the military enthusiasm of imperial France, and its tragical end, have begot the plaintive strains of Lamartine. The colonization of New England, by the pilgrim fathers, their manly assertion of liberty, and the sacrifice of all that is dear to mankind, for the very theory of freedom, is one of the most poetical, and noble spectacles which the world ever witnessed.

* HEINE.

The struggle of a young and uncorrupt race against the gigantic forests and rivers of a pristine world; the expiring groans of her children, and the noble enthusiasm of the Americans for their proud republic, form the theme of the poetry of Cooper. Whatever may be said of his imitation of Walter Scott, he is original in his scenes and conceptions, and will forever remain a rival competitor of the great master. His works have been translated into all European languages, and, despite of the illiberal criticism of his own countrymen, will be read and admired as long as there shall be a heart capable of enthusiasm for liberty. Whatever the Americans may now think of Cooper, he is, and will, probably, for a long time remain, the most manly and national representative of their literature.

Washington Irving's style is superior to Cooper's in elegance and finish; but his pictures are diminutive, and he succeeds best in sketches. His acquaintance with, and I may perhaps say, predilection in favor of European characters, rather pleases the Americans, who are flattered to see him ranked amongst the most classical English writers of the age. James K. Paulding is likewise one of the most fertile novelists of America. "The Dutchman's Fireside," "John Bull in America," "Westward, Ho," &c. are well known even in England, and are honorable productions of a descriptive mind. He has also written several plays, and a parody on Walter Scott's "Lay of the Minstrel," entitled "Lay of the Scotch Fiddler."

Among the lyric poets of the Americans, James G. Percival holds decidedly the first rank, though Bryant and Dana have, perhaps, more taste and elegance. He is a calm, contemplative genius, joining a powerful imagination to a masculine style, and a patriotic ardor which we only recognize again in the works of Fennimore Cooper. His poems, entitled "Clio," were republished in England, and he was the coadjutor of Webster in the publication of his dictionary. Bryant is editor of "The New York Evening Post," and Richard H. Dana, was, for a time, editor of the "North American Review." The best prose work of the latter is "The Idle Man," and amongst his poems the Buccaneer is justly entitled to the high reputation it enjoys in America. Some of the poems of Bryant have been lately translated into German, and were pronounced, by competent critics, to be equal to the best productions of British Bards.

John Howard Paine and Hillhouse are the Coriphei of American dramatic literature. The best works of the latter are "The Last Judgment," "Percy's Mask," and "Hadad." The plays of Paine appeared first in England, and, I believe, met with a favorable reception. The author has sinee returned to America, where some of them have been revived on the stage, and performed to fashionable audiences.

Dr. Bird, of Philadelphia, the author of several popular novels, is also worthy of considerable distinction as a dramatic writer. His Indian tragedy of *Oroloosa* was highly successful, though it was rather too full of stage trick and clap-trap. His *Gladiator* is a much superior performance. Though it has many faults, it possesses much redeeming merit; and the personation of Mr. Forest not only insures its permanent popularity in the United States, but obtained for it a most favorable reception before a London audience. The Bride of Genoa, by Epes Sargent, was produced in Boston, at the Tremont Theatre, in the spring of 1837, the popular and clever native actress, Miss Clifton, sustaining the principal male character. The play is founded upon incidents in the career of Antonio Montaldo, a plebeian, who made himself Doge of Genoa, in the year 1393, when he was only 22 years old. In the "History of the Revolutions of Genoa," he is described "as daring and ambitious, with a genius equal to the most extensive views, yet of a forgiving temper." Great license is taken with history in the conduct of the play, but the character of Montaldo is faithfully and well represented. The sxccess of this drama, on its production in Boston, was very decided, and the house, on the third night, crowded to overflowing with the most brilliant audience of the season. Its representation in the other principal cities of the Union will probably precede its publication, there being, unfortunately, no law in the United States securing to dramatic writers a compensation for the production of their published works on the stage. Another play, by the same author, a tragedy of the most powerful dramatic intewest, entitled

Velasco, is in preparation, and has, by competent judges, been pronounced vastly superior to the first ; if so, its complete success cannot for one moment be doubtful.

Besides these authors there is yet a number with whose names the British public are familiar. Miss Sigourney, Miss Sedgwick, (author of Hope Leslie,) Mrs. Child, (particularly known as a moral and political writer,) and Charles Brockden Brown (author of Edgar Huntly, Carwin and Wieland,) need no commendation from my pen. Nathaniel P. Willis, the youngest of the American minstrels, has earned glory and the minstrel's reward in England, and Mr. Theodore S. Fay is well known as the author of " Norman Leslie." Mrs. Child has just published a new novel, " Philothea," replete with imagination and classical learning, and imbued with that spirit of morality which distinguishes all her productions.

In the department of science and education a number of original writers have distinguished themselves, not only by composing text-books, but also by publishing works in the higher departments of knowledge. The philosophical works of Cousin have been translated and published in Boston ; and Dr. Nathaniel Bowditch has furnished the best translation of La Place's " Mécanique Céleste," with notes and figures (these were wanting in the original) occupying nearly one half of the work.*

* It is, perhaps, not unworthy of notice that Mr. Hamilton, in his learned criticism on American scholars, should have so far travelled out of his orbit, as to condemn them, because they thought themselves mathematicians without reading La Place, and philosophers without understanding Cousin. This idea the learned author introduces amongst a number of not less ingenious remarks on American college-education, compared to that of England. Now, whatever the advantages of an *English* collegiate education may be, La Place's Mécanique Céleste forms no text book either in a British or French university, and is not even among the works prescribed for the pupils of the *école polytechnique.* As regards the philosophy of Cousin, which, in fact, is based upon his intimate acquaintance with German metaphysics, I am inclined to believe that many a British scholar would have to renounce his claims to philosophy, if the works of that writer were to be made the criterion of his knowledge. Cousin is far from being generally understood by his own *countrymen ;* and we may, therefore, infer that he is not quite so intelligible to every *Englishman* as to the author of " Men and Manners." At any rate, the Americans possess a *translation* of Cousin, and until the English shall have shown the same taste for metaphysics, Mr. Hamilton's remarks on American scholarship can only prove injurious to his own countrymen.

Were these works published in a new, original language, no doubt could exist, in the mind of any European philosopher, as to their composing the most ample elements of a national literature; but, published in an European language an invidious comparison obtrudes itself involuntarily on the reader; and he declares them—perhaps against his will—as imitations of the classical literature of England. The Americans, as they increase in wealth and power, will enlarge also the field of their literature. It will be strongly tinctured with the spirit of freedom which pervades their country; their imagination will reflect the gigantic scenery of the New World, in comparison to which that of Europe (with the exception of Switzerland) represents but a miniature picture; they will have their epos, their lyric and dramatic poesy, but to an Englishman they will appear as so many annexations to British literature.

America has an European origin, an European language, and an European civilization; three circumstances which will always connect her with Europe, and establish a reciprocal action between the Old and New world. Every English classical poet will be read in America, as the works of every American author of celebrity will constitute part of an English library. Washington Irving and Cooper are now as much read in England as Scott and Bulwer in America; and there is no reason why a similar reciprocity should not exist in the future.

But the English classics, Shakspeare and Milton, will forever remain the models of Americans, as they are to this moment the beau ideal of the Germans. Genius belongs to no soil; its action is universal, and cannot be shut out from a country like an article of contraband. Where it is once admitted, it creates admirers; and from admiration to imitation the transition is too natural to suppose that the Americans alone should prove an exception to the rule. Besides, the national distinctions which characterise the people of Europe and America are gradually dying away: the feelings and sentiments of Americans are fast gaining ground, not only in Europe, but all over the world; and unless some forcible revolution take place must eventually become those of mankind in general. What changes of feelings have not the English and

French undergone for the last thirty years? What, those of the Germans? But every political change in the government of a nation must necessarily affect its literature. England, France and Germany furnish examples of this doctrine. There is less difference now between the sentiments of a liberal German and an Englishman, than there was, at the time of the American revolution, between the British and the inhabitants of the United States; and there is certainly more similarity between the writings of Byron, Schiller and Lamartine than could ever be discovered between those of Shakspeare and Racine. But if the literature of a people, speaking a different language is gradually losing its national characteristics, what can be expected from a literary branch of one and the same language?

Another circumstance checking the growth of a national, independent literature in America, is her constant and increased intercourse with Europe. The national peculiarities of a people—in which their literature always participates—are generally founded on prejudices, or religious superstition. Both these must yield to the superior light of Christianity and the knowledge resulting from actual observation.

The national features of the English, the French and the Germans, are not derived from the period of their civilization; but, on the contrary, from the times of their barbarism. The warlike manners of the French are still those of the ancient Gauls, the most characteristic features of the English are yet Saxon, and the best knowledge of the German character may yet be derived from Tacitus.

America was civilized in her very origin. The early settlers felt, thought, and believed as their brethren in Europe; or, at least, did not differ from them sufficiently to create permanent distinctions. The people who obstructed their progress and whom they conquered by arms, were not sufficiently powerful to call for an extraordinary demonstration of valor. It was not an expedition of Argonauts in quest of the golden fleece: it did not even partake of the military glory of the conquest of Mexico. The American Indians were a degraded race, without history, memory, or tradition. They seem to have been the remnants of a once powerful people,* whom a general plague or a series of internal wars had reduced to the condition of the most abject wretchedness. There was no renown attached to their subjugation; it was the victory of intelligence over the barbarism of savages. No poetry, therefore, attaches to the conquest of the American soil, and the history of it is only remarkable from its conjunction with that of Europe. It was the oppression of Europe which settled the American wilderness; it was the resistance against Europe, which introduced America into the ranks of nations. Previous to that period America had been a European province, and its history an appendage to that of England. America enjoyed the *political* existence of a nation before it had an *historical* one by geniture. No mythological fable is blended with her origin. Her children are not descended from the gods or the sun ; they are pious Christians, who, from simple colonists, have at once risen into a powerful national independence. Had the American Indians, at the time of the European settlements, been a strong organized nation, who, by amalgamating with the colonists, would have tinctured the manners of the settlers, and in turn received the superior arts of civilization, then a national literature, essentially different from the English, might, perhaps, have arisen from the conjunction; but it would have been that of the Indians, and not of the settlers ; it would have retarded the progress of independence for centuries, and, in its stead, given birth to another system of vassalage.

Another means of levelling national distinctions consists in the propagation of learning. The man of science belongs to no country, and has no prejudices except in favor of those who are his superiors in knowledge. In the common course of nature, the arts precede the sciences in every country, as poetry comes before prose : in America alone the sciences have preceded the arts, and thus *raised the nation beyond the tender susceptibility of fiction.*—Rousseau's motto,

" *Plus qu'on raisonne moins qu'on aime,*"

applies not only to man, but also to Nature. The poetry

---

* Their religion, rites, and even their bravery seem to warrant this conclusion.

and awe with which Nature inspires an untutored mind
are no concomitants of the demonstrative reasoning of
mechanical philosophy; and her terrors cease to be sublime when disarmed by the discovery of Franklin.* The
sciences, which teach us to subject nature to human will,
are most destructive of the imagination; and the universe
itself appears pitiable in the shape of an orrery. Even
the most profound researches of mathematical analysis
diminish the *poetic* grandeur of the heavens, by reducing
the infinite and boundless to the computation of the " *infinitely small.*"

> How immeasurably great, how infinitely sublime are the heavens!
> But the spirit of *littleness* pulled even heaven down.†

The Americans, as a nation, cannot be said to be inferior in science to any people in Europe; for not only
are its most useful branches more generally diffused and
applied in the United States than either in England or
France, but also the most abstruse departments of knowledge are cultivated and improved by men of competent talents. Their number, assuredly, is not as great as in Europe; but still they exist, and are sufficient to imprint a
character on the nation. But men of science, as I have
remarked before, belong to no country, and are, in themselves, incapable of giving a *national* impulse. They may
excite emulation and contribute to the development of
intellect; but they cannot create such lasting distinctions
and peculiarities, as we are in the habit of claiming for
the national literature of a people.

America has not passed through the different stages of
civilization, each of which leaves its historical monuments and a distinct impression on the people. There
was no community of religion, and hardly of feeling
previous to their common resistance against England! It
was the genius of liberty which gave America a national
elevation; and it is to this genius, therefore, we must look
for national productions. It is the bond of union, the confession, the religion, the life of Americans; it is that which
distinguishes them above all other nations in the world.

* What can be more averse to poetry, than the thunderbolt of Jove
made harmless when caught by a lightning-rod.

† "So unermesslich ist, so umendlich erhaben der Himmel!
Aber der Kleinigkeitsgeist zog auch den Himmel herab."
SCHILLER'S *Poems.*

But the genius of liberty, though it has chosen America for its permanent dwelling, overshadows, also, a portion of Europe. England, France, and Germany are roused by its summons ; and the poet of Europe, inspired by the same muse, kneels at the same altar, and worships the same God. Thus, the Americans, instead of being a distinct people, have become the representatives of liberty throughout the world. Their country has become the home of the banished; the asylum of the persecuted, the prospective heaven of the politically damned. Every people of Europe is represented in the United States; every tongue is spoken in the vast domain of freedom; the history of every nation terminates in that of America.

But this gigantic conglomeration, while it prognosticates the future sway of the United States, while it promises to revive the history of all ages and of every clime, is, nevertheless, one of the principal causes why America possesses, as yet, no national literature. Yet there is sufficient of English leaven in this enormous mass to penetrate even its uttermost particles. The fructifying principle is every where visible, and the fruits are not tardy of coming. But the seed is English, though the soil and the climate may give it a different development.

But, though the literature of America be not a legitimate child of the soil, it may become so by adoption, and as such form a most important and distinct branch of that of England. Compared to English literature, its position will, perhaps, be similar in rank to the respective political importance of the country ; and who can tell, but at some future period, when the British muse may have become silent, her younger sister may revive her memory, and proclaim her fame, and her glorious effusions, to all the nations of the world ?

Mr. Chasle, in the *Revue des deux Mondes*, expresses his belief that America is not the land of the muses ; because the commerce and continued occupation of her inhabitants preclude alike the commission of great crimes, and the leisure required for poetic inspiration. With him, the Americans are too happy a people. They marry at too early an age, live without intrigue, and prosper till they grow old. There is nothing so prosaic in the eyes of Mr. Chasle as steam-boats, rail-roads, and the building

of new cities. Where there is commercial and industrious activity, there is, in his opinion, no spot consecrated
to poetry.*

---

* *D'ailleurs,* "says Mons. Chasle," *il y a peu de mal-être en Amérique ;
la poésie souffre de cet état prospère.* LE MAL-ETRE FAIT LES GRANDS
POETES. (!)

How unfortunate must have been the times of Shakspeare! What
influence must they not have had on Goethe!

"*En Amérique,*" continues Mons. Chasle, "*dès qu'un citoyen est
mécontent, qu'un fils trouve sa légitime trop courte, qu'un banqueroutier
se lasse de sa cinquième banqueroute, il y a, pour tous ces hommes, la ressource du désert, ressource honorable et réhabilitante, colonisation inces-
sante et facile. On défriche, on exploite, on travaille, et nul n'y trouve à
redire. La société compte sur cet exutoire perpétuel. Mais aussi elle
n'a pas de Lord Byron, que les souffrances des salons grandissent* (!!) *et
irritent ; pas de chapelain Crabbe qui ait vécu à l'école de la faim et de
la souffrance ; pas d'Ebenezer Elliot qui se plaigne en vers éloquents de
n'avoir pas de pain ; pas de Lamartine, que les tourments de l'empire et
de la restauration aient ramené à la poésie réligieuse, pas de Béranger
qui exprime avec un sourire amer le désillusionement des peuples. Helas !
que d'amertume sans doute chez tous ces poètes ! Que d'angoisses dans
l'inspiration de leurs chants. L'Amérique septentrionale est trop heureuse
aujourd' hui de son* EXERTION *physique pour produire rien qui en approche.*"

Alas! how distant is yet the golden age of American Literature!
The coteries are yet too kind and condescending to produce a Lord Byron ; the people too well fed to become poets, and there is no man in
the United States who can sing " that he has no bread." No military
despotism nor political misrule has, as yet, brought sufficient misery on
the people to make their poets once more embrace the religion which
they never abandoned ; and there is no man to smile on their delusive
love of liberty and independence! As long as the West remains open
to the enterprise of merchants and settlers, as long as the soil is fertile
and the people willing to *exert* themselves to obtain an honest liveli-
hood, just as long will America be deprived of poets; who, in the opinion of Mr. Chasle of the *Revue des deux Mondes,* have this remarkable
property in common with the grey-hounds, that they show their talents
best when they are hungry.

Again he says, " *Il est* (the American) *trop paisiblement heureux, trop
facilement moral* (!) *par tempérament et par habitude. Sa déstinée
marche avec une simplicité trop grave. Il n'a pas même le loisir de se
créer ces douleurs de mélancolique rêverie, ces douleurs voluptueuses dont
nous cannaissons toute l'amertume et toute la sensualité, ces peines raffinées
qui sont des tristesses de luxe. L'état social dans lequel il vit l'oblige à
l'activité la plus constante ; tout ce qui l'entoure partage cette activité ;
les routes se creusent, les rainures se forment ; les bois s'abattent, l'eau
gronde dans les canaux : le sol est bouleversé ; les manufactures naissent ;
les machines sifflent, murmurent, enfantent leur produits ; les villes sor-
tent de terre comme le fungus après la pluie ; la vapeur et les chemins de
fer anéantissent l'espace et multiplient la terre. Poésie! Poésie! toi qui
veux le silence, l'ombre, le bonheur du repos ; toi qui n'es féconde que loin*

This rhapsody savors much of the French criticism of German literature, when, not more than fifteen years ago, "one of the members of the Academy" declared *in pleno* that the Germans could never become an imaginative people, because their sky was never blue. Mr. Chasle's observations are neither founded on philosophical observation, nor do they betoken the least knowledge of the human heart. All the feelings and passions which ever stimulated men to virtue or hurried them into the commission of crimes; all the disappointments of life which tune the heart to melancholy sadness; frustrated hopes, baffled ambition, "the pangs of despised love," and "the spurns that patient merit of the unworthy takes," exist in America as in Europe: the nation alone is as yet exempted from the tragedy. In all her combats, in all her struggles, the republic has been the victor, and the individual woe is buried in the general prosperity. There is enough of the drama in the lives of Americans, though it may escape the eye of a French critic.

de l'activité matérielle, et de la production brute, tu n'as rien à faire en un tel pays."

*   *   *   *   *   *   *

"*Je ne dis point que la vertu soit incompatible avec le génie. Non certes; peuples et individus n'achèteront pas le génie en adoptant le vice; mais une certaine exactitude de comptoir, une certaine piété de formule, une certaine régularité mécanique, éteignent le feu des arts, sans profit pour la véritable vertu.*" (!)

Less industry, less honesty, and less regularity in the manners and habits of the people, would probably be more congenial to the *génie d' artiste,* and to what Mr. Chasle calls "*une moralité haute, passionée, réligieuse, puissante,*" though it would be difficult for an Englishman to understand the precise meaning of a *high, passionate, religious, powerful* morality, which, to a logical mind, would convey nothing but a *contradictio in adjecto.*

But Mr. Chasle's idea of poetry will be better understood from the following *ultra*-liberal sentiment.

"*Si vous ôtez à la France sa sociabilité féconde en défauts et en illusions, sa galanterie ennemie des mœurs et de la fidélité conjugale, sa facilité d'impression et d'émotion, à l'Espagne son mépris romain pour la vie des hommes et son orgueilleuse etiquette, et son catholicisme terrible, e t son point d'honneur féroce, vous dessécherez la sève vitale du génie chez ces nations diversement grandes.*"

The English were probably ignorant of the fact stated by Mr. Chasle, that the want of conjugal fidelity in the French, and the bigotry and besottedness of the Spaniards, form the principal elements of their greatness. Many a generation must pass away before the Americans will catch the inspiration, and become as "great and poetical a nation" as the French or the Spaniards!

But there is something in their activity, in the enthusiastic ardor with which they penetrate into their hoary forests, and subject nature to their will, which is truly incomprehensible to Europeans. Most nations, in the early stages of their history, had to *fight* for their existence; every foot of territory was disputed by their neighbors, and it was through combat they became strong and powerful. The Americans had no such enemy to contend with, none to resist their expanding power, or to call their martial valor into action. Yet war and strife constitute the lives of nations as of individuals; and this war the Americans wage against the elements. There is something heroic in the voluntary banishment of a New Englander to fertilize the wilderness; there is sublimity in the sufferings and hardships of those exiles from the refinements of civilized Europe. The boldness and daring of the Western settler is really chivalrous, and surpasses even the achievements of the mariner. This is the Trojan war of the Americans, though they have not, as yet, found a Homer to immortalize their exploits. No Roman *virtus militaris* is nursed by their deeds, no terror and desolation mark their footsteps; but a nobler virtue is reared in the midst of those forests of a thousand years — a virtue which will outlast the memory of Greece and Rome —the *virtus civilis* of the Americans.

In the Western States the foundation is laying for the wealth and power of future empires. But, I repeat it, America is not yet settled; her youthful forces are yet employed in subduing nature and establishing governments. The first act of the American drama has hardly commenced, and should we already judge of its completion? Who can deny the capacity of Americans for literature, when the very first day of their national existence brought forth authors who could dispute the palm with the most fertile poets of Europe? Where is the French novelist whose works, in literary Germany, are read with as much delight as those of Cooper and Irving? There never was a nation incapacitated for literature, if once capable of civilization; the idea itself is a logical absurdity. Add to this that the Americans are already in possession of a classical language, capable of expressing thoughts with elegance and precision, and the assertion becomes a barefaced effrontery. In whatever contemptuous terms Europeans may speak of American literature, it is nevertheless a most powerful propagator of intelligence, and occupies and expands the mind until scenes of a different nature shall rouse it to increased poetic action.

But if the Americans are not all poets, they, at least, read poetry with an avidity which borders on gluttony. Poetry is produced and consumed in America in most enormous quantities. Besides the publications in the newspapers, of which they form the necessary condiment, there hardly passes a day without ushering a new volume into existence, which is greedily read, admired, censured —but at any rate—sold. There are, certainly, more poets among the Americans than prose writers, owing to a kind of musical impulse, which makes them express themselves in rhymes. But, above all, it is the prevailing taste of the readers, which calls for this extraordinary exertion on the part of the authors, as the *manufactory* of goods must increase with the *consumption*.

The Americans, as a nation, are the most reading people on the face of the earth. I can safely assert that there are annually more volumes read in the United States of America, than either in England, France, or German; but the favorite works are poetry, and next to them novels.

This tender and delicate taste is owing to the circumstance of the ladies reading more than the gentlemen; the latter being at a very early period of their lives engaged in business, or in a habit of improving their leisure hours with the more serious works on the sciences. Every volume of English poetry, every English novel, is reprinted in America within sixty days or less of its publication, and, in addition to these, five or six hundred native authors keep the press continually thronged, and contribute to the diversion of the public. The Germans publish annually a great number of books; but they are, in these respects, vastly inferior to the Americans; and, above all, they are not so much *read*. There exists in Germany a " Republic of Letters," but its fame has hardly reached the middle and lower classes. The German *literati* form a distinct class by themselves, and are supported and fed by *one another*, which accounts sufficiently for their want of corpulency. In America they prey upon the people at large, and their flushed cheeks and sprightly carriage show, at least, that they are not in want of the necessary beef and mutton. What consolation, after all, is it to an author to be read and admired by a few of his peers, while, in the mean time, he is starving in his garret ? The Americans, of all people, are the most grateful to their authors ; and there is many an European writer that would give half of his fair reputation for a share in the favor of the Trans-atlantic public.

Of scientific works, those on mathematics are most generally studied ; and next to them the works on natural philosophy, chemistry, and mineralogy, with which the greater portion of Americans (even of the inferior orders) are tolerably well acquainted. I have often been surprised at the philosophical explanations given by operative mechanics of the various processes of their art ; and I have seldom known one who, in so doing, would not use the most appropriate technical terms.

Elementary works on the sciences are read by all classes without distinction, and the authors of them have frequently become rich by the rapid sale of their works. Many of them are really possessed of intrinsic merit and originality, and have even been reprinted in England. Culburn's Algebra and Arithmetic have been published to the number of more than one hundred thousand copies ; Comstock's Philosophy has passed through four or five large editions, and new works in these branches are constantly issuing from the press.

The call for scientific works does not, in many instances, extend much beyond the elements ; but this is the case in all countries, and must be still more so in the United States, where a great proportion of the reading and studying community is composed of persons, who, in Europe, would never take up a book.

I have known but few American operatives, who, at the age of thirty or forty, were not willing to improve their early education by the study of mathematical and other works, to which they would apply themselves in the hours of rest. An American is never too old to go to school, and this is one of the happiest traits of his character. It is a feature which, as far as I remember, has not been observed by any English traveller. Mr. Hamilton is the on-

10*

ly one, who, in his " Men and Manners," observed, that,
in Boston, he listened to a lecture on the steam-engine,
which was evidently delivered by an operative mechanic,*
and was, in his opinion, remarkably clear and instructive.
He ought to have added that the greater number of his
hearers were also composed of mechanics, and of men of
butiness, who employed the hours of relaxation in the improvement of their mental faculties.   Had Mr. Hamilton
taken further information on the subject, he would have
learned that lectures on every branch of useful knowledge
are periodically delivered in Boston and Philadelphia,
and that the most respectable inhabitants of those cities
are in the habit of frequenting them for their favorite
recreation.   He might have enlarged on the influence
which such a prevailing taste must necessarily have on
the morals of the people, and to what improvements it
must lead in every department of science.   He might
have learned also that in almost every town and village
throughout the United States there exist associations of
gentlemen and operative mechanics for the promotion of
useful knowledge; † that the most learned and informed
of these lecture gratuitously to the others ; and that each
of these societies is provided with the necessary books
and maps for the study of its junior members.   He might
have seen that same operative of whom he speaks in his
work, instructing a class of other operative mechanics
and apprentices, in the elements of algebra and geometry,
and would have been satisfied with the proficiency of both
teacher and pupils.   But the learned author deemed it
sufficient to visit the library of Harvard College, near
Boston, and judged at once, from its meagerness (it contains at present little more than 40,000 vols.) that the
Americans will always remain tyros in the sciences.

The historical department of American literature is
more deficient than any other ; but historical writers seldom live in the period of a nation's prosperity, and when
they do, their history is poetry.   The Americans, moreover, from their great respect for their patriots, seem to be
more inclined to reading and writing biographies, which

---

* It was Mr. Claxton, of Boston, one of the most ingenious philosophical instrument makers of that city.
† These have received the name of " Lyceums."

furnish at least excellent data for history. Jared Sparks and George Bancroft are authors of great eminence, and deserve all possible credit for the honesty and scrupulousness with which they have collected the materials for a History of the United States; but the arrangement of their works (of George Bancroft's History of the United States, I have only seen the first volume) does not appear to be throughout suitable to the subject; and above all, there seems to be wanting that indispensable classification of greater and minor events, that subordination of inferior incidents to the leading facts, that philosophical view and calm contemplation of events as connected with the destinies of mankind, and the development of human character in general, which constitute the chief merit of an historian. The best history of the United States, published in America, was written by Marshal, in form of a " Biography of George Washington ; " and to this moment the ablest commentaries on the rise and progress of the United States of America are to be found in the lives and memoirs of her Statesmen.

But there is one particular branch, as I shall hereafter have occasion to remark, in which the Americans excel, and for the study of which they have made the most ample provisions. I would allude to the knowledge of geography, which in no country is so generally diffused as in the United States. The cultivation of this branch of learning is facilitated by excellent maps, published in all the large cities of the union, at prices even lower than those of Germany. The art of engraving or lithographing maps has been much perfected in Boston and Philadelphia, and from the latter city have issued the best and most correct publications of atlases. For charts, however, the Americans have generally recourse to the English, which, I believe, are preferred by all navigators, on account of their great correctness and minuteness of detail.

The mania for periodicals, which exists in all the large towns of Europe, has also spread to America, and accordingly the " North American " and " Quarterly " reviews, besides a number of " Monthly Magazines," bearing the names of " American," " Boston," " New England," &c. have been called into existence, not so much to encourage or damn the offsprings of American genius, as to talk promiscuously about the literature and science of Europe, and to afford the critic an opportunity of exhibiting his own profundity of knowledge. Something similar to it exists also in England, and particularly in Scotland, where the title of the book on which the critic expands is frequently the means of introducing his own reflections, without the least regard to the work he is about to review. A very inferior writer may thus find an opportunity of acquiring celebrity by coupling his name with that of an author of superior reputation, and passing sentence on him to whom the public look up with reverence. There is a peculiar arrogance in assuming the judge's seat without a jury or counsel for the defendant; and the vulgar are but too apt to believe in the wisdom of gentlemen in office. Neither is there an appeal from the judgment of these petty tyrants, except to the public at large, whose opinion is generally forestalled by the criticism of the reviewer. In Germany there exist already several literary journals, admitting of *critique* and *contre-critique*, and inserting neither one nor the other without the name of the author. A man knows in this way by whom he is wronged, and is not injured beyond the possibility of redress.

The American periodicals, like the English, are often devoted to politics; and party feelings and scandal are frequently mixed with learned dissertations on the sciences. The "Southern Review," which was published in Charleston, South Carolina, was probably the best periodical which ever appeared in the United States. Though its contributions were anonymous, they were evidently the effusions of the most prominent talents of the south; and though its editors were also unknown, Mr. Legaré, the late American chargé d'affaires at the Court of Brussels was named as its chief conductor. The principal English periodicals are all reprinted in the United States, and a collection of them appears, in New York, for not quite the price of any one of them in England.

When the bulk of these publications is considered, it is really astonishing that the Americans should find time to read half of them, with their own works and newspapers, without neglecting their more serious occupations—commerce, manufactures and agriculture. A *Revue Française* is published in New York, and a

French paper, "*Le Courier des Etats Unis*" is also established in that city. But no German literary establishment does, as yet, grace any city of the Union. The
German daily and weekly papers, which are published in
Pennsylvania, Ohio, Illinois and Missouri, do not deserve
that name. Several French classical authors have been
reprinted in the United States, but, with the exception of
prayer-books, no similar honor has as yet been done to a
German writer of eminence. Is there not one among the
five hundred periodicals of Germany which deserves being republished or read in the United States? Would
not a collection from the best of them, published, quarterly, in form of a translation, be an useful addition to American reading?

Amongst the periodicals dedicated to science, "Professor Silliman's Journal" occupies the first rank, and is
well known throughout Europe; the remainder, however,
contain chiefly extracts from English publications, with
very little original matter. "The Mechanic's Magazine,"
of New York, however, is a clever publication; and "The
Mathematical Diary," published by Professor Renwick,
contains nothing but original communications.

The best medical journals are "The American Journal
of Medical Sciences," of Philadelphia; "The Archive
of Medicine and Surgery," of Baltimore; "The Journal
of Medicine and Surgery," of Boston,—"The Medical
Magazine," published at the same city, and the "Journal
of Medicine and Surgery in the United States," published
in New York; besides a great number of others on different branches of the science.

On jurisprudence there are but few periodical publications in the shape of journals or magazines; but on theology there are several commanding the attention of the
public. The "Christian Examiner," published by the
Unitarians in Boston, contains essays on ethics and morals, written in a masterly style, but cannot strictly be called a theological publication, in the sense in which the
term is generally applied in Europe.

As to the number of newspapers published in the United States, nothing definite can be said about it, except that
it baffles all attempts at computation; there being hardly
a village or a settlement of a dozen houses in any part of

the country, without a printing establishment and a paper. The amount of knowledge and useful information circulated by these most powerful engines of civilization, is really enormous ; and, although no great depth of reasoning or proficiency of learning particularly distinguishes the fraternity of editors, common good sense is nevertheless the characteristic of an American paper ; as without this most necessary commodity it would be difficult for them to make the least impression upon the public.* The amount of circulation is prodigious, and greatly facilitated by the reduced postage.

Each paper, not carried out of the state in which it is published, or if carried out of the state not over one hundred miles beyond it, pays but one cent, and if over one hundred miles out of the state, never more than one and a half cent postage ; and it is even contemplated to abolish the postage on newspapers altogether. Printers of newspapers may send one paper to each and every other printer of newspapers within the United States *free* of postage, under such regulations as the Postmaster General may provide.† Thus, an inhabitant of Boston or New

---

* The first printing-press was established in Massachusetts, in 1638; and the first printing done in 1639. The first American newspaper, " The Boston News Letter," was published in Boston, in 1704. " The Boston Gazette" succeeded in 1719; and at the same time (Dec. 22d. of the same year) "The American Weekly Mercury " was published at Philadelphia. The first newspaper in New York, " The New York Gazette," was printed in 1725; and from that time newspapers were introduced into all the other colonies. All these journals, however, were subjected to a kind of censorship, which continued till the year 1755. It is, perhaps, not altogether unworthy of notice that the first three things printed in America were " *the freeman's oath*," " an *almanac calculated* for New England," and " *the psalms in metre*,"—three publications singularly expressive of the New England character.

† The rate of postage on Magazines and pamphlets is as follows:—

If published periodically, distance not exceeding 100 miles   } 1½ cent per sheet.

Ditto, distance exceeding 100 miles   2½ ditto.

If *not* published periodically, distance not exceeding 130 miles   } 4 ditto.

Ditto, distance over 100 miles   6 ditto.

" Every printed pamphlet and magazine, which contains more than twenty-four pages on a *royal* sheet, or any sheet of *less* dimensions, shall be charged by the sheet; and small pamphlets, printed on a half or quarter sheet of royal or less size, shall be charged with half the amount of postage charged on a full sheet."

York is able to read the New Orleans papers with little
more than an additional expense of four dollars fifty cents,
or less than one pound sterling *per annum;* and the inhabitants of the South are at the same cheap rate furnished with information from the North.

Of all the instruments which have been invented for
the emancipation of the human mind, the periodical
press is the most powerful. Its action is unceasing; its
force irresistible; its achievements more lasting than the
conquests of arms. The pen has disarmed the sword;
and the type-metal of the printer speaks louder than the
despot's cannon. This is as well understood in Europe
as in America. While England looks upon the liberty of
the press as the "palladium of her civil and religious
rights," * the French are constantly endeavoring to throw
off the shackles with which their cunning legislators have
at all times tied and disarmed it; and the petty tyrants of
Germany, while they hardly object to *large volumes* of
liberal sentiments, take great pains to enslave the *periodical* press by a most odious censorship, lest, little by little,
the minds of their subjects might catch the Promethean
fire.†

The most sublime idea expressed or read only once,
makes but a faint impression when compared to the effects
of unceasing, *daily repeated* sentiments, spoken by a thousand tongues, and repeated and rehearsed by thousands
of thousands. It is not so much the force of eloquence
with which these sentiments are uttered; it is the repetition of them which accounts for their power. The same
idea is expressed in a thousand different manners, until
finally one of them is suited to the capacity of the reader,
and produces the desired effect. The operations of the
press are slow, when compared to the effects of oratory;
but they are more lasting and universal. Few only can
be convinced by the power of speech, millions re-echo
the sentiments of the press. They are brought every day
to our doors : wherever we move, their action follows us;

* *Junius.*

† A work consisting of more than 20 sheets may be published in some
of the smaller states of Germany, without being previously submitted to
the censor; but all smaller publications and *papers* cannot be printed
without it.

in business or amusement, at home or abroad. Not a thought is expressed, not an idea is conceived, which is not destined to make the tour of the world; and what was formerly the property of a few, becomes now the common wealth of millions.

The periodical press, and the increased facilities with which its publications are distributed, have done more towards changing the face of the world, than was in the power of half a million of philosophers, or the bayonets of all the nations of Europe. But their action has only commenced; the future will show their power and influence on the destinies of mankind.

Nothing is more common in the United States, (and, perhaps, also in Europe,) than to hear persons speak disparagingly of country papers and editors; as if it were absurd for every hamlet to have its own press, and to express its own sentiments. I confess myself no partisan to this opinion, and this for reasons which I am about to explain.

Every society of men is capable of a certain intelligence, proportionate to their consciousness of power, and the degree of their moral and political independence. Nothing can promote either so much as the creation of a distinct organ for the assertion of both, or a means of extending their influence. Such an organ is created by the establishment of a newspaper, which, in every country where liberty of the press exists, must necessarily represent the feelings and sentiments of the majority of its readers. Besides the political and other information which a little community derive from it, at a much cheaper rate than would be possible, if they were confined to the reading of city papers, they have in it also a means of communicating their own sentiments to the inhabitants of the towns, and thus to establish a kind of reciprocity, without which they would be reduced to a state of mere passiveness. Political life and action is thus created in every village, and a general interest in the public prosperity produced throughout the country.

There is nothing so dangerous to a republic, or to the institutions of good government in general, as a morbid excitability in one or a few of the large towns, with a comparative inaction on the part of the country. France has, at all times, given a most melancholy demonstration of the correctness of this doctrine ; and her present situation is far from proving an exception to the rule. All the political life of France is concentrated at Paris, while the provinces are hardly able to re-echo the sentiments of the capital. Neither is the consent of the country deemed necessary whenever the Parisians think it expedient to change the form of their government, or to make concessions incompatible with the chartered liberties of the nation. There exists not even a means of *ascertaining* the sentiments of the country ; since it possesses no organ of public opinion, and is not even conscious of the right of being heard, when the national institutions are in danger. A licentious mob, or a profligate faction may thus rule the destinies of a nation without the least regard to the benefits of those for whom government is properly instituted.

The country will forever be the best moderator of the cities. The passions of men are sooner excited when living in continual contact with one another, where personal animosities and family quarrels lend to the fury of political parties, than where they are scattered over a large surface, mutually independent of one another, and therefore less anxious to make proselytes.

On this account large cities will always be the worst repositories of public liberty, while the country will prove its best guardian.* If the inhabitants of the cities have better means of gathering intelligence, those of the country have more leisure to think and reflect, and are less subject to the influence of parties. Each class of citizens has its peculiar advantages, and is entitled to an expression of its opinion : and it is the interest of the politician, and the duty of the legislator, to bestow on both an adequate share of attention.

But there is yet another point of view in which country papers appear to me particularly useful. Thousands of persons are, by their influence, made to read, who would hardly think of it, if no other publications than those of

* This, of course, must be understood of the farmers and planters in the United States, who are *all proprietors and independent of one another*—and not of the dependent farmers in England.

11

the large cities were at their command, whose sentiments
and opinions correspond but seldom with their own, and
from which they are too remote to be directly concerned
in their political proceedings. They prefer to read what
is dedicated to their immediate interests, and, by so doing,
obtain a vast deal of political information, which they
would not have been disposed to draw from any other
source.

It cannot be objected that the same, or even a greater
degree of information would be gathered from the periodical publications of the cities, which would, undoubtedly,
be read in lieu of those of the country. Independent of
their style being less acceptable to the taste of those readers, they would establish a system of tutorship and dependency, which would preclude the free exercise of their
judgment. The editor of a daily paper ought to be the
representative of public opinion, and not a dictator, or a
political pope, as in France, who preaches his infallible
doctrine to town and country, without restraint or fear of
contradiction. The editor of a city paper is always ready
to pronounce judgment in a cause in which he never
hears more than one party ; and, depending for subscrib-
ers principally on the population of the large towns, it is
not difficult to foresee in whose favor his judgment must
incline. How easily is not the fountain of such information troubled ! Does not the same sentence convey different meanings to men living at a distance from, and to
those who are eye witnesses of, certain scenes ? And, suppose the editor of such a paper to change sides, or to
abandon a cause which, to him, appears no longer plausible, (to say nothing of the possibility of his being bribed,) are not the great majority of his country readers
misled until they are made acquainted with the circumstances of his conversion ? And may it not in this manner
happen, that when there are but few organs of public
opinion, and those misled or won by the leaders of a party,
the opposition may, for a time, be left without a champion, or a means of asserting their rights ? Have we not a
happy illustration of all this in the history of the periodical press of France ? To how many parties was not the
Journal des Débats devoted ? How many times will it
yet change sides and opinions ? And yet it was always

edited with talent, and ranks now with the best periodical publications of France. Were there more papers published in the French *provinces*, their very number would be an obstacle to their being bribed; and the government, by silencing half a dozen editors in Paris, would not effectually gag the whole nation. I repeat it—the inhabitants of the country are entitled to, and ought to have, their own organs of public opinion, as they enjoy the privilege of sending their own representatives to Congress. In whatever contempt country politicians may be held by a certain party, they are, nevertheless, a wholesome check upon the leading politicians of the cities, and save the country alike from the tyranny of a factious mob, and a selfish and narrow-minded aristocracy.

Let no one say the people in the country ought to be differently employed from speculating upon politics ; or, that they ought to attend to their domestics concerns, and leave politics to the town. Such a guardianship would be fatal to their liberty and independence. The present times are neither made for Arcadian shepherds, nor for a patriarchal life, whatever poetry may be attached to either. Guardianship on the part of the rulers implies want of pupillarity in the governed, and contains the principles and essence of slavery. On this account I congratulate America on the great number of country papers, which circulate throughout the Union, whatever be the *literary* deficiencies of some of their editors. Their number, and the good sense which pervades them, atone practically for the want or elegance of style in any one of them ; as their great utility is a sufficient apology for their comparatively slender pretensions to refinement and taste.

CHAPTER VI.

WITH the exception of Protestant Germany, there is no country in which so much has been done for the education of children, as in the United States of America. In all the large cities of the Union there are public free schools, and there is scarcely a hamlet unprovided with the means of elementary instruction. The States of New England have, in this respect, taken the lead, and all others have since made the amplest provisions for this branch of national development.

In the State of Connecticut there is a school fund, from which the following dividends are made to each county.

Counties.	Children.	Dividend in Dollars.	
		Dollars.	Cents.
Fairfield - - -	13,524	12,171	60
Hartford - -	14,261	12,834	90
Litchfield - - -	12,601	11,340	90
Middlesex - -	7,337	6,603	30
New Haven - - -	11,789	10,788	30
New London - -	12,044	10,339	60
Tolland - - -	6,671	5,103	30
Windham - -	8,057	7,251	30
Total of Children	86,284	76,433	20

It appears, from this table, that there exists, in that State, a provision by which something more than four shillings sterling *per annum* are allowed to every child from four to sixteen years of age, for the purpose of education ; a liberality which, I believe, is unequalled in any part of the world.

Nor is this a solitary instance of American liberality in the department of instruction. The amount of tax raised in the State of Massachusetts for the support of common schools, averaged 350,000 dollars, or 70,000*l.* sterling *per annum*. The state of New York has a school fund of 2,116,000 dollars, or 423,200*l.* sterling, invested in 9580 school-houses ; and the expenses of common schools in that State amounted, in 1833, to 1,262,670 dollars 97 cents, or 252,514*l.* sterling, nearly.

Ohio, Pennsylvania, and South Carolina have also adopted the principle of free schools, and other States are gradually following the example. The inhabitants of Boston have made the most ample provisions for the education of children ; and the system of free schools, in that city, has become a model for imitation throughout the United States, where similar institutions are now fast rising into existence.

The ablest and most skilful instructers in the United States are natives from New England, who are generally supposed to be better acquainted with school discipline, and better versed in the art of communicating ideas, than the rest of their countrymen. Their religious habits, and the severity of their morals, seem to qualify them particularly for the task of " teaching the young idea how to shoot." It is computed that not less than sixty thousand New Englanders are employed annually in the instruction of children, in the different States ; which single fact is more creditable to New England, than all the praises which could be bestowed on the industry and ingenuity of her inhabitants.

I am afraid, however, that the pecuniary advantages of these gentlemen are not in proportion to their exertion, and that the vocation of an instructer is, after all, not the most honored in the United States. Much as the Americans appreciate the services of a teacher, they neither reward or esteem him according to his merits, and are

11*

hardly ever willing to associate with him on terms of fair reciprocity and friendship. The same feeling exists, in a still higher degree, in many parts of Europe, especially in England ; but then there is no reason why it should continue in America, in a country in which no disgrace ought to attach to any honest pursuit ; but in which, on the contrary, men should be honored, in proportion as they contribute to the moral and intellectual advancement of the State.

The correctness of this doctrine, however, is so well understood in the United States, that the people are ashamed of their own sentiments, and leave no opportunity unimproved to evince that respect for the vocation *in private*, which they are most deficient of showing on all public occasions. Many a fashionable gentleman of the large cities would be glad of the company of the instructor of his children to a *family* dinner ; but would be unwilling to introduce him to a party of friends, and would think himself disgraced, were he to be seen with him on 'Change.

The Americans have a nice sense of justice, and understand their own interest too well, to be entirely neglectful of the attention due to instructers of youth ; but the more fashionable part of the community are too modest to exhibit their sentiments in public. Much, however, has lately been done for the improvement of the condition of teachers ; and it is to be hoped that the newly formed "American Institute of Instruction," which among its members numbers already some of the most influential and wealthy men of the country, will at last succeed in raising the character of instructers, and thereby increase the sphere of their usefulness.

The salaries of teachers in the public schools in most of the States are mere pittances, when compared with the remuneration of professional men, or clerks in the counting-rooms of respectable merchants. The compensation of private instructers is, in general, higher, but still of too sordid a character to enable them to live as gentlemen.

This inadequate compensation of the most arduous labor, is not only unjust and ungenerous, but productive of the most serious consequences to the public. The profession of teacher is embraced by a large number of men, who, though qualified for the office, resort to it only as a temporary means of subsistence, which they quit as soon as an opportunity of preferment offers itself in some other quarter. The immediate consequence is an almost annual change of instructers, and the succession in office of novices unqualified by age or experience. No proper system of school-discipline can, in this manner be introduced by the teacher; because in children the *habit* of obedience does more than the law, and it is the principle of authority to grow stronger by usage. The branches of education themselves must be taught in a loose and disconnected manner; because every teacher has necessarily a method of his own, which can only be improved and modified by a more intimate acquaintance with his pupils. No great application on the part of the teachers or pupils can be expected under such circumstances. Neither can there exist between them that mutual relation of friendship and respect, which is the most powerful stimulus to exertion, and inspires a taste for the cultivation of the sciences, on the principle of emulation, more lasting than that which results from a momentary enthusiasm in their pursuit.

But the greatest evil arising from the too frequent changes of instructers in the United States is the unavoidable contempt to which it exposes the veterans in the profession. — Many of the most eminent lawyers, ministers, and physicians of New England have, during a certain period of their lives, been obliged to resort to teaching, either to finish their collegiate education, or to obtain the necessary means for the study of their respective professions. They have thus been in a habit of considering the employment of an instructer as a sort of relief from the most pressing necessities ; but not as *an end* to be proposed by a man who aspires at honorable distinction. This creed, once established in the minds of professional men, has communicated itself to all ranks of society ; so that, instead of the thanks of his fellow-citizens, an ancient instructer is only sure of being considered as a man of inferior talents; else he would have followed his colleagues in their professional career. As long as this opinion of instructers is entertained in the United States, the schoolmaster's task will be degraded.

Those whom necessity shall reduce to it, will look upon it as defaming their fair reputation, and embrace the first opportunity to leave it with disgust and detestation.

But with what zeal can a man devote himself to a profession, at once laborious and difficult, in which the greatest success is incapable of procuring distinction ? — which exposes him to unmerited contempt and reproach ? And why should a pettifogging lawyer or a quack, consider himself better than an honest and successfnl instructer?

> " Honor and shame from no condition rise ;
> Act well your part—there all the honor lies."

With regard to the plan of instruction, considerable improvements have been made within the last ten years. The mechanical Lancastrian system has every where been improved or superseded by the inductive method of Pestalozzi; which, as it is calculated to draw out the *thinking* faculties, is naturally better adapted for the instruction of republicans.

The branches of learning, which are best taught in American schools, and in which the pupils seem to be better informed than those of any school I have seen in Europe, are arithmetic, geography, geometry, grammar, and reading: those in which they are most deficient, are history and foreign languages. The taste for mathematics is so prevalent in the United States, that even the young misses study geometry and algebra, and this principally on account of their usefulness in strengthening and invigorating the intellect. Mechanics and astronomy, together with the elements of natural philosophy and chemistry, are taught in all female seminaries throughout the country; and there are some in which even plane and spherical trigonometry are introduced as regular branches of instruction.

There are many schools for young ladies entirely conducted by gentlemen ; and the undertaking has proved so profitable to the instructers, that many of the most distinguished professors of colleges have resigned their chairs, to assist in the education of women. By a singular *caprice* of the American coteries, the principals of these

schools are exempted from the odium which is generally
attached to the profession : they are the only instructers
in the United States who enjoy a fair share of the reputation and esteem, to which they are justly entitled by
their talents and labors.

The improvements which have lately been made in the
system of education in Germany have not passed unno-
ticed by the vigilance of Americans ; and a society is already formed at Albany, in the state of New York, charg
ing itself with the translation of the Prussian school-books.
— The object of the society is to improve the system of
instruction in the state of New York, and to adopt, instead
of the disconnected treatises now in use in the different
schools, the uniform system of the Prussian text-books.
This liberality of the Americans, with regard to the system of education in general, must, ere long, extend itself
also to the instructers.   It will raise the standard of their
profession, and remunerate their services in a manner
which shall induce them to follow their task from choice,
and not from necessity.   The high respect which is paid
to all persons engaged in the business of instruction in
Germany is, perhaps, the principal reason why it is so
cheerfully embraced by gentlemen of literature and science, and has done more for the improvement of common
schools, than all the laws enacted for that purpose.

To show in what low estimation teachers are held in
the United States, notwithstanding the general call for
public instruction, and the importance attached to it by
private individuals and legislative assemblies, I here insert
an extract from the " Annual Report of the Superintendent of Common Schools of the State of New York,"
made January, 1835.

" The incompetency of teachers " says the report " is
the great evil of the common school system of this State,
and it may, indeed, be said to be the source of the only
other material defect which pertains to it, — a low standard of education in most of the schools.   The evil, however, is by no means universal.   There are many teachers
of ample qualifications, and many schools of high standing, both as regards the nature and extent of their acquirements.   The principal obstacle to improvement is
the *low wages* of teachers ; and, as this is left altogether

to be regulated by contract, between them and their employers, there would seem to be no effectual remedy for
the evil, but to inspire the latter with more just conceptions of the nature of the vocation, and its high responsi-
bilities ; and of the necessity of awarding to those who
pursue it, a compensation in some degree suited to its
arduous duties and requirements. So long as the compensation of teachers is on a level with that which is commanded by the most ordinary employments, it is not to be
expected that men of the necessary talents will prepare
themselves for the business of teaching ; but it may justly
be said that there is scarcely any vocation, in which the
best talents can be employed to greater advantage. The
practice of paying " *low wages* " has, as might be expected, introduced into the common schools, teachers
wholly incompetent to execute their trusts, who have
brought in bad methods of teaching, and kept down the
standard of requirement for their pupils on a level with
that by which their employers have measured their qualifications.

"Although the compensation of teachers is still extremely low, it is gratifying to reflect that it is increasing. In
the districts heard from the number of schools kept during
the year 1833, an average period of eight months was
$9,392. The amount annually paid for *teachers' wages*
in the same district was about 665,000 dollars. This
sum, divided by the schools, would give each teacher 8
dollars 85 cents a month.* But it is supposed that female teachers are employed about half the time at a compensation of about 5 dollars (a guinea) a month.† In
this case, the average compensation of male teachers

---

* Equal to 1*l.* 16*s.* nearly, or about 9*s.* a week; in a country, where
the commonest day-laborer may earn from 50 cents to 1 dollar or 2*s.*
3*d.* to 4*s.* 6*d.* each day. The wages in the cities average still more;
and there is no servant or housemaid to be obtained at less than from
10 to 15*s.* per week, besides board.

† This is another sordid practice introduced throughout the United
States. Female teachers are employed for no other apparent end than
because they are less expensive than regular instructers. Women in
general (unless mothers) are not the most appropriate teachers of boys,
even in a nursery; much less are they capable of superintending the
more advanced education of male children. The system of instruction
in every branch of learning requires considerable modification accord-

would be 12 dollars and 70 cents (2*l.* 10*s.* 5*d.*) nearly.
By a similar estimate for the year 1831, contained in the
report of the superintendent made in 1833, it appears that
the average rate of *wages* was but 11 dollars 85 cents
(2*l.* 8*s.* 5*d.*) A similar estimate for 1832 would give 12
dollars 22 cents (2*l.* 9*s.* 5*d.*) Thus it appears that the
rate of wages is regularly advancing, although still altogether inadequate to the services rendered."

This report, which was evidently drawn up by a gentleman engaged in *improving* the system of instruction of
common schools, appears, nevertheless, from the unhappy
choice of terms, replete if not with contempt, at least with
little consideration for the vocation of teachers.   A regret
is expressed that instructers are not better paid ;   because
" *low wages* " are not apt to act as a premium on the skill
and application of *workmen ;* but the idea does not seem to
be for one moment lost sight of, that teachers are hire-
lings, whose labors are always to be commanded with
money, as the services of journeymen mechanics.   I am
not inclined to believe that the character of teachers in the
State of New York will improve as long as they receive
" wages ; " and am fully convinced that half the number
of teachers employed in that State, if they were qualified
for the business, would be more serviceable to the public
than two or three times their actual number, with their
present inferior acquirements, joined to the disadvantages
of their position.

Owing to the system of education generally introduced
in the schools of the United States, text-books written in
the catechising form (with questions and answers) are
preferred to more compact treatises.   In some branches
of education this method of instruction may be advantageous ;   but in others it must prove a serious evil.   Mechanical methods ought to be carefully avoided as begetting indolence in both teacher and pupil, and taxing the

ing as it is to be applied to the pupils of one or the other sex :* and on
this account I think female instructors as little qualified for the instruction of boys, as male teachers to superintend the education of young
ladies. The teacher ought to represent the parent, which to a boy
must be the father, and to a girl the mother of the child.†

*Schwarz. Erziehungslehre. Leipsig, 1829.
†Niemeyer. Grundsätze der Erziehung. Halle, 1825.

memory without exercising the nobler faculties of the mind. I do not think, however, that the Americans are, in this respect, more deserving of censure than the generality of the English; and they are certainly superior to the lamentable deficiency of French elementary instructers. But their system of instruction could not, as yet, be compared to that of Germany, either in method or discipline; although a vast number of improvements have already been adopted, and legislative assemblies and private individuals are constantly aiding the progress of elementary education.

There are two branches of instruction, however, which I consider to be better taught in America than even in Germany. I would refer to reading and speaking. The Americans, in general, take more care to teach a correct pronunciation to their children, than the English; and the Germans are almost wholly unmindful as to the correctness of utterance, or elegance of language. They are so much attached to the substance of thoughts, that they heed little in what form the latter are expressed, and are satisfied with teaching their pupils to understand what they are reading, or to comprehend with the eye what they are unable to express with clearness and precision. A German boy knows often more than he can express in his abstract and unmanageable language: an American says at least as much as he knows, and is seldom embarrassed except with the difficulty of the subject.

This readiness of the Americans to express with promptness and precision what they have once been able to understand, is as much owing to their system of education, as to the practical genius of the nation, and of immense advantage in the common business of life. An American is not as "manysided" as a German; but whatever he has learned he has at his fingers' ends, and he is always ready to apply it. A little, in this manner, will go a great way, and the amount of intellect and application which is thus penetrating every corner of the United States is prodigious, when compared to the seemingly slender means by which it is produced. Propose a question to a German, and he will ransack heaven and earth for an answer. He will descend to the remotest antiquity to seek for precedents; and, after having compared the histories of all nations, and the best commentaries on them in half a dozen languages, he will be so perplexed with the contradictory statements of authors, that his conscientiousness will hardly allow him to venture an opinion of his own. He will give you a most erudite *resumé* of the subject; acquaint you with all that has been said on it in Sanscrit and Arabic, and, after having made some remarks on the respective credibility of these writers, leave the conclusion to your own ingenuity. An American, with hardly one tenth of the learning, would have submitted the subject to *common sense*, and, ten chances to one, would have given you a satisfactory answer. The Germans are the best people in the world for collecting materials, but the Americans understand best how to use them. I know no better combination of character than that of German and American; and there is probably no better system of instruction than a medium between the theoretical rigor of the former, and the practical applications of the Americans.

The German system favors the development of the mind to the exclusion of almost all practical purposes; the American aims always at some application, and creates dexterity and readiness for action. One is all contemplation, the other all activity—the former is adapted to the abstract pursuits of philosophy, the latter to the practical purposes of life.

Each of these systems has its own advantages and disadvantages, and corresponds well to the genius of the respective nations among whom it is established. There is probably no better place than a school-room to judge of the character of a people, or to find an explanation of their national peculiarities. Whatever faults or weaknesses may be entailed upon them, will show themselves there without the hypocrisy of advanced age; and whatever virtue they may possess is reflected without admixture of vice and corruption. In so humble a place as a school-room may be read the commentaries on the past, and the history of the future development of a nation.

Who, upon entering an American school-room, and witnessing the continual exercises in reading and speaking, or listening to the subject of their discourses, and watching the behavior of the pupils towards each other

12

and their teacher, could, for a moment, doubt his being amongst a congregation of young republicans? And who, on entering a German academy, would not be struck with the principle of authority and silence, which reflects the history of Germany for the last half dozen centuries? What difficulty has not an American teacher to maintain order amongst a dozen unruly little urchins; while a German rules over two hundred pupils in a class with all the ease and tranquillity of an Eastern monarch?

In an American school every thing is done from conviction; in a German, obedience is from habit and precedent. How active is not the strife for consideration and power amongst a class of young Americans; how perfectly contemplative the same collection of Germans, intent only upon their studies and the gratification of individual tastes.

The majority of the pupils of an American school will imprint their character on the institution; the personal disposition of the teacher in Germany can always be read in the behavior of his pupils. There is as little disposition on the part of American children to obey the uncontrolled will of their masters, as on the part of their fathers to submit to the mandates of kings; and it would only be necessary to conduct some doubting European politician to an American school-room, to convince him at once that there is no immediate prospect of transferring royalty to the shores of the New World.

It has been observed, that with Americans mathematics come by instinct. This is true *with regard to the applications* of the science, which in America are as well, or better understood, than in any part of Europe; but there is no taste visible for the mere abstract knowledge of it, as is the case in France and Germany.

The Americans are born analyzers, and are better able to understand a principle from its application, than to seize a truth in the abstract, nor would they think such a truth an acquisition, unless they saw its practical bearings. I have known several excellent mathematicians in Boston and Philadelphia, but their talents were all of the order I have described; and I suspect, therefore, that they are not very eminent teachers. The method of instruction must necessarily be synthetic, and implies a process of reasoning, which, as far as my experience goes, is least acceptable to American palates. In politics analysis is the only means of arriving at fair conclusions ; but in the exact sciences it is less direct and secure, although it is the method of invention and the most fertile in applications. On the whole, I do not think that the Americans have a greater share of mathematical talent than Europeans; but they certainly apply it to greater advantage, and evince an acquaintance with the science in all their civil and political transactions. Mathematics with them are an active principle ; not an abstract science, as in Europe.

For history, the Americans seem to have the least fondness ; but they are great admirers of statistics, and have an astonishing memory of numbers. An American considers the history of his country as the beginning of a new era ; and cares, therefore, less for the past, than he does for the present and the future. Statistics is nevertheless a still-standing history,* and the key or index to the future fate of a nation. This truth is as well understood in America as in any other country ; and accordingly, the rage for statistical tables, as a means of obtaining knowledge in a quick and easy manner, exists in the United States to a still greater degree than in England or France. I have known few persons in Europe, as well acquainted with the imports and exports, revenue and expenditure, amount of national debt, standing armies and navies, &c. of their own and foreign countries, as the great mass of Americans.

Geography is well taught from excellent text-books, some of which have been translated into several European languages. The proficiency of the pupils in this branch is highly creditable to the instructers, and surpasses in minuteness and correctness that of most scholars of the same age in Europe.

But the most surprising fact, in the whole course of American education, is the *total absence of religious instruction,* in most of the elementary schools. This is entirely left to the care of the parents, and confined, principally, to the reading of the Bible and the hearing of

* *Schlözer.* Lehrbuch der Statistik. Göttingen.

sermons and lectures on the Sabbath. I confess myself
unable to judge of the expediency of this course, which
is perhaps rendered necessary by the great number of religious sects who send children to one and the same
school; but whatever its disadvantages may be, I am quite
certain there is as much theoretical and practical religion
in the United States as in any other country.

Before I conclude these observations on elementary instruction in America, I would mention a subject, which,
as yet, seems to have escaped the attention of most travellers, though it is sufficiently interesting in itself, and ex-
planatory of a great many peculiarities in the lives of
Americans. I would allude to the precocity of children,
which results from the plan of education pursued in
schools and at home, and perhaps, also, from the peculiar
climate of the country.

An American boy of ten or twelve years of age is as
much of a young man as an European at sixteen; and
when arrived at that age, he is as useful in business, and
as much to be relied upon, as a German at twenty-four,
or a Frenchman at fifty. Something similar to it may also
be found in England; but neither climate nor education
promote it to the same extent as in America. From the
earliest period of his life, a young American is accustomed to rely upon himself as the principal artificer of his
fortune. Whatever he learns or studies is with a view to
future application; and the moment he leaves school he
immerses into active life. His reputation, from the time
he is able to think, is the object of his most anxious care;
as it must affect his future standing in society, and increase the sphere of his usefulness.

As a school-boy, he has his opinions on politics and religion, which he defends with as much ardor as if he
were a senator of the republic, or a minister of the gospel. By the time he is able to read and write, he is already forming the plan of his future independence; and
I have heard boys from ten to twelve years of age enlarge
on the comforts and advantages of married life, with as
grave an aspect, as if they had been reciting a mathematical lesson, or discussing the merits of an essay on politics. They were calculating the prospects of domestic
happiness, as a merchant would the profits of a mercan-

tile speculation, or a banker his commission on a bill of exchange.

American children study the foibles of their parents and teachers, which they are sure to turn to their own advantage, and at the age of twenty-one are better judges of characters, and human nature in general, than many an European at the age of fifty. In girls this precocity is blended with bashfulness and modesty ; but the most characteristic feature of American children, whether male or female, is, nevertheless, an early development of the understanding, and a certain untimely intelligence seldom to be found in Europe.

The Americans have a much shorter period assigned to them, for the completion of their studies than Europeans; but the quantity of knowledge acquired in that time is really prodigious, and it is a wonder if the memory can retain one fourth part of it in after life. A child from four to five years of age is already obliged to be six hours a day at school, and to study perhaps two or three more at home ; and as it advances in age, the number and variety of these studies increase in a duplicate ratio. At the age of twelve, a boy will study Latin, Greek, French, Italian, Spanish, algebra, geometry, mechanics, moral philosophy, mineralogy, natural philosophy, chemistry, and Heaven knows what ! and manages at least to recite his lessons to the satisfaction of his *teachers.* I have never seen an attempt at any thing similar in Europe, and am satisfied of the utter impossibility of its success, were it to be hazarded in England or Germany.

If the time devoted to an American college-course were anyways in proportion to the intensity of application on the part of the pupils, the American seminaries would be the first in the world, and its professors and students the most remarkable for application and learning. But, unfortunately, the period of a collegiate education is limited to four years, which is about one half of what ought to be allowed for the completion of the course prescribed for an American college. Not much more than the rudiments of science can be acquired in so short a period ; and the American scholar, therefore, must chiefly depend on the resources of his own mind, and the assistance of libraries, to become eminent in any department of knowl-

12*

ledge, or to compete with men of learning in Europe. A number of American students are, for this purpose, annually visiting the Universities of Europe, especially those of Germany, and many distinguished scholars in the United States are as intimately acquainted with the literature of that country, as with the literary institutions of their own.

But if the Americans do not as yet possess the higher institutions of learning, which are the ornament of the most civilized states of Europe, the elements of a classical and mathematical education are, at least, disseminated throughout their whole country, and the means of laying the foundation of scholarship in every State of the Union. They had, in 1835, not less than seventy-nine colleges, thirty-one theological seminaries, twenty-three medical, and nine law schools.

There were also five Roman Catholic seminaries, viz. at Baltimore and near Emmitsburg, in Maryland; at Charleston, South Carolina; near Boardstown, and in Washington county, Kentucky, and in Perry county, Missouri.

In these colleges there were, in 1835, 639 instructers employed in teaching Latin, Greek, mathematics, philosophy, astronomy, and other elementary branches of learning to 7810 students; and besides, 220 professors in the higher departments of science for an average number of 5000 pupils. The number of alumni and students amounted to more than 33,000, and the number of volumes in the libraries, to 456,420; of which 277,770 belonged to the colleges, 113,220 to the students' libraries, and 65,430 to the theological seminaries. But since 1835, five new colleges have been established, viz., Haddington college in Pennsylvania, Shurtleff and McKendrean colleges in the state of Illinois, Columbia college in Missouri, and Buffalo college, on a munificent scale in the state of New York. It is to be observed, moreover, that out of the whole number of colleges, more than one half have sprung up since 1820, and nearly one third since 1830. Most of them were established in the western states, where civilization has scarcely penetrated within a dozen years; and the theological seminaries date nearly all from the period of 1820. We shall see, hereafter, how the remarks of some English writers agree with these facts.

When we speak of the merits of American institutions of learning, we ought not to forget that the United States are still *settling*, and not *settled;* and that, consequently, all the Americans have done thus far, for the promotion of learning, is rather to be considered as indicative of their taste and the high value they set on intellect, than as a fair specimen of what they will be able to accomplish in the course of time.

The attention of the public must be earnestly directed towards improvements in education, in order to establish, within the space of ten years, eight new colleges in a state, which has only been settled within the last forty years, as is, for instance, the case with the colleges of Oxford, New Athens, Hudson Gambier, Granville, Marietta, New Elyria, and Chagrin, in the state of Ohio. In the state of Kentucky, which, in 1790 contained but 73,677 inhabitants, of whom about one third were slaves, there are now six colleges, with nearly forty instructers. The state of Alabama, which in 1810 had but a population of 10,000 people, including slaves, had ten years later already a seminary of public instruction with six professors in the various departments of science. The state of Mississippi did not exist three years (it was only admitted into the Union in the year 1817,) without instituting a seminary of learning with ten professors; though its whole population, at that time, did not exceed 75,000, of whom about 33,000 were slaves. The college of St. Louis was incorporated in 1829, nine years after the territory of Missouri had been admitted into the Union as an independent state, though it contained at that time little more than 100,000 inhabitants, of whom nearly 25,000 were slaves; and a new college has been established since 1835, in that state. The college of Bloomington, Indiana, was established in 1827, though the whole state did not yet contain a single large town, (New Albany, the largest of them, containing in 1831 but 2500 inhabitants,) and the college of Jacksonville, in the state of Illinois, in 1830 ; the whole county of that name containing then little more than 1500 inhabitants. Judge Hall, in his oration, delivered at Vandalia (!) on the 4th of July, 1830, expressed his sentiments in reference to this college in the following manner :—*

"All who have explored this state, (Illinois,) agree in awarding to it the capacity to sustain a larger amount of population, than any other equal expanse of territory in the United States. *But it is the moral more than the physical character, which raises a state to a proud elevation among her sister republics.* Illinois is destined to have wealth and strength ; and it is important that she should also have intelligence, virtue, and refinement, to enable her to direct her mighty energies to the noblest ends. Industry and arts will soon make their abodes among us. Millions of freemen will draw their subsistence from our prolific soil. Let us train up our young republicans to virtue. *Let us educate the children, who, in a few years, must stand in our places.* Let us lead back their minds to the example of the pilgrims, who forsook their country and their homes, rather than violate conscience or offend their God."

Where such sentiments prevail the best hopes must be entertained of the future. The literary institutions of America may be as young as the states in which they are formed ; but they are, at least in proportion to their population, more *numerous* than in any part of Europe, Germany not excepted, and afford ample means of initiating beginners into the elements of science, at an expense of little more than one third of what is required, for similar purposes in England.

The academical course, as I remarked before, is completed in four years, at the end of which the degree of Bachelor of Arts is conferred without any of those rigid examinations which are customary in the universities of Germany. No dissertation is required, on a particular subject, and the candidates for academical honors are not obliged to become authors before they are pronounced to be scholars.† The merits of the students are computed from their daily recitations in the various departments of instruction ; and the system is, at least, daily productive of application, which, in the more scientific institutions

* I quote it here, because it is strongly expressive of the feelings of the people in general.

† This is the practice in Germany.

of Germany, is constantly deferred to the end of the "semester." An American student does not learn as much, at any one time, as a German, and his knowledge, therefore, is less connected and arranged ; but he acquires a great deal, little by little, and can, in this way, more easily follow his professors. The hardships of an American student are certainly less than those of a German ; but then he enters the university at a much earlier period, and quits it at a time when Europeans are yet at school.*

The degree of Master of Arts is conferred three years after that of Bachelor is obtained ; but is less desired in America, and consequently more seldom granted, than in England.

The academic morals I should pronounce to be a shade higher than those of English or German students, and the practice of duelling is, I believe, entirely unknown. But the German universities were at all times considered as a national institution ; which can hardly be said of the American colleges, established by the munificence of individuals, and maintained, frequently, for the promotion of the interests of a particular denomination of Christians.

The libraries of the American colleges cannot certainly, be compared to those of Oxford, or Göttingen, or Munich, and perhaps not even to those of much inferior institutions of learning in Europe. But in the natural and exact sciences a small number of works, principally modern, suffices to acquire proficiency ; and these, as far as I am acquainted, are found in all the larger colleges of the United States. Nine tenths of all the works to be found in European libraries are only referred to, as bearing on the history and literature of the sciences, and are hardly ever read by the younger students, who are too busily engaged with the new discoveries to devote any considerable portion of their time to the philosophical contemplation of their origin and progress.

For philological studies, the Americans have, until now, shown but little fondness, and the libraries of their colleges are, therefore, very deficient in this branch of knowledge. But then, where so much is constantly doing

* Compare the preceding remarks on American precocity.

for the education of youth, in other departments, it would be unjust to expend large sums in the purchase of books, on a subject which would only gratify a few individuals ; who ought sooner to visit Europe to gratify their thirst for a branch of knowledge the least useful in the life of a young republic, than tax their fellow-citizens at home with expenditure for which they could never make an adequate return.

But the greatest deficiency exists in the historical department, which scarcely furnishes matter for the history of America, and is lamentably defective in that of Europe. Of the whole range of studies pursued in American colleges, that of history is most neglected. The taste for it remains to be created ; and, as far as I can judge, no symptoms of it are, as yet, perceptible in the social institutions of the United States.

The theological libraries have also been complained of as being extremely deficient ; but most of the predominant religious sects in America draw their arguments directly from the Bible, and not from any human authority whatever, and have, therefore, less recourse to written documents. The Americans believe—and this not without their usual good sense—that an acquaintance with the temptations and trials of this world, and the motives of human actions, is as indispensable a qualification in a minister of the gospel, as the most critical knowledge of canonical laws, and require their religious instructers to be rather practical men, than skilled in the theological sciences.

Mr. Hamilton, in speaking of the education of the American clergy, after having made a number of valuable remarks on "timber and tobacco growers," concludes with the following bitter reflections :—

"Even to the present day, the value of education in the United States is estimated not by its result on the mind of the student, in strengthening his faculties, purifying his taste, and enlarging and elevating the sphere of thought and consciousness ; *but by the amount of available knowledge which it enables him to bring to the common business of life.*

"The consequences of this error, when participated in by a whole nation, have been most pernicious. It has unquestionably contributed to perpetuate the very ignorance in which it originated. It has done its part, in connection with other causes, in depriving the United States of the most enduring source of national greatness. Nor can we hope that the evil will be removed * until the vulgar and unworthy sophistry which has imposed on the judgment, even of the most intelligent Americans,† shall cease to influence some wiser and unborn generation.

" The education of the clergy differed in little from that of laymen. Of theological learning there was none, nor did there exist the means of acquiring it. It is probable that within the limits of the United States, there was not to be found a single copy of the works of the Fathers. But this mattered not. Protestantism is never very amenable to authority, *and least of all when combined with democracy*. Neither the pastors nor their flocks were inclined to attach much value to primitive authority, (?) and from the solid rock of the Scriptures, each man was pleased to hew out his own religion, in such form and proportions as were suited to the measure of his taste and knowledge. It was considered enough that the clergy could *read* the Bible in their vernacular tongue, and expound its doctrines to the satisfaction of a congregation not more learned than themselves.

" To the present day, in one only of the colleges has any provision been made for clerical education.‡ Many of the religious sects, however, have established theological *academies*, in which candidates for the ministry may, doubtless, acquire such *accomplishment* as is deemed necessary for the satisfactory discharge of their high functions."

Now, in the first place, the habit of studying a profession, principally on account of its *practical* applications, exist in all countries; though there are gentlemen in the

---

* I leave to the reader to contrast this declamation with the facts I have hitherto stated.

† Compare Judge Hall's Speech, alluded to, page 140.

‡ This remark is quite incorrect. Theological schools are attached to the universities of Yale and Harvard; as, also, to Princetown, New Brunswick, Kenyon, Western Reserve, Granville, and Lexington colleges. But the learned author seems to have been too much influenced by his holy zeal for religion, to inquire fully into the state of religious instruction in America.

United States, as well as in England, cultivating science *con amore*, such as the learnéd author of " Men and Manners," without ever thinking of applying their wisdom in practice. Necessity, however, has always been "the best teacher, as well as the mother of invention." I believe the instances are rare, in which persons are willing to devote themselves to the study of *theology*, without the hope of future promotion ; and the eagerness with which church livings are coveted in England, shows, at least, the unwillingness of the clergy to embrace the profession merely for the sake of "enlarging and elevating their sphere of thought and consciousness." Theology, jurisprudence and medicine are, in Germany, known by the name of " bread-studies " (Brot-studien,) because they are principally pursued for a temporal establishment ; and the number of those who apply themselves to them to become practical lawyers, physicians, or ministers, is, for the benefit of mankind, in all parts of the world, greater than that of those priests of knowledge whose sole object it is " to purify their taste," and to "enlarge and elevate the sphere of thought and consciousness."

The Americans consider their ministers as public servants, paid by their respective congregations in proportion to the degree of their usefulness. It is a principle with them to establish no sinecures, either in religion or politics ; and their clergy, therefore, have less fortune and leisure to employ in their personal improvement *as gentlemen*, though they have ample time for the cultivation of that more substantial knowledge in a minister, which teaches him to imitate the example of his great Master ; and, by winning the hearts of his congregation, and influencing their morals by his own irreproachable life, to become truly the pastor of his flock, and the friend and counsellor of every family in his parish. Such were the ministers of the pilgrims, and such, it is to be hoped, will be the ministers of the gospel in the United States yet for many a generation. And the people, with a simplicity which does credit to both their hearts and their understandings, value these qualifications in their clergymen higher than the strongest claims of the latter to the refined tastes of gentlemen.

The standard works on British Law have always been

republished in America, (mostly in Boston and Philadelphia,) and make part of every lawyer's library. To these must be added the numerous digests of American laws, the statutes of the different states, and the larger works of American jurisprudence. Several of these, among which are the works of Kent and Story, are sufficiently known to the profession in England to need no further notice in a work of this nature. An American lawyer has certainly greater difficulties to overcome to attain to eminence in his profession, than any other barrister in the world. Not only is he to be learned in the English law, which forms the basis of American jurisprudence, but he must also be familiar with the different statutes of each state in the Union, together with those of the United States themselves. The prerogatives of the general government, and those of the governor and legislature of each independent state, present often the nicest points of distinction, and afford ample scope for the ingenuity and discrimination of American lawyers. The most fertile in argument and scientific distinctions are, I suppose, those of Philadelphia, their fame being established by the adage, "This will puzzle a Philadelphia lawyer;" which is expressive of the same difficulty as the squaring of the circle in mathematics.

The reason why law-schools are not so numerous in the United States as other institutions of learning, is, because young men are in a habit of studying with some professional gentlemen of acknowledged talents and reputation — a custom which exists equally in England, and extends also to medical students in lieu of a *clinicum* for young practitioners.

The first anatomical operation in the United States consisted in the dissection of the body of a felon, who was executed in 1750. Six years later Dr. Hunter, of New York, a graduate of the university of Edinburgh, commenced a course of lectures on anatomy and surgery ; and in 1765 the first medical school was established under the superintendence of Doctors Shippen and Morgan, of Philadelphia. In 1767 another medical school was founded in New York ; but from that period till 1792 the progress of medicine was interrupted by the war of the American independence. A second medical institution was

13

established in New York in 1792, which was afterwards united with the first, under the name of " College of Medicine and Surgery."

The medical school of Massachusetts was established as early as 1782 ; but its celebrity commenced only with the year 1810, when it was transferred to Boston, and became one of the most flourishing institutions in the Union.

The fourth medical school in America is the work of Dr. Smith, of Dartmouth College, New Hampshire. It was founded in Hanover in 1797 ; and, since that time, similar institutions were established all over the United States.

Schools of pharmacy exist in New York and Philadelphia, and have, together with the " Journal of Pharmacy," much contributed to the improvement of this most useful science.

It may yet be remarked, that the Americans have made proper provisions for anatomy ; the bodies of felons and other persons buried at the States' expense, being, by law, due to the students of anatomy. The state of Massachusetts set the example, and many of the other states were prompt in its imitation. I mention this particularly, because no similar provision, I believe, promotes as yet the study of anatomy in England.

If, then, instead of scrutinizing particular institutions of learning, we consider the general progress of.education and science in the United States, and by what means that progress has been insured, we shall not accuse the Americans of indifference with regard to the higher attainments of the mind. The majority of their colleges and universities, and especially their public libraries, when compared to those of Europe, are, perhaps, yet in a state of infancy ; but they are daily enlarging, and their number increases even faster in proportion than the population of the Western States.

The Americans are fully aware of what they have yet to accomplish before they can rival Europe in the arts and sciences ; but they have certainly made a noble beginning, and are constantly improving in every department of knowledge. If they do not *import* a great number of scientific works from Europe, — a fault with which

Mr. Hamilton severely reproaches them — they *reprint* the more, and have also published many excellent translations from the French and German, among which it will be sufficient to allude to the works of La Place, Cousin, Heeren, and the German Conversation Lexicon. This, in a country like America, in which more than one half of the entire population have not as yet any fixed habitations, affords assuredly a strong proof of the high value its inhabitants set upon literary and scientific acquirements ; while at the same time it is the best refutation of the gratuitous charge, that the Americans are strangers to the pleasure arising from intellectual pursuits, or too much absorbed by trade and traffic, to bestow any considerable portion of their time on the cultivation of their mental faculties.

CHAPTER. VII.

GENERAL OBSERVATIONS ON AMERICANS. — DEFINITION OF
AMERICAN PATRIOTISM. — THE AMERICANS AS A MORAL
AND RELIGIOUS PEOPLE. — DIFFERENT RELIGIOUS DE-
NOMINATIONS IN AMERICA. — UNITARIANISM. — THE RE-
SPECT OF THE AMERICANS FOR THE LAW. — OBSERVA-
TIONS ON THE LYNCH-LAW. — ITS ORIGIN. — TEMPER-
ANCE AND OTHER BENEVOLENT SOCIETIES. — NATIONAL
CHARITY.

THOUGH the Americans, in general, have fewer prejudices than any nation in Europe, and possess, therefore,
less of a national character; though they have no community of religious feeling; yet there exists amongst them
an uniformity of thought and sentiment, which is sufficient
to mark them as a distinct people. These sentiments are
principally *political*, or have reference to their *habits of
industry*.

The Americans present the singular spectacle of a
people united together by no other ties than those of excellent laws and equal justice, for the maintenance of
which " their lives, their fortunes, and their sacred honors " stand mutually pledged. The American commonwealth consists of a community of reason and good sense;
its empire, therefore, is the largest, and its basis the most
unalterable on which the prosperity of a people was ever
established. They revere the theory and foundation of
their government, to which they transfer most of their
local attachments, their love of country, and those generous sentiments, which the contemplation of the gigantic
scenery which surrounds them is calculated to inspire.

There is, at present, no room for idylic poesy and ro-
mance ; but the energetic develop,ment of the nation may
soon furnish matter for an epopee

An American does not love his country as a Frenchman loves France, or an Englishman England : America
is to him but the physical means of establishing a moral
power — the medium through which his mindoperates —
" the local habitation " of his ʲpolitical doctrines. His
country is in his understanding ; he carries it with him
wherever he goes, whether he emigrates to the shores of
the Pacific or the Gulf of Mexico ; his home is wherever
he finds minds congenial with his own.

Americans have been reproached with want of love for
their native country ; but, with such an enlightened attachment to their moral and political institutions, it is
difficult to fix upon the limits of the empire which must
eventually be theirs, or upon the boundary line which they
shall not overleap in their progress. The patriotism of
the Americans is not confined either to a love of their
country, or to those who are of the same origin with them :
it relates to the mind, and to the habits of thinking and
reasoning. Whoever thinks as they do, is, morally speaking, a citizen of their community ; and whoever entertains
opinions in opposition to their established theory of government, must be considered a natural enemy to their
country.

The moral influence of this process of reasoning on the
prospects and future power of the United States is incalculable. It has made America the representative of a
doctrine which is fast gaining ground throughout the
civilized world ; it has extended her physical and moral
dominion, and created for her friends and allies in every
nation and in every clime. It has made her cause the
cause of humanity, and her success the triumph of reason
over ignorance and prejudice. What people could now
make war on America, without retarding the progress of
their own freedom ? What arm would not drop palsied
in aiming a blow at American liberty ? What mariner
would wish to extinguish the beacon-light which directs
the course of his navigation ? — It has made the Americans strong within themselves, and invulnerable from without. Their political doctrines have become the religion

13*

and confession of the people of all countries: like the truths of Christianity, they have had their apostles and their martyrs, and like those truths they are destined to become the universal faith of mankind.

Neither can the patriotism of the Americans be called a vague and indistinct feeling; on the contrary, it is clear and defined, and has a definite aim. It is not an instinctive attachment to scenes with which they are acquainted from childhood, or to men to whose familiar converse they are accustomed ; it consists in the love of principles, for which they are ready to make every sacrifice, and which in the outset they preferred to their homes.

The American pilgrims carried their country in their hearts, and their government in their minds. Their character was formed before they touched the soil which was to nourish them, and has ever since remained superior to local circumstances. The Americans entered the wilderness as masters, determined to subdue it; and not as children of nature, nursed and brought up in its bosom. They could not at first love what was not their own ; and when it became theirs, they had already changed its face.

The succession of changes was so rapid, that scarcely one could leave a permanent impression on their minds. They treated nature as a conquered subject; not as a mother who gave them birth. They were the children of another world, who came thither to burn, ransack and destroy, and not to preserve what ¡they had found. They burned the forests, dug up the bowels of the earth, diverted rivers from their course, or united them at their pleasure ; and annihilated the distances which separated the North from the South, and the East from the West.

All other nations have *gradually* merged from barbarism to civilization, and, in the successive stages of their development, been strongly influenced by the soil and the climate. But it is in proportion to the length of time nature retains her dominion over man, that he will cling to her as a child to its mother, or that local attachments to the soil and the country are formed. At the very settlement of America, (as I remarked in the last chapter,) the highest degree of civilization, the product of another clime, was at war with a pristine world ; and to this moment no permanent truce is established. Let the conflict be brought to an end, let man make his peace with nature—and she will once more become his companion, and make him love his native land.

I have said that the patriotism of Americans is not a vague and indefinite feeling, but that it consisted in a strong attachment to principles. I say so still. The principles which they cherish are those of liberty, and they are sufficient to raise them to a proud eminence amongst the nations of the earth. They establish a moral empire more durable than human feelings, and less susceptible of changes. I will now add that the Americans *love* their country, not, indeed, *as it is*, but *as it will be*. They do not love the land of their fathers ; but they are sincerely attached to that which their children are destined to inherit. They live in the future, and *make* their country as they go on.

It often appeared to me as if the whole property of the United States was only held by the Americans in trust for their children, and that they were prepared to render a religious account of their stewardship. See with what willingness they labor to secure an independence to their children!—with what readiness they take a part in the national improvements of their country!—with what cheerfulness they quit an already fertilized soil, and emigrate to the "far west," to make more room for their offspring ! —how ready they are to invest their fortunes in undertakings which can only benefit their progeny ! Are these no proofs of a genuine patriotism ? Is this not the most exalted love of country of which history furnishes us with a record ?

A mere local attachment to the soil, however it may influence the domestic happiness of a people, is, of itself, hardly capable of imparting that national impulse which directs the feelings and actions of individuals to a common centre, and makes them sacrifice their own private interests to the general good of the whole. It must be a spiritual essence, a community of the highest faculties of the mind, which shall make men look on one another as brethren, and unite them as members of one and the same family. It was the *spirit* of the Romans which created and preserved Rome ; as it was the highest principles of religion which united the Israelites into a nation, and led them out of the land of bondage. It was the love of political and religious liberty which led to the settlement of the British American colonies ; and the same feeling is yet sending thousands to the shores of the New World. It is the cement of the American confederacy, and the very essence of their commonwealth.

I am aware it will be urged that it is not so much the liberal institutions of America as the immense resources of the country, the fertility of the soil, and the vast extent of commerce, which are the causes of the constant emigrations to the United States. This, however, is but begging the question ; for, without those institutions, the resources of the country would not yet be developed, the soil would not yield its produce, and the commerce of the country would still linger under onerous laws.

It is the love of freedom, the hope of being exempted from burthensome taxes, and the expectation of being able to call their own what they shall earn by their honest toils, which causes most Europeans, and especially the Germans, to emigrate to the United States, in preference to the equally fertile but ill-governed states of South America. The security and good faith of the American government act at least as much as an enticing cause as the hope of realizing a competence.

The early settlements of the British North American colonies, their political progress, and the present prosperous condition of the United States, may be alike traced to the love of liberty, which, from the commencement, distinguished the Americans ; and the history of the individual states sufficiently proves that their inhabitants set a higher value on political and religious freedom than on the physical advantages of the soil, and the means of acquiring riches. "For what is good land without good laws ? "—said the early colonists of West Jersey, in their remonstrance against the usurpations of the Duke of York—" the better the worse. And if we could not assure people of an easy, and free, and safe government, both with respect to their spiritual and worldly property, —that is, an uninterrupted liberty of conscience, and an inviolable possession of their civil rights and freedoms, by a just and wise government,—a mere wilderness would be no encouragement; for it were madness to leave a free, a good, and improved country, to plant in a wilderness, and there adventure many thousands of pounds to give an absolute title to another person to tax us at will and pleasure ? "

" We have not lost any part of our liberty," continued they, " by leaving our country; for we leave not our king, nor our government, by quitting our soil ; but we transplant to a place given by the same king, with express limitation to erect no polity contrary to the same established government, but as near as may be to it; and this variation is allowed but for the sake of emergencies ; and that latitude bounded by these words, 'for the good of the adventurer and planter.' " *

Property, in some of the South American republics, is acquired with as much, or even greater facility, than in the United States ; but there is no security for its preservation, while the latter offer, in this respect, greater guarantees than any other country, England and France not excepted. There are no conflicting elements which threaten an immediate change or overthrow of her established institutions. The opposition in America is powerless, and never refers to the *principles* of government, but only to particular measures. No class of society in the United States is opposed to republican institutions, as there is no political party whose permanent interests are opposed to the majority of the people. Neither is the policy of the United States likely to involve the country in a foreign war; and if in a national broil the republic should become a belligerent party, her political and geographical position is such, that she has little to fear from an enemy.

The Americans have kept good faith with all nations ; and, by the most unexampled economy, discharged their national debt. Their credit is unrivalled, their honor unquestioned, and the most implicit confidence placed in their ability to fulfil their engagements. They have, thus far, received strangers with hospitality, and put no obstacles in the way of their progress. They have not monopolized a single branch of industry; but let foreign-

* *Samuel Smith's* History of New Jersey.

ers and native citizens compete fairly for an equal chance of success. They have established liberty of conscience, and compelled no person to pay taxes for the support of ministers of a different persuasion from his own. They have abolished all hereditary privileges ; but let all men start free and equal, with no other claims to preferment than that which is founded on superiority of intellect. In short, they have made their country the market for talent, ingenuity, industry, and every honest kind of exertion. It has become the home of all who are willing to rise by their own efforts, and contains within itself nearly half the enterprise of the world.

These are the true causes of the rapid growth of America, which, joined to her immense natural resources, must make her eventually the most powerful country on the globe. It is the principle of liberty, carried out in all its ramifications and details, which has produced these mighty results. The states of Buenos Ayres and Brazil contain immense fertile plains, blessed with a climate vastly superior to that of the United States, and watered by streams which may vie with the Mississippi ; but no earnest attempt seems, as yet, to have been made to settle them ; and of the thousands of emigrants from Europe, scarcely a handful have seen the La Plata, or ventured themselves on the Amazon. The physical advantages are on the side of South America; but every moral and political superiority is permanently established in the United States.

One of the greatest advantages enjoyed by the Americans, and which can never be sufficiently taken into consideration, consists in their being descended from the greatest and most enterprising nation in Europe. America, in her very cradle, was the child of freedom—wrapt in chartered rights and immunities. She was the offspring of a strong, healthy, well-conditioned mother, who was determined not to spoil her by foolish caresses, but rather hardened her constitution by premature exposure. To the noble blood of her mother, she joined the superiority of education obtained in the school of adversity ; and to the attachment of her parent to liberty, the sturdy love of independence.

The English have bestowed more blessings on humanity, by the establishment of their colonies, than any other nation in the world. To whatever quarter they have transferred their laws and institutions, they have contributed to improve the condition of the human race. The French, the Dutch, the Spaniards, and the Portuguese have also established colonies ; but these have never risen to political importance. They were no nurseries of freedom, but administered only to the sordid cupidity of their parents. Even in achieving their independence they fall into wreck and ruin ; and the sickly progeny of diseased parents can hardly survive their sires. Compare to this the active vigor of the British Colonies ; their legislative assemblies ; their administration of justice, and the liberty of the press established in most of them !

The Americans, after the war of independence, possessed the advantage of British laws and institutions ; from which they selected and retained all they deemed good, and rejected all that was obnoxious or inapplicable. It was a particularly fortunate circumstance that they could retain so much ; and thus the citizens of the young republic were already *accustomed* to conform to the majority of their new laws. Had the change in the legislation been sudden and radical, it would, perhaps, have been difficult, in the outset, to enforce that unlimited respect for the law, without which no liberal government can subsist, or must soon degenerate into anarchy.

But it was not so in America. Most of the statute laws of the States were of old standing, and the people willing to bow to them as the result of the wisdom of ages. This was a great step towards the consolidation and permanency of their government. They had, in most cases, only to *transfer* power instead of *creating* it anew ; and the people who were used to its existence were ready to lend it obedience.

The same principle is yet operating in the new settlements. Without any legislative assembly, or a special agreement for that purpose, every new colony in the Western States elects its magistrates, empannels its juries, and establishes its courts of justice, as if the settlers were the inhabitants of a county in Great Britain ; and without a positive code of their own, the English law is in force till abrogated by statutes. This establishes order and harmony in the beginning, and is the means of great savings of time and money. Instead of turning their early attention to the establishment of governments, and the enacting of suitable laws, the whole energy of the settlers is employed in improving the country, under the highest moral and political standard of legislation, adopted by the common consent of all parties. The Americans, by a singular dispensation of Providence, are enabled to profit by experience which they themselves have not made; and are enlightened by the wisdom of old age, in the vigor and buoyancy of adolescence.

But if the Americans have inherited advantages from England, they have not been the less anxious to improve them. They have not buried their talent, but put it out at interest. To the eminent qualities they possessed by virtue of their descent, they have added copious new ones; and have been studiously anxious to avoid the errors of their ancestors. Their laws and institutions furnish ample proofs of this assertion. They have promoted morality by the simple force of example; they have advanced the cause of religion without making appropriation for the clergy; they have facilitated the means of education, by establishing free schools throughout the country, and are entitled to the universal gratitude of mankind, by their philanthropic improvements in the discipline of prisons. They have gone farther; they have aided the progress of education in foreign countries, by establishing seminaries of learning in Greece, and sending missionaries and instructers to the islands of the Pacific, to spread the doctrines of Christianity among the Indians; and have set an example to their own progenitors in their efforts for the suppression of intemperance. They have joined their efforts to those of the most prominent philanthropical societies of Europe, and have softened the lot of fugitives from tyranny by the most liberal provisions of Congress. The absolute powers of Europe have designated America as an exile for political offenders—a conception which does credit to their ingenuity; but they ought to take heed, lest the banishment should become too attractive, and hasten the commission of crimes, for the sake of incurring its penalty.

But the strongest tie, which unites the Americans into

a powerful nation, is, nevertheless, the hope of acquiring property and consideration, which their institutions hold out to all persons, without distinction of birth or parentage. The idea may be prosaic ; but it is, nevertheless, a correct one. What unites the citizens of a country more effectually than their common stakes of rights and property ? The more they have to defend, the better will they defend it. Must not the stoutest patriotism relax in a country, in which a man is born only to be the footstool of those above him ; in which the most persevering exertion can hardly protect him against want, and in which he must leave his children without inheritance, to lead the same weary life as their father. How must it affect his pride and honest ambition, to be marked from his birth as an inferior being ; though the faculties of his mind ought to make him the peer of the favored! What stimulus to industry is there in the thought that labor is incompatible with respectability, and that the highest title to respect is the having *inherited* a fortune ?

The Americans alone, of all nations, have completely overcome these prejudices. In their country the same rights, the same privileges are offered to all ; industry is an honor, and idleness a disgrace ; all a man earns is his own, or goes unimpaired to his children ; no beginning is so humble but what it may lead to honor ; and every honest exertion is sure of its adequate reward. As long as the institutions of America are productive of such happy results, it is but natural that the people should cling to them as the principal cause of their boundless national prosperity.

Of all the writers on the United States, I remember but one,* who has enlarged on the general morality of the country, to show the intimate connection which exists between it and the stability of republican governments. This is a subject of much importance, and admits of a variety of detail.

Morality, I am aware, is philosophically separable from religion ; but I am fully convinced, that in practice, especially as regards the whole people, the separation is absolutely impossible. Neither the mere abstract love of

* Alexis de Tocqueville " *De la Démocratie en Amérique.*"
14

virtue, nor its perfect harmony with all other laws of nature, nor even the happiness which it is calculated eventually to produce, have ever been sufficient to restrain
either the lower or higher classes from the commission of
crimes against individuals or society in general. Religion,
in all countries, has been the broadest basis of national
virtue ; and the same holds of the United States of America. Although the most perfect tolerance exists with regard to particular creeds, yet it is absolutely necessary
that a man should belong to some persuasion or other, lest
his fellow-citizens should consider him an outcast from
society. The Jews are tolerated in America with the
same liberality as any denomination of Christians ; but
if a person were to call himself a Deist or an Atheist, it
would excite universal execration. Yet there are religious denominations, in the United States, whose creeds
are very nearly verging on Deism ; but, taking their arguments from the Bible, and calling themselves followers
of Christ, they and their doctrines are tolerated, together
with their form of worship.

The Unitarians, who are forming large congregations
in the Northern and Eastern States, taking for their motto the words of St. Paul, " Prove all things ; hold fast
that which is good," are, perhaps without knowing it, as
nearly as possible, on the verge of pure Deism ; but as
long as they conform to the usual form of prayers, to the
regular sabbath service and evening lectures, and partake
of the sacrament, they will be considered as good Christians, and enjoy the same consideration as any other sect
in existence. But their creed is far from being universally popular, especially in the Southern States, where it
is almost wholly confined to the trading classes, composed
of emigrants from New England.

The inhabitants of the South are principally Episco-
palians, and as much attached to authority in religion as
they dislike it in politics. They consider Unitarianism as
a religious democracy ; because it relies less on the authority of the Scriptures, than on the manner in which
the understanding of the clergy expounds them, and retains too little mysticism in its form of worship, to strike
the multitude with awe. I have listened to many excellent sermons preached by Unitarian clergymen, contain-

ing the most sublime morals which I ever knew to flow from the pulpit; but I hardly ever perceived a close connection between the text and the sermon; and whenever they entered upon theological doctrines, I have always found them at variance with themselves and each other. I write this with the fullest conviction that I do not, myself, belong to any orthodox persuasion; but, as far as logical reasoning and consequence of argument go, I think the Unitarians more deficient than any other denomination of Christians. I do not see how they can hold the ground which they have assumed: they must, in my opinion, go either further on the road to Deism, or retrace their steps, and become once more dogmatical Christians. The greatest objection I would make to Unitarianism is the absence of *love* in many of its doctrines; and the substitution of ratiocination in most cases, where the heart alone would speak louder than all the demands of a sedate, reasonable, modest morality. When I hear an argumentative sermon, I always remember the words of our Savior:

"Happy are the poor in spirit; for theirs is the kingdom of heaven."

And when I hear stoic virtues preached, I remember poor Magdalen,

"To whom much was forgiven; because she loved much."

Two reasons there are for the spreading of Unitarian doctrines in the United States. First, because its ministers are amongst the most highly gifted, and the more eloquent as they belong to a sect which is yet in the minority; and, secondly, because there is a class of people in America, who, aware of the moral and political necessity of religion, in order to restrain the vices of human nature, would do all in their power to preserve the text and practical applications of Christianity; while, at the same time, they would willingly dispense with certain ceremonies and popular beliefs, which, in their opinion, are not essential to religious worship. They call themselves "Unitarians;" because they dare not call themselves more, or rather less; and are better known by their opposition to orthodoxy, or what they think the extravagances of the Christian faith, than by any positive tenets

of their own. They agree, as far as I am acquainted, on
but one point, which is the denial of the Trinity, by denying the divinity of Christ ; but as to the *authority* for their
belief, it is too nearly related to a certain branch of the
applied mathematics, to require a particular comment.*

Many Unitarian preachers have published excellent
sermons, which have become popular, even in England ;
and as long as they refrain from attacking other sects,
and retain their purity of style, I can see no reason why
they should not be read by all denominations of Christians, as containing a concise, intelligible, and even eloquent code of morals.

I ought to observe, moreover, that the Unitarians in
New England form a highly respectable and intellectual
class of society, whose private lives and virtues offer but
little room either for moral or religious criticism. This
is probably the reason why Unitarianism is supposed to
become popular in the United States ; though it is, by the
great majority of the people, still looked upon as a doctrine incompatible with pure Christianity. But then we
ought to distinguish between cause and effect, and not ascribe exclusively to the doctrine, what may perhaps be
more easily explained by the peculiar position of its followers.

The Unitarians in the United States are not numerous :
they are, for the most part, in tolerable circumstances ;
and at the head of their persuasion is the oldest and best
university of the country.† No other religious denomination in America enjoys the same advantages ; and we
might, therefore, naturally expect some moral distinction
in favor of its adherents. But if Unitarianism should
ever become the creed of the great mass of the people,
it is more than probable those advantages would cease,
or, at least, be confined to a small number.

Religion gains more from the heart than from the abstract understanding ; and is more accessible through the

---

* I have heard the doctrine of the Trinity disputed on the ground
that *three* are not *one ;* as if any denomination of Christians considered
the trinity of God as more or less than *three different manifestations of
the same principle.* I thought these objections sufficiently combated in
Swift's sermon " On the Trinity."

† Harvard College—the most literary institution in the United States.

medium of the feelings, than through the most logical course of demonstrative reasoning. Man is naturally a sophist, and ever ready to adapt his creed to his actions, or at least to allow his conscience a certain latitude, incompatible with moral and religious justice.

The Christian religion addresses itself particularly *to the heart*, and is, on that account, accessible to all capacities, and adapted to every condition of life. Love and charity are its basis; and Christ himself has set the divine example in dying for the sins of this world. To strip religion of its awful mysteries, to explain the creation and redemption of man like a phenomenon in natural philosophy, and to make human intellect the ultimate judge of its truth and applications,—is to deprive it of its sanctity, and thereby of its influence on the majority of mankind.

I do not believe that the spreading of Unitarianism will serve to increase the respect for the Christian religion, or that its moral consequences will benefit society in general. Neither do I think it capable of becoming the universal religion of the people, whose affections and hopes require a stronger prop than the cold dictates of human morality.

> Venture then to hope; and fondly dream:
> Yonder world shall ev'ry pledge redeem,
> Of your true and faithful sentiment.*

Thus far, it does not appear that Unitarianism has made very rapid progress in the United States. The number of its congregations is still small when compared to those of other denominations of Christians, and, as far as I am acquainted, is not on the increase. This, however, is not owing to the want of zeal in their clergymen, but principally to the doctrine itself; which does not seem to captivate the feelings and sympathies of the great mass of Americans, however it may please and accord with the argumentative disposition of its followers.

> * Wage du zu hoffen und zu träumen;
> Wort gehalten wird in jenen Räumen,
> Jedem schönen gläubigen Gefühl.
> Schiller's *Thekla eine Geisterstimme.*

14*

The most numerous religious sects in the United States are the Methodists, the Presbyterians, and the Baptists.

The following table will exhibit a general summary of the different religious denominations in the U. States:—

Denominations.	Ministers.	Churches or Congregations	Communicants.
Congregationalists - - -	975	1,071	129,756
Presbyterians (Gen. Assembly)	1,914	2,648	247,964
Reformed Dutch Church - -	167	197	22,515
Associate Presbyterian Church -	70	169	12,886
Associate Reformed Church -	43	100	10,000
Cumberland Presbyterians -	400	. . .	60,000
German Reformed Church -	186	600	30,000
Baptists Calvinistic - - -	3,110	5,888	384,859
Free-will Baptists - - -	342	546	25,276
Seventh day Baptists - -	32	32	4,258
Six principle Baptists ·· -	12	23	2,137
Christian Baptists - - -	300	1,000	30,000
Mennonite Baptists - - -	200	. . .	30,000
Tunker Baptists - - -	40	40	3,000
Methodist Episcopal Church -	2,458	. . .	638,784
Methodist Protestants - -	70	. . .	30,000
Protestant Episcopal Church -	701	800	. . .
Roman Catholic Church - -	340	383	. . .
Evangelical Lutheran Church	191	627	59,787
United Brethren or Moravians	33	24	2,000
Unitarians (Congregationalists)	165	187	. . .
New Jerusalem Church - -	33	27	. . .
Universalists - - - -	300	600	. . .
Friends or Quakers - - -		500	. . .
Shakers or Millennial Church -	45	15	. . .

This table, which, it will be perceived, is incomplete, furnishes, nevertheless, twelve thousand one hundred and twenty-seven ministers, fifteen thousand four hundred and seventy-seven churches, and one million seven hundred and twenty-three thousand two hundred and twenty-two communicants. The Presbyterians enumerated in the above table belong, moreover, all to New England; and there are yet a considerable number in the other states. The number of Jews is computed at about fifteen thousand. It appears, then, that out of the whole population, including slaves and children, there are five communicants to every thirty-nine persons, one minister to every eleven hundred, and a church to every eight hundred and forty, nearly.

When we reflect that no tax is imposed for the support of ministers, or the building of churches, and that, consequently, all those establishments are the result of voluntary contributions of the people, the conviction will certainly be forced on our minds that the Americans are deeply impressed with the importance of religious instruction, and that, together with their freedom, they prize nothing so high as the sacred truths of Christianity. No more satisfactory evidence is required on this subject, than the fact that they are willing to *pay* for it; which is certainly a singular coincidence when contrasted with the political position of other countries. If there were an established religion of state, I doubt whether half the money could be raised for its support which is now cheerfully expended for the maintenance of twenty-five different doctrines.

The American ministers are continually striving to make proselytes, and, being usually paid in proportion to the number of communicants, anxious to increase the number of their respective congregations. I do not mean to say that this is the only motive of their religious ardor; but merely speak of the advantages of the system over all others, independent of the intrinsic merits of the ministers. The principle of paying most "where most work is done," or where it is done best, which is daily producing miracles in the United States, is even applicable to the clergy, and is productive of more good to mankind than could be produced with twice the funds in any country in Europe. Not only have the Americans a greater number of clergymen than, in proportion to the population, can be found either on the Continent or in England; but they have not one idler amongst them, all of them being obliged to exert themselves for the spiritual welfare of their respective congregations. The Americans, therefore, enjoy a threefold advantage : they have more preachers; they have more active preachers, and they have cheaper preachers than can be found in any part of Europe.

The religious habits of the Americans form not only

the basis of their private and public morals, but have become so thoroughly interwoven with their whole course
of legislation, that it would be impossible to change them,
without affecting the very essence of their government.
Not only are the manners and habits of a people, at all
times, stronger than the positive law, but the latter itself
is never readily obeyed without becoming reduced to a
custom.   It is to the manners and habits of a nation we
must look for the continuance of their government.   In
France, where the people have for ages been accustomed
to an absolute and despotic government, where every historical monument, every palace, every work of art, nay,
the very furniture of their rooms, speak monarchy, we
perceive constant anomalies in society, from the legislative halls down to the meanest public resort; simply because the people are accustomed to feel one way, and
constrained to reason and act in another.   They possess
yet the forms of religion, which have ceased to convey to
them a meaning; they have yet the splendor of a throne,
without any of the feelings of loyalty; they have all the
titles and pretensions of their ancient nobles, with the
most unbounded love of equality.   Yet, with all their political excitability, and their theoretical attachment to republicanism, they are constantly lulled asleep by monarchical principles, without offering any other resistance
than the sensation which the fact itself produces, when
set off by the pen of an editor.   An Englishman or an
American would *feel* the encroachment on his liberty;
because it would oblige him to change his habits, which
he is less prepared to do, than to surrender a positive
right.   American liberty is further advanced in the minds
of the people than even in the laws themselves.   It has
become an active principle which lives with, and animates
the nation, and of which their political constitution is but
a *fac-simile*.

Whatever contributes to confirm a people in the habitual exercise of freedom, is an additional guarantee of its
continuance; and whatever has been instrumental in procuring that freedom, or is associated with it in their minds,
must be preserved with religious care, lest liberty itself
should suffer in their estimation.   This is the case with
the doctrines of Christianity in the United States.   Reli-

gion has been the basis of the most important American settlements; religion kept their little community together—religion assisted them in their revolutionary struggle; it was religion to which they appealed in defending their rights, and it was religion, in fine, which taught them to prize their liberties. It is with the solemnities of religion that the declaration of independence is yet annually read to the people from the pulpit, or that Americans celebrate the anniversaries of the most important events in their history. It is to religion they have recourse whenever they wish to impress the popular feeling with anything relative to their country; and it is religion which assists them in all their national undertakings. The Americans look upon religion as a promoter of civil and political liberty; and have, therefore, transferred to it a large portion of the affection which they cherish for the institutions of their country. In other countries, where religion has become the instrument of oppression, it has been the policy of the liberal party to *diminish* its influence; but in America its promotion is essential to the constitution.

Religion presides over their councils, aids in the execution of the laws, and adds to the dignity of the judges. Whatever is calculated to diminish its influence and practice, has a tendency to weaken the government, and is, consequently, opposed to the peace and welfare of the United States. It would have a direct tendency to lessen the respect for the law, to bring disorder into their public deliberations, and to retard the administration of justice.

The deference which the Americans pay to morality is scarcely inferior to their regard for religion, and is, in part, based upon the latter. The least solecism in the moral conduct of a man is attributed to his want of religion, and is visited upon him as such. It is not the offence itself, but the outrage on society, which is punished. They see in a breach of morals a direct violation of religion; and in this, an attempt to subvert the political institutions of the country. These sentiments are all-powerful in checking the appearance of vice, even if they are not always sufficient to preclude its existence.

With Argus-eyes does public opinion watch over the words and actions of individuals, and, whatever may be their private sins, enforces at least a tribute to morality in public,

My meaning cannot be misunderstood.—It is but the open violation of the law, which comes before the forum of the judge; for our secret transgressions we shall have to account with our God. Public virtue must be guarded against the pernicious influence of example; vice must be obliged to conceal itself, in order not to tincture society in general. In this consists the true force and wholesome influence of public opinion. It becomes a mighty police-agent of morality and religion, which not only discovers crimes, but partly prevents their commission. The whole people of the United States are empannelled as a permanent jury to pronounce their verdict of "guilty" or "not guilty" on the conduct and actions of men, from the President down to the laborer; and there is no appeal from their decision. Public opinion may sometimes be unjust for a long time, especially in reference to politicians; but it hardly ever remains so, and there is no injury which it inflicts, which it is not in its power to remedy.

Another proof of the high premium at which morality is held in the United States, consists in its influence on the elections of officers. In Europe, a man of genius is almost privileged. If he be a poet or an artist, allowances are made for the extravagance of his fancy, or the peculiarity of his appetites. If he be a statesman, his individual wanderings are forgotten about the general good he bestows on the nation; if he be a soldier, the wounds he may inflict upon virtue and unguarded innocence, are pardoned for the sake of those he may have received in defending his country; and even the clergy have their offences excused, in consideration of the morals which they promote by their spiritual functions. No such compensation takes place in the United States. Private virtue overtops the highest qualifications of the mind, and is indispensable to the progress even of the most acknowledged talents. This, in many instances, clips the wings of genius, by substituting a decent mediocrity in the place of brilliant but vicious talents; but the nation at large is nevertheless a gainer in the practice.

It must be remembered that the Americans are already in possession of most political advantages other nations are striving to obtain; and that their principal care, therefore, is rather to *preserve* what they have acquired, than to enlarge their possessions; and for this purpose virtue and honest simplicity are infinitely preferable to the ambitious designs of towering talents. If morality, which is now the common law of the country, were once to be dispensed with in favor of certain individuals—if the exactions which are now made of every member of the community were to relax with regard to the peculiarly gifted, then the worst and most dangerous aristocracy would be introduced, which would not only shake the foundation of society, but eventually subvert the government. Talent, in a republic, must be valued principally in proportion as it is calculated to promote public good : every additional regard for it enriches only the possessor ; and the Americans are too prudent a people, to enrich and elevate individual, with the property and wealth of the nation.

The moment a candidate is presented for office, not only his mental qualifications for the functions he is about to assume, but also his private character are made the subject of criticism. Whatever he may have done, said, or listened to, from the time he left school to the present moment, is sure to be brought before the public. The most trifling incidents which are calculated to shed a light on his motives or habits of thinking, are made the subject of the most uncompromising scrutiny; and facts and circumstances, already buried in oblivion, are once more brought before the judging eye of the people. This, undoubtedly, gives rise to a vast deal of personal abuse and scurrility, and may even disturb the domestic peace of families; but then the candidates for office are comparatively few, while the people, who are to be benefited or injured by their election, are many ; they are all presenting themselves of their own accord, and the people compelled to be their judges; they have friends to defend and extol their virtues, and they must therefore expect to have enemies, who will endeavor to tarnish their fair reputation. We may have pity on a repentant culprit—we may be roused to indignation by the condemnation of an innocent person ; but we would not, on that account, abolish the trial by jury, or shut our courts of justice, which are instituted not only for the punishment but also for the

prevention of crime. The process of an American election resembles that of a Roman canonization : the candidate must be fairly snatched from the clutches of the
devil's advocate, before he can be admitted to the unrestrained enjoyment of paradise. If, in this manner, some
are prevented from becoming saints, who have a just title
to that dignity,—it may also serve to prevent a heathen
worship of idols, which would divert the people from the
true faith.

It is an erroneous maxim, to consider American institutions as they are calculated to affect individuals : they
are made for the people, and intended to benefit the
majority. The consideration of quality must necessarily,
in many instances, yield to the reflection on quantity ;
and a small benefit extended to large numbers, be preferred to a signal advantage conferred on a favored few.
The American government possessing little coercive
power, cannot introduce sudden changes either for the
better or worse, and is, therefore, less able to correct an
abuse if it is once introduced and sanctioned by the
majority, than any other government in the world.* It is
consequently of the greatest importance that public morality should be preserved at any price, and that the
people themselves should compose the tribunal before
which the offenders are to be tried. It is their noblest
privilege to be themselves the guardians of their moral
and religious rights, without which their political immunities would soon become crippled and destroyed. In
this manner they will not always secure the greatest
talents, but generally the moral integrity of their leaders ;
they will not easily sacrifice peace to national glory, but
promote the tranquil happiness of millions ; their career
will not be one of brilliant triumph, but it will be less
sullied with political crimes ; they will not give birth to a
Cæsar or an Augustus, but be spared the mourning for
Brutus.

Morality, in America, is not only required of a states-

* De Tocqueville entertains directly the opposite opinion—but seems
to have considered this matter rather in a *legal* than an *historical* point
of view. The laws may easily change—but not the *habits of the people*,
after they have once been generally adopted.

man, but is equally necessary in every occupation of life. The merchant who employs a clerk, the master-workman who employs a journeyman, the gentleman who hires a servant, will all make morality an indispensable condition of contract. In this they are as much guided by their own choice, as by the opinions of their neighbors and the community in general. An inferior workman of "steady habits" is almost always preferred to one possessed of the highest business qualifications, but with a doubtful moral characer. Thus, a married man will be sooner trusted than one who is single ; because "he has given hostage to fortune," and possesses what Bacon calls "an impediment to mischief." A man of sober habits will be sooner employed than one addicted to intemperance ; and a clumsy, but moral servant will more readily obtain a situation, than one who is expert and vicious. Religion will, in all, be considered as a pledge of morality ; and a lax observance of religious duties, as a bad index to their private virtues. In short, morality and religion are as indispensable to the laboring classes in the United States, as powerful and well-formed limbs, and a correct use of the understanding. They will often atone for a variety of other imperfections ; but without them every other qualification becomes useless, and only serves to aggravate the despair of success.

There is one particular sentiment pervading all classes of Americans, which, though something similar exists in England, is in no other country carried to the same extent, or productive of the same consequences. I mean the universal respect for women, and the protection offered them, to whatever order of society they may belong. *Ladies* are respected, or rather command respect, every where, especially in England ; but in no country are the penalties fixed by the law, or the received customs of society, on a breach of decorum, so severe as in the United States. The commission of such an offence not only excludes a man from society, but influences his business, his character, his reputation, his prospects in life, and every reasonable chance of success. No rank or standing proves sufficient to protect him against the denunciations of the public ; no repentance can atone for an offence once known to the world. Of all the crimes

15

against society, the Americans seem to be bent upon visiting this with the most unrelenting severity; of all that obtain forgiveness, this alone seems to form an exception.

Neither is this protection, as I have said before, only offered to *ladies*, or to those whose education and family entitle them to particular consideration, as is the case in Europe; it extends to all classes without distinction, and is even more favorable to the lower orders, than to those who are supposed to be above them.

If a man of fortune and reputation were to ruin an innocent girl, or be guilty of a breach of promise, were it but to a waiting-woman, it would no less affect his standing in society, and expose him to the revenge of the public. Neither ladies nor gentlemen would plead his cause; and his only chance of escape from punishment, would be to satisfy the injured party.

Where a feeling of this kind is so general, and acts alike on every member of society, it cannot be the result of a mere polite etiquette, but must be based on a *principle* which is deeply rooted in the mind, and forms part of the national code of morals. Its advantages in promoting early marriages, and preserving the sanctity of the marriage vow, are incalculable, and are the best comment on the rapid increase of population and the domestic happiness, which is enjoyed throughout the United States.

Let us compare this to the state of public morals in Europe. A gentleman being guilty of a breach of promise, or an offence still more heinous, with regard to a *lady*, will be called to an account by her relations or friends; he will have to settle the matter "as a man of honor;" and if he be so lucky as to escape uninjured, the affair is brought to an end. At the next drawing-room he will appear with additional *éclat;* there will be something *distingué* in his whole carriage and manners; while the most kind-hearted of the ladies will consider him a gentleman of "high spirit," and rather the more interesting, "as he has got himself into difficulty." He will, for a time, become the hero of society; where his first success will only facilitate the road to his next conquest.

If a young man of rank and expectations should happen to injure a woman in an inferior rank of life, the matter will be only considered as something a young gentleman is hardly able to avoid; or he will be pitied for his want of refinement in not making a better selection. And the woman? "Why! she must have been a fool to believe him. Why did she raise her expectations so high? She could not, in her senses, believe he would marry her." In short, the case is dismissed, as being too uninteresting to deserve a moment's attention.

An injured gentleman fares hardly better. He becomes the object of ridicule — while his rival moves on in his career, and has scarcely another consolation left, than that which belongs to all misery—of suffering in common with others. The *Code Napoléon*, and subsequently the *Code Français*, have very wisely abandoned this matter "to the censure of public opinion." There is a case in which the best law becomes useless; and this is when it is impossible to obtain justice *from want of an impartial jury.*

I consider the domestic virtue of the Americans as the principal source of all their other qualities. It acts as a promoter of industry, as a stimulus to enterprise, and as the most powerful restrainer of public vice. It reduces life to its simplest elements, and makes happiness less dependent on precarious circumstances; it ensures the proper education of children, and acts, by the force of example, on the morals of the rising generation: in short, it does more for the preservation of peace and good order, than all the laws enacted for that purpose; and is a better guarantee for the permanency of the American government, than any written instrument, the constitution itself not excepted.

No government could be established on the same principle as that of the United States, with a different code of morals. The American Constitution is remarkable for its simplicity; but it can only suffice a people habitually correct in their actions, and would be utterly inadequate to the wants of a different nation. Change the domestic habits of the Americans, their religious devotion, and their high respect for morality, and it will not be necessary to change a single letter of the Constitution in order to vary the whole form of their government. The circumstances being altered, the same causes would no longer produce the same effects; and it is more than probable, that the disparity which would then exist between the laws and the habits of those whom they are destined to govern, would not only make a different government desirable, but absolutely necessary, to preserve the nation from ruin.

The moral and domestic habits of the Americans must necessarily exercise an important influence on the acquisition and accumulation of property. A single man encounters often more difficulties in making his way through the world, than one whose early marriage has increased his stimulus to exertion. The man who has a family is doubly pledged to virtue, and has, in every additional member, a monitor to industry and frugality. In a country like America, where so much depends on individual enterprise, the effect of it, when anyways ably directed, can never long remain doubtful; especially when it is seconded and approved of by the community in general. Accordingly, there are but few single men largely engaged in commerce, or any other kind of enterprise, and less who, in that state, are capable of accumulating fortunes. The most enterprising merchants and ship-owners, the first manufacturers, and the proprietors of the largest estates in the country, are married men; and what is still more remarkable, have acquired their property, not before, but after, their marriage.

This example of prosperity in the marriage-state, and the consequently greater facilities of credit of married men, act as a premium on matrimony ; and enable men to provide for their wives and children, who, without them, might have been unable to provide for themselves. But when the foundation of a fortune is once laid, its increase and accumulation follow as a matter of course, unless some unexpected calamity should blast the hope of success. The moment a man is known to have acquired a little property by his own industry, he receives credit for ingenuity and perseverance, and is trusted on account of these virtues. His means become, in this manner, much more enlarged than his estate ; and it depends chiefly on the resources of his own mind, what advantages he will draw from his position.

But if the acquisition and accumulation of property in the United States is made comparatively easy, and credit given to those who succeed in it, a proportionally larger discredit must attach itself to those who are unfortunate and poor; and this is really carried to a melancholy extent, although, from the unexampled prosperity of the country, there are few to whom it will apply. A man, in America, is not despised for being poor in the outset— three-fourths of all that are rich have begun in the same way;—but every year which passes, without adding to his prosperity, is a reproach to his understanding or industry; and if he should become old without having acquired some property, or showing reasons which prevented his success,—if he should not enjoy a reputation as a scholar or a professional man,—then I am afraid he will be doubly punished;—by his own helpless situation, and the want of sympathy in others. But in this case, it is not the want of property, which deprives him of the consideration of his fellow-beings: it is the want of talent, ingenuity, perseverance, or enterprise, which might have insured his success. Hence an American will seldom complain of losses, want of business, or prosperity in general. The sympathy he might create in his friends would rather injure than benefit him; and would, at best, but destroy his credit with the rest. In the United States, if a man has made a bad bargain, he is sure to keep the secret to himself, lest his business talent should be doubted; if he has been unfortunate in a speculation, he will find a remedy in another, without lamenting the loss; and should he even be ruined, he will put on a good face, arrange himself with his creditors, and start anew, cautioned by his former experience.

This habit, of depending chiefly on themselves, produces in the Americans a spirit of independence, scarcely to be found in any other nation. It stifles complaints of all sorts; makes them support heavy times and calamities with patience; and inspires them with hope and energy when oppressed with loss and misfortunes. During a residence of many years in the United States, I have had frequent intercourse with all classes of society, but do not remember having heard a single individual complain of misfortunes; and I have never known a native American to ask for charity. No country in the world has such a small number of persons supported at

15*

the public expense; and of that small number one half are foreign paupers. An American, embarrassed in his pecuniary circumstances, can hardly be prevailed upon to ask or accept the assistance of his own relations; and will, in many instances, scorn to have recourse to his own parents. Even an unsuccessful politician will leave the field without a groan, not to appear overcome by his antagonist; and, whatever be his secret anguish, show a bright countenance to the public. Happiness and prosperity are so *popular* in the United States, that no one dares to show himself an exception to the rule; and avoiding carefully the semblance of misfortune, they generally succeed in reality, and become that which they have always been striving to appear.

Another feature of the American character, which is evidently entailed upon them from the English, is their unbounded respect for the law. Notwithstanding the frequent accounts of disturbances, (which for the most part are so exaggerated as scarcely to bear a semblance to truth,) there exists in the United States an universal submission to the law, and a prompt obedience to the magistrates, which, with the exception of Great Britain, is not to be found in any other country. If there be but a small force required in England to put down the popular fury, nothing of the kind exists at all in America; and we ought, therefore, not to wonder if, with the more frequent causes of popular excitement, and the total absence of any armed power to restrain it, there sometimes occur excesses, which disturb the public peace.

The lower classes in England are never called upon for an expression of their political sentiments, while in most of the states of the American Union, every man is entitled to vote, and becomes, by the constitution of his country, a judge of the actions of his rulers. His feelings, and his worst passions are constantly appealed to by political leaders and the press, and it requires a forbearance, which the operative classes in Europe can hardly be supposed to possess, in order, on trying occasions, to abstain from abusing these privileges. The American riots, moreover, which are so much the subject of conversation in England, hardly ever originate with the lower classes themselves; but are instigated by political partisans to forward their individual designs. They operate for this purpose on foreigners, who are too short a time in the United States to have made themselves acquainted with the law, and whose strange credulity is easily excited into abusive conduct.

But what are these riots, after all, but infringements on the police regulations of the cities—an improper expression of popular feelings on some vexatious occasion, *without the least attempt to effect a change in the law.* Compare to this the horrible scenes of the Manchester and Bristol riots in England! When has it been known that the lower classes in America disturbed the legislative assemblies, encroached on the dignity of the judges, refused to pay the taxes assessed by their representatives, or offered a permanent resistance to the law? The disorderly conduct above alluded to, is produced without premeditation, on the spur of the moment, and passes, like an April shower, without leaving a vestige of its occurrence. The damages, on such occasions, consist in one or two broken heads, and some black eyes, for which a proper fine is exacted; and the matter is dismissed from the court, as it is from the mind of the public, to engross the speculations of Europeans, who may feel concerned for the safety of America.

If instead of reading the exaggerated accounts of these riots in the American papers, (which are generally colored for a party purpose,) one will only pay attention to facts, and consider the small number of persons which, on such occasions, are arraigned and found guilty of wilfully disturbing the peace, he will soon be convinced that "the awful outrage on public decency" was committed by half a dozen intoxicated laborers, such as are nightly taken up in the streets of London, and dismissed, the next day, on paying the drunkard's penalty of "five shillings to the King." I have no hesitation to advance the opinion that all the magistrates of the city of New York are not, in this respect, as much occupied in a year, as some of the London magistrates in six months; and yet I would consider my person and property as much protected in London, as in any other city on the globe.

Another argument in favor of the peace-loving spirit of the Americans, consists in the fact of their preserving public order, notwithstanding the attempts to infringe upon it, by a few unruly persons, with no other means at their command, than their own good intentions, and the willingness of all classes, to assist the officers of justice. No military force is employed for this purpose. The riots are quelled by the civil magistrates, assisted by tha people, without the aid of an armed police. It is always the people themselves, who protect the peace and watch over the execution of the law; and as long as the public mind remains uncontaminated with the spirit of disorder, no fears need be entertained of any serious disturbances. To one rioter there are a thousand admirers of order, and a thousand more ready to preserve it with all the power in their hands. It remains yet to be observed, that in none of the riots which have taken place in the United States, the people manifested the least disposition for plunder. They have sometimes destroyed the private property of individuals, but in no instance shown the least design to enrich themselves by it; and there is, consequently, not a shadow of truth in the assertion, that there is " a war between the poor and the rich," originating in the hatred and envy of the former, of the superior advantages of the latter.

A favorite habit of many American editors is to charge all manner of riots to the turbulent spirit of the Irish. This is at once getting rid of the question, by transferring the guilt to the "foreign paupers;" and is at least, proving the fact, that if the poor are not always guilty of crimes, they may at least with impunity be suspected. If it be true that public peace is disturbed only by persons of the lowest occupation in life, and that the Irish, from their poverty, are often obliged to resort to the most menial labor in order to procure a living, it will readily be conceived that, on all such occasions, they are *likely to be amongst the number* of the guilty, without being themselves either the *instigators* or the *principal actors* in the riot. But it is also a well-known fact, that many of the constables, in all the large cities, on the Atlantic, are Irish, or of Irish extraction; and it is equally true, that whenever the peace of those cities is disturbed, these Irish officers are amongst the most active in endeavoring to re-establish it. If the Irish are charged with the commission of popular crime, because they are sometimes among the number of offenders, it is but just to take public notice of their virtue, when it is employed in checking its progress.

To one more fact I must refer before I dismiss this subject: — the burning of the Ursuline Convent at Charlestown, near Boston. I shall not enlarge on the fact itself, as it is already sufficiently known to my readers; but I would remark, that this was certainly not done by the Irish, and was in itself sufficient to provoke their utmost temper and worst passions. Yet, how have they borne it ? — The city of Boston is supposed to contain upwards of ten thousand Irish, principally servants and day-laborers ; and there were besides a large number of them employed on the rail-roads adjacent to that city. No armed force was stationed about the city, although watch was kept by private citizens, in order to give the alarm, in case of a popular movement. The tranquillity, however, was not disturbed for one moment, nor the least demonstration made of an attempt to rise in a body. Was this proving the turbulent spirit of the Irish ? or the impossibility of governing them by laws ? All that was done to calm their excitement, consisted in a meeting of some of the most respectable citizens, to express their indignation at the outrage which had been done to society, and more particularly to the feelings of the Catholics ;— and this honest declaration was sufficient to soothe the minds of the "unruly, the turbulent Irish." The conduct of the citizens of Boston was undoubtedly praiseworthy, and well calculated to reconcile the feelings of the injured : they gave on that occasion a new proof of their wisdom and experience in all matters relative to the administration of justice; but this cannot diminish the credit due to the moderation of the Irish, and the forbearance which they manifested on an appeal to their better feelings. I happened to be in Boston at that time, and was more than ever struck with the truth that *justice is the best peace-maker among nations.*

I have said before, that, notwithstanding the occurrence of popular disturbances, the Americans, as a nation, have a great respect for the law; they are indeed too

enlightened not to set, themselves, an example of obedience to the legal authorities of their country. They
know full well, that the minor laws being once infringed
upon, the general government is in danger. They understand admirably the connection which exists between
the most subordinate authority of the country, and the
highest administrative functions. In America it is the
common interest of all, which requires submission to the
law; for it is the majority who are offended, when an
insult is offered to the government.

The people must naturally be a more jealous sovereign
than a king protected by his crown: they have no power
to pardon offences against their majesty, and if they had,
they could not exercise it without danger of destroying
themselves. Clemency is more frequently a virtue of
kings, than a characteristic distinction of a nation. It is
the majority which governs and makes the law in a democratic republic, and opposition to it must therefore necessarily offend the people. No such opposition can, by
any chance, become popular; because the state of public
opinion is too well known to leave the majority doubtful.
If, in America, there were a strong aristocracy, who
should have the power of making the law for the people,
—then resistance to it might have a majority in its favor,
and disobedience be protected by the influence of the
largest number. No immediate prospect, however, of
such a state of things exists in the United States; and
as long as the majority govern, the majority must be in
favor of the law, and the minority deprived of the power
of resisting it.

There exists but one practice in the United States,
which seems to be at variance with what I have thus far
advanced; and yet, upon further consideration, I am almost inclined to consider it as a part of the common law
of the country. I would refer to the " Lynch law," of
which the most brilliant accounts are furnished in the
British papers. The Lynch law of America, it must be
remembered, is not a child of democracy; it is of a much
more ancient and illustrious origin, and occurs already in
the early history of the colonies. It was begot in those
happy times, in which religious customs took the place

of the law; and in which the ingenuity of the settlers recurred to the simplest means of obtaining the most summary justice. It is, in fact, of a patriarchal nature,
having for its motto the wisdom of Solomon,—"Do not
spare the rod." The pilgrim fathers, who settled the
New England States, were a highly religious people—
with whom the authority of the elders of the Church was
of more avail, than any positive law of Great Britain,
which, from its distance, and the manner in which it had
been abused into an instrument of oppression, had considerably lost of its force. Their little community was
more governed by mutual agreement and consent, than
by any written code, except that to which their ministers
pointed, as leading the way to salvation. The Bible
furnished them with precedents of the cheap, easy, and
salutary correction of flogging; and there was no reason
why their legislators should have attempted to improve
upon the wisdom of Moses.

The custom being once introduced and found expedient,
was gradually increased in severity as the rigid morals of
the puritans began to relax; until, towards the American
Revolution, when abuses had reached their climax, the
original method of "tarring and feathering" was substituted for the more lenient punishment of the rod. The
commencement being made with the excisemen in Boston,
was soon imitated in the other provinces; and being at
first employed in a patriotic cause, created an universal
prejudice in its favor. It became a national custom which,
as far as I remember, was only used in cases more or
less directly affecting the people. Thus, whenever an
individual gave a national insult, or did or practised any
thing which threatened the peace and happiness of the
people, they recurred to it as a domestic remedy; but I
am quite certain not with the intention of opposing the
regular law. They only resorted to it *ad interim*, till the
regular physician could be called in; and in most cases
effected a *radical cure*, without paying for the attendance
of the doctor. In this manner the Lynch law was executed on gamblers, disorderly persons, and latterly also
on a certain species of itinerant ministers, who, a little
too anxious for the emancipation of the Negroes in the
Southern States, had betaken themselves to preaching the

doctrine of *revenge*, instead of that of the *atonement*,* and thereby forced the good people, to apply the doctrine to those, who evinced the most zeal for its propagation. But as I have said before, the Lynch law is not, properly speaking, an opposition to the established laws of the country, or is, at least, not contemplated as such by its adherents ; but rather as a supplement to them, — a species of *common* law, which is as old as the country, and which, whatever may be the notion of " the *learned* in the law," has nevertheless been productive of some of the happiest results. I am aware there are different versions of the origin of " Lynch ; " but the above will be found to contain the essence and philosophy of all.

It remains for me yet to say something of the benevolent feelings of Americans, and of the national efforts which have been made in the United States for the suppression of vice, and the progress of virtue, not only in their own country, but in every quarter of the world. One of the most prominent of these, consists in the ardor with which they have labored for the suppression of intemperance, and the astonishing results which they have produced, since the commencement of this noble enterprise. The origin and progress of their proceedings are too illustrative of the American character, and have had too important an influence on the efforts of philanthropical societies in Europe, not to interest an English reader; and I will therefore venture to give a short account of them, taken principally from the " Permanent Temperance Documents of the American Temperance Society," published at Boston, in the year 1835. It will strongly corroborate my assertion of the necessity of combining morality with religion, or making the latter the practical foundation of the former, and the political proceedings of the country the regular sequel to both.

The first public meeting for the suppression of intemperance was called at Boston only as late as the month of February, 1824, when the question was proposed, —

What shall be done to banish intemperance from the United States?

---

* Some of these itinerant preachers absolutely called on the negroes to disobey the commands of their masters, and to rise in open rebellion, to achieve their political freedom.

After prayer " for Divine guidance," and consultation on the subject, the result was a determination to form an "American Temperance Society," whose grand principle should be abstinence from strong drink; and its object, " by light and love," to change the habits of the nation with regard to the use of intoxicating liquors. After stating the reasons for their determination, among which there was this, that *without trying to remove the evil, they could not free themselves from the guilt of its effects*, they resolved unanimously, —

1st. " That it is expedient that more systematic and vigorous efforts be made, by the Christian public, to restrain and prevent the intemperate use of intoxicating liquors.

2d. " That an individual of acknowledged talents, piety, industry, and sound judgment should be selected and employed as a permanent agent, to spend his time, and use his best exertions, for the suppression and prevention of the intemperate use of intoxicating liquors."

A committee was then appointed to prepare a constitution, and the meeting was adjourned to February 13, 1826. At that meeting a constitution was presented and adopted, the officers chosen, and the resolution agreed to,—

" That the gentlemen composing this meeting pledge themselves to the ' American Society for the Promotion of Temperance,' that they will use all their exertions in carrying into effect the benevolent plan of the society."

On the 12th of March following they met, and, after choosing eighty-four additional members from the Northern and Middle States, presented an address to the people, in which they stated that, after deliberate and devout attention to the subject, they had resolved, " *in the strength of the Lord, and with a view to the account which they must render to Him for the influence they exert in this world*," to make a vigorous, united and persevering effort to produce a change of public sentiment and practice with regard to the use of intoxicating liquors ; and, at the same time, called upon the wealthy and influential men in the country, to assist them in procuring funds for this purpose. This call was heartily responded to, at first, by the people of New England, and subsequently by every other state of the Union.

16

In January, 1827, the corresponding secretary of the society visited Boston, to obtain means for the support of a permanent agent. At the first meeting for that purpose, though the weather was exceedingly stormy, the amount subscribed was 3,500 dollars (700*l.* sterling;) at the second, 1200 (240*l.* sterling) more ; and at the third, 700 (140*l.*) In the adjacent villages 7000 dollars were additionally subscribed.

At the close of the year 1829, there had already been formed and reported more than 1,000 societies, embracing more than 100,000 members : more than 50 distilleries had been stopped, more than 400 merchants had renounced the traffic, and more than 1,200 drunkards had been reformed. So great became the influence of public opinion, even on the minds of common sailors, that on board the United States sloop of war " Falmouth," seventy of the men abstained from ardent spirits ; and between forty and fifty on board the " Brandywine " frigate. A later report shows that, out of the whole ship's company of that frigate, only 160 men drew their grog, and from January 1, 1830, till January 1, 1831, 150 vessels had left the port of Boston without carrying ardent spirits.

On the first of May, 1831, the number of temperance societies had already increased to 2,200, and that of the members to 170,000 ; which gives an addition of 1,200 societies with 70,000 members in the space of less than two years ! From their influence, and the state of public opinion, it was computed that 300,000 more had adopted the plan of not using strong drinks, or furnishing them for the use of others ; 1,000 distilleries had been stopped, and the use of brandy or whiskey excluded from more than 100 public houses.

The next year's report, containing the history of the society, and its operations from the commencement, as also the reason " why its principles should be extended through the world," was stereotyped and distributed through all parts of the United States, Canada, New Brunswick, and Nova Scotia. It was also sent to Mexico and South America ; to England, Ireland, Scotland, Denmark, Sweden, Russia, Germany, Malta, Palestine, and the Sandwich Islands ; imitating, in this respect, the benevolent efforts of the British Bible Society, for the Promotion of the Christian faith.

In 1832 a successful effort was made by the clergy, to exclude drunkards from the communion table, and to introduce the subject of temperance into the sermons to be preached on the Sabbath. The appeal of the society in favor of these measures, contained in their " Annual Report," is a singular specimen of American eloquence ; from which I cannot refrain to give some valuable extracts :—

" Never was an idea further from the truth, than that which represents the Temperance Reformation as only a secular concern, affecting principally the body—or confined in its influence to this world, or to time—to be discussed only on the week day, and that as a matter of convenience, expediency, or domestic comfort, pecuniary profit, or reputation, or respectability. Its principal influence, and that which in importance eclipses and swallows up every other, is upon the soul and for eternity. As much as the soul is worth more than the body, as much as eternity is longer than time, so much more important is its influence on the soul than on the body, and with regard to eternity than with regard to time. And till its influence on the character, prospects, and destiny of the soul for eternity shall be exhibited on the sabbath, from the pulpit, by the ministers of Christ, to every distiller and trafficer, and user of the drunkard's poison in the land, who does not, on account of doing evil, so hate the light, as to refuse to come to it, this engine of death eternal will not cease to operate, nor this citadel of Satan be demolished. Ministers may think that they could not be supported without the avails of the distillery, and the dram-shop, or the countenance of those who furnish or support them; and churches may think that it is not ecclesiastical for them to move, or for their members to act on the subject; and both may hope that other temperance agents, or societies will do the work, and accomplish the object without their assistance, and that they had better say nothing, and do nothing, but mourn in secret, and pray—though church members continue to carry on the traffic, and cause thousands eternally to die: yet it is not so." "No minister of Christ," says the author, "in doing the work of Christ, needs the gains of ungodliness; and no church of Christ is strengthened or sanctified by having rum-makers, and rum-sellers, and rum-drinkers for members. None such formed the family of the Savior, the company of his apostles, or any of that bright constellation, who, in their day, through faith and patience, entered in, and took possession of the promises. They were men of another sort. They could not look up to God and pray, ' Lead us not into temptation,' and then go away and tempt their fellow-men to ruin, and yet hope for his favor. They felt bound to do to others as they would that God should do to them. And if they did not strive to use their influence, not to corrupt and destroy, but to save others, they knew that God would not save them. Nor will he save any, who are not in this respect like them. In vain will they plead their connection with the Church, in arrest of condemnation for destroying their fellow-men. And if they continue that work of death, and the Church continues to hold them within its sacred enclosure, and spread over them the protecting banner of the cross, she will be judged as accessory, and held responsible for the mighty ruin. And when the overflowing scourge shall pass through, judgment will begin where, had reformation began and continued, it had brought out salvation, at the house of God.

" And whether the rainbow of mercy which has begun to appear, shall extend and encircle the world, or earth be enveloped in blackness and darkness, now, under Christ, hangs on the decision of the Church which he has purchased with his own precious blood. Let her members extract from the bounties of his kindness, the material for burning out the consciences of their fellow-men, — let them set it on fire, apply it, and make it a business to spread it through the community, and the smoke of their torment will cover the whole earth, and spread through all its dwellings, darkness, lamentation, and mourning, and woe. A fire in God's anger will burn perpetrators of such wickedness, even to the lowest hell. They would keep the jewels from the crown of his Son, and ruin the souls for whom he died.

" And when Ethiopia is rising and stretching out her hands, and the isles of the sea are receiving and obeying God's laws—when China is struggling to keep off death from her people — *Iceland* in supplication for deliverance is *melting*, and the whole creation groaneth and travaileth in pain — when the Savior, with a voice which pervades creation, is proclaiming, Who is on the Lord's side ? — Who ? — and the universe looks with intense gaze to witness the result ; — and when a single individual, by coming out openly and decidedly on the Lord's side, and sacrificing, in a single instance, money to duty, may roll a wave of salvation on the other side of the globe ; — shall professed members of that church which Christ has bought with his blood, take part with the enemy of all good, and assist in perpetuating his dark and dismal reign over souls, to endless ages ? — If they do, God will write, for the universe to look at, *To whom they yield themselves servants to obey, his servants they are.* And the Register, in blazing capitals, will be eternal. And though men who continue knowingly and habitually to do evil, and to hate the light, may, in this world, refuse to come to it, and when it approaches them may attempt to flee away, —in the future world it will blaze upon them, in one un-clouded vision of infinite brightness, and show the hearts of all who persevere in wickedness to be more black than darkness itself forever."

In another place the author is still more figurative and impressive. Alluding to the sermons to be preached on the Sabbath against intemperance, he says,—

" There is reason to believe that thousands and tens of thousands are now impenitent, unbelieving, and on their way to second death, who, had it not been for the sale of ardent spirits, had been ripening for glory, and honor, and immortality, and eternal life ; and that tens of thousands more have passed the boundary of hope, and are weeping and wailing, who, had it not been for this, might have been in heaven. And, in view of such things, shall we be told that temperance is only a secular concern ? that it affects only the bodies of men, not their souls ; and is a concern which relates to time only, not to eternity ? that it ought not to be discussed from the pulpit on the Sabbath ? Should Satan cause this to be believed, he would perpetuate intemperance to the end of the world. Shall the fires which make these poisons burn on the Sabbath, and the use of it tend to counteract all the merciful designs of Jehovah, in establishing that holy day? Shall Jehovah be insulted (!) by the appearance in the sanctuary of men, who use it on the Sabbath, and yet the Sabbath not be occupied by light and love to abolish the use of it? Shall it cause the word of the Lord, even from the pulpit, to fall as upon a rock, instead of being as the rain and the snow, that come down from heaven and water the earth, and thousands who might be trees of righteousness in the garden of the Lord, to stand like the heath in the desert, not seeing good when good comes, and yet the pulpit be dumb? or speak only on week days, when those who traffic in it have so much to do in furnishing the poison, that they have no time, and less inclination to hear.

"If we may not, in this warfare, fight, on the Lord's day, when he himself goes forth to the battle, and commands on the field—if we may not use his weapons, forged in heaven, and from the high place of erection pour them down *thick, heavy,* and *hot* upon the enemy,— we may fight till we die, and he will esteem our iron as straw, and our brass as rotten wood; our darts he will count as stubble, and laugh at the glittering of our spear. Leviathan is not so tamed. There is no coping with him; but with weapons of heavenly temper from the armory of Jehovah, on the day when he goes forth, and creation, at his command, stands still to witness the conflict. Then it is as conscience kindled from above, blazes, and thunders in the heart of the enemy, that he is consumed by the breath of the Almighty, and destroyed by the brightness of his coming."

This specimen of eloquence, which for its strength and quaint pathos might rival the Capuchin's sermon in Schiller's " Wallenstein," or be ascribed to the immortal genius of Abraham *a Sancta Clara,* exhibits, in the most striking manner, the influence of religion on public morals, and the fact that the Americans, far from having abandoned their puritanical notions of decency and propriety, are yet able, on important occasions, to bring the whole force of religious argument to bear on them; a circumstance which not only insures the continuance of their present customs and manners, but, by virtue of these, also of their political institutions.

During the year 1831 there had been added 50,000 members to the Temperance Society of the State of New York alone. In several counties the increase had been 200 per cent. These societies printed 350,000 circulars, and sent them to every family in the state, inviting each member, who had come to years of understanding, to abstain from the use of ardent spirits, and to unite with a temperance society. They also printed and sent round 100,000 "Constitutions for Family Temperance Societies," in which the members were to pledge themselves not only not to use ardent spirits themselves, but not to suffer them to be used in their families, or presented to their friends, or to those in their employment, except for medical purposes. Those who were, or afterwards were to become, heads of families, were to pledge themselves to teach their household the principle of entire abstinence, and to use their best endeavors to obtain their signatures to the Constitution. They were also to agree to place a copy of that Constitution in their family Bible, to which their children should be often pointed, as containing the will of their parents and they were to engage them ; as they revered the memory of their parents, sacredly to regard those sentiments.

In that year it was computed that 1,500,000 people in the United States abstained from the use of ardent spirits, and from the furnishing of it for the use of others : there were 4,000 temperance societies, embracing 500,000 members ; 1,500 distilleries had been stopped ; 4,000 merchants had ceased to traffic in spirits, and 4,500 drunkards had been reformed.

Nor were the efforts confined to individuals alone. On the 5th of November, 1832, the Adjutant-General issued an order prohibiting the further issue of ardent spirits to the troops of the United States, as a component part of their rations, and substituted 8*lbs.* of sugar and 4*lbs.* of coffee for every one hundred rations, as an equivalent for the ardent spirit formerly in use ; or, at those posts where the troops might prefer it, 10*lbs.* of rice to every one hundred rations, in lieu of eight quarters of beans allowed by the then existing regulations. The same order prohibited also the introduction of ardent spirits into any fort, camp, or garrison of the United States, and the selling of them by any sutlers to the troops.

In the month of December following, the committee issued circulars inviting the people of all states to *a national convention*, to be held in Philadelphia on the 24th day of May, 1833.

In February, 1833, a "Congressional Temperance Meeting" was held at the Capitol of Washington, at which Mr. Lewis Cass, then secretary of war, presided, and where the following remarkable resolution was adopted:—

"Resolved, as the sense of this meeting, *that the liberty and welfare of the nation are intimately and indissolubly connected with the morals and virtues of the people;* and that, in the enactment of laws for the common benefit, it is equally the duty of the legislative body *to guard and preserve the public morals from corruption*, as to advance the pecuniary interest, or to maintain the civil rights and freedom of the community."

Mr. Felix Grundy, senator from Tennessee, invited them not to stop there; he requested them to have their facts and arguments printed and circulated all over the country. "Let it be seen," continued he, "by the whole American people, that men in high places, men whom the people have elevated to represent them in the Congress of the United States, are the friends, the patrons, the active, zealous, and persevering promoters of the cause of temperance. Let them see that this blessed cause has taken possession of the capitol, and that it will hold possession, and, from this elevated spot, this stronghold of liberty, will extend itself over the whole country."

The American Temperance Society contained in that year 2,000,000 of members, out of an aggregate population of about 15,000,000, of which 2,000,000 are slaves; consequently, *every third man* in the country was engaged in suppressing intemperance.

On the last Tuesday, 1834, the "American Congressional Temperance Society" held its anniversary at the Capitol, and in that same year the number of societies had increased to 7000; the same number of merchants had ceased to sell ardent spirits; more than 1000 vessels belonging to the United States had sailed without them; and an insurance company in Boston agreed to return five per cent. on the premium of every vessel which had been navigated without grog : 4,500,000 temperance tracts had been printed by the "New York State Temperance Society" alone ; and addresses were published, in that same year, "to moderate drinkers, and those who furnish spirits to moderate drinkers," to "ministers of the Gospel of every name and in every country," and "to the members of the churches of Christ of every denomination throughout the world," to invite them to abstain from the use of ardent spirits, and to prevent the traffic in them ; and the society could finally close its Eighth Annual Report with the joyful hope of seeing their labors rewarded, expressed in these terms :—

"Great voices shall be heard in heaven, saying Alleluia ; for the Lord God omnipotent reigneth. Peace shall flow as a river, and righteousness as the waves of the sea. Joy and gladness shall swell every heart, and to the Author and Finisher of all good shall arise, as a cloud of incense from the whole earth, thanksgiving and the voice of melody."

From an attentive perusal of this short sketch of the history of the American Temperance Society, three important convictions will be forced on the mind of the reader, viz. that the Americans are yet capable of a strong religious excitement; that morality is, by them, considered a national cause ; and that their political leaders, convinced of the importance of moral and religious institutions, are willing to aid in securing and promoting their influence. Nor have they been less successful in making a political argument of it, to prove that the laws authorising men to traffic in ardent spirits, violate the first principle of political economy. Their reasoning on the subject is plain and impressive, and supported by facts well calculated to illustrate the proposition.

"The wealth of a nation," they argue, "consists of the wealth of all the individuals that compose it. The sources of wealth are labor, land, and capital. The land is, indeed, the product of the two former; but as it may be used to increase their value, it is considered, by writers on political economy, as one of the original sources of national wealth. Whatever lessens either of these, or their productiveness when employed upon each other, lessens the wealth of the country."

"Capital may be employed in two ways—either to produce new capital, or merely to afford gratification, and in the production of gratification be consumed without replacing its value. The first may be called capital, and the last expenditure. These will, of course, bear inverse proportions to each other. If the first be large, the second must be small—and *vice versa*. Without any change of the amount of wealth, capital will be increased by the lessening of expenditure, and lessened by the increase of expenditure. Although the manner of dividing makes no difference with the present amount of national wealth, it makes a great difference with the future amount, as it alters materially the sources which produce it, and the means of an equal or increased reproduction.

" For instance, a man fond of noise, and excited agreeably by the hearing of it, pays a dollar for gunpowder, and touches fire to it. He occasions an entire loss of that amount of property. Although the powder-maker and the merchant may both have received their pay, if it has not benefited the man, to him it has been a total loss—and if the sale of it was no more profitable than would have been the sale of some useful article, it has been an entire loss to the community. And if, by the explosion, the man is burnt, partially loses his reason, is taken off, for a time, from business, and confined by sickness to his bed, must have nurses, physicians, &c., the loss is still increased. And if he never recovers fully his health or reason, suffers in his social affections and moral sensibility, becomes less faithful in the education of his children, and they are more exposed to temptation and ruin, and he is never again as able or willing to be habitually employed in productive labor,—the nation loses a sum equal to the amount of all these put together. And if his example leads other men to spend, and to suffer in the same way, the loss is still further increased; and so on, through all its effects.

"And even though the powder-maker and the merchant have made enormous profits, this does not prevent the loss to the community, any more than the enormous profits of lottery-gamblers, or counterfeiters of the public coin prevents loss to the community. Nor does it meet the case, to say that the property only changes hands.

This is not true. The man who sold the powder made a profit of only a part of the money which the other man paid for it; while the latter lost not only the whole, but vastly more. The whole of the original cost was only a small part of the loss to the original buyer, and to the nation. The merchant gained nothing of the time, and other numerous expenses, which the buyer lost; nor does he in any way remunerate the community for that loss.

"Suppose that man, instead of buying the powder, had bought a pair of shoes; and that the tanner and shoe-maker had gained in this case, what the powder-maker and the merchant gained in the other; and that, by the use of the shoes, though they were finally worn out, the man gained twice as much as he gave for them, without any loss of health, or reason, or social affection, or moral susceptibility, and without any of the consequent evils; — who cannot see that it would have increased his wealth, and that of the nation, without injury to any, and have promoted the benefit of all?

"This illustrates the principle with regard to ardent spirits. A man buys a quantity of it, and drinks it; when he would be, as is the case with every man, in all respects better without it. It is to him an entire loss. The merchant may have made a profit of one quarter of the cost, but the buyer loses the whole; and he loses the time employed in obtaining and drinking it. He loses also, and the community loses, equal to all its deteriorating effects upon his body and mind, his children and all who come under his influence. His land becomes less productive; his capital, produced by his land and labor, is diminished; and thus the means are diminished of future reproduction. And by the increase of expenditure in proportion to the capital, it is still further diminished, till to meet the increasingly disproportionate expenses, the whole is often taken, and the means of future reproduction are entirely exhausted. And, as there is no seed to sow, there is, of course, no future harvest.

"This is but a simple history of what is taking place in thousands of cases continually; and of what is the tendency of the traffic in ardent spirit, from beginning to end. It lessens the productiveness of land and labor, and consequently diminishes the amount of capital; while, in proportion, it increases the expenditure, and thus in both ways is constantly exhausting the means of future reproduction. And this is its tendency, in all its bearings, in proportion to the quantity used, from the man who takes only his glass, to the man who takes his quart a day. It is a palpable and gross violation of all correct principles of political economy; and, from beginning to end, tends to diminish all the sources of national wealth.

"And are not the laws," continue they — alluding to the licensing of dram-shops,— "which sanction the sale of ardent spirits, horrible laws? Do they not tend, by their whole influence, to render the business respectable, to perpetuate it, and permanently to produce such results? Results none the less horrible because produced according to law; and which stamp the law that sanctions the business which produces them, with the dark, deep, and indelible impress of vice?" * * What moral right have legislators to pass laws which enable men legally to injure their fellow-men, to increase their taxes, and expose their children to drunkenness and ruin? * * *

"But it is said, the licensing of the traffic is a source of revenue to the state, and therefore the public good requires it. This revenue is much like the woman who sold her grain and her rags to purchase whiskey for her children. She said it was cheaper to keep them on whiskey than on bread; and as it made a market for her rags, it was a source of profit—in government language, of revenue. Her garments and those of her children were soon nearly all rags, and all sold; when her revenue had become such, that she and her children, as a public burden, were obliged, by a public tax, to be supported at the alms-house."

They then proceed to prove that in nearly every state of the Union, the support of paupers occasioned by the traffic in ardent spirits, draws annually sums from the public treasury equal to twice and three times the revenue raised by licensing dram-shops, and conclude their argument with reproaching the legislators — "Who build prisons, and license men to carry on the trade that fills them; erect lunatic asylums, and furnish their tenants; build alms-houses, and license pauper-making manufactories to fill them; augment four-fold the public burden, and ten-fold the personal and domestic wretchedness of the country. * * * And as to those who say "The object of licensing is not to encourage the sale and use of spirits, but to restrain and prevent it," there are two answers for them. The first is, it does not restrain and prevent it. It has been tried effectually for more than half a century; and its fruits have been manifested in the living wretchedness, and in the dying agonies of more than a million of men.— Notwithstanding all such restraints and preventions, the evil constantly increased, till it had well nigh proved our ruin.—The other answer is, *the licensing of sin is not the way to prevent or restrain it, but it is the way to sanction and perpetuate it; by declaring to the community that if practised legally, it is right; and thus preventing the efficacy of truths and facts in producing the conviction that it is wrong.* Let legislators, chosen by the people, and respectable in society, license any sin, and it tends to shield that sin from public odium, and to perpetuate it, by presenting for it a legal justification."

"He that justifieth the wicked, and he that condemneth the just; even they both are an abomination to the Lord."

The Americans have taken up the cause of temperance with an enthusiastic ardor, which entitles them justly to the gratitude of mankind. They have, in this single instance, done more for the suppression of vice throughout the world, than the united efforts of a host of princes could have accomplished. They have set to the world a national example of voluntary submission to the laws of morality and of God; and of the blessings which result from it to every condition of society. Their example has been imitated in every quarter of the globe, and is every where productive of the same happy results. From the islands of the South Sea to the centre of civilization in Great Britain, their efforts are hailed with cordial approbation, and promote the cause of humanity. If the Americans have borrowed their civilization from Europe, they have discharged a part of their debt by teaching her the virtue of temperance.

Nor is this the only instance in which the efforts of Americans have promoted the welfare of mankind. The example set them by the "British and Foreign Bible

17

Society " has been nobly imitated in the United States; and the American Bible Society possesses now, next to the English, the largest funds, and is most instrumental in promoting the interests of Christianity. Its affairs are conducted by a president, twenty-one vice-presidents, one treasurer, four corresponding secretaries, and thirty-six managers.

The receipts of the society, since its origin in 1816, were as follows:—

				Dollars.	Cents.
1817	-	-	-	35,877	46
1818	-	-	-	36,564	30
1819	-	-	-	53,223	94
1820	-	-	-	41,361	97
1821	-	-	-	47,009	20
1822	-	-	-	40,682	34
1823	-	-	-	52,021	75
1824	-	-	-	42,416	95
1825	-	-	-	49,693	08
1826	-	-	-	46,115	47
1827	-	-	-	65,192	88
1828	-	-	-	75,879	93
1829	-	-	-	143,184	33
1830	-	-	-	170,067	55
1831	-	-	-	125,316	79
1832	-	-	-	107,059	00
1833	-	-	-	84,935	48
1834	-	-	-	86,600	82
1835	-	-	-	100,806	26

Total in 19 years, - - 1,404,009 50
or about 300,000*l.* sterling.

The number of Bibles and Testaments, issued from the depository of the Society, till 1835, was 1,767,936; and that of the year 1835 alone, 123,236. Besides the issues from the depository, large sums of money have been granted to missionary establishments at Constantinople, Bombay, Ceylon, Burmah, China, and the Sandwich Islands, to aid the printing and circulating of the Scriptures in various pagan tongues into which they have been translated.

" The American Board of Commissioners " is another o ciety for the promotion of Christianity. The designs

of this society are stated to be " By disseminating prima-
rily the Christian religion, and subordinately all kinds of
useful knowledge ; to improve the social, intellectual, and
religious condition of heathen and other anti-christian nations ; and for this purpose to send abroad preachers, physicians, male and female school-teachers, mechanics, ag-
riculturalists, &c. ; who are employed in preaching the
Gospel, translating, printing, and putting into the hands
of the people the Holy Scriptures, religious tracts, school-
books, &c. ; in teaching and superintending schools,
training native preachers and schoolmasters, and administering medicine to the diseased ; and in teaching the
mechanic arts and husbandry." A more extensive plan
of charity was certainly never conceived by human beings, nor executed with more cheerfulness and perseverance. By this Society the New Testament has been
translated and printed in the Mahratta, the Armeno-Turkish and the Hawaiian languages ; and one or more of the
Gospels in the Cherokee, Choctaw and Seneca. Books,
portions of the Scriptures, and religious tracts, have been
printed in seventeen different languages, exclusive of the
English, viz. Italian, Greek, Armeno-Turkish, Ancient
Armenian, Arabic, Mahratta, Tamul, Chinese, Hawaiian,
Cherokee, Choctaw, Creek, Osage, Seneca, Ojibwa, Ottawa, and Abernaquois. The Board possesses nine printing establishments, two type and stereotype foundries,
and several bookbinders' establishments. The Society
employs 102 preachers, (7 of whom are physicians,) 9
physicians, 9 printers, 30 teachers, and 161 married and
unmarried females. The number of schools is 474 ; that
of the pupils, 37,311 ; and the whole number of those who
have been educated, not less than 80,000! There are also connected with the Society two seminaries for the education of native preachers and teachers, with about 250
students.

The funds of the Society, which consist entirely of voluntary contributions, and the income from the " Missionary Herald," a periodical published by the Society,
amounted, in 24 years, to about 288,000l. sterling.

The following table, taken from the " American Almanac and Repository of Useful Knowledge" of 1836 will show
the missions, the time when each was commenced, and the
number of stations, preachers, &c., connected with each.

Missions.	Commenced.	Stations.	Preachers.	Physicians not ordained.	Teachers, Printers, Farmers.	Females.	Total.	Native Assistants.	Pupils.	Church Members.	Printing Presses.
West Africa	1834	1	1			1	2				
S. E. Africa	1835	2	5	1		6	12				
Greece	1830	2	2			2	4		142		
Constantinople	1831	1	3			3	6		200		
Asia Minor	1833	4	6		1	7	14				1
Syria and Holy Land	1823	3	5	1		6	12		14	4	1
Nestorians (Persia)	1834	1	1	1		2	4	1			
Mohammedans (Persia)	1835	1	1				1				
Mahrattas	1813	2	7	1	4	11	23	1	2,000	28	3
Tamul People	1816	9	14		1	17	32	35	3,713	230	2
Siam	1831	1	3		1	3	7				
China	1830	21	3				3	2			1
Indian Archipelago	1833	1	3	2			5				2
Sandwich Islands	1820	14	24	1	5	35	65		30,000	782	3
East Cherokees	1817	5	3		4	14	21		430	250	
West Cherokees	1820	3	3	1	5	9	18		175	106	1
Choctaws	1818	6	6		3	10	19		160	195	
Creeks	1832	1	1			2	3		15	12	
Osages	1820	3	2		4	6	12		40	20	
Pawnees	1834	1	1		1		2				
Sioux	1835	2	2		1	5	8		45	70	
Ojibwas	1831	4	2		5	4	11		60	64	
Mackinaw	1823	1			2	6	8		37		
Stockbridge Indians	1827	1	1		1	1	3				
New York Indians	1805	4	3	1	1	7	12		280	210	
Explorers near the Rocky Mts.			1				1				
Total		94	103	9	39	160	308	39	37,311	1971	14

It will also be perceived that the funds and usefulness of the Society are on the increase; 14 new stations having been created since 1830.

The "American *Home* Missionary Society" was instituted in the city of New York on the 6th of May, 1826. The number of its missionaries and agents consisted, in 1835, of 719; and the number of congregations and missionary districts, aided by the Society, was 1050. Under their ministry about 25,000 individuals had been added to the churches of Christ; from 10,000 to 40,000 children were annually instructed in Sabbath Schools; and in Bible Classes, from 2,000 to 12,000 of all ages.

"The American Board of Commissioners for Foreign Missions" being under the patronage of the Congregational Church of New England, and the Presbyterian and the Reformed Dutch Churches of the Middle, Western, and Southern States, the *Baptists* formed another missionary society, under the name of "The Baptist General Convention of the United States for Foreign Missions." The object of the Society is "the propagation of the Gospel among the heathens, and the promotion of pure Christianity in Christendom." The funds received during the last year (1835) were 58,520 dollars, 28 cents, or about 11,704*l.* sterling.

17*

The Missionary Stations are	Mission-aries.	Assist-ants.
Valley Towns, Cherokees, North Carolina - -	4	5
Thomas, on Grand River, Michigan - - -	2	..
Sault de Ste. Marie, near Lake Superior - -	4	..
Tonawanda, near Niagara, New York - - -	3	..
Shawanoe, Kansas River, near Missouri - -	4	..
Delawares, near the junction of the Kansas and Missouri	2	..
Otoes and Omahas, Bellevue, near Great Plate River	3	..
Putawatamies, North of the Missouri - - -	2	..
Ottawas, South of Shawanoe - - - -	2	..
Creeks near the junction of the Arkansas and Verdigris	4	2
Cherokees, in Flint district, Cherokee county -	1	..
Choctaws, Choctaw agency, on the Arkansas -	..	1
Port au Prince, Hayti - - - - - -	1	..
Paris, France - - - - - - -	3	..
Hamburg, Germany - - - - - -	1	..
Liberia, Africa - - - - - - -	5	..
Maulmein, Burmah - - - - - -	10	8
Rangoon, ditto - - - - - - -	4	7
Ava, ditto - - - - - - - -	2	2
Chummerah, ditto - - - - - - -	2	..
Newville, ditto - - - - - - -	..	..
Tavoy, ditto - - - - - - -	5	3
Mergui, ditto - - - - - - -	..	2
N. Arracan, ditto - - - - - - -	2	..
S. Arracan, ditto - - - - - - -	2	..
Bankok, Siam - - - - - -	4	1
Total -	72	31

Eighteen churches are connected with these stations, embracing 1400 members ; and about 600 scholars are taught in the schools. One printing-press is employed in the Indian territory, and four in Burmah, from which publications are issued in seven different languages.

" The Baptist *Home* Missionary Society" has for its object to preach the Gospel in North America, (comprising Upper and Lower Canada.) The receipts of this Society during the last year, (1835) were 9000 dollars, or 1800*l.* sterling.

The Methodist Episcopal Church have also formed a missionary society. Its receipts, ending 1835, amounted to 30,500 dollars, or about 6,100*l.* sterling. It employed 14 preachers at Liberia (all colored men), and six school-teachers. The number of church members was 204, and about 200 children were taught at schools. Including other missions, the society had 144 missionaries, 16,430 members, and 32 teachers, and instructed 940 pupils.

The Protestant Episcopal Church have also formed a "Domestic and Foreign Missionary Society." Its receipts in 1834 amounted to 24,007 dollars 97 cents, or about 5,200*l.* sterling ; it employed 20 Missionaries in the Southern and Western States, two in Greece, and two in China.

For the *education* of young men for the ministry the "American Education Society " was established, under the superintendence of a president, one vice-president and twelve directors. This society offered, first, gratuitous assistance to young men ; *but finding that this encouraged idleness*, they fixed upon a definite sum to be granted to beneficiaries, throwing them for support, in some measure, on their own resources. In 1820, another method of assisting them *by loans* was adopted ; and an obligation required of them, to refund one half the amount received. This was found to operate so favorably, that since 1826 an obligation has been required *to refund the whole with interest*, after a reasonable time subsequent to the beneficiary's education, and his entrance upon the active duties of his profession. The notes, however, of foreign and domestic missionaries, and of ministers settled over feeble churches, may be cancelled at the discretion of the Board of Directors. The sum annually furnished is 48 dollars or 9*l.* 12*s.* sterling, to academical students, and 75 dollars or 15*l.* sterling, to collegiate and theological students. Since its foundation, the society have assisted 2,258 young men ; of those who received aid from the funds of the society, during the year 1835, 200 were connected with 17 theological seminaries, 538 with 37 colleges, and 302 with academical and public schools ;—making in all 1,040 young men connected with 152 institutions of learning. The whole amount *refunded* by beneficiaries, since they have entered on the ministry, is 14,111 dollars 16 cents, and their earnings, by preaching and school-keeping, 132,623 dollars, or 26,524*l.* sterling. The society publishes a journal, entitled the "American Quarterly Register."

The American Sunday School Union, after the plan of that established in Great Britian by Robert Raikes, is entirely under the direction of laymen. No clergyman can ever be an officer or manager of the society ; and to secure a more perfect concurrence of Christians, the agents, missionaries, and other persons employed by the society, are selected *indiscriminately from different denominations.* Its object is " the establishment and support of Sunday schools, and the distribution of the society's publications at the lowest prices, or gratuitously, *not only in America, but at the various Protestant missionary stations on the earth, where they are wanted for English readers,* as well as for the aid of compilers and translators in native languages." The reports of this society, up to May, 1835, show that there are, or have been connected with it, 16,000 schools 115,000 teachers, and 799,000 pupils. The publications cost 1 mill *per* page, (equal to about one-third of a farthing.)

" The American Tract Society " whose object it is to distribute tracts " for the promotion of morality and religion," has received during the ten years of its existence the sum of 225,304 dollars 25 cents, or above 45,000*l.* sterling, with which they have published 754 new publications, and distributed altogether 481,990,418 pages.

The most important feature of " the American Unitarian Association" is the establishment, in Boston, of a ministry for the moral and spiritual benefit of such of the poor as have no place of worship, and no religious instruction. The benefits which this ministry confers on the poor, in the person of the benevolent and eloquent Rev. Joseph Tuckerman, are incalculable ; and it is perhaps the most charitable institution in that philanthropic city.

On the whole, it appears that the receipts of the principal benevolent institutions in the United States during the year 1835 amounted to 815,302 dollars 23 cents, or 163,000*l.* sterling.

All these societies are formed for the promotion of morality, religion, and education ; and impose a tax of 3*s.* sterling *per annum* on every white inhabitant of the United States. When to this are added the ordinary taxes for the support of common schools, it will be found that the Americans pay more for the moral and religious improvement of society, than any other nation, England herself, in proportion to her population, not excepted. And yet they have been reproached with selfishness; with a sordid attachment to pecuniary gain and profit, and a total neglect of the nobler qualities of the mind! "Money," it has been added, "is the sole talisman of the Americans;" but not a word has been said of the manner in which they disburse it. Europeans could see no other causes of prosperity in the United States, than the *mercantile* habits of their inhabitants, and the immense natural resources of the country. But the time will come when they will be convinced of their error—when the moral progress of America will keep pace with her physical development, and her influence on mankind, in general, be hailed with joyful gratitude.

CHAPTER VIII.

THERE is, probably, no people on earth with whom business constitutes pleasure, and industry amusement, in an
equal degree with the inhabitants of the United States of
America. Active occupation is not only the principal
source of their happiness, and the foundation of their
national greatness, but they are absolutely wretched without it, and instead of the " *dolce far niente*," know but
the *horrors* of idleness. Business is the very soul of an
American : he pursues it, not as a means of procuring for
himself and his family the necessary comforts of life, but
as the fountain of all human felicity ; and shows as much
enthusiastic ardor in his application to it as any crusader
ever evinced for the conquest of the Holy Land, or the
followers of Mohammed for the spreading of the Koran.

From the earliest hour in the morning till late at night,
the streets, offices, and warehouses of the large cities are
thronged by men of all trades and professions, each following his vocation like a *per petuum mobile*, as if he never
dreamed of cessation from labor, or the possibility of becoming fatigued. If a lounger should happen to be pa-
rading the street, he would be sure to be justled off the
side-walk, or to be pushed in every direction, until he keeps

time with the rest. Should he meet a friend, he will only talk to him on *business :* on 'change they will only hear him on *business;* and if he retire to some house of entertainment, he will again be entertained with *business.* Wherever he goes, the hum and bustle of *business* will follow him ; and when he finally sits down to his dinner, hoping there, at least, to find an hour of rest, he will discover, to his sorrow, that the Americans treat that as a *business* too, and despatch it in less time than he is able to stretch his limbs under the mahogany. In a very few minutes, the clang of steel and silver will cease, and he will again be left to his solitary reflections, while the rest are about their *business.* In the evenings, if he have no friends or acquaintances, none will intrude on his retirement ; for the people are either at home with their families, or preparing for the *business* of the next day.

Whoever goes to the United States, for the purpose of settling there, must resolve, in his mind, to find pleasure in business, and business in pleasure, or he will be disappointed, and wish himself back to the sociable idleness of Europe. Nor can any one travel in the United States without making a *business* of it. In vain would he hope to proceed at his ease : he must prepare to go at the rate of fifteen or twenty miles an hour, or conclude to stay quietly at home. He must not expect to stop, except at the places fixed upon by the proprietors of the road or the steamboat ; and if he happen to take a friend by the hand an instant after the sign of departure is given, he is either left behind, or carried on against his intention, and has to inquire after his luggage in another state or territory. The habit of posting being unknown, he is obliged to travel in company with the large caravans which are daily starting from, and arriving at, all the large cities, under convoy of a thousand puffing and clanking engines, where all thoughts of pleasure are speedily converted into sober reflections on the safety of property and persons. He must resign the gratification of his own individual tastes to the wishes of the majority who are travelling on *business*, and with whom speed is infinitely more important than all that contributes to pleasure ; he must eat, drink, sleep, and wake, when they do, and has no other remedy for the catalogue of his distresses but the hope of

their speedy termination. Arrived at the period of his
sufferings he must be cautious how he gives vent to his
joy, for he must *stop quickly* if his *busy* conductor shall
not hurl him on again on a new journey.

Neither is this hurry of business confined to the large
cities, or the method of travelling ; it communicates itself to every village and hamlet, and extends to, and
penetrates, the western forests. Town and country rival
with each other in the eagerness of industrious pursuits.
Machines are invented, new lines of communication
established, and the depths of the sea explored to afford
scope for the spirit of enterprise ; and it is as if all
America were but one gigantic workshop, over the entrance of which there is the blazing inscription "*No admission here, except on business.*"

The position of a man of leisure in the United States is
far from being enviable ; for unless he take delight in
literary and scientific pursuits, he is not only left without companions to enjoy his luxuriant ease, but, what is
worse, he forfeits the respect of his fellow-citizens, who,
by precept and example, are determined to discounte-
nance idleness. That the influence of such a system
must be highly beneficial to the national standard of
morality, is, of itself, sufficiently evident, and another
cause for the comparatively small number of crimes committed in the United States, and the general correctness
of principle which pervades all clssses of society. There
is more philosophy and morality contained in the admonition of Dr. Panglos, "*Travaillons notre jardin,*" than
Voltaire intended to put in his mouth ; and this philosophy the Americans possess *by instinct.*

Labor is as essential to their well-being as food and
raiment to an European. This national characteristic
of Americans, together with their love of independence,
is a complete commentary on the history of all their
settlements, and the progress of manufactures and commerce. Thousands of persons who, as servants, or in
other inferior walks of life, might be able to provide for
themselves in the large cities, emigrate to the western
woods, to procure for themselves a larger field of enterprise and useful occupation. There is no hardship or
privation incident to the lives of new settlers, which their

robust and athletic constitutions would not willingly suffer, to gratify their insatiable desire after active and independent labor : there is no pleasure within the range of all a city can afford equal to the proud satisfaction of beholding the daily results of their indefatigable exertions. These phenomena it would be in vain to explain by the mere spirit of adventure. There are no gold mines in the western states; no active commerce equal to that from which they emigrate; no accumulated wealth to allure their covetousness. The riches of the soil can only be explored by active labor and a series of harassing details, connected with the sacrifice of every convenience of life: the commerce of the explored region is to be created by new roads and lines of communication, which call for new and increased exertion on the part of the settlers ; and it is only after a period of many years their sturdy industry can hope for an adequate reward of ease and prosperity. Such prospects are not apt to allure the weak, either in body or mind, and require a determination and steadiness of purpose totally incompatible with the vague and loose spirit of adventure.

Neither is there any thing in the character of the western people which could give the least foundation to such a suspicion. They are a hardy persevering race, inured to every toil to which human nature can be subjected, and always ready to encounter danger and hardships with a degree of cheerfulness which it is easily perceived is the effect of moral courage and consciousness of power. They are distinguished from the rest of the Americans, and, perhaps, the rest of mankind, by huge athletic frames of body, a peculiar *naïveté* in their manners, and a certain grotesqueness of humor, which, as far as I am acquainted, is not to be found in any other part of the United States. There amphibious nature—being obliged to make themselves, at an early period of their lives, familiar with the navigation of the western rivers—together with the boldness of their disposition, has won for them the characteristic appellation of "*half horse, and half alligator;* " which, in the language of the western Americans, is full as honorable a term as the "*preux chevaliers,*" applied to the chivalry of the middle ages; though they prefer the rifle and the

18

somewhat barbarous amusement of "*gouging*" to the more knightly combat with spears and lances.

It appears, then, that the universal disposition of Americans to emigrate to the western wilderness, in order to enlarge their dominion over inanimate nature, is the actual result of an expansive power, which is inherent in them, and which, by continually agitating all classes of society, is constantly throwing a large portion of the whole population on the extreme confines of the state, in order to gain space for its development. Hardly is a new state or territory formed, before the same principle manifests itself again, and gives rise to a further emigration ; and so is it destined to go on until a physical barrier must finally obstruct its progress.

The Americans, who do not pretend to account for this principle at all,* are nevertheless aware of its existence, and act and legislate on all occasions as if they were to enjoy the benefits of the next century. Money and property is accumulated for no other visible purpose than being left to the next generation, which is brought up in the same industrious habits, in order to leave *their* children a still greater inheritance. The laboring classes of Europe, the merchants, and even professional men, are striving to obtain a certain competency, with which they are always willing to retire : the Americans pursue business with unabated vigor till the very hour of death, with no other benefits for themselves than the satisfaction of having enriched their country and their children. Fortunes, which, on the continent of Europe, and even in England, would be amply sufficient for an independent existence, are in America increased with an assiduity which is hardly equalled by the industrious zeal of a poor beginner, and the term of "*rentier*" is entirely unknown. The luxurious enjoyments which riches alone can procure are neither known nor coveted in the United States ; and the possession of property, far from rendering them indolent, seems to be only an additional stimulus to unremitting exertion.

In this disposition of Americans the attentive peruser of history must evidently behold a wise dispensation of

---

* Compare the Remarks on American Literature, Chapter IV.

Providence, though it may, for a time, impede the progress of refinement and the arts. Without the spirit of enterprise and the taste for active labor, the immense resources of the country, and the facility with which riches are acquired, would become the means of individual and national corruption and the introduction of expensive habits, which would not only undermine the private morals of the people, but eventually subvert their republican government.

The sudden introduction of European refinements, if it were possible to make them universal, would, at this period, be the ruin of the American constitution. The framers of that noble work, perhaps the proudest achievement of the human mind, did not contemplate a state of society as it exists in Europe, and could, therefore, with safety repose the highest power and trust in the virtue and integrity of the people. America was then but thinly settled, and her population spread over a wide surface; her inhabitants were distinguished for the simplicity of their manners and the high moral rectitude of their character; they were a highly *civilized* people, though they could not have been called *refined* in the sense in which the term is applied in the fashionable circles of London and Paris. It was of the utmost importance for the safety of the government, which, at that time, was only an *experiment*, that the people should retain their simple habits, until age should give strength to the constitution, and accustomed the people readily to submit to the newly-instituted authorities. It was necessary for the rulers, as well as the governed, to acquire a *routine* of business, and to establish that mutual confidence in one another, without which every free government must soon be converted into despotism.

An *habitual* obedience to the law was to be created without the intercession of force, which, at the beginning of a republic, where the rulers and the governed are yet too nearly on a level with one another, partakes always more or less of the character of usurpation, and threatens the dissolution of government. This was the case with the republic of France, and hence its speedy overthrow. The habits and morals of a people are the surest guarantee of the continuance of any government; they are the life and essence of its existence, without which the constitution is but a dead letter. The charter must *live* in the minds of the governed, or it will soon be carried to the grave.

The thinly-scattered population assisted the government prodigiously in cooling the passions of the discontented, or in rendering them harmless. Even the multiplicity of interests and parties proved an additional security, as it weakened the power of the opposition, and prevented them from uniting under any one principle, the carrying of which might have endangered the safety of the constitution. Every liberal government must, in the outset, depend more on the *weakness of the opposition* than on its own strength, which it is dangerous to increase before the rights of the governed have become the common law of the country. The history of France furnishes a complete index to this truth, while a special providence seems to have presided over the destinies of America. It is with regard to this principle that the western settlers are of incalculable advantage to the government; for not only is by their means the population of the Atlantic states relieved of its annual increase, but new sources of wealth opened to the nation at large, which increase the occupation and prosperity of those who remain. Every new settlement requires laborers for the construction of roads, canals, &c., to facilitate its communication with the Atlantic states, and every new road and canal increases the commerce of the seaports.

But it is not the general prosperity of the people—though of course this must be counted among its happiest results,—it is their useful *occupation*, and the creation of new and powerful interests, which are of the greatest advantage to the government. Every new colony of settlers contains within itself a nucleus of republican institutions, and revives, in a measure, the history of the first settlers. Its relation to the Atlantic states is similar to the situation of the early colonies with regard to the mother country, and contains the elements of freedom. Every society which is thus formed must weaken the fury of parties by diminishing the points of contact—while the growing power of the western states becomes a salutary check on the spreading of certain doctrines, which are continually importing from Europe, and to the evil influence of which the Atlantic states are more particularly exposed.

The western states, from their peculiar position, are supposed to develope all the resources and peculiarities of democratic governments, without being driven to excesses by the opposition of contrary principles. Their number too augments the intensity of republican life by increasing the number of rallying points, without which the principle of liberty would be too much weakened by expansion. It is a peculiarly happy feature of the constitution of the United States, that every state has itself an independent government, and becomes thus the repository of its own liberties.

The inhabitant of Arkansas, Illinois, or Indiana, living on the confines of the state, and the very skirts of civilization, would, in all probability, be less of a patriot if his attachment to the country were only to be measured by his adherence to the general government. He would be too remote from the centre of action to feel its immediate influence, and not sufficiently affected by the political proceedings of the state to consider them paramount to the local interests of his neighborhood. Political life would grow fainter in proportion to its remoteness from the seat of legislation, and the energies of the people, instead of being roused by the necessity of action, would degenerate into a passive acknowledgment of the protection offered by the government. This is more or less the case in every country, except England and America, and perhaps the principal reason of their little progress in freedom. Hence the feverish excitement in their capitals and large towns, and the comparative inertness and palsy of the country.

Every town and village in America has its peculiar republican government, based on the principle of election, and is, within its own sphere, as free and independent as a sovereign state. On this broad basis rests the whole edifice of American liberty. Freedom takes its root at home, in the native village or town of an American. The county, representing the aggregate of the towns and villages, is but an enlargement of the same principle : the state itself represents the different counties ; and the con-

18*

gress of the United States represents the different states. In every place, in every walk of life, an American finds some rallying point or centre of political attachment. His sympathies are first enlisted by the government of his native village ; then, by that of the county ; then, by the state itself; and finally, by that of the Union. If he is ambitious, he is obliged to make an humble beginning at home, and figure in his native town or county ; thence he is promoted to the dignity of representative or senator of his state ; and it is only after he has held these preparatory stations that he can hope to enjoy the honor of representative or senator in the congress of the nation. Thus the county is the preparatory school for the politician of the state, and the state furnishes him with a proper introduction to national politics.

The advantages of this system are manifold. It creates political action where otherwise all would be passiveness and stupor ; it begets attachment to the institutions of the country by multiplying the objects of their political affection, and bringing them within the sphere of every individual ; it cools the passions of political parties, by offering them frequent opportunities of spending themselves on various subjects, and in various directions; it establishes a strong-hold of liberty in every village and town, and accustoms all classes of society to a republican government ; it enforces submission to laws and institutions which are the type of those of the nation ; and it furnishes numerous schools for young politicians, obliging them to remain sufficiently long in each not to enter the university of congress without age and proper experience. This system, while it lasts—and there are no symptoms of its being speedily abolished—will prevent novices in politics from entering the senate or house of representatives of the United States, and reserve the dignity of president for the wisdom of sexagenarians. In France, where no similar freedom and independence exist in the provinces, where the system of centralization is constantly forcing the whole political power into the capital and a few of the large towns, leaving the country without life, motion, or means of defence, all attempts to establish a rational system of liberty were confined to its superstructure, without enlarging its foundation. The most awful lessons of history have been taught to her people in vain ; and it seems as if they were the only nation who never profit by experience.

The western states of America are each a nursery of freedom : every new settlement is already a republic *in embryo.* They extend political life in every direction, and establish so many new fortified points, that the principle of liberty has nothing to dread from a partial invasion of its territory.

Every new state, therefore, is a fresh guarantee for the continuance of the American constitution, and directs the attention of the people to new sources of happiness and wealth. It increases the interest of all in upholding the general government, and makes individual success dependent on national prosperity. But every year which is added to its existence increases its strength and cohesion, by reducing obedience to a habit, and adding to the respect which is due to age. If it be true that the life of nations and political institutions resembles that of individuals, it is equally true, that the different periods of their development are exposed to the same dangers. One third of all that are born die in childhood ; the greater number of them are healthy during the period of their manhood, and all must eventually die of old age. Climate and soil breed particular diseases, which must be cured according to their peculiar constitutions; but of these, fevers and consumptions are the most dreaded. Violent cures are apt to weaken the system, but are often rendered unavoidable by a criminal delay of the proper remedies ; and a total neglect of them is sure to produce an incurable distemper. A child is exposed to more diseases than a man ; and so is it with a young country. America is fast approaching her period of pupillarity, and the constitution of a century will be established on a firmer basis than that of a dozen years. The people will have experienced its blessings, and cherish it as the venerable inheritance of their fathers. Each succeeding generation will be born with an increased respect for it, and will be taught, at school, to consider it as the basis of their happiness. Age always commands reverence ; and the people are not so easily persuaded to lend their aid in the destruction of a government under which they have prospered for

centuries, than of one within their own recollection and
of their own making, which they may hope to rebuild on
a new plan.   We quit reluctantly an old mansion, though
a new and better one should be offered to our habitation ;
and the force of habit and the endearment of time are
stronger than the force of principles or the power of argument.   I think that the Americans have, spontaneous-
ly, found the right track ; and that no better admonition
can be given to the young republic than the wise saying
of Dr. Panglos, which can never be too often repeated,
" *Que chacun travaille son jardin.*"

But the western territory of America is not wholly
peopled by emigrants from the Atlantic states ; a large
number of the inhabitants being settlers from Switzerland
and Germany.   The Irish, though emigrating to the
United States in large numbers, prefer, generally, a residence in a city, with such transient occupation as they
may find, to the quiet industry of the Germans, who are
more particularly attached to the cultivation of the soil.
The advantages of the German cultivators in the United
States over all other competitors are, indeed, numerous ;
but most of them arise from the manner in which they
emigrate, and settle in the various districts.

Whoever has witnessed the parting of a caravan of
Germans from their friends and relations, or their pro·
ceeding on the way until they reach the seaport of their
destination, will be convinced of their resolute determination to make America their home, and to assist each
other in their new vocation of settlers.   This I consider
the principal reason of their success.   Having no longer
an alternative before them, they apply themselves to the
cultivation of the soil, not as adventurers for the sake of
experiment, but as farmers, who mean to keep possession
of it.   They prefer the western states for their settlements,
and, being in this manner at once cut off from an uninterrupted correspondence with the country which gave them
birth, soon learn to make themselves a home in America.
They direct their undivided energies towards improving
their estates, instead of lingering in a state of indecision
with their eyes half turned towards their native land.
The habit of remaining together, and settling whole town-
ships or villages, serves to render their exile less painful,

and enables them, if the phrase be permitted, to transfer a part of their own country to the vast solitudes of the new world. They hardly feel that they are strangers in the land of their adoption, as long as each of them sees in his neighbor the friend of his youth, or the companion of his childhood. A man cannot be said to have left his home if he be not separated from his nearest relations, or from those who are most dear to his heart. In this manner the German emigrants in the United States preserve, to a great degree, their original simplicity of manners ; and, being frugal by habit, and sociable by nature, are soon able to rear their little hamlets by mutual assistance, and to give stability and permanency to their settlements. Being not much given to money speculations, their care is less to hoard riches than to improve and increase their estates, and, by that means, they hardly ever fail to become independent and opulent. They are less enterprising than the native Americans, especially the New Englanders, on which account they are often considered dull and inactive ; but they yield to no part of the population of the United States in unremitting labor and persevering industry. There are few of them grow rich by sudden turns of good luck ; but it is a comparatively rare case to see any of them behindhand in the management of their household ; and, preferring, from inclination, agriculture to commerce, they are less exposed to the caprices of fortune, and more certain of ultimate success. They are universally allowed to possess the finest farms in the United States, because it is their settled maxim not to hold more land than they are able to cultivate, and to keep it for their own use, and not for the purpose of speculation. The dwelling of a German farmer is generally humble ; but his granary and stables are of huge dimensions, and exhibit the provident husbandman. The improvement of his farm is with him a more urgent consideration than his own individual comfort. His cattle are the object of much solicitude, and his labor is the more productive as it is seconded by every member of his family.

It is a fact no less curious than remarkable, that these characteristics of German farmers apply to all of them, in whatever part of the country they may have formed their settlements; and that there is, in this respect, no difference between a settler in Pennsylvania, Ohio, Illinois, or the valley of the Mississippi. Neither the soil nor the climate seems to change their manners and customs. I have seen German settlers in Hungary and Transylvania resembling those of Pennsylvania, as much as one New Englander resembles another; but wherever they dwell, and to whatever country they may emigrate, I have always known them to be sober, industrious, and living on good terms with each other and their neighbors. Nor does time change their habits materially. The Moravian settlers of Georgia, who went to America under the kind auspices of General Oglethorpe, were in this respect substantially the same as those who emigrated previously to Carolina and Pennsylvania; and the description of the latter, given by William Penn, corresponds yet with those of the present inhabitants of that state.

Until recently, the emigrants from Germany were chiefly composed of agriculturists, with an occasional admixture of operatives; but the late unfortunate struggle for liberty in Germany has, within the last five or six years, caused the expatriation of a more intellectual class; and, accordingly, settlements have been made in the valley of the Mississippi and in the state of Illinois, by a body of Germans whose education fitted them rather for the drawing-room and the closet, than for the hardships of cultivating the soil. Yet they have cheerfully embraced their new vocation; and of physicians, lawyers, theological and other students, who arrived about three years ago in the United States, have become active husbandmen, though they were obliged to resign the romantic idea of founding a "*New Germany*" in the western territory of the United States. Immediately after their arrival they established a press and a paper, in which they published the history of their little settlement. Extracts from it, speaking in highly favorable terms of the climate and soil, appeared in nearly all the public prints of Germany; and large numbers of their countrymen are preparing for the same destination.

I ought yet to observe, in this place, that it is absurd to settle in America with the intention of hiring the labor of the poor. The price of it is high, and cannot always be commanded with money. The Germans especially prefer working on a farm, in which they have an interest, or the hope of ultimately possessing a part of it—which is the surest means of making them eventually independent. Proud, in his "History of Pennsylvania," observed already the singular circumstance of most of the poor laboring classes becoming rich, while men of property, commencing with large fortunes and estates, were gradually becoming poor; and alluded to the singular habit of some Germans of property, to hire themselves out as *servants*, until they obtain a sufficient knowledge of the climate and soil to commence business on their own account.

The quiet temper of the Germans does not allow them to take a very active part in politics, though their number would be sufficient to form a most powerful party. In Pennsylvania they have, nevertheless, acquired great influence, and the governors of that state have, for many years past, been selected from amongst their countrymen. This is a matter so much settled by mutual consent, that, even at the last election, when there were two democratic and one whig candidate for office, all three were taken from the ranks of the Germans, and none other would have had the least chance of success. In the state of Ohio, though it was originally settled by emigrants from New England, there are, at present, not less than from thirty-five to forty thousand German voters. The state of New York, though originally settled by the Dutch, contains, nevertheless, a large German population in several counties, especially in that of Columbia, which gave birth to Mr. Van Buren, the present vice-president, and, in all probability, the next president of the United States. The state of Maryland contains a large proportion of German voters; the population of Illinois is nearly one third German; and the valley of the Mississippi is being settled by thousands of new emigrants from Europe. I do not think it an exaggeration to state, that not less than one hundred thousand votes are annually cast by Germans, and that, in less than twenty years, their number will have increased to half a million. In the city of New York the Germans have already a great influence on the election of mayor and the other city officers; the number of those who are entitled to vote amounting now to three thousand five hundred.

Under these circumstances, "*the German vote*," as it is termed, becomes a matter of great solicitude with politicians of all ranks and persuasions; and, accordingly, newspapers in their own language are established in all parts of the United States where they have settled. In Pennsylvania alone there are now more than thirty German (mostly weekly) papers; and in Ohio and Illinois, as many more are published and circulated. A considerable number of them is also published in Maryland; and the "New York Staatszeitung" was entirely established by the democratic Germans of that city. If these papers were ably directed by a standard publication in any of the large cities, whose editor should understand the peculiarities of the German mind, the local circumstances of their settlements, and their relation to the general government, they could be made a most powerful political engine, which would give strength and perpetuity to any party in whose favor it should once declare itself.

But the Germans in the United States have, to this day, no powerful political organ to express their opinions and sentiments; and their policy, therefore, is but a reflection from the ruling doctrines of the other states: they are unconscious of their power, and more bent on increasing their numbers, than on concentrating their efforts, and directing them to a certain point. The Germans in America are not so easily excited as their brethren to the south or north, and are consequently often indifferent on a variety of minor questions, the connection of which with the more important principles of government, seems to escape their immediate notice. In this manner they are often defeated in their own ranks, and, contrary to their intentions and purposes, made the tool of insidious politicians. But no sooner is an important question of state agitated, than they unite again; and, despite of all efforts to disseminate discord by appealing to their prejudices and local interests,—an appeal which is hardly ever made in vain to the inhabitants of any other section of the country,—persevere in supporting the men and principles of their adoption.

They are not apt to speculate on politics, but rather act in accordance with general maxims, which are as liberal as possible, and of which they never question the utility, provided they agree with their ideas of moral and political justice. They seldom enter on details, but never desert a principle; and are, therefore, least actuated by motives of interest and selfishness. Their practical sense is republican; and, as I have previously observed, they are democratic almost by instinct.* But the time may come when they will be conscious of their power; and they will then form a party, the strength and importance of which will, in all probability, be beyond the computation of mere abstract politicians.

For the education of youth, the Germans in Pennsylvania and Ohio have as yet done little, when compared with the efforts of the New England states for the general diffusion of learning. In 1833 there were yet a large number of children in both states who could neither read nor write, and, although improvements are gradually making in the system of instruction, it is not to be expected, that, in this respect, an equality will soon be effected with the other states.† The reminiscences of the Germans in the United States of their former situation in Europe are not calculated to inspire the humbler classes with a particular regard for the sciences. They were oppressed by men of literary pretensions at home; and the unusual number of feed clerks with whom the kingdom of Wurtemberg (which furnishes the greatest number of emigrants) was yet, a few years ago, infested as with a plague, struck the peasantry of that country with horror for every thing which, in their provincial dialect, they called a "*schreiberle*" (little scribbler.) I remember some years ago, when travelling in Pennsylvania, to have asked a German at Easton, (a town situated about sixty miles from Philadelphia,) whether he would not be glad to see a college established in his place,‡ which would

---

* I have given the reason of this in chapter III.

† What I have here said of the state of education in Ohio, applies merely to its German population. The New England settlers have excellent schools and seminaries of learning.

‡ Lafayette College has since been established in Easton, even by the co-operations of some well-informed Germans of that place.

afford his children an opportunity of superior instruction ?
He merely shrugged his shoulders, and observed, *that his
sons should not go to it, as he intended them for active farmers, and not for lazy thieves, to live on other people's industry.* Not even the prospect of realizing a larger income
from his estate by the influx of students from Philadelphia and New York could quiet his apprehensions of the
abuse of learning; and the idea that any of his children
should quit the paternal estate in order to study a profession, which would change their simple manners into the
more fashionable carriage of gentlemen, proved a perfect
torture to his mind. There is so much philosophy and good
sense in this species of ignorance that one might almost
call it ingenious, though it contrasts sadly with the habits
of the more aspiring population of the eastern states,
who are never satisfied unless their sons are called doctors or lawyers.

The profession of the law is rarely embraced by Germans; and, accordingly, most of the gentlemen of the
bar, in the German settlements of the United States, are
either from New England or Ireland. The idea of going
to law strikes a German as something wrong and debasing, and in case he is obliged to have recourse to it, he
prefers to hire some one to do it for him. This is a sentiment which pervades, not only the German population
of America, but also a considerable portion of the people
of Germany itself. The profession of the law, to which
that of politics is so closely allied, is, by German writers
of eminence, in the most uncharitable manner, called a
prostitute amongst the sciences; because it is the only one
which, instead of proposing the investigation of absolute
truth, renders the noblest powers of the mind subservient
to mere temporal benefits, which are often incompatible
with honor or justice. The theologian, the mathemati-
cian, the physician, &c., are all paid for the investigation
and assertion of positive truth, or, at least, of what they
consider as such. The lawyer alone is knowingly feed
for its perversion. So privileged is he in his calling, that
we can hear him plead the cause of a notorious culprit,
or see him employ the best faculties of his understanding
to prove the correctness of that which he hardly credits
himself, without being prejudiced against his character.

But the prostitution of the mind is more abject than that of the body, and just in that ratio more humiliating and degrading as mind is superior to matter.

> Reason becomes madness; benefit a curse;
> Alas! that thou should'st be an heir!
> That right which has been born with thee,
> That right alone they know not.*

Nothing can be further from me than the belief that the practice of the law must *necessarily* be attended by such moral disadvantages ; but it is certainly liable to very great *abuses*. How often is not lawful right opposed to moral justice, and the advocate, through whose instrumentality the former is asserted, compelled to offend against the latter ? In how many cases does not the issue of a litigation depend on mere forms ?—on the omission of a word, or the want of precision of language, in a legal instrument ? And is not the advocate obliged to take advantage of all such circumstances ? It is true he does not appear in his own cause, but merely* represents his client. He only says that for his client which the latter himself would say if he were endowed with legal knowledge. But this does not rid the profession of the reproach to which it is unfortunately exposed; because, when the client is a knave, the superior skill of the advocate is employed in perfecting his craft, and in injuring his honest adversary.

Neither can the advocate previously examine the cause of his client, to satisfy himself of the truth or justice of the cause: he has not even *a right* to do so; for this would be constituting himself *judge* of the case, and give rise to the still greater abuse of turning away clients which are poor, or whose adversaries are rich and powerful. He is, in fact, obliged to take up the case *as it is stated to him*, or as it appears on trial; and it is but the verdict of the jury which informs him of its legal justice. He is compelled to start from premises, the correctness of which it is neither in his power or his duty to ascer-

---

* " Vernunft wird Unsinn, Wohlthat, Plage;
Weh dir, dass du ein Enkel bist!
Vom Rechte, dass mit dir geboren ist,
Von dem ist leider, nie die Frage."—Göthe's *Faust,*

tain or examine, and is, therefore, in the exercise of his
profession, less concerned in the investigation of absolute
truth than men of science in every other department.

The imperfection, however, does not properly exist in
the advocates, but in the law itself. The laws of nature
and of God are immutable, and in perfect harmony with
each other in their most remote consequences. Those of
men are the product of a finite intelligence, and are,
therefore, subject to frequent changes, and liable to disagree with each other. They are enacted for *specific* purposes, not always corresponding with the universal laws
of the world, but protecting the peculiar interests of human institution : they are adapted to circumstances, and
to the state of society in each country ; not to the abstract
properties of humanity, and are, therefore, often favoring peculiar trades and professions, at the expense of philosophical justice. Thus, the laws against forgeries, and
other crimes against property, are established for the protection of credit ; military and naval laws for the maintenance of discipline, &c. In all these cases the legislators consider, principally, the immediate advantages,
and not the moral consequences of the law ; their object
is to secure a direct and positive benefit, though in so doing they may infringe on the natural rights of individuals.
One principle is often sacrificed to another—as the minor
interests must yield to the community at large, and the
prosperity and happiness of individuals to the national
progress of the commonwealth.

It is this peculiar property of jurisprudence which distinguishes it from every other science, and tinges, in the
opinion of many, even the moral and intellectual character of advocates. Besides, the profession of the law is,
more frequently than any other, embraced for its worldly
advantages ; and Archimedes' reply to the scholar who
wished to study mathematics because their application
had rendered the country some service, applies *à fortiori*
to the lawyer : " He who worships the *goddess* must not
woo the *woman*."

The Irish are almost diametrically opposite to the Germans, in disposition and enterprise. The industry of the
lower classes consists more in bodily exertion than in its
direction to any definite purpose. Possessing, naturally,

great generosity of character, they are satisfied with acquiring what is necessary for the present, and share even
this with each other, without prudently heeding the future.
While they are thus content to be hired in large bodies
to dig canals or construct railroads, they neglect the more
useful cultivation of the soil, which would, at once, make
them independent and respectable. The second generation, however, fare much better. Being for the most part
brought up in the large cities, they have an opportunity
of benefiting by the superior means of instruction held
out so liberally in all parts of the United States, and to
raise themselves, by their talents and acquirements, to an
equality with the most informed and wealthy. Some of
the most eminent lawyers and statesmen of America are
of Irish extraction, and General Jackson himself is descended from an Irish family. They are a warm-hearted,
patriotic race, who require nothing but the cooling influence of a certain number of years' residence in the United
States, in order to become most useful and peaceable citizens.*

Individually, an Irish gentleman is more esteemed than
a German, and, perhaps, on account of the greater con-
geniality of thought and learning, a more useful member
of the American community. But, as a mass, the Germans are greatly preferred. They have done more, or at
least as much, as any class of Americans for the improvement of the country, and contributed largely, and in the
most systematic manner, to the development of its internal resources. The first American manufactures which
excited the jealousy of Great Britain were the German
paper, woollen and linen cloth manufactures of Pennsylvania ; and to this moment Pennsylvania and Massachusetts are rivalling each other in this species of industry.†
The mechanic arts are allowed to have made greater progress in Philadelphia than in any other city of the United
States; but the principal workmen are Germans,‡ and

---

* Compare the Irish character described in the chapter on American
prejudices.
† Proud's "History of Pennsylvania " and Graham's "History of
the United States."
‡ Of late, a number of English mechanics have emigrated to the
United States, and depressed the labor of the Germans.

many of the first merchants of that city are also descended from Germany. Such occupations are not apt to shed
a particular lustre on the names of individuals ; but they
characterise the whole body as a highly industrious and
useful class of society, which, by its smaller excitability
and *great steadiness of mind*, may, at some future time,
prove a salutary check on the inordinate ambition of a
faction.

The political influence of the Irish, which is the subject of so much discussion in the United States, as well
as in England, and to which one of the political parties
has ascribed all its recent defeats, is, in itself, exceedingly small, and only felt in some of the large towns on the
sea-coast. It is a well ascertained fact that a large majority of the *country*, and not of the *cities*, has voted in
favor of the present administration and the measures of
General Jackson ; and that almost all cities, with the exception of New York, have declared themselves against
them. Even the majority in the city of New York did
not materially influence that of the state, which was sufficiently great to compensate for a failure in any of the
large towns. The Irish are not nearly as unanimous in
their votes as the Germans, and do not hold sufficient
property in any one state to have an immediate influence
on the elections. The Germans, on the contrary, constitute, by themselves, a majority in Pennsylvania, and a
very respectable and wealthy party in many other states.
Being for the most part proprietors of the soil, their vote
is independent, which can hardly be said of the lower
classes of the Irish, who are mostly employed by the rich
capitalists. If the Irish, then, have voted for the administration, I take it for granted that they have done it from
principle ; because a view to their immediate interest
might, perhaps, have dictated an opposite course. Commerce and manufacture, from which the greater number
of Irish, at least indirectly, draw their subsistence, might
have invited them to vote differently ; whilst the farmer
in the interior is, by his very position more independent
of the monied institution of the large cities. The Irish,
were they united to a man, could not have the influence
and power of the Germans, with whom disposition, habit,
occupation, and property unite to make them what they

are, the stoutest democrats of the country. I am far from being instigated by any partisan spirit, either in favor of or against the Irish or Germans; neither do I speak of the correctness or injustice of their vote; but merely of the credit which is to be attached to it as *a moral and independent action.*

In the settlements of new districts it is seldom that Europeans are found to be actively engaged. This honor belongs almost exclusively to emigrants from New England, who may most emphatically be called the pioneers of the United States, and to whose enterprising spirit and recklessness of danger may be ascribed most of the valuable improvements of the country. They are, however, satisfied with tracing the road which the others are to follow, and occupying the most important stations: the intervals are afterwards filled up with settlers from other states and from Europe. The character of the New England emigrants has been too well described by Washington Irving for me to attempt to add to it more than is necessary to understand a certain political type, which may be observed in all states to which they have emigrated in large numbers. The talent of a New Englander is universal. He is a good farmer, an excellent schoolmaster, a very respectable preacher, a capital lawyer, a sagacious physician, an able editor, a thriving merchant, a shrewd pedlar, and a most industrious tradesman. Being thus able to fill all the important posts of society, only a few emigrants from New England are required to imprint a lasting character on a new state, even if their number should be much inferior to that of the other settlers. The states of Ohio and Michigan, and even a large part of the state of New York, offer striking instances of this moral superiority acquired by the people of New England; but it would be wrong thence to conclude that their own habits do not undergo an important metamorphosis, or that, in their new relations in the western states, they merely act as reformers, without being, in turn, influenced by the character of their fellow settlers. The change, however, is altogether for the better. Their patriotism, instead of being confined to the narrow limits of New England, — a fault with which they have been reproached as early as the commencement of the revolutionary war,* — partakes there more of a *national* character. The continued intercourse with strangers from all parts of the world, but more particularly from the different states of the Union, serve in no small degree to eradicate from their minds certain prejudices and illiberalities with which they have but too commonly been reproached by their brethren of the south. Tolerance, the last and most humane offspring of civilization, is, perhaps, the only virtue of which the New Englander is usually parsimonious; but even this seems to improve and to thrive in the western states ; and 1 have no hesitation to say, that, in this respect, the inhabitants of those districts are by far more emancipated than those of the Atlantic states, whatever advantages the latter may possess with regard to refinement of manners. I know of no better specimen of human character than a New Englander transferred to the western states.

To form a correct idea of the rapid increase of cultivated territory in the western states, it is only necessary to cast a glance at the unparalleled increase of population. The state of Pennsylvania, which in 1810 contained but 810,091† inhabitants, had in 1830, 1,347,672 ; increase, 537,581 : the population of the state of New York, which in 1810 was but 413,763, had in 1830 already increased to 1,913,508 ; increase, 1,499,745 : the population of Alabama was less than 10,000, but in 1830 already 308,997 ; increase 298,997, or nearly 2,990 per cent. in twenty years : that of Mississippi, which in 1810 amounted to 40,352, was in 1830, 136,800 ; increase in twenty years 96,448, equivalent to 239 per cent. : Tennessee contained in 1810 but 261,727 inhabitants, but in 1830, 684,822 ; increase 162 per cent. nearly : in Kentucky the population increased, in the same time, from 406,511 to 688,844, or by about 70 per cent. : that of Ohio advanced, in the space of time, from 230,760 to 937,637 ; increase more than 300 per cent. : the population of the same state was, in 1790, but 3,000 ; increased in 40 years, 31,154 $\frac{67}{100}$ per cent. : Indiana contained in 1810 but 24,520 inhabitants ; but in 1830 already 341,-

* Botta, " *Storia della guerra dell' independenza degli Stati Uniti.*"
† These numbers are taken from the census of 1810, 1820, and 1830.

582; increase more than 1,293 per cent. : but the population of Indiana consisted in 1800 only of 5,641 ; consequently the total increase in 30 years, or less than a whole generation, is more than 5,955 per cent. Illinois contained in 1810 only 12,282 inhabitants, which number was in 1830 increased to 157,575; equal to about 1,183 per cent.: Missouri had in the same space increased to seven times her original population ; that of 1810 being 19,833, and that of 1830, 140,074. The population of the eastern and southern states I have here omitted, because, though on the increase, they present nothing so striking as the rapid growth of the west. The states of Pennsylvania and New York, however, extend far to the westward, and thence arises their incredible augmentation of population.

More than nine tenths of all the people who emigrate to the west are *farmers* or *planters ;* and it is consequently chiefly the agricultural interest which causes the settling of the immense territory of the United States yet open to the spirit of enterprise. Commerce and manufacture, it is true, *follow* the path of the new settlers ; but they never lead the way to those regions, and are rather accessaries than originators of civilization. The continent of America might have been visited, like the islands of the South Sea, by a thousand enterprising merchants and navigators, without being for one moment redeemed from its savage state. It is but the actual cultivation of the soil, and the indisputable right to property arising from actual labor, which lays the foundation of states and empires, as it furnishes, perhaps, the only legitimate title to the possession of a country.

Let no sensitive European, therefore, complain of the barbarous cruelty of the Americans in chasing the Indians from the soil of their fathers, or in forcing them to flee from the approach of civilization to the unhospitable woods of the western territory. The American aborigine, with but very few exceptions, never possessed the soil on which they trod any more than the air which they breathed. They never cultivated it to any extent, nor had they, individually, any distinct title to it arising from actual labor. They held it in common with the beasts of the forest, and it was useful to them only as it afforded

them the means of prey. The English had as good a
right to call the ocean their own, because they moved on
it, as the American Indians to claim possession of their
continent because they roamed in its woods. There was
barbarity in the conquest of Lima and Mexico, the inhabitants of which were already in possession of many of the
arts of peace ; but there can be none in the quiet progress
of civilization in the United States, except what is provoked by the Indians themselves, and for which they
alone must remain accountable. The American settler
takes possession of a soil which has never been cultivated,
and which, therefore, has had no owner. He builds his
log-house in a country in which there is room enough for
the support of millions, and in which there are hardly a
few hundred stragglers to follow the track of the deer.
Is this robbery ? Is it cruel to civilize and improve a
country, and to open a new road to wealth and comfort
to thousands of intelligent beings from all parts of the
world, who would otherwise starve or be reduced to poverty, because in so doing they cannot avoid intruding on
the favorite hunting-grounds of some wandering tribes,
and disturb their game ? This, however, they do ; and,
with the deer, the American aborigines disappear from
the soil.

It is in vain to talk of civilizing them. If it could be
done which is more than doubtful, (considering the many
unsuccessful attempts which have already been made,)
hey would hardly be able to compete with their teachers
in any one human occupation calculated to secure a live-
lihood in a civilized country, and would, therefore, from
necessity, become outlaws to society, and incur the punishment of the law.* We cannot but regret the fate of
that doomed people ; but we can hardly think of rescuing
them from it, without being guilty of the most flagrant
injustice to the rest of mankind.

---

* The state of the Creek and Cherokee Indians furnishes a new
proof of this assertion. *Red Jacket*, an Indian chief of great eloquence,
in his answer to the missionaries, observed that it was very probable
God had intended the white and the red races for different purposes.
" To you," he said, " He has given the arts; to these He has forever
closed our eyes. Why should He not have given you another religion
also ?—*Red-Jacket's reply to the missionaries, by Thomas Jefferson.*

The power arising from the actual cultivation of the soil and the establishment of fixed habitations in a country is so irresistible and unsparing, that it must eventually triumph over all obstacles, and resist even the destructive consequences of wars. This is the reason why the British colonies in America prospered so rapidly, and finally finished by swallowing up Canada. The *military* force of the French settlements was vastly superior to that of the English; their lines of fortification extended from the mouth of the Mississippi to the river St. Lawrence; but they had no possession of the intervening territory by virtue of actual settlements, and the result soon convinced them that where the most property is accumulated, there also will be the strongest means of defence; on that side, consequently, must eventually incline the victory. But if the policy of the Anglo-Americans was sufficient to destroy so powerful a rival as the French, what can be expected from the unconcerted ill-advised resistance or attack of the aborigines, unskilled in military tactics, and not sufficiently strong, on any one point, to offer a serious impediment to the grasping power of the settlers?

Neither is it reasonable to suppose that the quitting of their favorite hunting-grounds can give the American Indians the same pangs which an everlasting farewell to the paternal soil, the scene of all early attachments, and the habitation of all that we love, fraught with the memory and tradition of centuries, can cause to a civilised nation. The Indians quit what never was precisely their own; they leave no object of memory or tradition behind; and, although the loss may be felt by the *tribe*, no *individual* is actually despoiled of his own. But it is the feelings of individuals which we must here consider; not that of the tribe or nation. A people cannot be said to feel the wrongs and pains inflicted upon it by another, except in proportion as the sufferings of the whole are felt and responded to by individuals. This, however, presupposes a degree of moral development, and a pitch of national enthusiasm, of which even history is sparing in furnishing us with examples, and of which certainly but few traces are to be found in the Indian character. Let no one mistake the *hatred* which the colored races bear to the whites, and to each other, for a strong love of country and an attachment to their native woods. Hatred of others is but a negative and barbarous qualification of nationality, and is by no means a necessary concomitant of its positive virtues. The hatred between the different races is something animal and instinctive, and is far removed from the noble disinterestedness of genuine patriotism. Whatever color poetry may lend to the removal of the Indians, it is, nevertheless, but the removal of a sick bed from a place where death is certain, to one from which it is more remote. Neither is it the death of youth or of manhood, but that of old age and decrepitude, which the Indian is doomed to die; and in his mouldering ashes germinates the seed of empires, destined to change the face of the world. This is but applying the universal law of nature to man: there is no life without death to precede it ; no seed without destroying the blossom ; no offspring without destruction to its genitors. One nation must perish to make room for another; and it is the peculiar good fortune of America that she can suffer these revolutions to go on without a feverish excitement of her vitals, or hurrying the succession of events by the horror and bloodshed of war.*

But the west would not be so rapidly settled if the cultivation of the soil did not promise a task rewarded with comfort and independence. There can hardly be a doubt of the fact, that the soil of the valley of the Mississippi is the richest and most fertile on earth ; and that, producing every thing which is necessary to the existence and comfort of man, it is intended to become the habitation of hundreds of millions.† Alexander von Humboldt gave it as his opinion, that America is the most fertile quarter of the world ; and it has since been computed that the whole population of Europe could find ample room and subsistence on the borders of the Mississippi alone. The whole population of the five great continents has

---

* What is termed " the Indian war," is nothing but a succession of skirmishes with a few of the neighboring tribes; and is only protracted because it is deemed too insignificant to warrant a general armament on the part of the United States. The case is very different with the French colony of Algiers.

† Compare De Tocqueville " De la Démocratie en Amérique."

been estimated at about one thousand millions; but what important change may we not expect in the condition of the human race, when we know that there exists a confederacy of republics capable of sustaining, with a greater degree of ease than was ever before shared by any portion of the human family, a population surpassing that of the entire globe? There is no country or tract of land on earth whose physical and geographical position are so well adapted to agriculture and commerce as that part of the American continent which composes the territory of the United States. Like China, America may be said to be independent of the rest of the world; inasmuch as she is capable of producing, not only what is essential to human existence, but also the luxuries inseparable from a certain degree of refinement. Her territory embraces every climate, from the extreme north to the furthermost south, and every species of vegetation intended for manufacture and commerce. But the facility of river communication, and the internal navigation of the United States, have no equal on earth, and may be considered the most durable cement by which the various states are united. There is hardly a settlement in the Union which has not more or less the means of communicating with some market town or city, and, therefore, not only the elements of prosperity in its domestic arrangements, but also the hope of obtaining the value of its produce, and thereby to become rich and independent. What is even the situation of China with regard to the commerce of the world, compared to that of the United States, when they will once be settled and extend from one ocean to the other? The largest empire, Russia, would require the Swedish peninsula, in order to hold a position at all to be compared to it; and even then, the extent of intervening country, the difficulty of communication, and the extreme northern latitude of her possessions, would deprive her of its principal advantages. A single glance at the map of the United States, and a slight acquaintance with the people who inhabit them, are sufficient to convince even the stoutest unbeliever that America is destined to become the first in agriculture, the first in commerce, and the first in manufacture of all countries in the world. It will touch the extreme east and west of the remaining

20

continents, and possess equal facilities of trade with the East and West Indies. It must become the centre of civilization ; and, from its equal proximity to both Asia and Europe, exercise a most powerful political influence on all nations of the globe. Europeans learn with astonishment the rapid progress of civilization and power in America; but all she has done to this moment is but a feeble prelude to the gigantic part which she is destined to perform in the universal drama of the world.

Already a most uncommon spectacle presents itself. Emigration to America is no longer confined to those parts of Europe which are over-peopled, (Wurtemberg and Ireland,) but communicates itself also to the less populated parts of Germany and France. Large numbers of the inhabitants of Old Bavaria and of the French province of Alsace are annually wandering to the United States ; and so inviting are the letters of those who are already settled, to their friends and relations in Europe, that some of the German governments have already been obliged to make provisions to arrest the *depopulation* of their country by law, and to enjoin the civil and military authorities to use their utmost influence to prevent emigration in the future. Neither is it only the lower and destitute classes who are daily embarking for the United States. On the contrary, the obstacles thrown in their way are such that only those who have property are able to receive their passports. There is now a law in Wurtemberg which obliges every subject, desirous of emigrating to America, to deposite the sum of 300 florins (640 francs) with the civil authorities of Stutgard, which sum is only remitted to him at the seaport of his embarkation. Thus every German emigrant, from that part of the country, must not only be able to provide for his journey to the seaport, but must also have a sum of 640 francs to spare, which is sufficient to pay his passage, and leaves him, on his arrival in America, with sufficient funds to proceed to the west. Much, indeed, has been said in America on the subject of foreign paupers; though it would be easy to prove, by the registers of emigration in Germany, that the emigrants from that country pay annually more than two hundred thousand dollars for their passage, independent of the money and goods which they carry to the United States.

And now, be the merits of this work what they may, I still flatter myself with the hope of seeing it translated into German; and as it will probably be read by many who will feel disposed to change the old for the new world, I will say a few words to these emigrants, equally applicable to those from other countries.

Let no one go to America merely on speculation ; but at once with the resolute determination of making it his home. Let him not expect to lead a life of comparative idleness; but, on the contrary, one of hard work and persevering industry, if he wishes to realise the fruits of his labor, and to become independent of the assistance of others. Let him remember that he is going to settle amongst the most industrious people on earth, whose constitution and government protect him, it is true, in the unmolested posession of property ; but that he *himself* must be the principal artificer of his fortune; and that *nothing but personal exertion* will ensure his ultimate success. Let him come unencumbered with farming utensils, machines, &c., which will only increase the expenses of his journey, without being of any real use in practice. Most of them he will be able to buy, in the United States, not only cheaper and of better quality, but also better adapted to the general use in the country. Many emigrants are in a habit of bringing ploughs, waggons, &c. to America, without reflecting, for one moment, that the expenses of transportation amount to more than their actual value ; and that it is more than probable that these implements may prove entirely useless or unmanageable in a different soil or on a different road.* Again, let them abstain from all mercantile speculations, of which they often know little or nothing, and which can never succeed, unless they are thoroughly acquainted with the state of the market. Let them remember, that, once out of money, they must sell their merchandise for what they will bring, not for what they are worth; that commerce requires capital and credit, and that without them they must necessarily become the tool of every trader and pedlar whom they may meet on their way.

* This is, to my knowledge, the case with several European farming utensils.

On their arrival in the United States let them not remain too long in the Atlantic cities. Every day they
stay there without occupation, is lost to their enterprise,
and diminishes their funds. Let them rather begin humbly
in the country, by working on farms, than become servants
in the towns, or commence business immediately on their
own account. If there are several members of a family,
let only those remain in the cities who have learned a
particular trade, or who may expect immediate employment: but it is far better for a whole family to move at
once to the west, where they may find occupation much
more suitable to their habits than they can hope to find
on the sea-coast, where a too sudden transition from rural
life to the refinement of the towns may prove destructive
to their morals. Let them bear in mind, that in the
cities, though individuals may prosper, they will hardly
be able to raise themselves to an equality with the native
inhabitants; whereas in the country, and especially on
new land, they must, by persevering industry, become as
respectable and powerful as the rest of their fellow-citizens. In the country they will enjoy an hundred indul-
gences of which they must necessarily be deprived in the
cities. They will there be allowed to follow their own
inclinations and habits, which they must never expect in
a large city, in which they must necessarily conform to
the manners and customs of the majority.

Let them, above all things, abstain from politics, before
they have had time to study the institutions of the country, and to know the government under which they are
going to live. A too hasty adoption of principles, before
they have thoroughly weighed them, may be fatal to their
own influence, and interfere with their prospects in life.
It is the duty of every European settler to make himself
acquainted with American laws and manners, in order
to judge for himself to what party he is to lend his support. The Germans especially ought to show more zeal
in acquiring the English language, without which it is
impossible to understand the true meaning of a thousand
things with which it is important they should be rendered
familiar. The American papers contain infinitely more
information than any of the German ones I have seen;
which, with but few exceptions, contain nothing but

mutilated extracts from the daily American press, in a language of which it is difficult to say whether it is less German or English.

I have said before, that in order to succeed in any one undertaking, but especially in farming, it is necessary that the proprietor should work himself, and not merely be an idle spectator or employer of the labor of others. I will now add, that without *personal* exertion on his part, he will not only be unable to advance, but absolutely fail and be ruined. America, (thanks to her institutions and the infinite resources of the soil,) is not yet a country for a gentleman farmer; a circumstance which has been much regretted by Mr. Hamilton, but which is the cause of much rejoicing to every unbiassed and intelligent inhabitant of the United States. An American prefers cultivating the smallest patch of his own, to working on the largest farm of his neighbor, and rather emigrates further to the west, than consent to become, in any manner or degree, dependent on his fellow-beings. The Germans who are found willing to hire themselves out on an estate are seldom content to serve for wages, but wish to be paid in land or produce, and become thus partners, instead of servants to their employers.

"But America," says Mr. Hamilton, "is not the place for a gentleman farmer. The price of labor is high, and, besides, it cannot always be commanded at any price. *The condition of society is not yet ripe for farming on a great scale.* (!) There will probably be no American Mr. Coke for some centuries to come. The Transatlantic Sir John Sinclairs are yet *in ovo*, and a long period of incubation must intervene before we can expect them to crack the shell." What a beautiful metaphor! It is to be hoped they will never be hatched. "As things at present stand," continues he, "small farmers could beat the great ones out of the field. What a man produces by his ow nlabor and that of his family, he produces cheaply; what he is compelled to hire others to perform, is done expensively. It is always the interest of the latter to get as much as he can, and give as little labor in exchange for it." Why does he not say, in few words, *a man works harder for himself than for others?* "Then arises the necessity of bailiffs and overseers; fresh mouths

20*

to feed and pockets to be filled; and the owner may consider himself fortunate, if these are content with devouring the profits, without swallowing the estate into the bargain."

When the condition of society in America will "be ripe" for the English system of farming, then the progress and prosperity of the United States will be on the decline. What is the farming system in England but a sort of tail to the feudal system, which, though it may have its advantages to the proprietors where it is once established, cannot benefit a country where it is to be newly introduced. And what is the Irish system of "tenants at will" but one of the many melancholy forms under which the misery of her people is entailed from one generation on another? It is not the *unfortunate* state of society which, in America, diminishes the number of gentleman farmers; it is the unexampled *prosperity* of the country, and the distribution of wealth throughout the whole population, which raises them at once above the condition of servitude. Whoever emigrates westward, goes thither on his own account; for, if he be an honest man, he can buy land on credit, or for a trifling amount of cash; and under such circumstances it is not to be supposed he will hire himself out to others. The present condition of the United States is such that but few are exempted from labor, and even these are not proud of their distinction. No disgrace attaches to industry, nor does the term "gentleman" necessarily imply a man who has nothing to do.

Large real estates neither contribute to the general prosperity of a country, nor are they very congenial with liberal institutions. The present prosperity of France and of some of the minor states of Germany is universally allowed to be produced by the division of property; and where such a division can be effected *in the outset*, without injustice to any one class of society, it would be absurd and criminal not to promote it. No hired laborer can be expected to do as well as he who works for himself; and it is therefore the interest of the country at large to have as many proprietors as possible. The greatest quantity of labor will be produced by the greatest number of persons interested in it; and the greatest

profits realised where they are obtained with little assistance from others. These truths are so generally understood, that even at the late diets of Hungary and Transylvania, the lower nobility* wished to change the law of
expropriation of the peasantry, by allowing them to
possess freehold estates by the same tenure as themselves; "because," they observed, "our property when
divided will be worth more than it is entire, and we shall
sell the fragments for more than the whole." Now,
while the policy of such an arrangement is acknowledged
in all civilised parts of the world, while even the nobility
of Hungary and Transylvania are willing to try so wise
and salutary a measure, is it not strange that so enlightened an author as Mr. Hamilton, in so enlightened an
age as ours, should publish, in "the most enlightened
country of the world," a work in which he derides the
American system of independent farming?   Of what
immense advantage is not the division of property in a
country like the United States? Is it not, in a degree,
necessary to the continuance of its republican institutions? Does the greater number of proprietors not increase the number of those who have a direct stake in
the government? Is not independence of suffrage best
secured by independence of property? There are, assuredly, proprietors of large tracts of *uncultivated* land ;
but no sooner are settlements made upon them, than they
are portioned out in little lots, and cultivated by men
of small fortunes. This is, indeed, one of the means of
realising fortunes out of real estates. Land, in America,
is treated like any other kind of merchandise; it is
bought in large quantities, and *retailed in small lots.*
Without this policy the population would not have increased so rapidly during the last twenty or thirty years,
and many of the western farms, which are now in a
thriving condition, would yet be as uncultivated as the
borders of the Pacific. Nothing but the love of independence could induce those sturdy settlers to make the
wilderness their home. If they wished to consult their

* The Hungarian diet is composed of two chambers, the magnates
and the nobles, or the lower and higher nobility. Each free town
counts as one nobleman in the lower chamber. No person can possess
real estate, except a nobleman or a citizen of a free town.

ease, they might become servants in the cities or cultivated districts ; for they have no chance of finding it in the
western woods. The willingness of the rich to work, and
the disposition of the poor to prefer hard independent
labor to easy, well-paid servitude, are the principal
causes of the increasing prosperity of the United States.

The unwillingness of the poorer classes of Americans
to hire themselves out as servants, and the little satisfaction with their lot when circumstances compel them to
do it, furnish a subject of incessant complaint with the
wealthier, and more aristocratic families. The theme is
too fertile for European tourists not to profit by it, and,
accordingly, their works are adorned with copious descriptions of the ludicrous pretensions of American servants. I admit at once that there are but few native
Americans who would submit to the degradation of wearing a livery, or any other badge of servitude. This they
would call becoming a man's man. But, on the other
hand, there are also but few American gentlemen who
would feel any happier for their servants wearing coats
of more than one color. The inhabitants of New England are quite as willing to call their servants " helps,"
or " domestics," as the latter repudiate the title of
" master " in their employers ; and as it is a matter of
agreement between them, I do not see that either party
is actually injured.

It is true, an American servant will not suffer the treatment of a liveried vagabond ; but then it is the meanest
gratification to be permitted to treat a fellow-being with
contempt. Neither is an American servant that same
indolent, careless, besotted being as an European. He
knows how to read and write, and is sure to understand
arithmetic ; he takes an interest in politics, reads the papers, and attends public meetings and lectures. He is a
member of the militia, pays poll-tax, and is entitled to
vote.* His mind is constantly engaged in making plans
for the future ; and, far from being content to remain all
his life a servant, he is earnestly contemplating his chance

* I heard, myself, an American servant tell of the gentlemann " he
lived with," *that he liked him very well; but always crossed him in politics.* His master knew this ; but kept him in his employ, because he
was, in every other respect, a trustworthy servant.

of success in some trade. No sooner has he earned a few dollars than he sets up a shop; and there are many of them who finish by becoming respectable merchants. With these hopes before him, it could not be expected that he would always be a ready, cringing sycophant; but it does not follow that he must necessarily be unwilling to do his duty, or to accomplish that which he has agreed to do with promptitude and cheerfulness. I am quite convinced that American servants work harder, and *quicker* than even the English; and that, from their greater intelligence, they are, on the whole, the most useful.

An American gentleman has seldom more than one man-servant, who is at once porter, footman, bottler, and, if necessary, coachman to the family. He cleans the boots, brushes the clothes, washes the windows, cleans the house, waits at table, goes to market, keeps the reckoning, and is, in one word, the *factotum* of the household. He does that which it would at least take six others to accomplish, and, notwithstanding his high wages, proves a cheaper servant than could be obtained in Europe. He is always at home, always busy, and hardly ever spending his leisure hours at a public-house. So far from being unable to *procure* good servants in America, the only difficulty consists in *keeping* them; there being but few amongst them whose capacity for trade will suffer them to remain satisfied with what they think an inferior condition.

As to female servants, few complaints, I believe, are made of their want of fidelity or submission, though they require a treatment very different from that to which the same class are accustomed in Europe. Despite of Mrs. Trollope's masterly sketches of American domestics, she could find nothing to impeach either their honesty or morality; (which, no doubt, the *fair* author would have been glad to do if it had been in her power;) and one instance, in particular, which she gives of the pride of a young girl, in her own service, who would rather starve than eat in the kitchen, and whom she always found obedient yet bathed in tears, exhibits a nobility of sentiment, of which certainly not a trace is to be found in her lady's writings.

The waiting-women at the inns and taverns are possessed of a peculiar dignity of demeanor, which effectually

prevents every improper approach, on the part of the vis-
iters, and, being generally tolerably well educated, it is
easy to perceive at once, that they are in many respects
vastly superior to some of the sots whom they are obliged
"to help." The superiority of the women over the men,
which is everywhere perceptible in the United States, extends equally to the servants; and it is, consequently, a
rare case for one of these fair " helps " to marry a fellow-
domestic. They are generally joined in wedlock to some
respectable mechanic; and, acquiring property by frugality and industry, finish by taking the stations of their former employers.

Much has been said on the relative position of the rich
and poor, by men who enjoy great reputation as scholars
and statesmen. Yet I believe their arguments are more
founded on theories and analogies, than on actual observation of the different classes of society in the United
States. There is no distinct line of demarcation between
the rich and the poor, as in Europe; the deserters from
both ranks, but especially from the latter, being more numerous than those who remain; and the number of new
comers putting computation altogether out of the question. Neither is there that envy amongst the laboring
classes which characterizes the "canaille" of Europe,
and manifests itself by an indiscriminate hatred of all
whose fortunes are superior to their own. Exemption from
labor, the beau ideal of the French and Italians, is not
even desired by the industrious population of America;
and the poor, are willing to protect the possessions of the
rich, because they expect themselves to need that protection at some future period. In all the hues and cries
against the bank, there was not the least manifestation of
a desire to despoil the rich of their property: all that the
people contended for was, in their opinion, an equal
chance for acquiring it. They wished to put down that
which they deemed a monopoly and an impediment to
the progress of the small merchant; but never dreamed
of plunder. This question has been sadly misrepresented
in Europe, and accompanied by pictures of the cupidity of
the lower classes, to which it would be difficult to find the
originals in the United States of America.

CHAPTER IX.

COMMERCE OF THE UNITED STATES.——SYSTEM OF CREDIT.
——AMERICAN CAPITALISTS.——BANKS.——MANUFACTURES.——
MECHANIC ARTS. — WAGES AND HOURS OF LABOR.——IN-
GENUITY OF AMERICANS.——NAVIGATION.——SAILORS.——THE
FISHERIES.——SHIP-BUILDING.

DESCENDED from the first maritime nation, and invited
by a sea-coast of more than sixteen hundred miles, possessed of the most excellent harbors, the Americans need
but follow their natural impulse, and improve the advantages of their geographical position, in order to become
the most powerful commercial nation on the globe. The
water is the native element of the Transatlantic republican ; and it is upon the ocean he appears truly great and
heroic. Even the navigation of the American lakes and
the great western rivers presents a spectacle unequalled
in any other part of the world. In no other country is
so large a portion of the whole population engaged in
navigation——in none other is the water treated with the
same familiarity as the land. The Americans are the
most amphibious bipeds on the face of the earth ; and
such is the abundance of water communication in the interior, that a man will hardly call on his next neighbor
without embarking on board of some steam-boat.

With the unparalleled spirit of enterprise, and the mercantile genius of her inhabitants, it is impossible that America should not develope all the mighty resources which a
country, whose shores are bathed by two oceans, and
whose interior is intersected by a thousand mighty streams,
must naturally offer to its merchants and seamen. At the

present time, at which probably not more than the one-hundredth part of the facilities of navigation are improved, the mercantile navy of America is but second to that of England ; but in skill, energy, and boldness inferior to none in the world. Compared to the entire population, the number of her ships and mariners is greater than that of any existing nation, and forms a broad and noble basis for her future maritime power. It is the merchant's service from which the navy is recruited, and without which it is impossible to educate sailors for the use of men-of-war. The naval power of every people has increased with its commerce, and, in the event of a war, the question is not so much how many ships she could muster in her docks, but rather how many she could man and navigate. The American navy is perhaps the smallest which ever protected so extensive a commerce ; but, in case of need, the United States could, in one year, build as many vessels, *and man them*, as any other nation, save England, could get ready for sea. The materials for ship-building are cheap, the skilful workmen numerous, and experienced sailors to be found in every harbor. The history of the American flotillas on the lakes, and the achievements of their frigates on the ocean, prove sufficiently the celerity and energy which they are capable of developing on important occasions, and that, notwithstanding the small number of government ships, America must be ranked amongst the first maritime powers.

It is the commerce of the United States which not only furnishes a market for the increasing manufactures and the immense natural productions of the soil, but constitutes also the right arm and strength of the national defence of the country. It is not merely an accessory to the arts of civilization ; it is not resorted to merely as a means of obtaining riches; it is a *national* occupation, imbued with all the spirit and energy of character which distinguish the American community.

An American merchant is an enthusiast who seems to delight in enterprise in proportion as it is connected with danger. He ventures his fortune with the same heroism with which the sailor risks his life ; and is as ready to embark on a new speculation after the failure of a favorite project, as the mariner is to navigate a new ship, after his own has become a wreck. An American carries the spirit of invention even to the counting-room. He is constantly discovering some new sources of trade, and is always willing to risk his capital and credit on some *terra incognita*, rather than follow the beaten track of others, and content himself with such profits as are realised by his competitors. This is undoubtedly the cause of a great number of unfortunate speculations and subsequent failures; but it constitutes also the technical superiority of the American merchant over the European. He is an inventor, not an imitator ; he *creates* new sources of wealth instead of merely *exhausting* the old ones. Hence his vigilance and application. The ordinary routine of business is not sufficient to ensure his success; he must think, invent, speculate ; for it is more by ingenuity and foresight, than by the regular pursuit of trade, that he can hope to realise a fortune. None of the present French or Dutch fashions of trade, would now prosper in the United States. Fortunes there are not made by small savings, but by large and successful operations. It is not by small savings, but by large and successful operations. It is not by hoarding money, but by employing and investing it, that property accumulates in America; and the inexhaustible riches of the country open daily a thousand new roads to industry and commerce.

The majority of Americans are, perhaps, not as good financiers as the Dutch, but they are more enterprising and successful merchants ; they are willing to run greater risks, in order to secure larger profits; and it may be said of them that their minds expand in proportion to their stakes in trade.

What, after all, can be more despicable than the character of a miser such as Holland teemed with since the decline of her active commerce, when, with the largest capital in the world, her merchants became money-lenders, and the creditors of all Europe ? What difference is there not between some of those haggard-looking, dirty, usurious financiers, and an active, liberal-minded, enterprising merchant, the support of an hundred small traders and mechanics, whom he trusts or employs in the various ramifications of business. Let any one compare the present population of Amsterdam to that of New York. The

21

aspect of the one is gloomy, contracted, sordid — that of the other all gaiety, frankness, and liberality. Except to a man of business, a residence at Amsterdam is wholly devoid of interest. Everywhere he meets the same greedy pursuit of money ; the same *avaricious* abstinence from all which contributes to pleasure. Even the ordinary conveniences and comforts of life are enjoyed only by a few of the oldest and richest families ; the rest lead a life of privation. How very unlike this is the picture of New York ! Every thing there bears the aspect of ease and cheerfulness. The streets are wide and airy, the houses of the wealthier classes are decorated with taste, and the whole population bears the impress of opulence and prosperity. In spite of the hurry and bustle of business during the day, the evenings of many of the wealthy families are devoted to social intercourse, and their doors are open to the reception of friends. No one can accuse the American merchant with want of hospitality. He is liberal and generous in his dealings, affable and obliging in his intercourse with strangers, a sincere friend, and a calm reflecting politician. The extent of his speculations prepares his mind for sudden success or ill fortune, and he is able to sustain losses with a degree of fortitude and equanimity which is utterly beyond the comprehension of ordinary men of business in other countries. His mind becomes enlarged by the extent of his enterprise, and becomes naturally superior to the niggard calculator of groats.

There seems to be something ungenerous in the mere business of a money-broker, charging his one quarter or one half per cent. commission, and hoarding a fortune by the small droppings from the estates of those who are actively engaged in commerce. One of the meanest occupations of men is the mere computation of numbers; but it may become destructive to the noblest faculties of the mind, when these numbers represent nothing but money. The first of all the sciences, mathematics, when unconnected with philosophy, may serve to enslave the mind and deprive it of imagination and fancy. Even the astronomer, who is solely confined to his ciphers, without seeing in them the laws and type of his God, degenerates into a mechanical book-keeper of the universe, without having an interest in its noblest transactions. The business of trading and jobbing in stocks is not only mean in itself, but may in many instances prove a serious injury to commerce. It may absorb a large portion of the capital which would otherwise be invested in merchandise, and give a wrong direction to the national industry of a country. The merchant must needs be influenced by the fluctuations of exchange, and must provide against them; but it is the gambler alone makes a living by them.

It has been observed, in all countries, that in proportion as active commerce declines, in that same proportion opens the game for the *agioteurs* on 'change; and there is no more certain mark of spreading demoralization than to see the people at large take an active part in it. It is then sure to dry up the fountains of wealth and virtue, and to convert thousands of industrious men into so many vagabonds and beggars.

Very remarkable, and not devoid of historical interest, is the comparison between the rise and progress of commerce in Holland, and the equally rapid success of trade in the United States of America. There are so many points of resemblance in the histories of both countries, so many similar causes which stimulated their inhabitants to exertion and prompted their ingenuity, that I cannot refrain from directing the attention of my readers to some of the principal facts which became the elements of their respective greatness. In speaking of the commerce of the United States, it must be remembered, however, that during the war of independence, and immediately after it, trade and traffic were principally confined to the New England states—neither the south, nor Pennsylvania, nor even New York, being, at that time, possessed of a considerable mercantile navy, or participating largely in commercial enterprise. What, therefore, I have to say of the origin of American commerce, will apply, principally, to the New England States, though its progress, of course, refers equally, and even more, to New York than to any other state in the Union.

Three principal causes there were to rouse the activity of the Dutch, and develope those mighty energies for which they have long been distinguished; the utter insufficiency of the soil to minister to their physical wants, the necessity of protecting themselves against the fury of the element which continually threatened to ingulf them, and their long-protracted struggle for political and religious freedom against the then greatest power of Europe. The physical obstacles which they had to overcome whetted their ingenuity and directed their enterprise to commerce and the fisheries; while the war with Spain, and their being excluded from the Portuguese ports, obliged them to seek the trade in Indian commodities at its source in the East and West Indies. The New England states were similarly circumstanced. Their soil, especially that of the province of Massachusetts Bay, was generally barren and rocky, and obliged the settlers, at an early period of their history, to resort to other means of subsistence than mere agriculture. The sea they had less to dread; but the severity of the climate, the merciless hatchet of the Indian, and their remoteness from the centre of civilization and from succor, taught them to rely principally on their own strength and industry. The continued wars with the aborigines, their defence against the incessant encroachments of the French, and, finally, their struggle for independence with England, were well calculated to develope all the energies of which they were possessed, and to direct their early attention to the establishment of a powerful navy.

The fisheries had become not only a means of supplying their wants, but a source of national wealth; as the herring-fisheries had at one time been the source of prosperity to Holland. During the war with Spain, the Dutch made immense prizes by the capture of Spanish vessels on the coast of America and in the West Indies, which enabled them, in part, to defray the expenses of the war. The Americans had to proceed to the coast of Africa for the very powder which they required to carry on the revolutionary war, while their privateers were scouring even the coasts of Europe, to annoy British trade at its strong hold, at home.

All nations seem to grow powerful in proportion as their early existence is threatened by some mighty foe. Rome grew strong in its wars with Carthage; Holland became the first maritime republic by its struggle against the greatest monarchy; America accomplished her independence by challenging into the field the most enterprising nation on the globe. The first war with England laid the foundation to the American navy; and as it was the most powerful nation they had to contend with, they had no other alternative than either to become great themselves, by surpassing every moral and physical obstacle to their progress, or be conquered and swallowed up by their superior antagonist. A series of circumstances combined to make them accomplish the former; and they have since kept possession of the ground they have assumed, and even succeeded in enlarging it.

The Americans must either have become equal to the English in navigation, or forever resign the thought of becoming a commercial nation; and confine themselves chiefly to agriculture. England possessed immense advantages over America by her possessions in the East and West Indies, and the geographical position of her North American colonies, from which she might have checked the growing trade of the United States.

The Dutch conquered a portion of the Spanish colonies, and established themselves in the East Indies on the ruin of the Spanish influence. The Americans could not hope to reap any such signal advantages over any European colony established in the East; and had, therefore, no other means of competing with their European rivals than those which were furnished by the skill of their navigators, and the enterprise and ingenuity of their merchants. The Americans had to purchase commodities from the European settlements in the East and West Indies in order to sell them again to European nations at a less price than they were sold by the merchants of those countries. They had, therefore, to employ all their sagacity in trade to compete with them. They had to make shorter passages, navigate their ships at a less rate, and content themselves with smaller profits. But it was even the disadvantages under which they labored which developed their commercial energies; and without a single possession in the East and West Indies, they have now more private ships engaged in the India trade than any European nation, save England. The number of American ships trading to the Dutch settlements in the East Indies was, more than ten years ago, already superior to that of all the ships employed by the Dutch East India Company, and they have since wrested from Holland a large portion of her trade to Russia and all the ports of the Baltic.

But if the commercial importance of the United States was ,in the outset, favored by circumstances similar to those which promoted the trade and navigation of the Dutch; if, in the course of their progress, the Americans were powerfully assisted by the long wars between France and England, acting on their commerce, as the civil wars of France and Germany acted on the prosperity of Holland, they were equally fortunate in avoiding most of the evils with which the commerce of Holland was incumbered even during its most flourishing period, and which, ultimately brought on its rapid decline. Some of these were inseparable from the political and geographical position of Holland ; the rest were owing to misgovernment. To the former we must reckon the oppressive taxation, which was rendered unavoidable by the long war with Spain, and subsequently with France, and the struggle of the republic for supremacy with the growing power of England ; to the latter belong the introduction of monopolies, the excessive accumulation of capital, and the consequently reduced profits in trade, and the introduction of the financiering system by which the Dutch became the money-lenders of Europe.

But to understand this subject properly, and, at the same time, to be enabled to draw a correct inference from it with regard to the future prospects of America, I must be pardoned for alluding to a work with which the English are already familiar through the pages of the Edinburgh Review ; * but which sheds too great a light on the history of commerce of all nations, and especially on that of the United States, not to be once more introduced to the attention of British readers. I would refer to the " *Recherches sur le Commerce de la Hollande*," published at Amsterdam in 1828. From an attentive perusal of the work, and a proper comparison of the history of Dutch commerce with that of the United States, the conviction will be irresistible that political and religious free-

* July, 1830.

dom were the two most prominent moral causes which promoted the trade of both nations, and that every attempt to circumscribe that freedom either by the establishment of monopolies or any other prohibitive system, must arrest the progress of commerce, and become an impediment to industry. There can be no stronger argument in favor of this proposition than the answer of the Dutch merchants themselves to the queries addressed to them by the Stadtholder William IV.,— *Why the trade of Holland had been rapidly declining, and by what means it was to be re-established and placed on its ancient footing?* In replying to these questions the merchants were obliged to enter fully on the moral and physical causes which co-operated to raise Holland to her former proud eminence, as also on the reasons which led to her gradual decline. Their arguments were all based upon facts, and are the more entitled to credit as they proceeded from practical men, who had themselves experienced either the benefits or the disadvantages of the various systems of Dutch policy. They may therefore be supposed to contain a valuable lesson for all trading communities, and particularly for the prosperous Americans. I shall here repeat their statements, in order to apply them to the history of commerce in the United States.

The causes which favored the trade of Holland are divided into three classes, viz. the natural and physical, the moral and political, and the adventitious and external.

,, I. The natural and physical causes are the advantages of the situation of the country, on the sea and at the mouth of considerable rivers; its situation between the northern and southern parts, which, by being in a manner the centre of all Europe, made the republic become the general market, where the merchants on both sides used to bring their superfluous commodities, in order to barter and exchange the same for other goods they wanted.

,, Nor have the barrenness of the country, and the necessities of the natives arising from that cause, less contributed to set them upon exerting all their application, industry, and utmost stretch of genius, to fetch from foreign countries what they stand in need of in their own, and support themselves by trade.

"The abundance of fish in the neighboring seas put them in a condition not only to supply their own occasions, but, with the overplus, to carry on a trade with foreigners, and out of the produce of the fishery to find an equivalent for what they wanted, through the sterility and narrow boundaries and extent of their own country.

"II. Among the moral and political causes are to be placed the unalterable maxim and fundamental law relating to the free exercise of different religions; and always to consider this toleration and connivance as the most effectual means to draw foreigners from adjacent countries to settle and reside here, and so become instrumental to the peopling of these provinces.

"The constant policy of the republic to make this country a perpetual, safe and secure asylum for all persecuted and oppressed strangers,—no alliance, no treaty, no regard for, or solicitation of any potentate whatever, has, at any time, been able to weaken or destroy this law, or make the state recede from protecting those who fled to it for their own security and self-preservation.

"Throughout the whole course of all the persecutions and oppressions that have occurred in other countries, the steady adherence of the republic to this fundamental law, has been the cause that many people have not only fled hither for refuge with their whole stock in ready cash, and their most valuable effects, but have also settled and established many trades, fabrics, manufactories, arts, and sciences, in this country, notwithstanding the first materials for the said fabrics and manufactories were almost wholly wanting in it, and not to be procured but at a great expense from foreign parts.

"The constitution of our form of government, and the liberty thus accruing to the citizen, are further reasons to which the growth of trade, and its establishment in the republic may fairly be ascribed; and all her policy and laws are put upon such an equitable footing, that neither life, estates, or dignities depend upon the caprice or arbitrary power of any single individual; nor is there any room for any person, who, by care, frugality, and diligence, has once acquired an affluent fortune or estate, to fear a deprivation of them by any act of violence, oppression or injustice.

"The administration of justice in the country has, in like manner, always been clear and impartial, and without distinction of superior and inferior rank—whether the parties have been rich or poor, or were this a foreigner and that a native; and it were greatly to be wished we could at this day boast of such impartial quickness and despatch in all our legal processes, considering how great an influence it has on trade.

"To sum up all—amongst the moral and political causes of the former flourishing state of trade, may be, likewise,' placed the wisdom and prudence of the administration; the intrepid firmness of the councils; the faithfulness with which treaties and engagements were wont to be fulfilled and ratified; and particularly the care and caution practised to preserve tranquillity and peace, and to decline, instead of entering on a scene of war, merely to gratify the ambitious views of gaining fruitless or imaginary conquests.

"By these moral and political maxims were the glory and reputation of the republic so far spread, and foreigners animated to place so great a confidence in the steady determination of a state so wisely and prudently conducted, that a concourse of them stocked this country with an augmentation of inhabitants and useful hands, whereby its trade and opulence were from time to time increased.

"III. Amongst the adventitious and external causes of the rise and flourishing state of our trade may be reckoned,—

"That at the time when the best and wisest maxims were adopted in the republic as the means of making trade flourish, they were neglected in almost all other countries; and any one reading the history of those times, may easily discover that the persecution, on account of religion throughout Spain, Brabant, Flanders, and many other states and kingdoms, have powerfully promoted the establishment of commerce in the republic.

"To this happy result, and the settling of manfacturers in our country, the long continuance of the civil wars in France, which were afterwards carried on in Germany, England, and divers other parts, have also very much contributed.

"It must be added, in the last place, that during our

most burdensome and heavy wars with Spain and Portugal, (however ruinous that period was for commerce, otherwise) these powers had both neglected their navy ; whilst the navy of the republic, by a conduct directly the reverse, was at the same time formidable, and in a capacity not only to protect the trade of its own subjects, but to annoy and crush that of their enemies in all quarters."

Every word of section 1st and 2d is directly applicable to the history of the United States; and a large portion of the adventitious causes which protected and favored the commerce of Holland have equally found a parallel in the progress of trade in America. The central position of Holland with regard to Europe, is but the counterpart to the superior situation of the United States with regard to the rest of the American continent and the West Indies. The United States have become the mart of the whole South American and Mexican produce, while the city of New York has become the centre of the bullion trade in the world. They are, besides, the principal market for European manufactures, and export them again, or their own, to all other parts of the globe.

The barrenness of the soil, which is stated as one of the causes which prompted the Dutch to industry and application, applies, it is true, but to a small portion of the United States, comprising a part of New England ; but then the New Englanders, as I have said before were the first merchants of America, and the rest of the inhabitants were, from the newness of their settlements, incapable of availing themselves of the advantages of the soil, and, with regard to manufactures, entirely dependent on Europe. The fisheries, therefore, were early resorted to as a means of support, and are yet a rich source of national wealth to the Americans. They have carried this branch of industry further than any other nation, and there are whole towns and districts in the United States employed by the whale fisheries alone.

The moral and political causes which favored the growth of Dutch commerce are still more coinciding with those which operated in favor of the United States. The religious freedom and tolerance of America have been the cause of the settlement of whole states, as was, for instance, the case with the quakers in Pennsylvania, and the establishments of the puritans in New England. They were the immediate motive of emigration to America of thousands of Europeans from England, as well as the continent, and, more than any other, instrumental in peopling the country. In like manner have the United States offered " a safe, secure, and perpetual asylum " for all persecuted and oppressed strangers, and have, in this manner, added to their population, capital, manufactures, commerce, and arts and sciences. Nor has the constitution of the United States been surpassed by any political instrument, in the degree of liberty and protection which it affords to the lives and properties of citizens. It gives equal rights to the rich and the poor, and administers justice independent of rank, titles or hereditary distinctions. The good faith which the Americans have kept with all nations, their keeping aloof from European politics, and the care and caution with which they have always endeavored to preserve peace, whenever it could be done without injury to their national honor, have made European capitalists willing to entrust money and property to the rectitude and enterprise of Americans; and at this moment an investment of capital in the United States is considered as safe, or safer, than any European investment which can be made.

With regard to the adventitious causes which have increased the commercial prosperity of the United States, it may equally be asserted that the erroneous course of legislation in other countries has acted as a premium on the ingenuity of the American merchants. The monopolies of the English and Dutch East India companies created the India and China trade of the United States; and though the late system of free bottomry must necessarily interfere with its further progress, it is no longer able to crush it. The Americans have become experienced and skilful in the trade; they have enriched themselves by its profits, and have created the capital by which to carry it on. They have procured themselves customers in every part of the world; and it will require a long and tedious opposition to drive them from the vantage-ground they have assumed.

If the civil wars in France, Germany and England contributed largely to the mercantile greatness of Holland, those of the French revolution gave the Americans almost a monopoly, and made them the carriers of all Europe. But if this was a fortunate circumstance, which gave them an opportunity of becoming skilled in navigation and commerce, they have improved it to the utmost extent of their power ; and, by a system of unremitting industry and perseverance, have, since the establishment of peace, *retained* most of the advantages for which they are indebted to the war. This is the point of culmination of the whole history of American commerce, and here the history of Holland and the United States are at issue.

After the universal peace of 1815 all nations were at liberty to pursue trade, and increase their mercantile navies as it suited their genius and circumstances. The competition of England and France, which proved so injurious to Dutch commerce, after the peace of Aix la Chapelle, now threatened to annihilate the American. The United States possessed no colonies either in the East or West Indies; they had less capital than any of the principal mercantile nations ; they were at a greater distance from the principal European marts, and they had to pay higher wages to their seamen. But, notwithstanding all these difficulties, the American shipping has since that period increased even more rapidly than before, and their ships are now generally preferred to those of all other nations.

Two principal causes were assigned by the Dutch merchants for the serious decline of their trade : enormous taxation, and the competition of France and England. The former induced the merchants of other countries to export their superfluities in their own ships, to the countries where they were needed, and to barter them for other commodities, which they equally brought home in their own bottoms. By this means they avoided being taxed by the republic ; and the latter lost its carrying trade, and ceased to be the mark of Europe.

The immense internal resources of the United States, and the principle of rigid economy introduced into every branch of their government enable them to avoid a similar calamity. The American commerce is as free from direct taxation as it is from monopolies; and these are, probably, the principal reasons of its uninterrupted progress, notwithstanding the increased competition of all Europe. The extortions and barbarities of the Dutch East India Company, its small capital, which did not exceed 6,500,000 florins, or about 541,700*l.* sterling, and with which they monopolized a trade which might have employed millions of the sums the Dutch were then obliged to lend to other countries for want of some better investment, and the infamous means by which they absorbed and diminished the spice-trade in the East Indies, were all instrumental in checking the progress of their trade, and were, in effect, a premium on the industry of other nations.

The United States, on the contrary, laid it down as a maxim that trade, in order to prosper, must be free, and, therefore, granted the same privileges not only to all native citizens, without distinction, but also to all foreigners who chose to settle, reside or trade, in any American city. By this means no particular kind of trade is made to absorb an undue portion of the capital of the nation, or is embraced and cultivated to the detriment and neglect of other branches; and foreigners, from all parts of the world, establishing themselves permanently in the United States, make them, in a measure, the central station of their commerce.

But the progress of commerce in the United States gives rise to yet another consideration, which, at this moment, is of universal interest. The question may arise whether the trade of America is increased or diminished by the want of colonies in the East and West Indies; and whether such colonies, independent of the political advantages which they afford to the different nations of Europe, actually increase the profits of their merchants. Under the former system of trade, colonies unquestionably augmented the commercial prosperity of a nation. They were, in fact, considered as an investment of property in order to realise a greater per-cent-age on capital. Each nation guarding jealously the produce of its own colonies, with a view to establish a monopoly, success in trade, was, of course, in a great measure dependent on the possession of the most important maritime and commercial stations; and, accordingly, we have seen the nations of Europe at

22

war with each other for the possession of colonies in the
East and West Indies.

But the commerce of the world has since undergone
an important change. The principle of free trade succeeds rapidly to that of monopoly. The colonies themselves have risen into importance; and their trade, instead of being confined to the mother country, is open
to the competition of foreigners. They have attained a
political consequence, and their interests and commerce
require a different policy from that which led to their establishment. Europe is no longer the only consumer of
Indian commodities; a large portion of them being used
in the United States and other parts of America, and
much also being bartered for the produce of other colonies, or consumed at home. In proportion as the colonies
become settled, a portion of the national wealth becomes
permanently transferred to them, and is employed in enriching *them* instead of the mother country. The money
invested in plantations proves a drain on the capital of
Europe; and the interest of that money is again chiefly
invested in the colonies.* Neither does the traffic in their
produce benefit exclusively, the merchants of the mother
country; because other nations being at liberty to trade
with the colonies on nearly the same terms, the planters
naturally give the preference to those customers from
whom they may, in return, receive those commodities at
the cheapest rate, which they themselves stand most in
need of. By this means they have, to a certain extent, become commercially independent, and pursue now themselves the trade, and realise the profits on it, for the exclusive advantage of which the nations of Europe were
induced to establish them. Their interests are no longer
identified with those of the mother country, and their
riches are no longer a part of the national wealth. Mean-
while the expenses of their governments increase with
the extent of cultivated territory and the political consideration to which they become entitled by the number
and possessions of their inhabitants. The mother country,

---

* It must be observed, that these remarks apply principally to those
colonies where the English have formed permanent settlements, and
which have attained a powerful political consequence by the establishment of provincial assemblies.

which bears a great part of these expenses, is obliged to
concede to them every year new rights and privileges
which render them still more independent, and give
greater liberty to their commerce. Thus it may be said
that in proportion as the colonies increase, the profits of
the mother country diminish; they become every year
more expensive to the government, and a direct tax on
the country which gave them birth; making but inadequate and indirect returns by the facilities which they
afford to its commerce, and imposing a heavy duty on
many articles of European commerce, which must act as
a premium on the trade of America.

The Americans have no drawbacks, whether originating in colonies or otherwise, on their commerce. They
have not to expend large sums to favor a particular
branch of trade, and thereby tax all the rest; they have
not to create artificial interests which force a portion of
the national wealth into an unnatural channel, or alienate
it from home; and they never have any considerable
portion of their capital invested, without bearing them
interest. The profits realised in trade return directly
home to their country, and there beget new wealth.
America has no fixed possessions out of the United States,
and has no other interests to protect than her own. Her
merchants need not pursue any particular branch of
trade longer than it is profitable, or yields greater returns
than they can hope to realise from any other kind of
industry. The American trade, therefore, is more free
than that of any other nation; for it leaves the articles of
commerce, the place of purchase, and the best mart of
their sale entirely at the option of the dealers. It gives
them the greatest latitude of speculation, and the largest
field for enterprise. It is connected with the smallest
taxation to the merchants and the community at large,
and enables them to become *general dealers*, without
being obliged to become *store-keepers*, in any particular
part of the world. The expenses of trade are thus reduced, and American merchants successfully compete
with those of Europe, notwithstanding their apparently
small profits, and the *seeming* disadvantage of their
position.

That the internal resources of America have most

powerfully contributed to extend the commerce of the United States, no one can reasonably deny; but the policy of the country, its laws and political institutions, and the peculiar mercantile genius of the inhabitants, have done the rest. I do not believe that any other nation, placed under similar circumstances, would have developed the same commercial talent, and none could have succeeded without the political freedom of America.

For shopkeeping, the Americans seem to have less talent than any people in Europe. They lack the patience which is necessary for retail trade, and exhibit evidently less taste in the display of their goods, than either the French or the English. The shops in New York and other large cities are well stored with every description of merchandise from India and Europe; but the economical habits of the people do not allow them to expend any considerable sums in decorating their premises. In this they follow the inclination of their customers, who do not like to pay for the outfit, but value merchandise only according to its intrinsic worth and usefulness.

Good articles, at a cheap rate, command the greatest patronage; and no fashionable preference being generally established in favor of one or the other shop or its locality, the retailers follow the example of the merchants, and avoid every unnecessary expense which would tax their trade and reduce their profits. Neither do they seem to have any particular regard for the *quality* of their customers; but endeavor to increase their number, which can only be done by reasonable prices adapted to the means of the multitude.

The American shopkeeper depends on the public at large, and has, therefore, no inducement to gratify the fancy of particular classes by an attempt at expensive refinements. He prefers a trade in the commonest articles, to the dealing in costly fashions; and, by a peculiar mercantile instinct, is better satisfied with small profits on large sales, than with large profits on small ones. The Americans, of all nations in the world, understand least how to buy and sell things on a small scale, and are least in the habit of increasing their estates by the proportional smallness of their expenditure. I do not mean to say that they are an extravagant people, or fond of the higher elegancies and luxuries of life; but a certain degree of comfort, and even affluence, is shared by all classes of society, and is alike indispensable to all.

Of all nations in Europe, the French seem to be best adapted to the business of retail trade. They understand the whole art of buying things at five *sous*, and selling them again at six, without growing weary and impatient. They are a people who can enjoy life in every form and variety; and are generally more remarkable for excelling in the minutiæ of a particular department, than for the readiness with which they endeavor to enlarge it. They are frugal and industrious by nature, and, perhaps, as happy in their limited sphere, as the most enterprising nation in the world, and more certain of moderate success. They know best how to proportion their expenses to their income. They always manage to save something, be it ever so little; but they are less active and enterprising than either the English or Americans. Most of the small shopkeepers in Paris have their principal stock in trade at the window; but then there is taste in its arrangement, and ingenuity in its display. If they are asked for an article, they will enter upon an exposition of its qualities with a minuteness of detail, and a prodigality of reasoning, which will satisfy the inquirer at once that they are at home in their department, and not anxious to quit the premises.

To a French shopkeeper, his *boutique* is the universe. He there commences and finishes his observations; and, though sometimes subject to political aberrations, returns to it willingly, as the principal scene of his usefulness. An American, and especially a New Englander, has in his very constitution more or less of the spirit of a merchant. He cannot with good grace stoop to the retailing of ribbons and pins; and if, from a want of funds or credit, he is obliged to resort to so humble a beginning, he is eagerly panting for an extension of business, and will seize upon the first opportunity to disengage himself from so disagreeable a task.

In the large Atlantic cities of the United States, the retailers of goods follow the same routine as the merchants. They receive and give extensive credit, employ a book-keeper and a number of clerks, and, though there

22*

are generally more than one partner in a firm, manage to live and maintain their families in a style to which the same classes in Europe are almost entire strangers. Many of them are themselves importers, or supply the retailers in the country; and there is, perhaps, not one who would not willingly risk half his fortune to increase his facilities of trade. They are seldom content with their present situation, which they are always ready to improve by circumstances, and are only by great misfortunes and losses debarred from becoming respectable merchants.

Rousseau, with more irony than flattery to either sex, commended the business of shopkeeping to women; and it must be allowed that the women of France, at least, are most remarkably fit for that purpose. Whether he intended to increase the profits in trade by the petty manœuvres of which he judged females alone capable, or whether he wished to preserve the minds of men from a task which he thought humiliating and destructive to the higher powers, I know not; but certainly his advice has been followed in France, and the general morality of the people is far from being improved by it. The American shopkeeper's wife and daughters are never seen at the scene of business, for which they are neither intended nor qualified; and, being unable to assist him in trade, are more happily employed in preserving the purity and sanctity of his fire-side. They give him that which he would otherwise be obliged to resign—a home in the bosom of his family.

Trade, in America, does not consist in the mechanical purchase and sale of goods. The prices of articles are not so stable as in Europe, and depend in a far higher degree on the state of the money-market at home and abroad, and on the political prospects of the country. These it is not in the power of ordinary minds at all times justly to estimate; and it is therefore only the well-informed and the shrewd, who can reasonably hope to succeed. Fortunes are sometimes made by unexpected turns of good luck; but in the far greater number of instances, they are the result of well-planned and executed speculations; and none of them are preserved without prudence and good sense. In every other country the number of inherited fortunes is greater than that of the acquired ones; in America the case is entirely the reverse, most of them being the result of severe application to business, accompanied by sobriety and frugality of habits.

It is a circumstance worthy of observation that almost all the enterprising merchants of New York, Boston, and the other seaports, sprung from nothing, and that in nearly all instances, good sense and industry have gone further than mere capital, with inferior qualifications for business. It would be difficult to explain so general a phenomenon *merely* by the general prosperity of the country, the fertility of its soil, and the millions of acres of land yet left to be explored by the people. The fortunes of farmers and mechanics might be accounted for in this manner; because in these occupations it is personal labor chiefly which insures ultimate success. But in the case of the merchants, I would more willingly ascribe the source of prosperity, first, to the increased facilities of credit, and secondly, to the willingness of the rich capitalists to invest their money in trade. A young beginner with talents finds always a partner with money, —in many instances a silent one,—while the son of a rich man either studies a profession, or receives less of that practical education which alone can fit him for business.

There is, probably, no other country in which credit is so purely personal as in the United States. In England it is already more so than in France ; but in the rest of Europe it is chiefly based on property, and consequently with few individual exceptions, beyond the grasp of mere intelligence, honesty, and industry. In this manner, the investments of money are, assuredly, more secure; but the floating capital always less than the real amount of property, and active commerce, whose soul is credit, almost entirely out of the question. The money lent on real estate or any other security is no *bonus* paid to the personal qualifications and probity of the borrower, and cannot, properly, be said to constitue a trust. It does not actually *increase* his means ; for he obtains it only as an advance on something of still greater value. It may be of great advantage to him at the moment, because it enables him to dispose of, and employ, a certain part of the value of his estate without being compelled to renounce its possession ; but the transaction is as far removed from the operation of credit, as the accommodation of a pawn-broker who lends on pledges.

It is with the utmost difficulty that a poor German or a Frenchman succeeds in the acquisition of property : his progress is slow and tedious, and his facilities of credit never much in advance of his actual stock in trade. In America the case is different. Men there are trusted in proportion to their reputation for honesty and adaptation to business. Industry, perseverance, acquaintance with the market, enterprise—in short, every moral qualification of a merchant increases his credit as much as the actual amount of his property. The facilities of a beginner are even greater than those of a person established for some time, unless the latter have given evidence of his superior fitness for business. An American is more willing to trust a young man who has to *establish* a reputation by faithfully discharging his engagements, than one whose fortune is made, and who, on that account, is less dependent on the opinion of others. "A young man," he says, " is naturally more enterprising; he has a much longer career to run, and will, therefore, do more to win *golden opinions* from his friends, than one who has advanced to old age, and can neither atone for or correct the follies of his youth."

Neither are American capitalists, as I have said before, contented with so small a per-centage on their money as Europeans ; but rather venture a certain portion of their fortunes, in order to realise a greater income ; and are, consequently, always ready to trust and employ those who possess more mind than capital, or to go into partnership with them. Thus the amount of floating capital in the United States is not merely based on the gross value of real and personal estate, but also on the moral qualifications of the merchants, and the resources of the country which *it is the genius of the people* to develope. The figures on 'change denote not merely money and merchandise ; but represent also the intelligence, enterprise, economy and probity of the people : they are the index to the mind as well as to the property of the merchants.

The influence which this method of transacting business must exercise on the extension of commerce cannot, for one moment, be doubtful. The advantages arising from it, to the country at large, are incalculable. It enables merchants to extend their transactions to sums vastly superior to their positive means; holds out facilities of trade to persons who would otherwise be entirely dispossessed of them, and has a decided tendency to bring foreign capital into the market. Where the greatest profits are realised, and the greatest amount of business transacted, to that place will capital emigrate — be it India or China, England or the United States. Millions are thus circulating in many an American town, which would otherwise be confined to a small and limited trade, and thousands of people, who are now engaged in commerce, and employed in enriching themselves and the country, would be obliged to resort to manual labor, to obtain for themselves a bare subsistence. But it is not the country where the greatest capital is owned, but, on the contrary, that in which the greatest amount of it circulates, which must eventually become rich and powerful; and, with the present prospects of America, no limit can be assigned to her future prosperity.

The advantages of the American system of credit are not only felt in the operation of commerce; they have also a strong *moral* influence on the people, and it is principally this which commands our serious attention.

Where credit is solely based on property, there it must naturally stifle the spirit of enterprise, or confine it to a small class. A large number of those who possess fortunes will only be intent on the most sordid means of increasing it, and every additional pound which they amass is a fresh obstacle to the progress of a poor beginner. Meanness and avarice must take the place of a well-directed extensive commerce, and petty *savings* and usury be substituted for *activity* and liberal industry. That such a process is humiliating to the mind, and entirely incompatible with that generosity of feeling which we associate with the character of a gentleman, will hardly be disputed; and it is therefore not surprising that in those countries the position and employment of a merchant should be looked upon as debasing the nobler faculties.

In Germany, with the exception of three or four commercial cities, which by the Confederation are allowed to have their own government, the merchants hold a very inferior rank in society ; and there is no officer, civil or military, or no man of liberal education, in general, who would not be considered to confer a favor by his intercourse with any one connected with trade. Not so in America. The business of a merchant, in the United States, is rather calculated to expand and liberalise his mind than to contract and destroy it. His firm represents not only his property, but also the intelligence, industry, and enterprise of which he is possessed. His credit increases not only with his capital ; but is founded also on his personal qualifications, and the innate or acquired superiority of his intellect. He can supply the deficiency of capital by a more enlarged sphere of knowledge and experience, and is thus, by his moral advantages, raised to an equality with the more wealthy and prosperous. The rich are obliged to employ the talents of the poor in order to increase their wealth ; and the latter may, in turn, hope to become opulent and independent. Commerce, in this manner, is not monopolized by a few wealthy families, but becomes the national occupation of the whole people, in which all, who have talent and industry, have an equal chance of success.

An American merchant obtains and gives more credit than an European, and has, therefore, a wider range of speculation and action before him, than one possessed of the same capital in any other country. His mind becomes enlarged with the development of the immense national resources which form the basis and element of his enterprise. One half of the internal improvements of the country would yet be *in embryo*, or not even thought of, were it not for the liberality of the merchants and capitalists who have furnished the money, or the talents and industry of beginners who were willing to take charge of the enterprise. Without the system of personal credit, neither commerce, nor manufactures, nor even agriculture would have advanced with the same rapidity of progress ; and fertile districts, animated by the arts of civilization, and provided with schools and seminaries of learning, would yet be the abode of the deer, and the haunt of the American Indian.

The extensive and diversified commerce of the United States, the peculiar manner of transacting business, and the great number of persons who participate in it, cause an incessant contact of all classes of society, which cannot but be beneficial to all, but particularly advantageous to the merchant. He is made more intimately acquainted with the wants, means, and feelings of the mechanic, the manufacturer, the agriculturist, the politician, and the professional man—all of whom have a more direct influence on his prosperity, and are directiy or indirectly interested in his success. His information extends with his business, and he becomes, from necessity, a shrewd observer and judge of human actions and motives. He is continually watching the current of events, the changes of public opinion, and the different directions of industry; for if he fail to profit by them before they are generally known, he is sure to be distanced by his numerous and more vigilant competitors.

Again, credit being personal, and business done to a much larger amount than is covered by property, it is not sufficient for him to know the fortunes and present means of those whom in the course of his ordinary transactions he is obliged to trust: he must be able to judge of their honesty, their talent for business, and the motives which they may have for fulfilling their engagements. He is thus compelled to study characters, while his own is made the subject of the severest scrutiny; and becomes as skilful in discovering the personal qualifications of others, as he is solicitous to banish from his own conduct all that can give rise to premature judgments or suspicions. This is the reason why the American merchants enjoy such a high reputation for shrewdness and sagacity; and why they are universally allowed to be excellent judges of men and their actions. Mr. Hamilton observed a similar feature, but did not trace it to its right source.[*]

* " Of whatever solecism of deportment they are themselves guilty," says Mr. Hamilton, " The Americans are admirable, and perhaps not very lenient judges of manners in others. * * * With them vulgar audacity will not pass for polished ease, nor will fashionable exterior be received for more than it is worth. I know of no country where an impostor would have a more difficult game to play in the prosecution of his craft, and should consider him an accomplished deceiver were he able to escape detection amid observation so vigilant and acute."

To the advantages of their position in society, the American merchants join, for the most part, those of a superior education, and there are many of them, especially in the city of Boston, who have completed a college-course. To this we must add the information acquired by travelling at home and abroad, and their consequent freedom from a variety of prejudices inseparable from men who have not had an opportunity of observing and judging for themselves. Many of them have taken an active part in politics; and, although they were not always so successful as in trade, have at least exhibited a penetration and comprehensiveness of mind which are seldom surpassed by professional legislators. There are merchants in the Senate and in the House of Representatives of the United States, and the same may be observed in the Senate and House of Representatives in each individual state. To sum up the whole, the American merchants, as a body, are a well-bred, intelligent and liberal-minded set of men, and in point of sagacity, judgment, and general information, inferior to no class of society either in America or Europe.

One serious objection which has been made against the American system of credit, is the great number of failures which are its necessary consequence. Now, granted that there occur more failures in the United States than in any country of the same population in Europe, it does not follow that, considering the amount of business, and the number of those who engage in it, there is more injury sustained from bankruptcies than either in France or England; on the contrary, it is more than probable that the profits, realised in any kind of trade, bear a better proportion to the losses sustained by insolvent debtors than in any other country.

To judge correctly of the frequency of failures in America, we must not only consider the vastness of speculation based on a comparatively small capital, but also the fact that in the United States there exists as yet no bankrupt law to exclude persons of whatever employment

This panegyric of American sagacity the learned author intended only for their judgment of manners; but a little further investigation would have convinced him that it has a more solid foundation, and applies equally to the moral and intellectual qualifications of men.

or trade of the advantages enjoyed by merchants. Mercantile speculations are not confined to any one class; the tradesman, the mechanic, the agriculturist, the lawyer, the physician, and even the schoolmaster have their share in them; and, considering the liabilities of all these persons, we shall find the number of those who actually avail themselves of the benefit of the " act for insolvent debtors," not only small, but incapable of affecting the community. If the facilities of credit were less, the number of failures would, undoubtedly, be less also ; but in the same ratio would also diminish the facilities of trade, and the profits arising from an active and liberal commerce. The nation would be deprived of one of its principal sources of prosperity, and thousands of enterprising individuals prevented from participating in an extensive business. Those who are against the credit system of the United States, ought for the same reason to oppose navigation, on account of the frequency of shipwrecks.

The American banks are all banks of issue, discount and deposite, and, in the large Atlantic cities, extremely well managed. I believe there are but very few instances known in which any of them have failed in Boston, and those of New York and Philadelphia enjoy equally the highest credit. Their number, however, is prodigious, which is, perhaps, one of the principal reasons why they are less secure than those of Europe. The system of credit in the United States renders them, of course, liable to frequent losses ; but they are, nevertheless, one of the principal engines in the rapid improvements of the country, and increase the facilities of intercourse and business.

All that can be said in their favor or against them, refers to the American credit system, of which the banks are but the auxiliaries, and is, consequently, already implied in what I have said on that subject. To avoid repetition, therefore, I shall content myself with stating, in the following table, the amount of banking capital and bills in circulation, in each state ; from which the reader may form an estimate as to the extent to which this principle is applied in practice. The table refers to the commencement of the year 1834, and does not include

23

the United States Bank with a capital of 35,000,000 of
dollars, and its numerous branches. Nor is it necessary
to add that since that period numerous other banking
institutions have sprung up, and are daily rising into existence, which, of course, must render all such statements incomplete. A table of this kind can only serve to
exhibit the *ratio* which exists between capital and credit,
and perhaps not even that with mathematical precision.

State.	No. of Banks.	Capital.	Bills circulated.
		Dollars.	*Dollars.*
Maine - -	14	2,727,000	1,303,671
N. Hampshire	24	2,454,308	1,063,145
Vermont -	17	911,980	1,234,178
Massachus'tts	102	28,236,250	7,889,110
Rhode Island	51	7,438,848	1,264,394
Connecticut	21	5,708,015	2,557,227
New York -	79	27,846,460	15,471,328
New Jersey	22	6,375,000	5,840,000
Pennsylvania	41	17,084,444	10,366,232
Delaware -	4	2,000,000	504,000
Maryland -	22	9,270,091	2,441,698
Virginia -	4	5,694,500	5,598,392
N. Carolina	3	1,824,725	981,114
S. Carolina	7	3,156,318	3,724,442
Georgia -	13	6,534,691	3,055,003
Alabama -	5	4,308,207	2,054,471
Mississippi	2	3,666,805	2,100,426
Louisiana	12	23,664,755	4,793,730
Tennessee	2	2,242,827	2,110,880
Kentucky	3	1,875,418	838,091
Ohio - -	20	5,986,625	1,945,917
Indiana -	1	150,000	75,000
Illinois - -	1	200,000	100,000
Missouri * -	—	—	—
District of } Columbia }	8	3,355,305	1,109,389
Florida - -	6	1,000,000	600,000
Michigan -	3	2,250,000	428,000
Arkansas † -	—	—	—
Sum total	487	175,962,572	79,449,838

* There was no bank in that state, except a branch of the United
States Bank.

† There was no bank in that territory, except a branch of the bank
of Maryland, which failed in March, 1834.

Most of the southern banks have a number of branches which are included in the amount of capital given above. The bills of the United States Bank circulating in 1835 amounted to twenty-two millions of dollars, and the specie in its vaults to 13,912,577 dollars 47 cents. There were twenty-nine banks selected for the deposits of the government with a capital of 34,847,203 dollars, which issued bills to the amount of 15,521,997 dollars.

The bank capitals in the different states, for the year 1834-5, compiled *from official returns*, as stated in Bicknell's "Philadelphia Counterfeit Detector," were as follows.

Maine	-	-	-	-	Dols. 2,724,000
New Hampshire		-	-	-	2,455,000
Vermont	-	-	-	-	911,000
Massachusetts	-	-	-	-	29,409,650
Rhode Island	-	-	-	-	7,438,848
Connecticut	-	-	-	-	5,708,015
New York	-	-	-	-	31,781,460
New Jersey	-	-	-	-	6,375,500
Pennsylvania	-	-	-	-	17,084,444
Delaware	-	-	-	-	2,000,000
Maryland	-	-	-	-	9,270,091
Virginia	-	-	-	-	5,694,500
North Carolina	-	-	-	-	3,324,725
South Carolina	-	-	-	-	7,331,318
Georgia	-	-	-	-	8,034,691
Alabama	-	-	-	-	4,308,207
Mississippi	-	-	-	-	11,000,000
Louisiana	-	-	-	-	33,664,755
Tennessee	-	-	-	-	5,242,827
Kentucky	-	-	-	-	10,000,000
Ohio	-	-	-	-	5,086,125
Indiana	-	-	-	-	1,500,000
Illinois	-	-	-	-	1,700,000
District of Columbia	-	-	-	3,355,305
Florida Territory	-	-	-	1,000,000
Michigan Territory	-	-	-	2,250,000

Total - 219,250,549 dols.

From 1811 *till* 1830, 165 banks are known to have failed, with an aggregate capital of 24,212,339 dollars. The number of failures, therefore, averaged between eight and nine *per annum*, which is not yet *one* for *every two* states of the Union, and consequently but a small drawback on the extensive benefits of the system.

After what I have said of American commerce and merchants, it will perhaps be not unwelcome to some of my readers, to have some numerical details about the imports and exports of the United States. The following are taken from official reports ; and it will be perceived from them that the exports in 1834 surpassed those of 1830 by 7,174,654 dollars; and that in the year following (1835) they increased by further 23,312,811 dollars, making in all a total augmentation of 30,487,465 dollars in five years.

		Dollars.
The exports of 1830 (the year ending September 30th) amounted to		73,849,508

		Dollars.
Of which there were—		
Domestic produce	- -	59,462,029
Foreign ditto	- -	14,387,479
Total	- - -	73,849,508

Those of 1834 were	- - - -	81,024,162
Of which—		
The sea yielded	- - -	2,071,493
The forest,	- - - -	4,457,997
Vegetable food,	- - -	10,884,052
Tobacco,	- - - -	6,595,305
Cotton,	- - - -	49,448,402
Other agricultural products,		453,028
Manufactures,	- - -	5,998,012
And other articles not } enumerated,	-	1,115,873
Total	- -	81,024,162

		Dollars.
Finally, the exports of 1835 to	- -	104,336,973

		Dollars.
Of which there were—		
Domestic produce	- -	81,024,162
Foreign ditto	- -	23,312,811
Total	- -	104,336,973

The imports in 1835 were   - -   126,521,332
Those of 1830   - - - -   70,876,920

Increase in five years   -   55,644,412

The amount of imports and exports in American vessels is to that in foreign vessels as six to one nearly. (In the year 1830 it was 51 : 8, or $6\frac{1}{6}$: 1.; and in 1834 as 175 : 32, or $5\frac{15}{32}$: 1.)

It will also be perceived from those statements that while in 1830 the exports surpassed the imports by 2,972,588 dollars, the balance of trade has, in 1835, been turned against America. This, however, was owing to particular circumstances connected with the history of the United States Bank, and the great depression of foreign exchange, which must always act as a premium on the importation of foreign goods.

To form an idea of the increasing navigation of the United States, we need only reflect on the amount of tonnage which at the beginning of the year 1833 was registered in the principal seaports and districts as follows :

New York, (State of New York)   -   298,832
Boston, (Massachusetts)   - -   171,045
Philadelphia, (Pennsylvania) - -   77,103
New Bedford, (Massachusetts)   -   70,550
New Orleans, (Louisana)   - -   61,171
Portland, (Maine)   - - -   47,942
Baltimore, (Maryland)   - -   47,129
Bath, (Maine)   - - -   33,480
Salem, (Massachusetts) - -   30,293
Nantucket, (Massachusetts)   -   28,580
Barnstable, (Massachusetts)   -   28,153
Waldoborough, (Maine)   -   24,948
New London, (Connecticut) -   24,225
Penobscot, (Maine)   - -   22,115
Newburyport, (Massachusetts)   -   20,131
Providence, (Rhode Island)   -   19,136
Belfast, (Maine)   - - -   18,576
Plymouth, (Massachusetts)   -   17,669
Portsmouth, (New Hampshire) -   17,126
Norfolk, (Virginia)   - -   15,790

23*

Passamaquoddy, (Maine)	- -	13,370
Gloucester, (Massachusetts)	- -	13,266
Wilmington, (North Carolina)	-	13,265
Charlestown, (South Carolina)	-	13,244
Vienna, (Maryland)	- -	13,129
Bristol, (Rhode Island)	- -	12,879
Bridgetown, (New Jersey)	- -	12,690
Fairfield, (Connecticut)	-	10,892
Alexandria, (District of Columbia)	-	10,599
Pittsburgh, (Pennsylvania)	-	10,091

Total - - 1,197,419 Tons.

exclusive of the tonnage of steamboats. If we allow
since 1833 but an increase of ten per cent., (which I think
is small, considering the rapid progress of commerce and
manufactures,) we shall have the actual amount of tonnage in the thirty principal districts 1,317,160 tons; and,
considering the low rate at which ships are generally
registered in the United States, and the districts not enumerated in the above statements, I do not think that two
millions of tons would exceed the actual amount of American tonnage. This, for a country whose independence
has been acknowledged little more than half a century, is
certainly enormous, and a gigantic index to her future
mercantile importance.

The following TABLE will exhibit the NUMBER of
AMERICAN and FOREIGN VESSELS, with their TONNAGE,
which entered into each of the DISTRICTS of the UNITED
STATES during the Year ending on the 30th of Septem-
ber, 1835; also the TONNAGE of each DISTRICT on 31st
December, 1834.*

* We must, here, again remember, that the mercantile transactions
of that year offer no fair average of the active commerce of the United
States. (Compare the remarks, page 269 on the Imports of 1835.)

Into	American		Foreign		Total	
	No. of vessels	No. of Tons.	No. of vessels	No. of tons.	No. of vessels	No. of tons.
1. Passamaquoddy (Maine)	41	4,086	913	61,885	954	65,971
2. Machias do.	1	98	....	....	1	98
3. Frenchman's Bay do.	....	....	5	461	5	461
4. Penobscot - do.	17	2,985	1	48	18	3,033
5. Waldoborough do.	3	1,072	....	....	3	1,072
6. Wiscasset - do.	4	1,512	....	....	4	1,512
7. Bath - - do.	31	7,843	....	....	31	7,843
8. Portland - do.	139	28,878	23	2,095	162	30,973
9. Belfast - do.	12	1,770	2	163	14	1,933
10. Kennebunk - do.	4	739	....	....	4	739
11. Saco - - do.	2	272	....	....	2	272
12. Portsmouth (N. Hampshire)	25	6,445	2	119	27	6,564
13. Vermont (Vermont)	206	36,595	....	....	206	36,595
14. Newburyport (Mass.)	26	5,087	1	136	27	5,223
15. Gloucester do.	10	2,048	....	....	10	2,048
16. Salem - do.	72	10,877	....	....	72	10,877
17. Marblehead do.	8	1,198	....	....	72	10,877
18. Boston - do.	754	158,712	2	140	10	1,338
19. Plymouth - do.	10	2,143	404	35,708	1,158	194,420
20. Dighton - do.	34	6,891	1	72	11	2,215
21. New Bedford do.	99	26 573	8	1,235	42	8,126
22. Edgartown do.	86	17,958	2	165	101	26,738
23. Providence (Rhode Island)	52	10,296	5	554	91	18,512
24. Bristol - do.	24	4,782	10	1,022	62	11,318
25. Newport - do.	21	3,813	....	....	24	4,782
26. New London (Connecticut)	30	6,735	5	958	26	4,771
27. New Haven do.	59	9,796	2	258	32	6,993
28. Middletown do.	5	692	....	....	59	6,796
29. Fairfield - do.	5	766	4	310	9	1,002
30. New York (New York)	1528	374,602	....	....	5	766
31. Sag Harbor do.	18	5,317	48	91,063	2,008	465,665
32. Cape Vincent do.	588	111,295	....	....	18	5,317
33. Champlain do.	201	31,203	467	86,929	1,055	198,224
34. Oswegatchie do.	282	49,570	....	....	201	31,203
35. Sackets Harbor do.	167	33,575	349	44,195	631	93,765
36. Oswego - do.	248	27,364	....	....	167	33,575
37. Genessee - do.	46	9,724	293	61,873	541	89,237
38. Niagara - do.	69	17,850	141	19,721	187	29,445
39. Buffalo - do.	214	15,673	157	49,526	226	67,376
40. Newark (New Jersey)	3	621	66	4,268	280	19,941
41. Perth Amboy do.	1	118	1	127	4	748
42. Philadelphia (Pennsylvania)	348	68,177	....	....	1	118
43. Baltimore (Maryland)	265	47,901	68	10,816	416	78,993
44. Snow Hill do.	1	53	61	15,522	326	63,423
45. Georgetown (Dist. Columbia)	2	269	....	....	1	53
46. Alexandria do.	27	5,314	3	314	5	583
47. Norfolk (Virginia)	55	7,369	6	799	33	6,113
48. Richmond do.	12	2,888	77	11,839	132	19,208
49. Petersburg do.	12	4,617	1	329	13	3,217
50. Tappahannock do.	3	322	....	....	12	4,617
51. East River do.	1	81	....	....	3	322
52. Cherrystone do.	1	459	....	....	1	81
53. Wilmington (N. Carolina)	84	11,796	24	2,733	6	459
54. Newbern - do.	20	2,011	1	97	108	14,529
55. Camden - do.	30	2,608	....	....	21	2,108
56. Edentown - do.	2	187	....	....	30	2,608
57. Plymouth - do.	2	139	....	....	2	187
58. Washington - do.	23	2,277	5	266	2	139
59. Beaufort - do.	2	229	....	....	28	2,543
60. Ocracoke - do.	2	262	1	137	2	229
61. Charleston (S. Carolina)	115	22,466	127	30,938	3	399
62. Savannah (Georgia)	48	10,448	85	25,429	242	53,404
63. Brunswick do.	6	1,019	3	372	133	35,877
64. Key West (Florida)	159	6,000	4	830	9	1,391
65. Pensacola do.	10	1,428	....	....	163	6,830
66. Mobile (Alabama)	75	16,834	42	14,050	10	1,428
67. Mississippi (Louisiana)	518	97,680	316	58,690	117	30,884
68. Cuyahoga (Ohio)	19	1,061	75	3,757	834	156,370
69. Sandusky do.	2	70	9	744	94	4,818
70. Detroit (Michigan)	29	1,114	17	617	11	814
					46	1,731
Total	7,023	1,352,653	4,269	641,310	11,292	1,993,963

The FOREIGN TONNAGE, VESSELS and CREWS were distributed as follows.

Flag.	No of vessels enter'd	No. of tons.	CREWS.		No. of vessels clear'd	No. of tons
			Men.	Boys.		
British	3,682	529,922	32,575	1,101	3,650	523,417
French	65	14,457	775	13	57	14,354
Spanish	162	24,497	1,761	25	177	26,245
Hanseatic	95	28,218	1,304	12	98	28,421
Swedish	64	15,661	780	7	56	13,479
Danish	18	3,570	175	6	17	3,186
Dutch	17	3,112	162	2	12	2,148
Russian	1	250	12	- -	1	330
Prussian	5	1,272	59	- -	4	942
Austrian	9	3,125	154	- -	7	2,509
Portuguese	5	511	43	- -	7	917
Belgic	3	980	42	- -	3	979
Grecian	1	321	16	2	1	321
Tuscan	1	205	10	—	—	—
Sardinian	3	689	45	- -	2	414
Sicilian	5	1,078	65	2	7	1,228
Haytien	1	139	6	—	—	—
Mexican	123	11,057	1,177	- -	122	10,531
Central American	1	80	5	—	—	—
Brazilian	4	663	38	- -	5	845
Columbian	4	503	31	- -	3	402
Buenos Ayrian	-	- -	- -	- -	1	156
Total	4,269	641,310	39,235	1,170	4,230	630,824

The manufactures of the United States have kept equal pace with the extension of commerce. The states of Massachusetts, Pennsylvania, New York, and New Jersey have taken the lead ; but the same spirit of enterprise is manifesting itself in every quarter of the Union. America possesses all the requisites of a manufacturing country—water, coal, and a highly ingenious inventive population. Wages are higher, and coal and iron dearer than in England ; but the taxes are lower, living cheaper, and raw material, especially cotton, hemp, flax, alkalies for glass, hides and tanning matter, obtained at a less rate in the country. The water-power of the United States, moreover, exceeds that of all other countries in the world, and is a cheap substitute for steam ; and the increasing coal-pits in Pennsylvania and Virginia will soon yield fuel for warming buildings at nearly as cheap a rate as in England. Besides, the mineral resources of the country are scarcely known; and from the number of iron mines and coal-pits, which are already in successful operation, the conclusion is but natural that many more will be discovered, as the increasing scarcity of wood will direct the attention of the people to this source of national wealth.* Large coal mines have recently been discovered in Ohio and Kentucky; and the attempt to use anthracite coal on board of steamboats has already been made, and succeeded: but in proportion as American coal is capable of taking the place of the English, the Americans will become independent also in this respect of the mother country.

The progress of manufacture is most powerfully seconded by the inventive genius of the people. The daily improvements in machinery and the mechanic arts are

* " Copper is found from Ouisconsin to the falls of St. Anthony's, on the shores of Lake Superior, in such abundance and purity, that the Indians make hatchets and ornaments from it. The whole region of the upper Mississippi is mineral, abounding in lead and copper ore."— *Missouri Advocate.*

The American gold region was not known till 1824; but the subjoined table, from the " American Almanac and Repository of Useful Knowledge," which was compiled from official documents, will show the amount of gold obtained from it, from 1824 to 1834 inclusive.

Year.	Virginia.	North Carolina.	South Carolina.	Georgia.	Tennessee.	Alabama.	Total.
	Dols.	Dols.	Dols.	Dols.	Dols.	Dols.	Dols.
1824	- -	5,000	- -	- -	- -	- -	5,000
1825	- -	17,000	- -	- -	- -	- -	17,000
1826	- -	20,000	- -	- -	- -	- -	20,000
1827	- -	21,000	- -	- -	- -	- -	21,000
1828	- -	46,000	- -	- -	- -	- -	46,000
1829	2,500	134,000	2,500	- -	- -	- -	139,000
1830	24,000	204,000	26,000	212,000	- -	- -	466,000
1831	26,000	294,000	22,000	176,000	1,000	1,000	520,000
1832	34,000	458,000	45,000	140,000	1,000	- -	678,000
1833	104,000	475,000	66,000	216,000	7,000	- -	868,000
1834	62,000	380,000	38,000	415,000	3,000	- -	898,000
Total	252,500	2,054,000	199,500	1,159,000	12,000	1,000	3,679,000

equalled in no other country, and show the natural adaptation of the Americans to every thing based on the computation of numbers. In this consists the practical mathematical talent which every American possesses " by intuition," and which renders him, instinctively, a calculating merchant, an ingenious mechanic, an able navigator, and an inventive manufacturer. His mind is constantly occupied with some plan or enterprise; and, being naturally inclined to investigation, he discovers daily new means of creating and increasing capital, improving trade, and constructing machines to diminish the amount of manual labor. *The high price of labor is an additional premium on successful inventions*, and the facilities of navigation and water-power indicate to him sufficiently the proper direction of his efforts.

The opinion of those who maintain that the high wages in the United States must, for a long time yet, retard the progress of manufactures, is practically refuted by the number of flourishing establishments, which are constantly springing up in every part of the country; and, more especially, by the profits realised by their projectors, the number of hands which they furnish with employment, and the general prosperity of all who are directly or indirectly interested in their success.

That there was a time when the manufactures of America were in a critical state, is as well known in England as in America; but then they were in their infancy, without experience or knowledge of the business in which they had engaged, and from the large profits realised at the commencement of their operations, tempted to increase their activity to a degree which was disproportionate with the consumption. They consequently glutted the market, and having, at the same time, to compete with large importations from Europe, saw their profits at once diminished beyond the possibility of continuing the business. Many of them failed, and others were nearly reduced to the same situation. But there were, nevertheless, a considerable number of those who possessed sufficient capital to escape from the period of trial; and there are few who have not profited by the experience of former years, and become more prudent and cautious in their operations.

Another objection made to the progress of American manufactures, was the necessity of their being protected by a high and oppressive tariff, which was thought to operate so unequally and unjustly in the different states that, at one time, it threatened to sever the union. This tariff has since been modified; the protection offered by it to many articles of manufacture, has been diminished by more than one half; and what is the consequence?—an *increase* of production, and a general prosperity amongst manufacturers, at a period which proved the severest trial to every species of trade and commerce. American manufactures are no longer confined to the domestic market; they have found the way to South America, the East and West Indies, and even to China. Their progress is assisted by the increasing navigation of the United States, and by the liberal and enterprising spirit of the merchants. But there is a set of sceptics who will listen to nothing that is not proved mathematically; and to those no appeal can avail unless it be made in numbers. Numbers are universally allowed to contain the most positive argument; and I cannot hesitate, therefore, to submit to the unbelievers of whatever country, the subjoined statements taken from official documents placed before the Congress of the United States at the first session of the twenty-fourth Congress, March 4th, 1836, by Levi Woodbury, Esq., Secretary of the Treasury.

Table, showing the Exports of Cotton Manufactures of the United States to different parts of the world.

Years.	To S. America and Mexico.	To India and Africa.	To China.	To the West Indies.
	value in dols.	*value in dols.*	*value in dols.*	*value in dols.*
1826	900,000	10,000	14,000	99,000
1827	900,000	13,000	9,000	66,000
1828	800,000	22,000	14,900	46,000
1829	1,800,000	37,000	26,000	49,000
1830	1,000,000	75,000	56,000	47,000
1831	900,000	66,000	49,000	41,000
1832	900,000	83,000	88,000	53,000
1833	1,900,000	120,000	215,000	86,000
1834	1,500,000	186,000	152,000	127,000

The yearly value of cotton manufactures in the United States was, in 1815, twenty-four millions of dollars, but, in 1832, it had increased to thirty millions, and during the following five years it has further increased by $17,-500,000, the aggregate amount being $47,500,000, or 9,500,000 pounds sterling. The capital employed in manufactures in 1815, was forty millions ; but in 1835, eighty millions of dollars; increase in twenty years 100 per cent.* The augmentation in the growth of cotton, and its exportation to Europe and other parts of the world is still more remarkable, as will be seen from the following table, also taken from the official documents of the Secretary of the Treasury.

* It must not be forgotten that the most unfortunate period of American manufactures followed immediately the conclusion of the late war with England; and that in the years 1817, 1818, and 1819 fewer hands were employed in manufactures than during the previous years.

Number of Pounds of Cotton exported from the United States.

Years.	England.	France.	Russia.	Holland and Belgium.	Spain.	Spanish West Indies.	Trieste.	Hanse Towns.	Italy and Malta.	All other Places.
1821	93,500,000	27,333,333	304,680	4,186,096	284,832	772,296	34,976	748,110	897,804	2,506,777
1822	101,000,000	21,500,000	713,789	1,970,258	-	445,964	210,138	2,955,581	1,956,253	450,762
1823	142,500,000	25,000,000	309,678	4,650,548	-	-	177,789	2,356,594	217,663	833,332
1824	92,000,000	40,500,000	501,645	432,976	-	3,853	-	292,852	-	227,529
1825	140,000,000	30,000,000	133,934	1,420,225	-	-	-	577,109	980	509,031
1826	131,000,000	62,333,333	15,262	4,592,439	-	-	33,311	2,012,679	-	1,820,116
1827	217,000,000	70,500,000	147,101	5,861,400	7,990	-	183,204	3,389,514	148,170	1,440,547
1828	151,750,000	53,500,000	649,791	3,780,988	-	-	980,354	3,386,108	407,068	1,072,448
1829	157,000,000	67,500,000	227,883	9,595,337	-	-	4,071,247	6,857,796	1,056,387	1,261,925
1830	211,000,000	75,000,000	111,376	8,561,193	32,210	-	2,814,477	4,123,047	235,265	638,877
1831	205,500,000	48,000,000	761,735	972,659	555,098	-	2,778,858	2,416,765	305,695	2,243,741
1832	217,250,000	75,000,000	838,951	3,920,016	2,283,875	-	1,654,775	4,075,122	530,274	2,250,190
1833	227,750,000	76,750,000	1,447,405	2,673,253	758,216	-	1,107,600	1,870,620	-	1,759,615
1834	266,750,000	79,900,000	1,260,494	6,096,462	892,967	-	3,805,312	6,612,895	190,842	1,153,382
1835	252,000,000	100,333,333	974,801	5,694,358	878,219	-	4,943,061	2,788,147	12,952	1,493,760

The whole cotton crop of 1835 was estimated at four hundred and eighty millions of pounds, growing on upwards of two millions of acres. The capital invested in the growing of cotton was estimated at eight hundred millions of dollars, or one hundred and sixty millions pounds sterling. The whole amount of capital, therefore, invested in the growth and manufacture of cotton, amounted, in that year, to eight hundred and eighty millions of dollars.*

In 1816 an official report made to Congress showed that forty millions of dollars capital were invested in cotton manufactures, and twelve millions in woollen. It was stated also that the whole amount of cotton consumed in the United States did not exceed 90,000 bales, and the value of the goods manufactured did not amount to more than sixty millions of dollars. At present the manufactures of all kinds amount annually to two hundred and fifty millions of dollars, of which more than twenty-five milllions are exported, and the rest consumed in the country.†

I will now subjoin some tables from " Pitkins's Statistics," showing the progress of cotton manufactures in twelve states; but especially in that of New York, and the town of Lowell, in the state of Massachusetts. This town, it must be remembered, has only become the seat of manufacturing establishments within the last fourteen years; but is now connected by a railroad with the city

---

* To this the official document remarks:—"One of the beneficial effects of our present active cultivation of cotton is, that while it yields the greatest agricultural profits in proportion to the capital in land and stock, it has a sure tendency to diminish the quantities of rice, tobacco, indigo, grain, and cattle raised in the cotton districts in America, and keeps up the price of those articles in a manner highly favorable to those who raise them. The moderate quantity of rice produced in 1801 and 1802 is a positive evidence of this profitable truth. The North American rice is of the *best class.* The body of our rice planters raise but three quarter crops from their attention to cotton. Having so much less to sell, the market is not glutted. The price is consequently not low. It is favorable. The growers of Indian corn in the southern states have also turned to raising cotton. Hence Indian corn and pork are every where better supported in price to the general benefit of our *farmers.* Much corn will go from counties *out* of the cotton district to counties *in* the cotton district, for sale and consumption. So will fish, and all eatables and drinkables."

† History of the Rise and Progress of Manufactures, by George S. White.

of Boston, and employs a capital of five millions four hundred and fifty thousand dollars in the manufacture of cotton goods.

TABULAR VIEW of the Cotton Manufactures in 12 of the American States in 1831.

States.	Capital.	No. of spindles.	Yards of Cloth.	Pounds of Cloth.	Pounds of Cotton used.
	Dolls.				
Maine	765,000	6,500	1,750,000	525,000	588,500
N. Hampshire	5,300,000	113,776	29,060,500	7,255,060	7,845,000
Vermont	295,500	12,392	2,238,400	574,500	760,000
Massachusetts	12,891,000	339,777	79,231,000	21,301,062	24,871,981
Rhode Island	6,262,340	235,753	37,121,681	9,271,481	10,414,578
Connecticut	2,825,000	115,528	20,055,500	5,612,000	6,777,209
New York	3,671,500	157,316	21,010,920	5,297,713	7,661,670
New Jersey	2,027,644	62,979	5,133,776	1,877,418	5,832,204
Pennsylvania	3,758,500	120,810	21,332,467	4,207,192	7,111,174
Delaware	384,500	24,806	5,203,746	1,201,500	1,435,000
Maryland	2,144,000	47,222	7,649,000	2,224,000	3,008,000
Virginia	290,000	9,844	675,000	168,000	1,152,000
Total	40,614,984	1,246,703	230,461,990	59,514,926	77,457,316

N. B. The state of Pennsylvania includes five hundred thousand dollars, and Delaware one hundred and sixty-two thousand dollars for the capital employed in hand-looms. The cotton consumed amounted to 77,757,316 lbs., 214,822 bales of the average 361 $\frac{86}{100}$

The following Table contains the price and distribution of labor.

States.	Number of Mills.	Number of Looms.	Males employed.	Wages of males per week.	Females employed.	Wages of females per week.	Children under 12.	Wages of children.
				dls. cts.		*dls. cts.*		*dls. cts.*
Maine	8	91	84	5 50	205	2 33	—	—
N. Hampshire	40	3,530	875	6 25	4,090	2 60	60	2 0
Vermont	17	352	102	5 0	363	1 84	19	1 40
Massachusetts	256	8,981	2,665	7 0	10,678	2 25	—	—
Rhode Island	116	5,773	1,731	4 25	3,297	2 20	3,472	1 50
Connecticut	94	2,609	1,399	4 50	2,477	2 20	439	1 50
New York	112	3,653	1,374	6 0	3,652	1 90	484	1 40
New Jersey	51	815	2,151	6 0	3,070	1 90	217	1 40
Pennsylvania	67	6,301	6,545	6 0	8,351	2 0	—	—
Delaware	10	235	697	5 0	676	2 0	—	—
Maryland	23	1,002	824	3 87	1,793	1 91	—	—
Virginia	7	91	143	2 73	275	1 58	—	—
Total	801	33,433	18,560		38,297		4,691	

The Cotton Manufactures in the State of New York, as stated in Williams's New York Annual Register for 1835, were as follows:

Counties.	No. of Mills.	Amount of Capital.	No. of Spindles in use.	Pounds of Cotton manufactured annually	Pounds of Yarn sold annually.	Yards of cloth produced annually.	No. of persons employed in the establishment.
		Dolls.					
Oneida - - -	20	735,500	31,596	1,705,290	175,080	5,273,200	2,354
Renselaer - -	15	525,000	16,606	854,300	147,110	2,790,315	1,621
Dutchess - -	12	445,000	17,690	833,000	185,500	1,952,000	1,974
Otsego - - -	11	304,000	15,344	618,543	56,000	2,322,000	1,077
Columbia - -	7	218,000	13,266	559,000	199,000	1,150,400	1,265
West Chester -	5	115,000	9,400	486,000	438,000	- -	280
Washington - -	5	100,000	3,606	168,800	23,500	717,650	275
Herkimer -	5	35,000	2,296	106,237	33,500	269,912	128
Saratoga -	4	144,000	5,752	270,000	- -	1,210,660	460
Jefferson -	3	170,000	6,020	327,000	22,600	1,004,720	595
Ulster -	3	140,000	5,796	410,000	330,000	115,000	475
Orange - -	3	135,000	4,200	251,000	4,000	740,000	460
Madison -	3	30,000	1,998	35.000	31,500	- -	35
Tompkins -	3	28,000	812	55,500	1,000	199,063	97
Onondaga -	2	62,000	2,160	125,000	5,000	460,000	225
Monroe -	2	55,000	2,648	208,000	105,000	300,000	320
Clinton -	2	16,000	884	25,000	- -	100,000	70
Rockland -	1	100,000	3,500	200,000	40,000	460,000	500
Schenectady - -	1	77,000	2,000	118,000	20,000	416,000	200
Chenango -	1	75,000	4,474	200,000	- -	800,000	225
Seneca -	1	70,000	4,000	190,000	- -	550,000	150
Cayuga - -	1	70,000	2,692	180,000	8,000	180,000	138
Franklin -	1	10,000	—	—	—	—	—
Suffolk -	1	10,000	576	36,000	33,000	- -	30
Total	112	3,669,500	157,316	7,961,670	1,867,790	21,010,920	12,954

It will be perceived from this table that the number of persons supported by manufactures in the state of New York, the most *commercial* state in the Union, and comprising immense *agricultural districts*, amounted, nevertheless, in 1832 to more than three fifths per cent. of the whole population, which at that period was estimated at two millions nearly.

The valuation of property in that state, from the comptroller's report of January, 1835, was as follows:

Real estate   -   -   350,346,043 dollars.

Personal estate -   -   108,331,941 ——

Total   -   458,677,984 ——

The capital invested in manufactures amounted therefore to $\frac{369}{458}$, or nearly one per cent., and with the increase since 1831, amounts now, probably, to more than two per cent. of the whole assessed property of the state.

The whole bank stock of that state was as follows:

State banks	- -	31,481,460 dollars.
Savings' bank	- -	3,855,517 ——
Total	-	35,336,977 ——

But the amount of capital invested in manufactures, allowing but ten per cent. increase since 1831, (which I think rather small, considering the vastness of manufacturing enterprise throughout the Union,) was probably more than 4,000,000 of dollars, and consequently nearly one eighth of all the capital invested in banking.

But what is the estimate of the state of New York compared to that of Massachusetts! The whole population of this state is not much more than 600,000, and the number of males and females employed in manufactures may now be estimated at 15,000, making $2\frac{1}{2}$ per cent. of the whole population, or one person out of forty engaged in manufactures. The valuation of property in that state was, in 1831, 208,236,250 dollars, (of which the city of Boston furnished more than 80,000,000;) but the capital invested, at that time, in manufactures, was 12,891,000 or 13,000,000 dollars nearly. The ratio, therefore, was more than six per cent. of the whole assessed property of the state; and it has increased since that period. The bank capital of the state was reported (in 1834) to be 29,409,450 dollars. Allowing the capital invested in manufactures to have increased since 1831 only by ten per cent., we may estimate it as something more than 14,000,000 of dollars; which would make the property invested in manufactures equal to nearly *one half* of the banking capital in the state. The statistics of a single town,—that of Lowell,—will show the unprecedented increase of manufactures in that state.

24*

LOWELL COTTON MANUFACTORIES.

(From Pilkins's Statistics, 1831.)

Companies.	Capital.	Mills.	Spindles.	Looms	Fem. employ'd	Males.	Yards per week.	Bales per week.
	Dolls.							
Merrimack	1,500,000	5	26,000	1,000	1,200	500	125,000	86
Hamilton	800,000	3	15,000	500	700	200	70,000	65
Appleton	500,000	2	9,500	350	475	60	80,000	86
Lowell	500,000	1	4,000	132	200	175	42,000	58
Suffolk	450,000	2	10,000	352	475	60	90,000	86
Tremont	500,000	2	10,000	410	475	60	120,000	86
Lawrence	1,200,000	4	23,000	750	1,050	100	170,000	160
Total	5,450,000	19	97,500	3,494	4,575	1,155	697,000	627

Thus, one small town employed, in 1831, nearly 6000 persons in cotton manufactures alone, and produced more than two-thirds of a million of yards per week, or about thirty-six millions of yards per annum. Of these, eight millions were printed; and including these (which sold at from 10 to 28 cents—5½d. to 15d.—per yard,) the whole may be estimated at 10 cents per yard; making 3,600,000 dollars, or £720,000 sterling *per annum.*

The different periods at which these companies were incorporated show sufficiently the rapid increase of manufacture in that town.

The Merrimack Company } 1822, commenced 1823.
    was incorporated in }

"   Hamilton   -   -   1825   ——   1825.
"   Appleton   -   -   1828   ——   1828.
"   Lowell   -   -   -   1828   ——   1828.
"   Suffolk   -   -   -   1830   ——   1832.
"   Tremont -   -   -   1830   ——   1832.
"   Lawrence   -   -   1830   ——   1833.

But in 1835 (as appears from a letter dated Lowell, April 20th, 1835, inserted in White's " History of Manufactures") the Merrimack company had increased the number of its spindles to 34,432, and that of its looms to 1253; they employed 1321 females, 437 males, and manufactured 172,000 yards per week. The Hamilton company had increased their spindles to 19,000, and the number of looms to 600; they employed 800 females and 200 males, and manufactured 78,000 yards of prints and drillings per week. The Appleton company had increased the number of spindles by 1500; the Lowell company by more than 500; and the Suffolk company by 250, in the space of three years.

There were, besides, incorporated a "Locks and Canals company," with a capital of 600,000 dollars, for supplying water-power to the various manufacturing establishments; (this company had an extensive machine shop, for the manufactory of cotton and woollen machinery, railroad cars, engines, &c., and employed 200 men,) and the Middlesex company with 500,000 dollars for the manufacture of broadcloths and cassimeres. The latter consumed annually 470,000 lbs. of wool, and 1,500,000 teasels. They ran two mills, 3120 spindles, 98 looms, and gave employment to 240 females and 145 males; making 6000 yards of cloth per week.* The same company have since enlarged their business so as to manufacture, *additionally*, 500 yards of satinet per day; using upwards of 2000 lbs. of wool per day.

The above establishments consumed annually 11,239 tons of anthracite coal, 4750 cords of wood, and 50,549 gallons of oil. The total amount of cloth made was between thirty-nine and forty millions of yards, and the amount of cotton used, between twelve and thirteen millions of pounds. The bleacheries used 310,000 lbs. of starch, 380 barrels of flour, and 500,000 bushels of coal per annum. The wages amounted to 22,500 dollars, or £4,500 sterling per week.

This is the progress of manufactures in a single town of 15,000 inhabitants; and similar improvements have taken place in the establishments at Smithfield, Pawtucket, Fall River, Slaterville, Greenville, Cabotsville, Paterson,† Newark, Cincinnati, Pittsburg, Lancaster, Philadelphia, &c.

* In 1805 all the woollen manufactures in the United States could not furnish 6,000 blankets for the use of the army!— *White's History of Manufactures.*

† "This town contained (1827) already fifteen cotton manufactories, with 24,000 spindles; two factories of canvass with 1,644 spindles, employing 1450 persons, whose annual wages amounted to 224,123 dollars. The town contained also extensive machine-shops and iron works. It consumed annually 620,000 lbs. of flax, and 6000 bales of cotton; spun 1,630,000 lbs. of cotton yarn, 430,000 lbs. of linen yarn; produced 630,000

The water-power of these places is, as yet, far from being employed to one half, or even one fourth of the extent to which it is capable of being used in manufactures; and there is, besides, a vast amount of power in other places which is entirely disused. The water-power of the town of Lowell (the manufacturing establishments of which I have just described) is capable of propelling more than one hundred times the present machinery; that of Lancaster, Pennsylvania, is almost inexhaustible, (the town being built on the river Susquehanna;) and the same may be said of the water-power of all the manufacturing establishments in the neighborhood of the large rivers. Whatever advantages Great Britain may, at this moment, enjoy over the United States with regard to the cheapness of coal, America possesses in the multitude of her streams, rivulets, and waterfalls, the most efficient means of propelling machinery at a cheaper rate than can be procured in any other country.

As an appendix to the foregoing, I shall here subjoin a table which was attached to a report made by Mr. Parker, to the senate of the state of Pennsylvania, on the 4th of March, 1835, showing the amount of anthracite coal, mined and brought to the market, in each year from the year 1820 to the year 1834, inclusive.

Year.	Lehigh.	Schuylkill.	Lackawana	Total No. of Tons.
1820	365	- - -	- - -	365
1821	1,073	- - -	- - -	1,073
1822	2,240	- - -	- - -	2,240
1823	5,823	- - -	- - -	5,823
1824	9,541	- - -	- - -	9,541
1825	28,393	5,306	- - -	33,699
1826	31,280	16,835	- - -	48,115
1827	32,074	29,492	- - -	61,567
1828	30,232	47,181	- - -	77,413
1829	25,110	78,293	70,000	173,403
1830	41,750	89,984	42,000	173,734
1831	40,965	81,854	54,000	176,819
1832	75,000	209,271	84,500	368,771
1833	124,000	250,588	111,777	486,365
1834	106,244	226,692	43,700	376,636

yards of cotton and linen duck, 3,354,000 yards of cotton cloth, and exported 796,000 yards of yarn; and new manufactories were then building."—*Report of the Society for establishing useful manufactories in New Jersey.*

This table evidently exhibits the increasing facilities even as regards coal, and these added to the water-power, must render America one of the first manufacturing nations of the world. The only difficulty, then, consists in the comparatively high wages now given in the United States; but this is an objection which the increased competition of every succeeding year has a natural tendency to remove, and is therefore, of itself, incapable of preventing America from becoming, in this respect also, the successful rival of Europe.

But it is not only the large manufacturing establishment, but also the grand manufacturing scale on which most of the mechanic arts are exercised in the United States which merits particular attention. It is the peculiar genius of the American people to excel in all kind of trade; and there is scarcely an article which does not furnish them with new means of exercising their ingenuity. Thus a large trade is carried on, by the people of New England, in painted chairs, which are sent by thousands all over the United States, and exported also to South America and to the West Indies. The shoe trade of some of the towns in the neighborhood of Boston is hardly less remarkable, the value of nearly two millions of dollars having been manufactured last year, and sent to the west alone. The state of Connecticut possesses the most extensive wooden clock manufactories in the world—affording them at about half the price of those made in the Black Forest. The glass manufactories of New England, Pennsylvania and Maryland, produce not only some of the finest specimens of pressed and cut glass, but carry on an extensive trade with South America and the West India islands. The gun manufactories of Lancaster, and the steel manufactories of Paterson, are established on a large scale ; the manufactories of paper and iron ware have long since competed with the importations from England; and the bronze manufactories of Philadelphia bid fair to rival those of Birmingham.

The following TABLE, taken from Williams's "New York State Register," will exhibit a SUMMARY of MANUFACTURES in that STATE, according to the Census of 1835:

	Number.	Value of raw materials used and manufactured.	Value of manufactured Articles.
		Dollars.	Dollars.
Grist mills -	2,051	17,687,009	20,140,435
Saw mills - -	6,948	3,651,153	6,881,055
Oil mills - -	71	214,813	275,574
Fulling mills -	965	1,994,491	2,894,096
Carding machines -	1,061	2,179,414	2,651,638
Cotton manufactories -	111	1,630,352	3,030,709
Woollen manufactories	234	1,450,825	2,433,192
Iron works - -	293	2,366,065	4,349,949
Trip hammers -	141	168,896	363,581
Distilleries - -	337	2,278,420	3,098,042
Asheries - -	693	434,394	726,418
Glass manufactories -	13	163,312	448,559
Rope do.- -	63	664,394	980,083
Chain cable do. -	2	20,871	28,625
Oil cloth do. -	24	63,119	95,646
Dyeing and printing do.	15	1,999,000	2.465,600
Clover mills - -	69	95,693	110,025
Paper mills - -	70	358,857	685,784
Tanneries - -	412	3,563,592	5,598,626
Breweries - -	94	916,252	1,381,446

This is but the statistics of manufactories in one state ; but New England and Pennsylvania are in this respect powerful rivals of New York, and, of late, large manufactories have also been established in the western states, and in the northern districts of Virginia.

The book trade, and especially that of school-books, is almost wholly monopolized by the eastern states; the hundreds of thousands of " arithmetics," "geographies," " grammars," and " spelling-books," which are annually printed and *consumed*, surpassing, by far the number of similar publications in Europe.* Large fortunes have been realised by the authors and publishers of these books, and their success has invited others to follow their example.

I believe I am correct in introducing this subject under the head " manufactures and commerce ;" because the making of school-books in the United States partakes more of the enterprising spirit of trade, than of the timid scrupulousness of literature ; and the sale of them is only inferior to that of " bread-stuffs, and beef." Nothing is left undone, by the authors and venders of these books, to procure an extensive sale of a commodity so useful to the minds of the young ; teachers and school committees are furnished gratis with every new work which issues from the press ; and whole editions are given away to schools, to procure the introduction of a book. In order that both author and vender may be as much as possible interested in the sale, the copyright, instead of being bought by the bookseller, (as is done in most parts of Europe,) is disposed of for a per-centage on the profits, which on school-books averages from five to ten per cent. on the nominal retail price of the work. The author or compiler is thus paid according to the success of his book, and the publisher risks only the expenses of printing and publishing the first edition. Hence an American author, the moment he has written a school-book which promises to be largely introduced, commences his peregrinations to the western ands outhern states, in order, by his personal influence and reputation, to support the merits of his work ; and perhaps, also, to earn a commission on the sale of it. The whole is considered as a commercial transaction ; and the immense competition of authors and publishers has had a decidedly happy influence on the merits and low prices of American school-books. There are several book-selling establishments in Boston and Philadelphia, trading altogether in school-books ; and I am quite certain, that their joint sales of elementary works alone, amount to more than a million of dollars *per annum*. I have seen

---

* These books being generally printed on bad cotton paper wear out so rapidly, that it is by no means unfrequent for children to change them several times in the course of a year.

the sixtieth edition of an arithmetic; the fiftieth of a geography, the seventieth or eightieth of a spelling-book, and Heaven knows how many editions of "Peter Parley."*

In the mechanic arts the Americans are the successful imitators of the English; which accounts for their being already superior, in most of them, to the French and Germans. Furniture is made in Philadelphia, Boston, and New York, much better than in any part of the continent of Europe, Paris itself not excepted; and the New England "rocking-chairs," the *ne plus ultra* of all comforts in the shape of furniture, have acquired an European reputation. It is not so much the elegance as the excellent adaptation to the purpose for which they are intended, which distinguishes every article manufactured in the United States. One sees at once that the maker must have been a thinking creature, who understood all the time what he was about, and left nothing undone which could materially improve the usefulness of his handicraft. An American mechanic does not exercise his trade as he has learned it: he is constantly making improvements, studying out new and ingenious processes, either to perfect his work or to reduce its price, and is, in most cases, able to account for the various processes of his art in a manner which would do credit to a philosopher.

A certain *mechanical* perfection, arising from a greater division of labor and long-followed practice in a narrow, circumscribed trade, is, assuredly, less to be found in America than in England, and has frequently given rise to the unjust complaint, that American mechanics can make nothing equal to the English. This, however, is an idle assertion, contradicted by reason and experience. A number of articles are made as well in the United States, and cheaper, than in England, and if, in other instances, their productions are not so good, the reduced prices are more than in proportion to their inferiority; and rather

---

* This is a work, consisting of about one hundred volumes, containing a Liliputian encyclopedia of all sciences, trades, and professions for children. Most of them are written in the form of dialogues or narratives, and contain nothing less than the stories of Rome, Greece and America, together with essays on mythology, natural philosophy, geography, mathematics, ethics, and moral philosophy. They were published in the form of *pocket* editions, the best adapted to their species.

show the unwillingness of the consumers to pay a proper price for them, than the incapacity of the workmen to produce a superior quality. Besides, there is nothing which could prevent experienced English workmen from settling in the United States, if they were sure of earning there more than at home. In several cases, they have attempted to do so, and experienced the quickness with which Jonathan learns and improves.

There is no branch of industry, in which the Americans do not participate, the moment any profits are to be realised from it ; and it is, in nearly all cases, the state of the market, or some more lucrative and attractive employment, which prevents them from manufacturing articles in the same style as in other countries. If they are not in a habit of subdividing labor as in England, in order to reduce handiwork as much as possible to an equality with machinery, they may, perhaps, in a few cases, be unable to work so cheap and with so little loss of time ; but *individually* they must become superior to mere mechanical workmen. The man who knows the different parts of a watch, and their mutual adaptation to the mechanism of its regular movement, is evidently superior to him who all his life manufactures only the wheels, without troubling himself about the machine in which they are to operate,—as a man who understands a *principle* is superior to the *empiric* who is only acquainted with the routine of particular cases. In China, where the division of labor is carried to its greatest extent, the laboring classes are reduced to mere machines. Their skill is, assuredly, astonishing ; but they acquire it with the extinction of every mental faculty : the whole nation partakes more or less of this mechanical stupefaction, and is " great in every thing that is small, and small in every thing that is great."

In the United States it is of the greatest importance that no part of the whole population should remain entirely ignorant ; but that, on the contrary, all should become accustomed to thought and reflection. The various processes of the mechanic arts offer a thousand opportunities for the exercise of the reasoning faculties ; and I deem it a particular advantage of the American operatives, that they are placed in a situation to improve them. The high price of labor, and the peculiar habits of the people, contribute much to facilitate the means of instruction; and the natural disposition of Americans prompts them to avail themselves of the advantages of their position.

Where a man has to labor all day in order to obtain for himself and family a bare subsistence, there it is impossible for his mind to act with a proper degree of freedom. The physical wants are too urgent to allow him sufficient respite for thought and reflection, and the only thing coveted, after the cravings of his stomach are appeased, is the necessary rest to restore his physical abilities. In America, not only the master mechanic, but also his journeymen, have the means of earning more than is required for a mere living; they are able to procure for themselves comforts which would hardly enter the imagination of similar orders in Europe. They are enabled to command a portion of their time; and their minds being free from the anxieties of a precarious life, and less vitiated by a desire of frivolous pleasures, are better qualified for study or improvement,—the only sure means by which they can hope to better their conditions. Their domestic habits, and the custom of spending the Sabbath at home, are highly favorable to the development of their mental faculties, and in this respect, of immense advantage to the general morals of the people. The majority of the lower order of European workmen hardly think of becoming independent, or doing business on their own account; and, being less sustained by hope, in the exercise of their physical powers, need more relaxation and amusement than the Americans, who consider the hardest of labor but an introduction to something better which is to follow. The American operatives are sustained by the very efforts they make, and need not have recourse to the sordid pleasures of debauchery, or the bottle, in order to plunge themselves into a momentary and brutal oblivion of their present necessities.

I wonder the superior condition of the laboring classes in America has not been taken notice of by any English tourist, (if we except Mr. Hamilton's philosophical dialogue with the Scotch baker,) while they were so tediously minute in describing the fashionable coteries! No drawing-room, in any part of the world, is without its second and third-rate performers, and their number in America may even be greater than in Europe. Nor will I deny that an American exquisite is, *per se*, an inferior being. A man, in Europe, may be a coxcomb, or a buffoon, in a manner peculiar to his own country, in which case he is still a *national* character; but to be a slavish imitator of the follies of others, in a country where they are only known to be despised, presupposes a degree of presumptuous imbecility, for which no excuse can be found in the customs and manners of the people. If Englishmen censure Americans for imitating the fashions of Europe, they ridicule them justly for not being wiser than themselves, or for succeeding less in an unprofitable enterprise. But, let them turn their attention to the thousands with whom they hardly come in contact on their tours; let them observe and watch the elevated character of the merchants, the skilful industry of the mechanic, the sober regularity of the workmen, and they will find ample room for a more charitable exercise of their judgment; they will then find the true strength and superiority of the American *people* over all other nations on the globe. They will find no humiliating imitation in the trade and commerce of the United States. They will see the arts exercised on a most liberal and extensive scale; the character of workmen raised by emulation to that of respectable citizens; and, instead of machines or mechanical operatives, they will discover everywhere intelligent beings, capable of accounting for every process, and improving it constantly by their own ingenuity. In no other country could they behold a similar spectacle; in none other witness the same emancipation of the mind. In England and Scotland a most generous beginning has been made to arrive at similar results; but the improvements have not yet penetrated to all classes, and for many a generation, America yet will be unrivalled in the moral elevation of her citizens.

A great deal has been said, by American and foreign writers, on the subject of trades' unions and other societies of operatives known under the name of "workies," and especially about their cries for "equal and universal education." I confess I never knew that the workmen wished to *arrest* the progress of education, in order to reduce the moral superiority of the higher classes to a sordid level with themselves, but, on the contrary, understood them to covet the same opportunities of mental improvement, which are enjoyed by the wealthier portion of the community. I am quite certain there is no class of Americans so utterly degraded in their moral sentiments, as to wish for universal ignorance, or a comparative mediocrity of talents, in order to protect and excuse their own imbecility. The workmen of New York, Boston, and Philadelphia, have struck for the " ten-hour system," on the ground that if a man work more than ten hours a day, " *he is unfit to read and improve his mind in the evening, or to superintend the education of his children;*" a plea which expresses certainly a very different desire from that of destroying the opportunities of acquiring superior knowledge. The wages of American workmen are high; but then it is seldom known that they make an improper use of their money; and they abstain entirely from the European custom of spending in one or two days, the whole earnings of the week. They understand not only how to make money, but also the art of saving it; and the amount of capital deposited in the various savings banks of the country furnishes the strongest evidence of the prudence and frugality of their habits. As long as these last, I cannot possibly persuade myself that the institutions of the country are in danger, whatever be the aberrations of individuals, or whole classes, in their respective political orbits.

The system of credit, established in manufactures and commerce, extends also to the business of the mechanic, and in some instances even to the workmen. An American shoemaker will give his note of six or eight months for leather ; a tailor his, in exchange for cloth ; a carpenter will buy timber, a printer his type, a blacksmith his iron, on nine, or twelve months' credit, and will in turn take the notes of his customers. Trades-people are in this manner as much subjected to sudden changes of fortune by fluctuations of exchange, and venture as much in the investment of their capital, as the active merchant ; and nothing, therefore, is more common than a combination of the two characters in one and the same person. The mercantile genius of the country pervades all classes of society, and by its universal influence unites them effectually to a large homogeneous whole, in which the most diversified qualities of individuals bear yet the mark of the general character.

I have, in the beginning of this chapter, briefly touched on the subject of navigation as connected with commerce; it remains for me yet to enlarge upon the character of seamen. The United States, and especially the northern and eastern states, furnish, in proportion to their population, a greater number of sailors than can be mustered in any other country save, perhaps, England; and possess, besides, the advantage of employing those of all other nations in the regular service of their merchants. The high wages, and the protection offered them by the government, are sufficient inducements for thousands of foreigners to enlist annually on board of American vessels; and there are comparatively few amongst them, who, once accustomed to the service, are again willing to quit it. Their task, it is true, is more severe than on board the ships of other nations, but then they are paid in proportion, and their provisions are better than those of the common sailors of other countries.*

With these additional expenses, the question may be asked, how it is possible for Americans to realise any

---

* De Tocqueville, in his work "*De la Démocratie en Amérique*," traces the progress of navigation in the United States to the same source. He compares the American method of navigating ships, to the new military tactics invented by the generals of the French republic; which were victorious until imitated by their enemies. "*Les Américains*," says the French jurist, "*ont introduit quelque chose d'analogue dans le commerce. Ce que les Français faisaient pour la victoire, ils le font pour le bon marché.*"

"*Le navigateur européen ne s'aventure qu'avec prudence sur les mers; il ne part que quand le temps l'y convie; s'il lui survient un accident imprévu, il rentre au port; la nuit il serre une partie de ses voiles, et, lorsqu'il voit l'océan blanchir à l'approche des terres, il ralentit sa course et interoge le soleil.*"

"*L'Américain néglige ces précautions et brave ces dangers. Il part tandis que la tempête gronde encore; la nuit comme le jour il abandonne au vent toutes ses voiles; il répare en marchant son navire fatigué par l'orage, et lorsqu'il approche enfin du terme de sa course, il continue à voler vers le rivage, comme si déjà il appercevait le port.*"

"*L'Américain fait souvent naufrage; mais il n'y a pas de navigateur qui traverse les mers aussi rapidement que lui. Faisant les mêmes choses qu'un autre en moins de temps il peut les fatrir à moins de frais.*"

25*

profits on the navigation of their ships? This query is answered, by the much smaller number of sailors, and the greater rapidity of passages. They make four passages where other ships make two or three, and save in time, what others save in wages. Again, making their sailors work harder, and keeping them constantly employed, they manage their ships with less hands, and are better able to maintain discipline. The intrepidity of American seamen is proverbial, and is sometimes bordering on recklessness. They are known to carry sail until rent by the blast, and to pursue their course amidst the howling and raging of the storm. It does not follow, however, (as De Tocqueville believes,) that, on that account, they are less safe than the ships of other nations. Being continually exposed to dangers, they are better prepared to meet them; and carrying sails to the last moment they will hold, they are accustomed, when urged, to execute the necessary changes and manœuvres with greater promptness and precision. There never is the least confusion on board of American ships; and I am not quite certain whether fewer hands, equally and steadily employed, are not more conducive to order and good management, than a large number of sailors accustomed to less work, and in a habit of relying on one another. To this we must add, that a person who is six weeks at sea, is naturally exposed to more accidents, than one who performs the same passage in four or five; and that every day saved in this manner from the tediousness and peril of a long voyage, increases the comfort and safety of the passengers and crew. The preference given to American ships by the merchants of most European ports, argues strongly in favor of the skill of their commanders; and the great patronage bestowed on the New York packets, is the surest indication of the willingness of the people of all countries to trust their lives and their property to the experience and science of American navigators.

I have remarked before, that a large number of sailors employed in the American merchants' service, are foreigners; but I do not remember having known many of them advance to mates and masters of vessels. The officers of American ships are generally natives of the

United States, and, without any national prejudice, it is easy to assign the reason.

A sailor is a jolly, jovial, careless being, all the world over. He thinks less of the future than men of any other occupation in life, and being provided against physical wants, gives himself up to merriment. "Perils," says Bacon, "love to be rewarded with pleasure;" but the American sailor's reward is promotion. Being generally better educated than the seamen of other nations, and prudent and economical by instinct, a Yankee tar will not only think of advancement on board of his ship, but speculate also on the probability of becoming a merchant. Encouraged by the success of so many others before him, and, as is often the case, by that of his own commander, he employs his leisure hours rather in the study of navigation, than in frivolous recreations, which would only retard his progress in life. He is, perhaps, as gay as any other sailor; but above all things he is a Yankee, and as such, intent upon bettering his condition, and, in this laudable undertaking, seconded by his employers. If he does not succeed, it is in most cases his own fault; for it would be difficult to conceal either talent or inferiority from such watchful eyes as those of his officers, who, with very few exceptions, have gone through the same career themselves, and are consequently the best judges of his ability and character.

There exists, if I mistake not, a strong aversion amongst American merchants, to trust themselves or their property to the care of captains, who, in the language of sailors, "have crept through the cabin window;" while, on the other hand, they are most liberal patrons of those who by courage and dexterity have acquired a just title to their favor. Hence merit is sure of its reward, and there is no stronger inducement to exertion.

Neither have the Americans, (judging correctly of the importance of their maritime power,) left any thing undone which could serve to promote the education and industry of sailors. The merchants of the large Atlantic cities have liberally contributed towards the establishment of churches exclusively for the religious instruction and improvement of mariners; savings banks for sailors have been formed under the auspices of the most enlightened citizens, who have volunteered their services as presidents and directors; and a project for the establishment of naval schools, to educate seamen for the merchants' service, is now before the Congress of the United States, and will probably pass at the next session. Religion, and voluntary abstinence from the use of ardent spirits, have had a prodigious influence on the moral habits of the sailors, and have saved thousands of them from that mental degradation to which they are continually exposed by their occupation and habits of life, and into which they are often misled, even by the best features of their character.

I have been so fortunate as to hear several sermons preached by the Rev. Mr. Taylor at the seamen's church in Boston, and have listened with intense pleasure to his pathetic exhortations to industry and sobriety. He had himself been a sailor on board of an American man-of-war, and understood admirably how to touch the feelings of his audience. His expressions were occasionally intermixed with seamen's phrases, which, it was easy to perceive, produced the desired effect. He would sometimes, in the midst of a sermon, call upon individuals, and especially on captains of vessels, to use their personal influence in suppressing the vice of intemperance, and to exhort the men under their command to a proper worship of God, and the obedience of His laws. It was a moving scene to hear those sturdy navigators reply in the affirmative, and pledge their honor and their faith to fulfil the injunctions of their preacher. Mr. Taylor possesses evidently great powers of oratory, which he employs in the most humane and charitable manner, for the benefit of his fellow-creatures. His church is always crowded, and in the countenances of his hearers may be read the effects of his eloquence. I have never listened to sermons more deeply imbued with the spirit and sanctity of religion, than those of "the sailors' minister;" and I can only wish, for the sake of his noble and disinterested undertaking, that he may preserve his original simplicity and vigor of style, and not be misled into an unprofitable imitation of the flights and tropes of his colleagues.

The American sailors, though they may be inferior in numbers, are morally superior to those of most nations;

and it is for this reason they are generally promoted to mates and captains of vessels; while the others, more easily satisfied, are content to remain seamen all their lives. Whatever be the extent to which the navy of the United States may, at any time, be increased, there will always be a sufficient number of *native officers* to command their ships; and as long as this is the case, the American navy will be as national an institution as that of any other country.

Suppose the Americans at war with any nation save the English, and Congress obliged to increase the naval power of the country; then, whatever be the number of ships which may be added to the navy, (and the facilities of ship-building are great,) there will always be found a sufficient number of British seamen, ready to enlist in the service, from no other reason than because the same language is spoken, and higher wages paid, on board of American vessels, than they can obtain by serving on board of the ships of their own country. But the number of such British seamen joined to that which the American merchants' service would furnish, would by far surpass the force which could be mustered by their enemies. Whatever inferiority the navy of the United States may present in point of number, the facility of increasing the establishment, when required, is greater than in any other country ; and in this consists the strength of a maritime nation. Every new merchant-man which is launched from the stocks, is an addition to the naval force of the country, and increases the means of national defence; with this difference only, that instead of increasing the national *expenditure*, it increases the national *wealth*, and directs the industry of the people to new sources of general prosperity. At the *beginning* of a maritime war, the Americans would have to act on the defensive ; but it would depend on their own will, and on the unanimity of their sentiments, whether they are to continue in that state, or assume an attitude which would at once command the respect and attention of any power in Europe.

Another means of increasing the naval power of the United States is furnished by their fisheries. The navy of every country requires for its existence and maintenance, a certain constant trade and employment, which

shall act as a school for apprenticing young mariners.
Such is the coal-trade of England, and the fisheries of
the eastern states of America. The whale, mackerel,
and cod fisheries of the United States occupy and enrich
a large portion of the population of New England, and
produce the hardiest and most enterprising sailors for
the service of the merchants' navy: by their means, large
fortunes are amassed in the midst of towns and villages
which are built on barren rocks, and which, but for the
bold spirit of their inhabitants, would be left without the
natural means of subsistence.

The fisheries, in the year 1834, yielded 2,071,493 dollars, nearly equivalent to £420,000 sterling.

These were distributed as follows:—

Dried fish or cod fisheries	-	630,384 dollars.
River fisheries	- -	223,290 —
Whale and other fish oil	-	740,619 —
Spermaceti oil	- -	50,048 —
Whalebone	- -	169,434 —
Spermaceti candles	-	257,718 —
Total	-	2,071,493 dollars.

But it is not so much the pecuniary benefit, as the incalculable advantage arising from it to the education of
seamen, which gives to this branch of industry a national
importance. The hardiest seamen of the United States
are from that part of the country, and more than one
half of all the officers employed in the navigation of
American ships are natives from New England.

Most remarkable, for the manner in which they are
carried on, are the whale fisheries of the United States.
The equipment of the ships and crews employed in that
trade resemble a privateering expedition—officers and
sailors receiving, in a measure, prize-money instead of
regular wages. Every man on board has a share in the
profits, which is according to his rank and employment.
Being thus paid according to what they earn, the crews
are willing to bear greater hardships, and are indefatiga-

ble in the chase. Every moment they remain on shore they consider as lost; and it is not unfrequent to see an American whaleman return from the Pacific Ocean with a full cargo of oil, without having once touched the land since he left home. The American sailors become thus inured to the worst dangers and hardships of the sea, and accustomed to the severest toils which fall to the lot of seamen. They become habituated to every species of privation, and find the merchants' service in which they may subsequently engage comparatively easy and cheerful.

Ship-building is another branch of industry in which the Americans excel. They are universally allowed to build the fastest vessels ; but considerable doubts were entertained as to the expediency of building them principally for making short passages. Experience has since shown these apprehensions to have been ill-founded; for it is now an uncontested fact that the American ships are, in all quarters of the world, the successful competitors of those of every other nation. The packets especially, are renowned for their speed and the elegance of their construction ; and they have had the preference, thus far, over all other ships sailing for American ports. The postage on letters conveyed by them from Great Britain and Ireland alone, amounts annually to more than £120,000 sterling, and the number of passengers to and fro, to from forty to fifty thousand. This is certainly a strong argument in favor of expedition, and is more than sufficient to prove that the Americans have found the proper way of building and navigating ships, and that they understand admirably to supply their inferior tonnage by a greater number of fast-sailing vessels.

The successes of the Americans during the last war with England, were by English officers themselves attributed to the skilful manner in which they navigated their ships, and especially to the superior construction of their large frigates. These were built in such a manner as to unite all the advantages of small, fast-sailing vessels, with the heavy calibre of seventy-fours, and were consequently capable of attacking and defending themselves against heavy ships of the line, while they were more than a match for ordinary frigates. The first idea of these vessels was conceived by the Americans, and has since been imitated by all other maritime powers. But the same spirit of invention, which has already been triumphant, may, in time of danger, contrive fresh expedients to ensure once more the success which is inseparable from genius.

CHAPTER X.

INTERNAL NAVIGATION OF THE UNITED STATES.—RAIL-ROADS.—CANALS.—FACILITIES OF TRAVELLING.—THEIR INFLUENCE ON THE POLITICAL CONDITION OF THE PEOPLE.—STEAM-BOATS.—PUBLIC AND BOARDING HOUSES.—HOSPITALITY OF AMERICANS.

No country is, by nature, favored with such large navigable streams as America; but it may also be added that none has done so much to improve its internal navigation. From the mighty Mississippi and its noble tributaries the Ohio and the Missouri, down to the smallest and most insignificant creek or inlet, the American waters are covered with steamers, boats, and rafts of all descriptions; and where the natural communication was not sufficient, the want has been supplied by canals. In the year 1831, there were on the western waters alone, one hundred and ninety-eight steam-boats running, and one hundred and fifty had been worn out or lost by accidents. The whole number of boats, therefore, built on those waters since 1811 was 348, of which one hundred and eleven were built in the city of Cincinnati alone.

But the Americans were not satisfied with improving merely what nature had done for them; they went further. They connected the western waters with those of the Atlantic, and the lakes with the Gulf of Mexico; and established an artificial water communication by means of canals, which, in extent is nearly half the length of the Mississippi, the largest river in the world. Mr. Pitkins, in his "Statistical View of the Commerce of the United States," estimates the number of miles of canals in the United States completed on the first of January, 1835, or which would not long after be completed, at two thousand eight hundred and sixty-four, and their cost, at $ 64,573,099, or £ 12,914,620 sterling. —"When the cost of the railroads in the United States," continues he, " is added to that of the canals, it will be found that there has been, or will soon be expended in this country, on these two kinds of internal improvements alone, a sum not less than ninety-four millions of dollars," —about nineteen millions pounds sterling ;—"and this has been done, principally, since 1817." According to this statement, which I think rather falls short of the truth than exceeds it, the Americans have expended, in that branch of improvement alone, the sum of one million pounds sterling annually, which is more than twenty per cent. of the whole expenditures of the national government.

The extent of railroads was nearly seven hundred miles, without including any of the large projected schemes for extending them to the west, and connecting the southern states with those of the east and north. These, however, have already been partially carried into execution ; and it is to be expected that in less than twenty years a traveller in the United States will be able to traverse the country from the western extremity to the shores of the Atlantic, and from the borders of Canada to the Gulf of Mexico, without being once obliged to slacken his speed, or to exchange a locomotive car or a steam-boat for the less expeditious method of a carriage drawn by horses.

The railroads, in progress, or completed, in the month of January, 1835, exceeded sixteen hundred miles in length, and their cost was in " Pitkins's Statistics " estimated at thirty millions of dollars or six millions pounds sterling nearly. This statement, however, must, I think, fall short of the truth ; as there were, in the state of New York alone, fifty incorporated railroad companies, with a capital of upwards of thirty-four millions of dollars, or six millions eight hundred thousand pounds sterling ; and similar companies were chartered in all other states.

The following of these RAILROADS were completed at
the close of the year 1836 ;

Length.

			Length
1.	The Railroad from	Buffalo to Black Rock	3 miles.
2.	—	Ithaca to Oswego -	29 —
3.	—	Albany to Schenectady	16 —
4.	—	Troy to Ballston -	$24\frac{1}{2}$ —
5.	—	Rochester to Carthage	3 —
6.	—	Saratoga to Schenectady	22 —
7.	—	Utica to Schenectady	77 —

Total $174\frac{1}{2}$ miles.

The following RAILROADS were commenced :

Length.

The Railroad from	Auburn to Syracuse -	26 miles.
—	Buffalo to Niagara Falls	21 —
—	Catskill to Canajoharie -	68 —
—	Prince St. to Haerlam -	7 —
—	Hudson to Massachusetts line	30 —
—	Lockport to Niagara Falls	24 —
—	Brooklyn to Greenport -	98 —
—	N. York city to Lake Erie	505 —
—	Saratoga Spr'gs to Whitehall	41 —
—	Rochester to Utica -	45 —

Total 865 miles.

At the last session of the legislature of New York in
1836, no less than forty-two new railroad companies were
incorporated, of which the most important ones were the
Attica and Buffalo, Auburn and Ithaca, Batavia and
Lockport, Brooklyn Bath and Coney Island, Courtlandt-
ville and Oswego, Herkimer and Trenton Falls, Lansing-
burgh and Troy, Chittenango and Cazenovia, Oswego and
Utica, Rochester and Genessee Port, Schenectady and
Troy, Staten Island, Syracuse and Binghampton, Syracuse and Brewertown, and Utica and Syracuse Railroads. — The state of New York alone, therefore, will in

a few years have ninety-two railroads, facilitating the intercourse of its principal towns and villages, or connecting them with the railroads of other states in order to establish lines of communication with the southern, western and eastern parts of the country.

The same spirit of improvement is stirring in the other states. In the state of Maine there has been completed (in 1836) a railroad from Bangor to Orono ; a company for another to extend from Portland to Dover, New Hampshire, has been incorporated at the last session of the legislature, and three new ones have been projected, one of which is to extend from the coast of Maine to Quebec. In the state of New Hampshire, two railroad companies have been incorporated, both of which have already commenced operations ; and in the state of Vermont four others, with an aggregate capital of 4,000,000 of dollars. In the state of Massachusetts, there are already completed three principal railroads, viz., from Boston to Providence, from Boston to Worcester, and from Boston to Lowell. Each of these has again its branches extending to other towns in the state, or connecting them with the railroads of the state of New York. The " Western Railroad," which was incorporated by the legislature of Massachusetts in 1833 was commenced in 1836, the tate having subscribed to it the sum of 1,000,000 dollars. This railroad will extend from Worcester to the Connecticut river at Springfield ; thence to the boundary line of the state of New York, where it will be connected with three different railroads, one leading to Albany, another to Hudson, and a third to Troy. From Albany a railroad to the westward is already completed as far as Utica ; from Utica to Buffalo a new railroad has recently been incorporated ; and from Buffalo it is to be continued through the states of Pennsylvania, Ohio, Indiana, and Illinois to the borders of the Mississippi; which will establish a direct line of communication between Portland, in the state of Maine, and New Orleans, in the Gulf of of Mexico. In addition to these, three new railroads were incorporated by the legislature of Massachusetts at its last session in 1836 ; one of which, from Boston to Salem, Newburyport and Portsmouth, N. Hampshire, is already in progress. In the state of Connecticut, three railroads are now in progress, and five new ones have been incorporated ; in New Jersey, three railroads are completed, and three new ones in progress ; in Pennsylvania thirteen are completed, and eight or ten in progress ; and in the small state of Delaware one is completed, and another in progress.

The Baltimore and Ohio railroad was incorporated by the legislature of Maryland in 1827, and is to extend from the city of Baltimore to the banks of the river Ohio, distance 360 miles. In 1835, eighty-six miles of this road were completed at an expense of 3,106,507 dollars. The company had in operation ten engines, fifty passengers' cars and 1,200 wagons for transporting merchandise. It is to be observed, moreover, that the company did not import their machinery from England, but relied entirely on the ingenuity of American workmen ; and they are now believed to possess locomotives of the best kind, and with the most powerful engines. For the prosecution of this railroad, the legislature of the state has recently subscribed 3,000,000 dollars, and the city of Baltimore other 3,000,000 dollars. Two other railroads have been completed in that state, and three new ones incorporated. In the state of Virginia three railroads of thirteen, fifty-nine, and thirty miles in length respectively, were completed in 1830 ; three new ones were commenced, and eighteen others incorporated since 1835, with a joint capital of 12,595,000 dollars, or £2,519,000 sterling. In the state of North Carolina six new railroads are projected, and some of them commenced. In South Carolina there exists already a railroad from Charleston to Hamburg, distance 136 miles ; and another is projected on a huge plan. It is to extend from Charleston to Cincinnati (Ohio,) distance 607 miles, connecting the valleys of the Ohio and the Mississippi with the Atlantic ocean. The expenses of this road are estimated at $15,000,000 or £3,000,000 sterling. In the state of Georgia there are completed two railroads, and three others are in progress, extending 90, 200, and 210 miles in length respectively. In the state of Alabama nine railroads are commenced ; in the state of Mississippi three, and in the state of Louisiana one railroad is completed, and five or six others in progress. In Kentucky two railroads are completed, and three or four

in progress. In the state of Ohio twelve railroads were
incorporated in 1832, of which the "Mad river and lake
Erie railroad," which is to extend 153 miles, was commenced in 1835, and thirty miles of it completed in 1836.
In 1835, twenty-eight new railroad companies were incorporated in that state with a capital of more than
20,000,000 dollars or £4,000,000 sterling. In the state of
Indiana four railroads are projected. In the state of
Illinois there were chartered in 1835 nine railroads of
which the "Alton and Galena railroad" alone was to be
350 miles long; and at the last session of the legislature
(in 1836,) fourteen new ones were incorporated. In the
state of Missouri two railroads are projected; and the
legislature of the state of Michigan, a state which has
only been recently admitted into the Union, has already
chartered four railroad companies, and a large number
of others are projected. The whole population of that
state is averaged only at 120,000, and consisted, according to the census of 1834, only of 85,856 inhabitants.
Several railroads have been projected also in the Florida
territory, and one or two of these are now in progress.

The canals of the United States are not of so late a
date, but are nevertheless constructed chiefly since 1820.
Ten years' improvements however, with so new and enterprising a people as the Americans, are sufficient to change
the aspect of things, and to give the whole country a new
character. The attention of the Americans has within
the last five or six years chiefly been turned to the construction of railroads; but I must be greatly mistaken if
canals would not, in many instances, answer the same
purpose; and they would, under particular circumstances,
be far less expensive. The natural facilities of water
communication seem to invite the Americans not to neglect this branch of internal improvement; and the profits
realised on the principal canals now in operation, ought
to be a sufficient inducement for speculators to invest
their capital in so useful and national a branch of industry.

The principal CANALS in the United States, completed
in January, 1835, were the following;

Blackstone canal	- -	45 miles.
Black river	- - -	76 —

Cayuga	-	-	-	- 20	miles.
Champlain	-	-	- 63	—
Chemung	-	-	- 23	—
Chenango	-	-	- 96	—
Chesapeake and Ohio (not					
yet completed)	-	- 340	—
Chesapeake and Delaware	14	—
Delaware	-	-	- 60	—
Delaware and Hudson	- 108	—
Delaware and Rariton	- 42½	—
Dismal Swamp	-	- 23	—
Erie	-	-	-	- 363	—
Farmington	-	-	- 78	—
Lehigh	-	-	-	- 46½	—
Middlesex	-	.	- 27	—
Miami	-	-	-	- 66	—
Morris	-	-	-	- 97	—
Ohio	-	-	-	- 334	—
Oswego	-	-	-	- 38	—
Pennsylvania	-	-	- 277	—
Santee	-	-	-	- 22	—
Schuylkill	-	-	- 110	—
Union	-	-	-	- 80	—
Wabash and Erie	-	- 200	—

Total 2,759 —

That the construction of canals in the United States has in most cases been a profitable undertaking, yielding on an average from ten to twelve per cent. interest *per annum* on the capital invested,* will appear from the sub-joined report of the canal commissioners of the state of New York, which may be relied on as official, as these canals are owned by the state itself.

* In one or two instances some private canal companies have de-clared a dividend of 102 per cent. *per annum!*

Name.	Length in Miles.	No. of Locks.	Cost in Dolls. & Cts.
Erie - - -	363	84	7,143,789 86
Champlain - - ⎱ Glen's Fall's Feeder ⎰	76	34	1,257,604 26
Oswego - -	38	14	565,437 35
Cayuga - - -	21	11	236,804 74
Chemung - - ⎱ Navigable Feeder - ⎰	39	53	331,693 57
Crooked Lake - -	8	27	156,776 57
Chenango Feeders -	113	109	1,960,456 28
	658		11,652,562 96

The average cost, per mile, therefore, was 18,000 dollars, or £3,600 sterling.

The Tolls received in the year 1835 were as follows:

	Dollars.	Cts.
Erie and Champlain canals - -	1,492,811	59
Oswego - - - - - -	29,180	62
Cayuga and Seneca - - - -	20,430	11
Chemung - - - - - -	4,720	44
Crooked Lake - - - - -	1,829	63
Total -	1,548,972	39*

which is 13⅓ per cent. nearly of their cost. The tolls on these canals have been annually increasing ever since the completion of the enterprise. In 1831 they amounted to 10½ per cent., in 1832 to 10⅖ per cent., in 1833 to 12⅖ per cent., in 1834 to 11½ per cent., and in 1835, as I have just stated, to 13⅓ nearly, of the whole cost of the canals.

The following table will show the increase of tolls during the last five years.

Comparative View of Tolls for Five years.

Canals.	1831.	1832.	1833.	1834.	1835.
	Dolls. Cts.	Dolls. Cts.	Dolls. Cts.	Dolls. Cts.	Dolls. Cts.
Erie - -	1,091,711 20	1,085,612 28	1,290,136 20 ⎱	1,294,649 66	1,492,811 59
Champlain	102,896 23	110,191 95	132,559 02 ⎰		
Oswego -	16,271 10	19,786 20	22,950 47	22,168 02	29,180 62
Cayuga -	12,920 39	13,893 04	17,174 69	18,130 43	20,430 11
Chemung -	- -	- -	694 00	3,378 05	4,720 44
Crooked Lake	- -	- -	200 84	1,473 40	1,829 63
Total	1,223,801 98	1,229,483 47	1,463,715 22	1,339,799 56	1,548,972 39

* Chenango canal is not yet in operation; but was to be completed in November, 1836.

Pennsylvania has always been the rival of New York with regard to internal improvements; and it will therefore be not improper to give a short statement of the canals of that state.

Pennsylvania possesses twelve state canals, extending $601\frac{1}{2}$ miles in length, and two state railroads of 81 and 37 miles respectively, making jointly a distance of 720 miles, exclusive of the improvements carried on by private companies.

The following TABLES will exhibit the LENGTH and COST of each CANAL, together with the AMOUNT of TOLLS received during the last Five Years:

Name.	Length in Miles.	Cost.	
		Dolls.	*Cts.*
Delaware Division - -	$59\frac{3}{4}$	1,238,027	69
Eastern Do. - - -	43	1,283,733	46
Juniata Do. - - ⎱ Feeders - - ⎰	$132\frac{1}{2}$	2,490,290	13
Western Do. - -	$106\frac{1}{2}$	2,758,937	71
Feeders - - -	- -	64,255	00
Susquehanna Do. - -	39	1,039,256	77
West Branch Do. - -	$25\frac{3}{4}$	421,771	00
North Branch Do. -	$55\frac{1}{2}$	1,096,178	34
Wyoming Do. - -	17	342,796	55
Lycoming Do. - -	$41\frac{3}{4}$	⎱ 1,205,573 ⎰	77
Feeders Do. - -	$4\frac{1}{4}$		
Beaver Do. - - -	$30\frac{3}{4}$	476,401	48
Franklin Line Do. -	$22\frac{1}{4}$	442,558	34
French Creek Do. -	$23\frac{1}{2}$	441,455	45
Total -	$601\frac{1}{2}$	13,301,235	69

AMOUNT of TOLLS received since 1830.

				Dolls.	*Cts.*
In 1830	-	-	-	27,012	90
1831	-	-	-	38,241	20
1832	-	-	-	50,909	57
1833	-	-	-	151,419	69

				Dolls.	*Cts.*
1834	-	-	-	309,789	15
1835	-	-	-	684,357	77

Total	-	1,261,730	28

Nor have the other states been behindhand with regard to internal improvements of this sort. There was one canal constructed in the state of Maine; four others in New Hampshire; four in Massachusetts; two in Connecticut; three in New Jersey; one in the state of Delaware; three in Maryland; six in Virginia; three in North Carolina; six in South Carolina; one in Georgia; two in Alabama; four in Louisiana; and two in the state of Ohio, viz. the "Ohio Canal," from Portsmouth on the Ohio to Cleaveland on Lake Erie, 307 miles in length, with 152 locks, and the "Miami Canal," sixty-five miles in length, with thirty-two locks; and there were, besides, eight new canal companies incorporated by the legislature of that state.

The legislature of the state of Indiana passed a bill in January, 1836, providing for a loan of 10,000,000 dollars to be expended in "improving river navigation, and constructing canals, railroads, and turnpike roads." In consequence of this bill, three canals, two railroads, and two macadamised turnpike roads have been commenced in that state, and are now in active progress. In the state of Illinois, two canal companies were recently incorporated, one of which, with a capital of 7,000,000 dollars, is to construct a canal from Chicago on Lake Michigan, to Ottawa on the Illinois river, distance ninety-five miles. The breadth of this canal is to be thirty-six feet at the bottom, sixty at the surface, and its depth six feet. Thirty-six miles from Chicago, the canal must be cut twenty-four miles through solid rock, from seven to twenty-eight feet in depth, making this part alone cost 4,000,000 of dollars. The commissioners advertised in July, 1836, for 10,000 workmen, offering them from twenty-five to thirty dollars (five to six pounds sterling) a month.

The post-offices and post-roads have increased in the same proportion as the canals and railroads.

In the year 1790	{ the number of Post-Offices was	75
------	1800 it was already - - -	903
------	1810 - - - - -	2,300
------	1820 - - - - -	4,500
------	1830 - - - - -	8,400

The gradual extension of post-roads will be best perceived from the following official account, showing the increase of miles in every ten years, from 1790 till 1830 inclusive.

In the year 1790	- - - -	1,875 miles.
------	1800 - - - -	20,817 —
------	1810 - - - -	36,406 —
------	1820 - - - -	72,492 —
------	1830 - - - -	115,176 —

The mails are now carried on these routes (daily or otherwise,) 25,869,480 miles per annum; viz. 16,874,050 in four-horse post-coaches and two-horse stages; 7,817,973 miles on horse-back, and in sulkies; * 909,959 miles in steam-boats; and 270,504 in railroad cars.

When we reflect on the multitude and extent of these improvements, the incredibly short time in which they were executed, the high price of labor, and the comparatively small and thinly scattered population of the United States, we shall irresistibly arrive at the conclusion, that in this particular branch of national industry, the Americans have done more than all other nations taken together. Even the rapid improvements in England appear diminutive, when compared to the vastness of American enterprise, and the continent of Europe cannot even furnish a term of comparison.

If the whole population of the United States were engaged in constructing railroads and canals, they would find ample employment in completing those which are now projected or commenced, and might for years be enployed in that branch of industry alone. What is truly surprising is, that a people, in number scarcely surpassing one third of the population of France, and spread over so large a surface, should, in addition to

* A species of light, uncovered gig.

these works, find the necessary time for the cultivation and extension of commerce, manufactures, and the mechanic arts! No other nation did at any time engage in such a variety of industrious pursuits, and none can boast, in any one of them, of a greater rapidity of progress.

The AMOUNT of POSTAGES received in the several States during the year 1834, and the number of Post-Offices in that year, were as follows :

States.	Dollars.	Number of Post-Offices.
Maine - - - -	48,717	446
New Hampshire - -	23,429	289
Vermont - - -	26,043	287
Massachusetts - -	172,567	469
Connecticut - - -	51,604	252
Rhode Island - -	19,002	46
New York - - -	430,426	1,687
New Jersey - - -	29,817	269
Pennsylvania - - -	343,406	1,148
Delaware - - -	6,465	39
Maryland - - -	89,235	233
Virginia - - -	114,554	891
North Carolina - -	38,746	557
South Carolina - -	60,755	300
Georgia - - - -	79,925	360
Alabama - - -	50,514	231
Mississippi - - -	26,450	126
Louisiana - - -	61,905	72
Tennessee - - -	43,858	470
Kentucky - - -	53,987	399
Ohio - - - -	100,652	883
Indiana - - - -	20,835	313
Illinois - - - -	14,789	204
Missouri - - -	19,518	145
District of Columbia -	17,724	3
Michigan Territory -	12,537	139
Florida - - - -	8,292	51
Arkansas - - -	4,100	78
Total - -	1,969,852	10,387

The Postages of the principal Cities were as follows:

New York	-	-	-	-	192,493 dollars.
Philadelphia	-	-	-	-	118,354 —
Boston	-	-	-	-	77,925 —
Baltimore	-	-	-	-	62,505 —
New Orleans	-	-	-	-	48,840 —
Charleston	-	-	-	-	30,562 —
Cincinnati	-	-	-	-	20,991 —
Richmond	-	-	-	-	20,336 —
Albany	-	-	-	-	16,601 —
Total in nine cities	-	-	-	588,607 —

(The income from the Post Office is principally spent in establishing new roads and lines of communication, and extending the usefulness of the department.)

The following Table will show the Rate of Travelling on the Mississippi and the Ohio, (taken from the Wheeling Virginia Gazette.)

Up the River.	Distance in Miles.	Total Distance.	Dolls.	Cts.
From Wheeling				
to Wellsburg, Ohio - -	16	16	0	75
to Steubenville, Ohio -	7	23	1	0
to Wellsville, Ohio - -	20	43	1	50
to Beaver, Pennsylvania -	26	69	2	50
to Pittsburg, Pennsylvania	27	96	3	0
Down the River.				
to Marietta, Ohio - -	82	82	2	50
to Parkersburgh, Virginia -	10	92	2	50
to Point Pleasant - -	78	170	5	0
to Gallipolis, Ohio - -	3	173	5	0
to Guyandotte, Virginia -	37	210	6	0
to Portsmouth, Ohio -	50	260	7	0
to Maysville, Kentucky -	47	307	8	0
to Ripley, Ohio - -	13	319	9	0

27

Down the River.	Distance in Miles.	Total Distance.	Dolls.	Cts.
to Cincinnati, Ohio - -	46	355	10	0
to Port William, mouth of Kentucky - - -	79	434	11	0
to Madison, Indiana -	13	447	11	0
to West Port, Kentucky -	20	467	12	0
to Louisville, Kentucky -	20	487	12	0
to Rome, Indiana - -	100	587	15	0
to Troy, Indiana - -	35	622	15	0
to Yellow Banks, Kentucky	25	647	15	0
to Evansville, Indiana -	40	687	18	0
to Henderson, Kentucky -	12	699	18	0
to Shawneetown, Illinois -	53	752	18	0
to Smithland, mouth of Cumberland - -	63	815	18	0
to Mouth, Ohio - -	66	881	20	0
to New Madrid, Missouri -	75	956	22	0
to Memphis, Tennessee -	150	1,106	25	0
to Helena, Arkansas -	85	1,191	26	0
to Vicksburg, Mississippi	307	1,498	30	0
to Natchez, Mississippi -	110	1,608	30	0
to New Orleans, Louisiana	300	1,908	35	0

These prices of passage include boarding. The fares of deck-passengers are about one fourth of these, the passengers finding themselves. To New Orleans it is still less, being only 8 dollars, or about 36s. for a distance of nearly 2,000 miles. The deck is covered and contains berths. The passage to Louisville is performed in two days and a half, and to New Orleans in from eight to ten ; returning about double that time. The ordinary speed is twelve miles an hour down, and six up the river. It must be observed, moreover, that there are boats which charge less than the above rates, the price depending upon the number of boats in port, and the abundance or scarcity of passengers.

The liberality with which the prices of passage are fixed ought not to escape the attention of the peruser of the above table. No additional charge is made for carrying a person fifty or sixty miles further, although it may happen, that by so doing he may have " the benefit of another meal." Thus the fare from Wheeling to Rome, Indiana, (587 miles,) is 15 dollars; and from Wheeling to Yellow Banks, Kentucky, (sixty miles further,) the same. From Wheeling to Evansville, Kentucky, (distance 687 miles,) the fare is 18 dollars ; and to Smithland, mouth of the Cumberland, (128 miles further,) no additional charge is made. The same holds of the distances to Vicksburg and Natchez, in the state of Mississippi.

The increased facilities of intercourse, thus created between the different states, cannot but produce the happiest results. They lessen the expenses of travelling, and enable emigrants from Europe and the eastern states, to proceed south or west at a trifling expenditure of time and money; they enhance the value of real estates throughout the Union, by shortening the distances which exist between the towns and country ; they increase commerce and open a market for the produce of the west, which would otherwise be beyond the line of natural communication ; they are the means of spreading civilization and learning throughout the country, by bringing the wilderness of the west in contact with the arts and sciences of the borders of the Atlantic ; and lastly, the most important of all, they amalgamate the different elements of which the population of the United States is composed to a large homogeneous whole, and strengthen the bond of union between the different states by so interweaving their individual interests that a separation could not be effected without a severe diminution of prosperity to all. The last two consequences are, from their moral and political importance, the most desirable of all, and are, of themselves, sufficient to create a permanent interest.

Those who are continually dreading or prophesying the dissolution of the Union, and whose fertile imagination is already employed in portioning out the territories of the west, south, east, and north, consider merely the physical inequalities of those states, without reflecting, for one moment, on the moral causes which have a tendency directly the reverse of what they anticipate. One

of the reasons which they allege for the impending dissolution, is the vast extent of territory of the United States,
and the consequent diversity of feeling and sentiment
created by the difference in the soil and climate. They
pretend that the south, the west, and the north have each
their peculiar interests, incompatible with the general
prosperity of the whole; and that so far from considering
themselves as children of one and the same family, the
inhabitants of the different states cherish a kind of sectional feeling, which is diametrically opposite to the
lofty inspirations of national character. I confess myself no partisan to such an opinion, and shall take another
opportunity (in the next chapter) of explaining my sentiments on that subject. I shall be satisfied, for the present, to consider the question only as far as it relates to
distances.

Distance is a relative idea, and is not properly measured by the number of miles, at which one place is
situated from another ; but rather by the *time* which is
required to *move* from one to another. This is so far
true, and so popular a view of the subject, that the notion
of expressing distance by *time* has become familiar to all
people ; the unit of comparison being generally the distance walked in an hour. Thus, in Germany, a traveller
will learn that a certain place is situated *three hours* from
another, and in Westphalia two or three *pipes*, indicating
the number of pipes which may be smoked on the way to
it.* These numbers are evidently *relative;* for a man
may increase or slacken his pace, and thereby diminish
the time required for accomplishing the distance. If, instead of walking, he mounts on horseback, the distance
will become still less ; and so on, in proportion to the
velocity with which he proceeds on his way. An object
removed half a mile from a lame person is, to him, almost an infinite distance ; but it would be dreadfully
near to the mouth of a cannon. Numbers, in general,
convey no positive idea; because the largest of them
may become infinitely small, and the smallest of them infinitely large, in proportion to the units of which they
represent the respective aggregates. We judge of the

* *Kaestner's* " Anfangsgründe der Mathematick."

whole physical world not as it *is*, but as it *appears* to our senses, and is capable of affecting our happiness. Thus the universe appears infinite to our finite senses; because we lack the term of comparison (the common measure ;) but it does not follow from it that to an understanding less limited and finite than our own, it may not bear an approximate ratio, and it is philosophically and mathematically certain, that, to the infinite Being, its relation is fixed aud invariable.* Thus, whatever is calculated to change our relation to the physical world, may actually be said to change the physical world itself, and *vice versâ*. Now, I maintain that such a change has taken place in the physical position of the United States ; and that, therefore, the people themselves must have changed their relation to the objects around them, and to each other.

To an American the United States can hardly be as large as France appears to a Frenchman ; the different states being actually less separate and distant from one another than the different departments of that kingdom. An inhabitant of Cincinnati, or of Charleston, is a nearer neighbor to a gentleman residing in New York, than an Alsacian is to a Parisian; because he is actually less removed from, and comes oftener in contact with him, than is the case between the two inhabitants of France. Whatever difference in manners, customs, and opinions there may exist between them, will have a tendency to be smoothed down by habitual intercourse and exchange of thought ; and prejudices, which are principally founded on ignorance or an imperfect acquaintance with the motives of others, must at last yield to individual conviction, and the knowledge acquired from observation. How many prejudices which existed betwen the French and the English have been explained away since the unrestrained intercourse between the two nations ! How many Englishmen, since the year 1815, have passed over to France with the expectation of finding a race of

* " A finite quantity is infinitely large when compared to an infinitely small one; a finite one, infinitely small with regard to one which is infinitely large; but the ratio between two infinite quantities may be expressed by numbers, and is constant."— *Tobias Mayer,* " *Höhere Analysis.*"— *Carnot,* " *Métaphysique du Calcul infinitésimal.*"

dancing monkeys, or ferocious tigers, and have in their stead discovered a polite, chivalrous and highly civilised nation! And how many Frenchmen, on the other hand, have come over to England to behold a people scarcely emerged from barbarism, whose principal amusement consisted in hunting, horse-racing, and cock-fighting, in order to become satisfied of what they have yet to learn in order to equal that people in depth of thought, energy of action, and the wisdom of its legislation. The mutual intercourse between the two nations has acted beneficially on both. Instead of hating one another, with that hatred which characterised the barbarism of their former wars, the people of the two countries have become friends, and are now united by the strongest ties which ever connected two nations not speaking the same language. They have learned to respect each other, and to imitate each other's virtues. The treasures of intellect of the one have become the common wealth of the other; and their former misguided passions and mutual rancor (which it was the the interest of certain politicians to kindle and nourish) are now dying away from want of aliment.

But if such are the effects of the increased intercourse of two nations naturally strangers to one another, what may we not hope for with regard to the people of the different states of America, where the same cause operates in a multiplied ratio, joined to an extensive internal commerce which affects all interests, and is strongly assisted by the ties of consanguinity, and the charm of one and the same language? So far from discovering in the progress of America any symptoms of the future dissolution of the Union, I can see in it only new pledges of its stability and duration. It grows stronger every year by the increased community of interests; and what the Americans did not wish for, when their stakes in the government were divided, they cannot reasonably desire or promote, when their cause becomes one and the same.

Neither is there any remarkable division of sentiment perceptible in their actions. On the contrary, it is una- nimity which characterises all their proceedings. The Americans have nothing to gain, but a great deal to lose, from a separation of the Union; and the regulations of their internal commerce are such, that a chaos of confusion, and a total suspension of business, would follow the slightest attempt at so preposterous a measure.

The climate is another cause supposed to act strongly on the minds of men, and to produce lasting national differences.* This, undoubtedly, does not change with the facilities of intercourse ; but the men who live in it may be able to effect an alteration, and thereby render themselves less subject to its influence. A person who lives six months of the year in one climate, and the remaining six months in another, cannot be said to be subject to the vicissitudes of either ; and the same will hold of him who is so little confined to any one place, that it is difficult to ascertain which is his habitual residence. This is the case with the Americans. Nearly one half of the whole trading population (and this is no inconsiderable portion of the whole) is constantly engaged in travelling ; and in the summer season, when, on account of the water communication, travelling becomes cheaper than it is in the winter, or early in the spring, every class of society, men and women, the aged and the young, join in it as a favorite amusement. The Americans seem to know no greater pleasure than that of going on fast, and accomplishing large distances in comparatively short times. Towards autumn, and at the beginning of winter the wealthier population of the north repair to the south, to escape the inclemency of an eastern winter or spring,† and during the hot months of summer the rich planters of the south retaliate upon their brethren to the north, by enjoying the cooling breezes of New England.

This continued motion of the Americans, which resembles, on a huge scale, the vibrations of a pendulum, is productive of very important results. It saves the southerners from the enervating influence of the excessive heat of their latitudes, and enables the northerners to familiarise themselves with the south. It acts as a constant moderator between them ; and this the more so as the facilities of travelling increase, and the expenses in-

* Montesquieu in his " *Esprit des Lois* " certainly ascribes to it more than its due influence.

† The months of March, April, and even part of May, in New England, are the most trying to the constitution, but the " *fall* " is beautiful, and superior to the same season in Europe.

cidental to them diminish. The constant intercourse of the southerners with the inhabitants of the north, and of the latter with the former, and the consequent necessity of conforming to the peculiarities of both climes, prevent the formation of those habits which belong exclusively to either, and are eminently calculated to diminish thos e moral and physical differences, which the remoteness or the vicinity of the equator seems to have permanently established among men.

Thus, in whatever light we may view them, whether we consider their physical or moral influence, their effects on civilization, or their promotion and encouragement of commerce and every branch of industry, we shall see, in the internal improvements of the United States, one of the most powerful means of producing harmony and good fellowship amongst the different states, and must therefore hail them as the harbingers of peace, and that friendship which I am confident will last as long as liberty shall find an asylum in the legislative halls of America. If freedom should once be lost, if the United States should fall a prey to some victorious enemy, if an ambitious faction should succeed in enslaving the people and directing the national efforts and energies to their own sordid ends, then it matters not what relative position the different states may assume : of a parcel of slaves it is immaterial which is foremost and hindmost in the ranks, or whether they are all chained alike to the yoke. But as long as the people are sovereign, the prospects of the country will remain unclouded ; and the Union will be preserved, notwithstanding the puerile declamations of those who would be the most inactive in time of danger, as they are now the most apprehensive in time of peace.

But has not, it will be asked, the Union been already in danger, at the late question of the tariff? To this question I would resolutely reply in the negative : the Union was *not* in danger. The nullification doctrine of South Carolina was the result of a fever produced by imprudent exposures, which has since yielded to the proper remedies ; but which did not threaten the continuance of the Union any more than a transient head-ache the life of a robust young man. It merely shows that prudence is necessary, even to the strongest constitution ; and that, in the terms

of an old English adage, " an ounce of preventive is worth
a pound of cure." Now that the sickness is passed, the
Americans have time to reflect on its origin, and the best
means of preventing its occurrence in the future. If it
should come again, it will not find them unprepared ; but
they are too wise a people to fall twice into the same
error. I consider the late proceedings in South Carolina,
and the subsequent measures adopted by Congress, as a
timely warning, which has brought the different states to
a consciousness of their true position, and the dangers
which await them if they swerve for one moment from
the true intent of their compact. The American Union
has now nothing to fear from a similar attack ; and is
just as much more secured against all such evils than
before the tariff question was started, as the mariner who
is prepared for a storm is safer than he who is only accustomed to sail with light breezes.

The internal improvements of the United States have
for a time been the rallying cry of a certain party, and
they have also had their champion in the person of Mr.
Henry Clay, senator from the state of Kentucky. To
understand this matter properly, it must be remembered,
that there does not, nor ever did, exist a party in the
United States, *averse* to internal improvements generally;
and the line of demarcation, therefore, consisted solely
in the *means* by which the different parties intended to
carry their plans into effect. Mr Clay's friends held that
the surplus revenue of the United States had best be spent
in internal improvements, (which more or less had to
benefit individual states,) while the present administration
saw in it a means of corrupting the elections, by " bribing
the people with the people's money." Both parties were
heartily in favor of improvements ; but the one wished to
employ for that purpose the money of the government,
while the other were willing to leave them to the enterprise of individual states, and to tax only those with the
expense of them, who, from their proximity, were most
benefited by the measure. Whatever glory may be attached to the doctrine of *national improvements* of Mr.
Clay, that of the administration is equally strongly re-
commended by good sense and *national justice.*

Mr. Clay's principles would have enabled the government to act powerfully on the political sentiments of individual states, and was too nearly allied with the system of *central zation* not to excite the apprehensions of the people. Spending the surplus revenue in the construction of national roads, might have amounted to an indirect taxation of the people, and would have delegated to Congress a power, which, by the constitution, it was not intended to possess. The least preference shown to any individual state (and it would have been impossible to benefit them all in the same ratio) would have roused the jealousy of the others; and as the number of those whom it would have been in the power of government to benefit must needs have been smaller than that whom it must necessarily have disobliged, Congress itself would eventually have lost a portion of its popularity.

It would have been exceedingly imprudent, in the president or the senate of the United States, to take a particular state into favor, or to extend their protection even to the weakest and most needy of them. Any such guardianship would have affected the independence of the individual states, and could hardly have failed to bring them into collision with the general government. Besides, it is very doubtful whether the great end, for which these sacrifices were to be made, would have been actually realised. It remains to be proved that the paternal care of the general government would accomplish more than the pride and emulation of individual states; and that people, in general, are more willing to preserve and improve what is *given* them, than what they *acquire* by their own individual exertion.

It is a principle of the New Englanders to tax the community with the support of common schools; because "people are more willing to send their children to school *when they pay for it*, than if education were to be had at no expense;" and I am strongly inclined to extend the same process of reasoning to the grand idea of national improvements. But, be this as it may, experience has shown that, in America, national undertakings of this kind are less apt to succeed, and less gratefully received by the states whom they are intended to benefit, than individual enterprise, in which they are obliged to invest their own money. The great western road has been an

immense expense to the government, but met with so
little favor and co-operation on the part of the states
through which it runs, that the latter could hardly be prevailed upon to charge themselves with the repairs of the
part which was finished, much less to do any thing in aid
of its construction or continuation. When Congress proposed to gather a toll for the purpose of defraying the expenses of the necessary repairs, Pennsylvania and some
of the other states violently opposed the measure, on the
ground that it would compromise their sovereignty. It
was therefore abandoned, and in its stead an additional
300,000 dollars (£60,000 sterling) voted out of the
treasury of the United States to finish the road, and surrender it to the individual states, to keep and use it as
they may. This apparent laxity of the Americans to
seize upon advantages offered them by others, evinces a
disposition diametrically opposite to Malvolio's, "Some
are born to greatness; some acquire greatness; and
some have greatness thrust upon them." The Americans
are altogether for *acquiring* greatness, and are therefore
least apt to run *mad*, and expiate their follies in *chains*.

The increased facilities of intercourse, and especially
the use of steam, are yet productive of another happy result, scarcely less deserving attention. The reduced expenses of travelling enable thousands of persons, who
would otherwise be obliged to remain stationary, to try
their fortunes abroad, or to journey for information.
Life consists in motion; and, as far as that goes, the
United States present certainly the most animated picture
of universal bustle and activity of any country in the
world. Such a thing as rest or quiescence does not even
enter the mind of an American, and its presence would to
him be actually insupportable. The rates of fares and
passages are so low, and so well adapted to the means of
the great bulk of the population, that there is scarcely an
individual so reduced in circumstances, as to be unable to
afford his " dollar or so," to travel a couple of hundred
miles from home, "in order to see the country and the
improvements which are going on." On board the
steamboats, meals are generally included in the price of
passage, which, during a certain part of the season, is so
reduced by opposition, as hardly to pay for the board

alone ; in which case it is almost as cheap, or cheaper, to travel than to stay at home.

The influence of these proceedings on the minds of the laboring classes is incredible. Instead of being confined to the narrow circle of their own acquaintances, and occupied chiefly with the contemplation of the steeple of their own native village, they have the same opportunity of widening the sphere of their knowledge by travelling and personal observation of the manners of different people, which in other countries is enjoyed by gentlemen of moderate fortune, and from which the same order in Europe is almost entirely excluded. The absence of post-chaises or any other vehicles exclusively for the conveyance of wealthy travellers, compels the latter to accomplish their journeys in company with such men as they may chance to meet on the road ; and if these happen to be mechanics or traders, an exchange of thought and sentiment takes place, which is often profitable to both parties. The laboring classes, which, in this manner, are brought in contact with the more polite orders of society, can hardly fail to improve in manners ; and the higher and wealthier classes, who in most countries are totally ignorant of the sentiments and wants of the lower orders, receive, in turn, much valuable instruction, which, as it passes from one individual to another, is sure of finally reaching the halls of Congress. A mutual loss and compensation takes place, and the facilities of travelling are, again, employed in equalizing conditions.

Much has been said on the anomalies of conduct of American travellers, especially on board of steamboats ; and unjust comparisons have been drawn between them and the passengers in European boats, sufficiently prejudicial to the former. No allowance, however, seems to have been made for the different materials composing these companies, and the peculiar usages established on board of American boats. Were the passengers in European steamers composed chiefly of small traders, hawkers, journeymen mechanics and operatives of all descriptions, and permitted to sit down at the same table with the polite and wealthier classes, to partake of dainties which they only know from hearsay, without any additional charge, I, for my part, would not wish to witness "the solecisms of deportment" of which they might be guilty. Add to this a liberal quotum of brandy, which on board of some of the steamboats is still handed round,* to be used at discretion, and it will be easy to fancy a picture which would more than shock the tender sensitiveness of an English tourist. When these circumstances are taken into consideration, it will appear that what English writers have *not* said about American travellers, is the highest encomium they can possibly bestow on their conduct; and that, notwithstanding the severity of their criticism on "American manners," they were not aware of the class of society with whom they journeyed. Their negative reasoning goes further than their positive assertion, and furnishes the best proof that the dress, language and manners of the inferior orders of Americans partake so much of the characteristic of education, that Europeans *mistake* them for those of gentlemen.

The American steamboats on the western rivers, and along the coast of the Atlantic, are of a very superior construction, both as regards speed and elegance of accommodation for passengers. They are now principally built on the low-pressure principle; but have generally engines of very great power. The ladies' cabin, which is usually on deck, is separated from that of the gentlemen, and the latter have no admission to it except by the consent of all the occupants. At breakfast, dinner and tea, the ladies are invited down to take their seats at the head of the table, (meals being generally served in the gentlemen's cabin,) after which the gentlemen are permitted to take theirs; and the usual ceremonies being passed, active operations are commenced on all sides with an activity of spirit, which allows no one to remain for a long time an indifferent spectator of the scene.

After dinner, the ladies, accompanied by their respective gentlemen, are seen walking off to their apartment, while those of the latter, who have no such *sweet incumbrance*, indulge in the luxury of a cigar, or take a solitary stroll on deck. Few are waiting for the pastry or the desert, though

* The temperance societies have abolished this custom on board of most of the steamboats.

both are generally of the best kind; because it would oblige
them to remain too long in a state of quiescence, which is
contrary to their nature, and incompatible with their notions of comfort.

The great advantages of American boats over those of
Europe consist chiefly in their much greater proportions
and consequently larger accommodations; in the elegance
of their furniture, the cheapness of the fares, and the
great rapidity with which they accomplish their passages.
Many of them contain state and drawing rooms, and all
the conveniences to be found in the best hotels. One or
two waiting women are always in attendance on the
ladies, while the gentlemen are blessed with the indispensable attendance of a barber. Some of the larger boats
are ornamented with a piano and other musical instruments; and, in order that a "feast of reason" may not
be wanting, a circulating library awaits the pleasure,
principally of the ladies; the gentlemen being on such
occasions either satisfied with the "news of the day," or
deriving more substantial comfort from a well-furnished
bar, containing the juice of the grapes of all climes,
together with a little of the less flavored brandy and
whiskey. On the western waters there are temperance
boats, which furnish no such articles; and it is more than
probable that the progress of temperance will banish
them also from on board the steamers of the Atlantic
states.

The public houses, with the exception of those in the
large cities, are frequently owned by the proprietors of
the road, or kept by persons interested in the steamboat
or railroad companies, who contract for the conveyance
of passengers. This adds much to the comfort and expedition of travelling. Instead of being tormented by the
officious offerings of an hundred cards, as is the case in
Europe, an American traveller, on his arrival at a stop-
ping place, is spared the trouble of inquiring for the best
inn or hotel, by being at once carried to that which is
prepared for his reception. Every thing there has its
regular price; so much for dinner, so much for supper,
so much for the use of a room, &c.; so that it is easy to
calculate, to the uttermost penny, the expenses of a journey
of many hundred miles. No head waiter, waiter, chamber-

maid, porter, &c. are impeding his progress on the en-
suing morning, by throwing themselves between his
pocket and the boat or coach; but, on the contrary, he
finds, on rising, his luggage already conveyed to the
starting-place, and the strictest injunctions given to the
servants, not to make any demands on the passengers.
The only money given to servants on such occasions, is
about 6d. for cleaning boots and brushing clothes, and
even this is left at the discretion of the traveller. A
very different custom, however, prevails in the hotels of
the large cities. Many of the servants there, being bred
in Europe, *expect* at least, if they do not actually demand,
certain remunerations for their services, besides the wages
which they receive from their employers; and in the
city of New York, one is hardly welcome without them.
But then they are not nearly as exorbitant as either in
England or France, and depend, still, principally on the
good will of the donor.

The charges made in the hotels comprise generally
board and lodging, and average from one dollar (4s. 6d.)
to two dollars and fifty cents (11s. 3d.) per day. In the
country they are much lower; good boarding and lodging being obtained for three or four dollars (from 13s. 6d.
to 18s.) per week. In the interior and the western states
the price of board and lodging is still less; averaging
from one dollar fifty cents to two dollars per week, or
about 1s. 3d. per day. No wine, of course, is included in
these prices; but there are four good meals served every
day, viz. breakfast, dinner, tea, and supper, at each of
which a profusion of meat is brought on the table, and in
many instances cider, beer, and even brandy are handed
round, without any additional charge.

The hotels in the large cities contain, besides the bar, a
ladies' and a gentlemen's drawing-room, a number of
sitting and smoking rooms, for the gratuitous use of the
boarders—a news-room, and one or two large dining-
rooms. These are all elegantly fitted up, and supply, in
a measure, the want of private parlors, which are not
easily obtained at an American hotel, and for which the
charges are about as high, or higher in proportion, than
in England. The *table d'hôte* contains all the luxuries of
the season, in the shape of viands, condiments and pastries

which are to be found in the market, dressed partly in the French and partly in the English fashion, together with the fruits of the country, and such supplements as are imported from Europe and India. In the summer a profusion of ice keeps water, hock and champaign in a state of delightful coolness, and becomes as indispensable an article of consumption as fuel is in winter, or beef and bread at every season of the year. Dinners served at private rooms, or served at particular hours, are, nearly as expensive as in London; but are seldom called for by native Americans. Wines in general, and of all kinds, are good, but dear; the best Madeira from three to ten and twelve dollars (13s. 6d. to 45s. and 54s.) a bottle; hock from two to three dollars (9s. to 13s. 6d.;) claret the same as hock, sherry from one dollar to two dollars and a half (4s. 6d. to 9s.,) and champaign from two to three dollars (9s. to 13s. 6d.). Port is little drank in the United States. English porter or ale is generally 50 cents or 2s. 6d. per bottle.

The high price of wines in the American hotels is the more surprising, as claret and hock pay but a small duty, and may be procured at a wine-merchant's at about one half or one fourth the prices I have named. But then, every charge being low, the only chance of profit of an inn-keeper in the United States is on the wines, of which the Americans profess to be the best judges, and for which, therefore, they are required to pay in proportion to their knowledge.

One of the peculiarities in the lives of Americans consists in the practice of boarding. Single and married men, and whole families, prefer this mode of life, to taking lodgings by themselves, or going to the expense of housekeeping. Whatever inconvenience may be attached to this habit, it is, nevertheless, commendable on the score of economy, and, to a newly married couple, is the means of saving a number of servants. Many young men, who cannot afford renting a house, (which in America is very expensive,) are in this manner enabled to marry a little sooner than their means would otherwise allow them, and find, in their new state, an additional stimulus to industry. Some of the boarding-houses are fashionable, and are kept by ladies of good families, whose reduced circumstances have compelled them to resort to this means of procuring an honest subsistence. An American lady, whose husband dies without making a provision for her, or who is suddenly reduced to poverty by reverses of fortune, finds a ready expedient in keeping a *school*, or a *boarding-house*, to extricate herself from the most urgent embarrassment. Moral and physical aliment is sometimes extended by the same hands—in which case the establishment is termed a *boarding-school.*

The accommodations in most boarding-houses are good, and there are some of them established on the plan of regular hotels. The price of board averages from one half to two thirds of that of the regular inns, besides saving the enormous expense of wine, which either need not be called for, or is furnished at a much lower rate than at taverns. Gentlemen may also drink their own wine—in which case little or no charge is made for corkage.

Good board for mechanics may be procured, in New York, or any other city on the Atlantic, at from two to three dollars per week, (9s. to 13s. 6d.) and, in the interior, it may be obtained still cheaper. The wages of a journeyman mechanic in those cities, average from one dollar to two and even three dollars a day, (4s. 6d. to 9s. and 13s. 6d.) and are therefore often five or six times as high as their living. A single day's labor is often sufficient to support them a whole week, enabling them to save the earnings of the remaining days, or to employ them for other purposes. This, I believe, cannot be said of the same class of men in any other country—there being none in which the operatives are possessed of estates of three, four, and five hundred pounds, as in the United States. It explains also why the American operatives, with very few exceptions, have carried their points when they struck for higher wages. They could hold out longer without work than their employers could well spare them. They possess property, and with it the advantages of credit.

Having thus enlarged on boarding-houses and taverns, I would willingly say a few words on those excellent accommodations which the Americans, and especially

28*

the inhabitants of the southern states, offer so liberally to all strangers who feel disposed to accept them. I mean the good offices tendered by their hospitality. The houses of the people in the northern and eastern states are not generally constructed for the reception of strangers, (although this is by no means a characteristic of their dwellings,) and their kind feelings, therefore, confine themselves usually to invitations to dinners and parties; but the house of every southerner contains a number of apartments, solely fitted up for the reception of guests; and so rigid are they in performing the duties of hospitality, that, even on *leaving* their estates for the east or the north, they provide for the strangers whom chance may happen to bring under their roofs whilst they are absent.

A traveller will always be offered the use of a good room, an excellent larder, and a well-stocked cellar, on the estate of a planter, whether the owner be at home or abroad. No letter of introduction is required for that purpose; it is sufficient that the stranger should have the exterior and manners of a well-bred man: it matters not from what country he comes, or what place he calls his home. A person may travel with his whole family and a numerous retinue, and will still be welcomed by his hospitable entertainers. This custom has made inns and taverns in the southern states almost useless; and their accommodations, therefore, are much inferior to similar establishments of the north. But a southern planter will be sorry if a traveller take lodgings at an inn, while his own plantation is near; and will often wait on him in person, to invite him to the cheer of his house.

Nor is it merely in the extension of hospitality, and, in general, in the friendly reception of strangers, that Americans evince the kindness of their dispositions. They are ready to assist foreigners with their counsel, with their influence, and, in many instances, with their fortunes. They are patient in their explanations, indefatigable in their services, and, of all people in the world, the most ready to make allowances for national and individual peculiarities. I know no country where a well-educated foreigner could be so certain of an honorable reception, as in the United States, or where he would so soon be apt to make acquaintances and friends. He will not remain there long without forming some tie or attachment, and must be unfortunate indeed, if he cannot make it his home. Whatever be the motives of persons in visiting the United States, few will quit them without cherishing a grateful remembrance of their hospitable inhabitants.

CHAPTER XI.

THE southern states of America have so many distinct
features, and their interests are, by Europeans, supposed
to be so much opposed to those of the north, that an inquiry into their peculiar situation, and the feelings and
sentiments of their inhabitants, cannot but be interesting
even to an English reader. The south and the north
have, in all countries, been considered as natural enemies
to each other, and an apparent reconciliation between
them as resting on no permanent basis. With regard to
the southern and northern states of America this natural
enmity seems to be fostered and increased by the introduction of negro slavery, the life and existence of one,
and the dread and horror of the other party.

Slavery, in the northern states has been attacked with
every weapon which morality, religion, politics, superstition and revenge could forge; whilst the inhabitants of
the south have been defending themselves with the anguish of despair, and that unanimity of sentiment, which
a sense of their common danger inspires. The contest
is still going on, and, in its ultimate consequences, is
supposed to threaten the Union. There are those who
prophecy an unavoidable dissolution of it in less than
twenty years; while others, in their zeal to anticipate
events, will not suffer a delay of ten; and there is a class
of religious fanatics who would wish the crisis still nearer
at hand. They seem to have a peculiar predilection in
favor of three grand divisions of the United States, viz.

the north, the west, and the south, which, it seems, would best suit their conception of national grandeur.

I do not confess myself converted by either of these doctrines; but, on the contrary, maintain that the Union of the United States will last as long as their individual prosperity, the period of the decline of which, I trust, is, at this moment, beyond the power of human calculation. I believe it as remote as the downfall of Great Britain, an event on which the continental politicians have speculated for more than two centuries, without extricating themselves from the puzzle; and which they supposed to be prepared by the national debt of England in the same manner as the American catastrophe, by the fatal influence of the negroes. Contrary to their expectations, however, they have seen England's power increase, and every new page of her history proclaim her national renown; while the military chieftain, who threatened her peace, was hurled from his proud elevation, with the same overwhelming fatality which had favored his ill-boding progress. The destinies of England seemed to be under the protection of a special providence, which strengthened her leaders in the battle and the cabinet, as if the cause of humanity had been identified with that of her freedom. Nor was it otherwise. England was the avenger of Europe, as she is now the only protector of liberty in whose honor the nations may trust, possessing the will and the power to oppose the incursions of barbarism.

America is laboring in the same cause. She, too, is wedded to freedom, notwithstanding the introduction of slavery, and the denunciations of bigoted partisans. But her freedom, her honor, her power, and her existence, are explicitly pledged in the Union. If this palladium of her liberty should once be lost or destroyed, peace would no longer dwell with her; the different states would become mutual oppressors, and revive the history of Italy in the middle ages, with its horrors and bloodshed. Internal commerce would be burdened with onorous duties; the mouths of rivers would be shut to the enterprise of merchants, and industry, in all its branches, groan under exorbitant taxes. The expenses of government would be multiplied in an hundred-fold ratio, while the national credit would die with the national pledge. Each state would have to maintain its standing army; for, the first division being made, the subdivisions would follow, and create the instruments of tyranny. The lofty patriotism of *Americans*, which now embraces a world extending from one ocean to the other, would shrink into a local attachment; and their minds, now expanded with ideas of national progress, would contract into the sordid compass of unworthy prejudices.

These awful consequences of a separation of the Union are known to every American, and there is no offset to them in any most distant advantage which one or more individual states might hope to derive from it. I cannot be persuaded, therefore, that it will ever be in the power of any one man, or set of men, to induce the inhabitants of a particular district to secede from (revolt against) the Union, unless a case should occur in which it were physically impossible for that district to comply with the rigor of the laws. In this case, the oppressed party would be reduced to the mournful alternative of choosing between immediate destruction, or a more remote, but not less certain death and ruin. But then it would not be the rebellious district, but the majority of Congress, which would have passed such unnatural laws, which would have infringed upon the social compact, and dissolved the Union *theoretically*, by whatever physical or moral force they might succeed in maintaining it.

But, even in this case we, might suppose the majority, which is capable of enacting these laws sufficiently strong to enforce them, even to the total ruin of the injured party. For, unless that majority were overwhelming, redress might be hoped for, from a change of opinion, and the injury borne with patience; or the law itself would have too little moral force to be executed with that rigor, which nothing but the consent of all parties could justify in a democratic republic.

I know of no national question, capable of producing this effect, unless it be a controversy on the abolition of slavery, on which subject Congress has no more power to legislate than on any other belonging to the internal government of the states; and from which, therefore, it must ever refrain, if the dissolution of the Union is not to egin at the capitol.

The question of the tariff does not bear the smallest resemblance to it; for it was at least one in which all the states were interested, though, perhaps, not in the same equal proportion which a strict adherence to justice might have rendered desirable. Few financial measures can operate alike on all states ; but the sympathy for the suffering party can, on that occasion, never amount to a direct opposition to the law ; unless it were established that the power of repealing this law has been taken away from the people, and the hope thereby lost of obtaining legitimate redress.

No such apprehensions were entertained with regard to the tariff of the United States ; and, on this account the conduct of South Carolina was generally condemned, though her grievances were readily redressed by the justice and good sense of the nation. Neither would the doctrine of nullification have spread in South Carolina itself, if the people in that state had not unfortunately believed that the law of the tariff was but the precursor of others still more oppressive, and intended to interfere with their slaves. The inhabitants of that state had, in this respect, previously suffered from the undue interference of northerners,* and their feelings, therefore, were in a morbid state of excitement, which required but little additional injury to burst into open indignation.

If the south could be assured that the north would never interfere with their slaves, all fears of dissension would vanish; for there is not one single subject capable of being brought before Congress which could operate so unequally on the different states, or injure a portion of them *beyond the possibility of redress.* I do not believe the south will ever secede from the Union, unless the north drive them away from it, which can hardly be their intention or policy. Such a campaign on the south can never become generally popular ; because it is as unprovoked as unjust, and could at best but distress the victors. It would be a war on the rights and privileges of others, without adding to the number of their own.

But I have anticipated the subject, and will, no doubt, be considered as an advocate of the *principle* of slavery.

* By itinerant preachers and publishers of incendiary pamphlets.

Nothing, however, can be further from my thoughts. Slavery cannot be defended on philosophical or religious grounds ; but where it once exists, is is but reasonable to look to the proper means by which it is to be abolished ; and not to choose those which, without advancing the moral condition of slaves, ruin and destroy their proprietors. The question admits of three distinct considerations, viz. the legal, the political, and the moral. Let us begin with the legal one.

The slaves in the southern states are the property of the planters, a kind of property which is not transferable, except amongst themselves, and which would be of no value to the inhabitants of the northern states. When the northern states emancipated their slaves, it was really because the expense of maintaining them was greater than the profits obtained from their labor, and because the same kind of work could be obtained as cheap, or cheaper, by hiring the services of the whites. The negroes, moreover, are the foundation of every other species of property in the southern states; for wit hout them, real estate would be of no value, as it is physically proved that neither the climate nor the soil will ever admit of the independent labor of the whites. It is evident, then, that if the negroes be emancipated, they must be *retained* to cultivate the plantations, and the proprietors obliged to hire them ; which amounts to paying interest on their own capital. This single point presents at once three formidable obstacles to the abolition of slavery.

1. They constitute a species of property which the planters cannot dispose of for any valuable consideration, and which, therefore, must be paid for by the liberators, by means of voluntary contributions or taxations.* The amount of this property is immense, as it may be computed at more than half the value of all real estate in the United States—the southern land being, on account of its productions, and especially those of cotton and rice, more valuable than any other in the country. The capital invested in the growth of cotton alone, was estimated at

* I have not yet heard of the amount which the abolitionists of the northern states have subscribed for this purpose; but feel quite certain it falls yet short of £20,000,000 sterling.

eight hundred millions of dollars, or one hundred and sixty millions pounds sterling.*

2dly. If the southern planters were deprived of their negroes, they would be entirely left without support. They cannot themselves cultivate the soil, on account of the climate; neither could they in that case *hire* labor, unless the means of doing so were furnished them; because, by taking away their negroes, their property and their credit would at once be destroyed; and they are neither by education nor habit prepared for any other occupation in life.

3dly. It would be impossible for them to retain the free negroes on their estates, unless an exorbitant price be paid for their labor; for they naturally prefer any other employment, especially that of house servants, to field-labor in any of the states. The cultivation of the soil they deem more irksome and tedious than almost any other human occupation; *and they would have the means of emigrating to the north.* The planters, therefore, would be involved in additional loss; because it would be impossible for them to produce cotton, rice, sugar, &c. as cheap as these articles are obtained in other parts of the world; and they would not even be certain of producing them at all. It would consequently be necessary to *compel* the negroes to remain, which is equally impossible in an open country, and in states where the negroes are more numerous than the whites.

Here we see at once the immense advantage of position which the British possessions in the West Indies enjoy over the southern states of America. *The negroes cannot emigrate thence to other fertile countries and obtain a higher price for their labor;* and in case they should threaten to leave the plantations in a body, a military and naval force could more easily frustrate their designs on an island, than on the continent, where the states are only separated from one another by imaginary boundary lines. Thus, from the simple consideration of property, it appears that the abolition of slavery in the southern states of America would amount to a spoilation of the property of the plant-

* Compare pages 277 and 278, Chapter X.

29

ers, together with the exclusion of the means by which property may be acquired.

But this is not all. To understand the whole force of this argument we must inquire in what manner the southern planters became possessed of that property ; in what manner they have retained it, and what right the inhabitants of other states have, to make that property the subject of legislation.

Slavery, we shall find, was almost forced upon the southern planters. Its introduction in Virginia served to increase the commerce of the mother country by augmenting the produce of the colonies. A premium, therefore, was held out to slave ships ; and the negroes being once introduced into one state, the inhabitants of the others were obliged to imitate the example, if they wished to make their plantations as productive as those of their neighbors.* The settlers who came after them and chose the southern states for their residence, proceeded thither in consideration of the prospects held out to them by the introduction of slaves. For, unless they had been promised the undisturbed possession of negroes, they might have invested their capital more profitably in the northern and western states, where they would have been able to increase it by their own labor.†

Many settlements in the southern states were effected under the promise of slavery : it was a *conditio sine quâ non* in the outset ; and now that their property is invested and bears interest, they are called upon to surrender it without being compensated for the loss !

The attempt to cultivate the southern soil without the

* Previous to the revolutionary war, the assembly of North Carolina passed a law prohibiting the further importation of slaves; but it was disallowed by England.

† The climate of South Carolina is such, that, during the hot months of summer, the planters are obliged to retreat to *the cities*, though these be infected with the yellow fever ; because the fever which rages in the country (on the plantations) is still more dreadful and fatal. At the commencement of the warm season, therefore, the wealthier planters travel to the north, while men of moderate fortunes retreat to the cities or pine-barrens, which remain exempt from the epidemic. I have known wealthy planters who had made thirty or forty trips to the north (of 600 miles each) without feeling the inconvenience of their annual passage.

assistance of negro slaves, was made in the settlement
of Georgia, but did not succeed, and the British government therefore was obliged to concede to that state also
the right of introducing slaves.

But what position did the southern states assume with
regard to those of the north during the revolutionary war ?
Did they not join the northern states on this condition,
that the north should not interfere with their internal
regulations of government? Was the slave question not
implicitly implied in this clause? Did the north not
solemnly agree to this stipulation ?—The southern states
would never have joined the bold measure of Massachusetts, if they had not been promised the undisturbed
possession of their rights and privileges, which had been
granted to them in their charter by the kings of Britain.
They could not have been supposed to join the other
states in an attempt to resist arbitrary taxation, and
suffer themselves to be despoiled of their property by
their own brethren! Without the co-operation of the
south, and especially that of Virginia, which at that time
was, with Massachusetts, the most powerful province of
America, and subsequently produced the ablest statesmen
to preside over the councils of the republic, it is more
than doubtful whether the northern states would have
been able to withstand the power of England, and establish an independent government. But it is highly probable that if the south had remained faithful to the cause of
the king, their rights and privileges would not soon have
been taken away from them ; and if Parliament had
agreed not to interfere with their internal regulations of
government, it is not to be supposed that they would have
been molested in the quiet possession of their property.

The British provinces on the continent of America
were always more independent of the mother country
than the islands of the West Indies. Some states enjoyed almost sovereign power, and, with the exception of
the Navigation Act, which prevented them from trading
directly with any other country but England, enjoyed all
the privileges of independent states. The southern states
were, at first, exempted from the heavy denunciations
which the British Parliament hurled against the rebellious
province of Massachusetts, with a special view to separate

the south from the north: even some of the obnoxious
taxes were repealed, and yet the south clung to the north
with all the attachment of a sister, freely sacrificing her
wealth and her children for the protection of the liberties
of the Union. This was done at the commencement of
the struggle, and subsequently to the declaration of independence.

The inhabitants of the south had greater sacrifices to
make during the revolutionary war than those of the north
or east, and their position was far more precarious. The
king's party in the southern states was powerful, and
the horror of a civil war added to their resistance against
Britain. Their coast, too, was more exposed and unde-
fended, and their situation rendered double perilous by
the proximity of the Indians, and their own slaves. If,
at that time, the inhabitants of the south could have
dreamt of an interference with the domestic institutions,
they would assuredly have preferred remaining under the
protection of England, to joining such dangerous friends
in America. But not the least symptom of such an intention was manifested by the north. Congress was only
to have the right of regulating commerce, declaring war
or concluding peace, raising troops for the national defence of the country, and establishing a navy for the same
purpose. The right of interfering with the internal regulations of the states was expressly denied to it, and consequently also the right of interfering with the slaves.
This incapacity on the part of the general government to
legislate on the subject of slavery has lately been corrobo-
rated by a large majority of Congress, which, I trust,
will postpone the question of arbitrary interference in-
definitely, and destroy the hopes of the abolitionists.

But I think the northern states have yet another duty
to perform. They ought to imitate Congress in pronouncing their *individual* incapacity to interfere with the
regulations of the south, and add to it an expression of
public opinion on the unlawful interference of the abolitionists with the fundamental laws of the Union. Any
attempt to *compel* the south to renounce the system of
slavery, either by encouraging the slaves to oppose the
will of their masters, or obliging the latter to surrender
their rights to the will and pleasure of the majority of

the north, would be tantamount to an assumption of sovereignty over the southern states, contrary to the original compact by which they are admitted as *equal* and *independent*. It would be a most violent usurpation of power and jurisdiction, incompatible with the federal constitution. It would be giving liberty to the negroes, by trampling on the rights of·the whites; or, which is the same, reducing the inhabitants of the south to *subjects*, by elevating their slaves to a sordid equality with the black servants of the north. The north would in this case be the aggressor; not the south, who would but defend their own rights, and the principles of their original compact.

The different states of the United States are as independent of one another, as any two sovereign powers in Europe; and the north, therefore, has no more right to interfere with the laws of the south, than England has to demand of France the emancipation of her colonial slaves, because the government of Britain has emancipated the negroes in the West Indies.

On the question of abstract right, therefore, the pretensions of the abolitionists are ill-founded. Historical origin, acquired and paid for privileges, and the most solemn obligations of contract are on the side of the planters, while nothing but ideal justice, without the least regard to the means by which that justice is to be obtained, seems to second the views of the former. An extension of franchise to the negroes effected by such means as the abolitionists propose, would be slavery to the white inhabitants of the south, and only serve to redress a theoretical wrong, which is scarcely felt by the injured party, by the most flagrant injustice to those, who know and are jealous of their rights.

I am fully aware there are those whose motto is "*reason is older than law*," and who maintain that no right can be acquired, unless it be founded on justice, even if an hundred generations should have had possession of it, and abused it to the prejudice of others. To this objection, which is purely *philosophical* and not *legal*, I would only remark that abstract reason never founded or preserved a state, and that according to this motto the very institution of government is an act of philosophical in-

29*

justice. Do not the individuals who unite to form a state make a contract in which they bind their posterity? Have they a philosophical right to do so? Do they not relinquish certain rights which belong to them as men, in order to give power to the abstract person which they call the state or the government?—Do they not often sacrifice their own individual prosperity to that abstract person?—And are not these sacrifices unequal when compared to the benefits which accrue from them to the different members of society? Is not a state itself a surrogate for reason, established to act as a mediator between absolute, philosophical right, and the *means* by which that right is to be secured?

Whenever a question of abstract justice arises, the sequel, by what means can it be obtained? must follow; though I am willing to admit, that the best state or government is that which possesses the best means of obtaining philosophical justice. In the variation and adaptation of these means, consist the different changes of government: the philosophical rights of men are always the same and invariable, and must remain so to the end of time.

From the very definition of a state, then, it follows that mere philosophical justice must be sacrificed, when the government lacks the means of administering it; or when the means devised for that purpose are in direct opposition to other rights still more precious, and clearly established. No right can grow from an absolute wrong, and the act which claims to be just must not be accomplished by injustice.

Neither is the question of slavery, as it now stands in the United States, one of philosophical justice *between the north and the south;* but simply one of contract. I do not pretend that the southern states have not themselves the right of abolishing slavery, whenever they shall have found the means of performing this act of humanity; it will even be their duty to do so as soon as it can be accomplished without destroying the government itself;—for it would be absurd to sacrifice the government to one of the purposes of government :—but with regard to the north, it is a morbid sensation of wrong, which they themselves do not suffer, and from which they have no right to seek relief, because they have solemnly agreed not to interfere with it. They have received a valuable consideration for that agreement, in all the sacrifices which the south has made to the north; and after having accepted these, it would be a breach of trust, honesty, and good faith, to infringe on the conditions of the compact.

The government of the United States was not instituted to redress individual wrongs, but for the purpose of procuring justice for the nation, and defending her against a common antagonist. The different states which were parties to that compact, did not consider it necessary, for the safety of the community, to surrender their sovereignty, and have, therefore, only made such concessions to the government of the confederacy, as they deemed necessary to effect a strong and permanent Union. The administration of justice was expressly reserved to the states, except with regard to offences committed against the laws of Congress; and they were treated as *independent*, by the head of the general government. Every new state which has since been admitted into the Union, was admitted as an independent state, with the same indisputable title to their own domestic government,—the privilege of enacting laws for the regulation of property, and the administration of justice. Now, if the United States do not possess, and never did possess, the right of interfering with the internal policy of the south, what right has any one state of that Union to infringe upon the strictest neutrality? In case of interference, the northern states would not claim justice, but assume the judge's seat, and deal it out at their pleasure. And in what cause? In one in which they have not been appealed to; in which no complaint is made to them, and in which they themselves are the offenders, and hasten the commission of the crime.

The case does not bear the slightest resemblance to the peculiar circumstances of any European nation. It is indeed one without a parallel in history, and to which it would be absurd to apply any modern or ancient precedents. There never existed a government similar to that of the United States; nor was slavery, on the principle of the southern states, ever introduced in any country.

The American slaves belong to a different race, a different continent, and a different clime. They have no community of sentiment, attachment or habit, with the other inhabitants of the country. Their physical and moral conformation are different from that of the whites, and there exists a natural (instinctive) dislike between the two races, which will forever prevent their uniting into one and the same family. In short, there is not a principle of liberty in any part of the world, which, in its application to negro slaves, would not have to be considerably modified in order to produce results, in the least degree similar to those which are anticipated from its application to the condition of other men.

So far, I have spoken only of the legal considerations which forbid the interference of the north with the system of slavery to the south : let us now consider the matter in its political bearings. Let us inquire what influence the emancipation of the slaves would have on the tranquillity, prosperity, and final progress of the whites ?—and what results it would produce with regard to the condition of the negroes ?

It has often been remarked that America is the only country which is yet tainted with slavery, while even the most absolute powers of Europe condemn it, as contrary to the laws of God and humanity. There are *republicans,* they add, more unjust to their fellow-beings than any monarch ever was to his subjects, or any aristocracy to the common people.

However plausible this argument may at first appear, there is not a shadow of truth or substance in it. For the northern powers of Europe, who would give liberty to the negroes, would only elevate them to an equality with their subjects, who are themselves slaves; and the aristocracy of Europe never dreamed of *feeding* and *clothing* the people, in order to lay claims to their labor. The lower classes of many countries in Europe are so overburdened with taxes, that they are compelled to commit their bodies to the most painful hardships in order to procure a subsistence ; and are not less laboring for the comfort and convenience of the higher classes, than the slaves for their masters in America; with this exception perhaps, that when they grow old and decrepit, they are not provided for by their rich employers, as the negroes by the American planters; and their children are equally exposed to famine. As regards the freemen to the north of Europe, they belong, body and property, to their respective sovereigns, who may tax them, or command their lives as they think fit, and compel them to serve as soldiers, while their wives and children may beg their bread on the high roads.* Is there no cruelty in separating a poor husbandman from his house and home, and letting his family starve, in order to lead him to the slaughter? The affecting scenes of such departures, for the martial glories of the camp, are nevertheless well worth being compared to similar barbarities in the southern states of America; only that the Americans fight their own battles, and employ their negroes exclusively for domestic and peaceable purposes.

There is no moral freedom in a country in which the people are only the tool of the higher classes, or so taxed as to be scarcely able to procure what is necessary for their physical support. The man who has been laboring all day, and, after his scanty repast, turns wearied to his wretched bed, is not apt to dream of liberty. Let his political condition be what it may, he remains the slave of his body, the cravings of which will ever overpower his reason. Liberty, in order to be prized, must be joined to the possession of property, or, at least, to a reasonable chance of its acquisition; and unless this hope can be held out to the negroes, it is more than doubtful whether emancipation would improve their condition.

In none of the states, where the negroes have been emancipated, have they been able to rise above the condition of inferior servants; in none have they thus far acquired respectability or property.† I will not, now, enter upon the causes of this result, but merely state it as a *fact*, which, whatever may be the reason, is never-

* I have known Prussian and Austrian invalids, who were permitted to beg, in consideration of the services they had rendered to their respective countries; and in order the better to succeed in their new vocation, the Austrians were presented with hand-organs.

† If, in a very few instances, negroes have acquired moderate property, their case is rather an exception to the rule,—hundreds of them being hardly able to procure situations as under-servants.

theless general throughout, and therefore deserving of
the most serious consideration. The physical condition
of the liberated negroes of the northern states, is by far
worse than that of the southern slaves; and they are consequently much more exposed to the commission of crimes
and the punishment of the law, than any other class of
human beings in America. Whether under these circumstances their moral advantages are increased, is still more
doubtful; for without the means of making themselves
respected or respecting themselves, they cannot value
either morality or virtue, and are, in most cases, at a loss
how to define either one or the other.

Let us now consider the circumstances under which the
negroes were emancipated in the northern states of
America, and lately, in the British West Indies, and compare them to those in which the southern planters are
placed, in order to see what analogies there exist between
them.

The northern states, as I have said before, perceived
that the evils of slavery overbalanced, by far, the advantages which they derived from it; and became greater in
proportion as the latter were on the decline. In every
state where slavery is introduced, the increase of the white
population is proportionably less, but that of the blacks,
greater than in a free state. The slaves are better fed,
better clothed, and have fewer cares than the free negroes, who, in the northern states, are daily diminishing,
and must, in course of time, become entirely extinct. In
a *colony* it matters little whether the white population increases or not. As long as it is small, property will not
suffer subdivision; and the planters, on acquiring a fortune, may return to their own country to enjoy it. But
the case is altered when that colony becomes an independent state, in which every citizen has a permanent residence and a home. It then becomes necessary to consider the *lasting* advantages of the country, and among
these will be found but few accruing from slavery.

In the first place, slavery is a severe tax on the planters, which none but the richest can pay, and for which
no other produce save that of the southern climes will
make an adequate return. The owner of slaves has to
support them before they are able to work; he has to

comfort them in sickness, and has to provide for them in old age. He is subject to great losses by deaths and diseases, and, by his own interests, invited to spare their health and abilities. A farmer in a free state only pays for the labor he *receives*, and, what is still better, can make his own labor available. He neither supports children nor old men ; and, in case of illness, provides himself with other servants.

Again, slavery introduces a strong physical force into the state, which requires supervision, and cannot be entrusted to any but the masters themselves. But this is not all. Slavery either enhances the price of white labor, or excludes it entirely from the soil. It therefore checks all manner of trade, and confines even commerce to the exportation of produce, and the importation of such articles as are actually required for consumption. For the same reason it checks the progress of manufactures and every other species of industry, which advances the prosperity of a state. Slavery, therefore, was an *impediment* to the progress of the northern states, and they felt it as such, especially the laboring classes. What therefore could have been more natural, than for them to devise a means, to remove so great an obstacle to their individual and national advancement. Not only was slavery a burthen to them ; but they could abandon it without any of those difficulties which would accompany emancipation in the southern states. The work which was done by their slaves, they knew would be readily performed by poor emigrants from Germany and Ireland, at a less cost than the negroes, and the climate admitted of their personal exertion in trade and commerce. Property, instead of being principally confined to real estate, must take a thousand different channels, and enrich every class of society. They could hope to subdivide estates without diminishing their relative value. This cannot be done in the south. An estate with ten negroes is not worth one tenth of one with an hundred slaves ; and a further division would entirely destroy its value. The expenses of a large southern estate are nearly the same as those of a small one ; but the profits on the latter are hardly sufficient to cover them. In the northern states, on the contrary, large estates are seldom as productive as small ones, which the proprietor can oversee and cultivate with little assistance.

All these circumstances were in favor of independent labor: the north had every reason to hope that labor would be *hired* cheaper than they were able to *purchase* it; and the climate itself was unfavorable to the constitution of the negroes. The negroes were too precarious a property, and required too constant an attention to be kept with profit or safety. I do not mean to say that morality and religion had not their due influence in persuading the minds of the people; but it is but reasonable to suppose, that even the sacred commandments of God are less apt to be resisted when they agree with the interests of men.

The southern states are very differently circumstanced. The produce of their soil enables them to pay for their slaves, and more than compensates for the losses by mortality and disease. If they surrender their slaves, no European emigrants will fill their places; because the climate of the south is fatal to the constitutions of the whites, especially as regards field-labor; but agrees with the conformation of the negroes. The south, therefore, can never compete with the north in any species of free labor, and is, consequently, obliged to derive its wealth from the soil. If the negroes were free, they would be a *set of privileged workmen;* because they alone would be capable of cultivating the soil. The southern planters would be obliged to pay a higher price for their labor; they would no longer be able to extend or diminish their operations at pleasure, and, at the same time, would be prevented, at home, from investing their money in some other business. The negroes would become powerful, while their masters would become poor; and were they as economical, enterprising, and sagacious as the whites, could not fail finally to possess themselves of the estates, and drive the whites from the country.

The situation of the planters in the West India islands is much more analogous to that of the inhabitants of the southern states of America. Soil and climate are alike favoring the natives of Africa, while they breed death and diseases amongst the whites. It is, I believe, generally admitted that without the assistance of negroes, it would be impossible for the proprietors to live there; nor could they personally cultivate their estates. They are dependent for manufactures on other countries; and their active commerce is confined to the exportation of their produce. But the West India islands do not form so many independent states entrusted with their own governments. They possess no elective franchise on the principle of that introduced in the United States, which gives the whole power to the people, and are, therefore, not injured in their political rights by the emancipation of their slaves. They do not entirely depend for safety *on their own resources;* but are protected by a powerful army and navy, the expenses of which are defrayed by the government of another country; and, being islands, are more easily protected than the scattered inhabitants of a vast continent. They have not the same attachment to the soil, and consider it not as their home. They are the subjects of Great Britain, and look on their estates as a merchant on his stock in trade. They possess no sovereignty which is compromised by the manumission of their slaves; but are provinces of a mighty empire, which stands pledged to protect their lives and properties.

Neither had they any *direct* influence on the government of that empire, as the southern states of America have upon the deliberations of Congress, and were, therefore, neither answerable for the errors of that government, nor apprehensive of giving to the negroes the power of making laws for the benefit or ruin of the country. They had less to lose, less to fear, and less to answer for. They were obliged to accept a measure which they themselves never proposed, and may, in consequence, lose their property, but not their country.

Neither is it at all probable that the West India proprietors would have accepted the measure, if it had not been forced upon them by the Parliament of England. Those who are obliged to live with the negroes, have, naturally, greater prejudices against them, than the philanthropist who respects in them the abstract dignity of man. The dangers of life and property, to which a proprietor is exposed, are not apt to influence a legislator at a distance of three or four thousand miles from the scene; but they have a most powerful effect on those who are immediately exposed to them. The experiment is but just being tried ; and the result, thus far, is not so inviting to the southern planters of America, as is represented generally to the British public.

But there is yet another question which I would pro- pose to English philanthropists. Would they have been as ready to exert themselves for the emancipation of the negroes, if the latter had been mixed with the population of *England*, or if their number had surpassed that of the native subjects of Britain ? The population of England is now above fourteen millions. Suppose eight or nine millions of these were negroes, or a race of beings whose whole civilization is thus far propt on that of other countries, and whose independent advancement in the arts and sciences is wholly problematic ;—suppose, I say, it were known that they are possessed of strong animal passions and propensities, naturally repugnant to the English ; would they have been willing to arm these eight or nine millions, and give them the same rights and privi- leges which they themselves possess, or the same share in the government of their country, even after a certain lapse of years, *when the least misuse of that power would lead them to inevitable destruction ?* Why are there those who would not grant these rights to the Irish ? a people be- longing to the same human family, capable of the same feeling, and possessed of those admirable qualities of mind which produced a Wellington, a Burke, a Sheridan, or an O'Connell !

The negro population of the United States may now amount to about two millions five hundred thousand, and it is in many of the slave-holding states more numerous than that of the whites. These states do not contain a single fortified place, capable of withstanding a siege ; they do not even contain a town surrounded by a moat or a wall, and no garrison or detachment of a standing army, to protect them in case of a revolt. They could not even avail themselves of the strength arising from congregation. Their habitations are scattered over a wide surface of land, and their families are surrounded by ne- groes. A man's wife and children might be murdered, and his home be a prey to the flames, before tidings could reach his next neighbor, or before measures could be con- certed for the preservation of the lives of the whites.

The army of the United States consists scarcely of seven thousand men, including officers and privates, scattered over the forts and seaports of the country. Their whole number, therefore, would not be sufficient to quell a negro insurrection in any of the southern states; and until the militia could assemble, one half of them might be put to the sword.

Such is the position of the southern planter in the United States. He has not the means of defending himself against a possible attack of the negroes, yet he is desired to make them free and arm them : he has no property except that which is invested in negroes, yet he is desired to surrender it, and then to protect his country ; he is incapacitated for every other human employment, and yet he is to be molested in the possession of his estate, and taxed for the support of the government. No compensation is offered for his losses ; no additional means provided for his personal safety ; no citadels built for the protection of his wife and children.

But he is supposed to do more. He is to grant to the negroes the right of suffrage ; for, unless he did so, his negroes would still be slaves—though, of course, less obedient and manageable slaves. He is then to surrender to them the power of legislation ; for they compose in many states a majority, and would, therefore, be able to carry whatever measure they might choose to propose. Thus all that man holds most sacred, life, property, justice, and the law itself, would be placed at the mercy of the negroes, in order to favor an experiment, which in case of a fatal issue, would engulph the happiness of millions !

A law for the emancipation of the negroes in the United States is not like any other law, which may be repealed, whenever it is found to produce mischief. It is a die which is cast forever ; for the power once departed from the whites, could not be made to return thither, without the horrors of a war, and the total extinction of the black race in the southern states of America.

And what influence would the liberation of the slaves have upon the councils of the nation ? At the present moment the southern states are strongly connected and allied to one another by their common interest in slavery, and by the necessity of a common defence against a possible interference with their domestic arrangements on the part of the northern states. If their negroes were emancipated, this common interest would, in a great measure, be destroyed. The southern states could not assist each other in case of a rebellion ; because each of them would in this case be too much occupied at home : they would have to make their peace with the inhabitants of the north, and implore or purchase their protection.

The southern states would become rivals of each other ; because, labor being free, and the negroes the only persons to perform it, the latter would be apt to give the preference to some particular states, and bent upon deserting the others. The southern influence in Congress would be wholly destroyed ; for, not only would the states be divided amongst themselves, but each state again between the whites and the negroes. There would be no power to check or direct the passions of their emancipated slaves, as their superior numbers would make them the legislators of the country. Thus the physical, moral, and political existence is threatened by the abolition of slavery ; and it is therefore but prudence and duty to pause and reflect, before hazarding so great an experiment.

I do not pretend to describe the situation of the West India planters ; but it can scarcely be doubted that their prosperity is on the decline. The emancipation of negroes may precipitate events, and must at least, for a time, render the position of the proprietors precarious. The white and black races can never be made to amalgamate, and where they exist mutually independent on one another, must always assume an attitude more or less hostile to each other's interests. The physical power is on the side of the Africans—the moral strength will always rest with the whites. The climate of the West Indies does not favor the increase of the latter, and destroys even their moral energies. There is a point beyond which intellect cannot triumph over physical obstacles, and there may be a time in the future history of the British West Indies, when the small number of whites, supported even by the presence of a powerful navy, will not be able to overcome the onslaught of the multiplied negroes, who, for aught I know, may be destined to become masters of the country. Let the feud be once began, and the proprietors must quit their plantations; for it is only in the garrisoned towns, where they may hope for protection and safety.

The power of intellect in repelling barbarous masses consists in the discipline of numbers, and in that peculiar elevation to which men are raised by their mutual influence on one another. This superiority, which the white race has always enjoyed over all others, cannot avail them individually, and especially not on their plantations, where physical force must decide. Once driven thence, their combats in the field would not profit them. They cannot have a force in every direction, and it would be the negroes who would fight for their homes; while the planters would, in a measure, become the invaders. They might visit the transgressions of the negroes on their heads; but they could never return to their plantations, and trust in the good faith of the conquered. Whatever might be the issue of such a war, its ultimate consequences must be the desertion of the colony by all who hold real estates. Without negroes they could not be cultivated; and their presence would be dangerous to the planters. A wise government may delay the commencement of hostilities; but it is difficult to foresee by what means their occurrence is to be rendered impossible; and until that security is obtained, the West India planters must sleep, with the sword of Damocles over their heads.

But in case of a war between the blacks and the whites, the southern planters of America would be in a still more deplorable condition. They could not even escape from their negroes, and seek the protection of the seaports. Whither could the inhabitants of Tennessee, Alabama, and Missouri flee for assistance? Whichever way they would turn, they would again meet their enemies. Their only salvation would be to stand and fight the unequal battle, let the consequences be what they may. Suppose they should conquer, would their foes not again increase and threaten them with a similar war? Can there be any hope of permanent peace between two so unequal parties? The negroes in the southern states increase

30*

faster than the whites. To whatever number, therefore, they might be reduced by a war, they would again become more numerous than the whites; and then the battle would renew. It is only by an immense moral superiority of the whites, that the blacks are kept in subjection, or suffered to increase without disturbing the peace of the country. Any material change in their present position would make them assume an attitude hostile to the whites, and sow the seeds of discord. The negroes would have all to win, the planters all to loose, while the battle-field would be nearly one half of the United States. It would be a war in fury unequalled in history ; for the hatred of the two races would sanction every species of cruelty, and drown the voice of humanity in a desperate struggle for existence. No quarter would, none could be given, consistent with the principle of safety ; neither could peace be established except by the total extermination of one of the belligerent parties.

Let us now consider the moral and philosophical merits of the question. There is something so revolting to the mind, in the very idea of slavery, that I can easily conceive why Europeans generally should be so averse to the doctrine. No man has a right to consider his fellow-being as his property, and to dispose of him according to his pleasure. The first perpetration of such a crime degrades both the slave and the master, and is equally injurious to both. The master becomes dependent on the slave, as much as the slave on his master, whatever be the power which the latter may exercise over the former. It is apt to lessen the feelings of humanity in the oppressors, and to fill the slaves with the most fiendly passions of revenge against their unnatural extortioners. The slave must either rise in resistance, or become so abjectly destitute of feeling as to be unworthy of protection or pity.

These are truths admitted as axioms by all men. It remains for us only, to give the definition of slavery. If we define it as an abuse of power, in one man, and a forced submission to that power in the other, we shall find that it exists in almost every part of the world ; though it is disguised in a variety of shapes, and often in the form of justice. We must, therefore, seek for a more

narrow definition, perhaps in these terms : " Slavery consists in *reducing* or *retaining* those, who would otherwise
be our equals, in a state of servitude, by means of absolute force." I have added " *absolute*," because the idea
of violence is most revolting to our feelings. We would
hardly commiserate a slave, who should have voluntarily
submitted his person to the will and pleasure of another,
in order to obtain a subsistence. But even this definition does not apply to the negroes. It remains to be
proved that the African negroes are equal to the whites ;
and that in forming part of the same state, in any other
condition, they would not be subjected to the will and
pleasure of the latter. If it could be made out that the
negroes are naturally inferior to the whites, or incapable
of enjoying the same rights and privileges without endangering the safety of moral and political institutions ;
if it could be established that their physical passions are
greater, and their judgment and understanding more
limited than those of the white race, then these facts
would, at least, contain an *apology* for *retaining* the
negroes in bondage ; though it would not establish a *right*
to abuse their inferior capacities.

When I speak of slavery, I speak of what exists, and
not of the principle which established it. The first introduction of slavery, I consider as an act of abomination, which, in its fatal retribution, has retarded the
progress of the white race wherever it was admitted.
But the states which are now burdened with it, must
naturally adopt a different method of reasoning. They
must start *from given premises*, and not from general
principles. They must apply their philosophy to a particular case, not to humanity in general.

It is very certain that the negroes would not have left
Africa, if they had not been carried away in European
vessels ; and it is equally certain that they would not
have been introduced into America, if they had not been
brought thither to be sold. They have since increased
in numbers, and become naturalised on the American
soil. They have had the means of acquiring a certain
degree of civilization, and have, in their intercourse with
the whites, assumed a particular character. This character, in its relation to the original African, and to that

of the American people, we must now consider, in order to pronounce on the claims of the blacks to a philosophical equality with the whites. But before I proceed further, I must state that I write this as a German, and not as an American partisan ; as a person whose education made him detest slavery in all its various ramifications, whether the slaves were black or white ; and as one who has no further interest at stake than that which is identified with truth. I have lived in several slave-holding states, in North and South America, and have had an opportunity of impartial observation. I never held any property in the least connected with slavery, and was a stranger to the inhabitants of those countries.

I must then give it as my honest conviction, that the negroes *are* an inferior human race, and *not* capable of enjoying, without excess, the same degree of freedom as Americans. In order not to be misunderstood,—as the latter clause will hold of the people of many other countries,—I will add, that I think the negroes wholly uninclined to, and entirely incapacitated for, living in a state of society similar to that of the whites ; and that, *if they were capable of forming such a state of society, they would not form it* WHILE SURROUNDED BY THE WHITES.

With regard to the mental inferiority of the negroes, the argument may be divided into an examination of the reasoning of those who pretend that they are equal to the whites, but only backward in education, and a proper illustration of facts, calculated to establish the proposition.

Those who take it for granted that the negroes have the same capacities as the whites, belong generally to a set of philosophers accustomed to reason *à priori;* in whose minds the idea of humanity is so abstract and exalted, that they cannot apply it to any particular race, without bestowing on it its inestimable attributes. "They are men," they say, "why should they not be possessed of the same qualities as men ? " In vain will any one plead the difference in color, conformation of limbs, and especially the different formation of the skull. "They possess the main physical characteristics," they will reply, and "therefore the principal qualities of the mind." But the argument is exactly the reverse. They have very marked distinctions from any other race of men; and where nature points out a physical disproportion, we may in all cases safely conclude that a moral one corresponds to it.

And how does history support their arguments? All other people have either themselves laid the foundation of their civilization, or, of their own free will, imitated the refinements of others. The negroes have been known to the remotest people of antiquity, but always in the same state in which we know them now, though they have had commercial intercourse with foreign nations, and visited, in part, other countries. What are their manners and customs now? The same as two thousand years ago. It is usual for a people to express their natural inclinations in their favorite amusements, among which the national dance occupies the foremost rank. The Scotch dance is expressive of strong martial inclinations; the German waltz bears the strongest characteristic of the peculiar frankness and gaiety of the Germans; the French quadrille expresses the desire of pleasing by graceful attitudes; the fandango is indicative of unrefrained passion; but the original negro-dance is stamped with the marks of brutal sensuality. So are their ornaments. Those of the bodies consist chiefly of the entrails of animals; those of the interior of their houses, of ordure.

The same brutality they evince in their worship. Their idols are the most hideous, and their adoration the most ferocious of any people with which we are acquainted; and they are almost entirely destitute of that noble virtue of barbarous nations, for the sake of which we willingly pardon a number of other faults—bravery. Compare the negroes to the American Indians. The former with his frightful gods and base cowardice—the latter with his sublime belief in the "Great Spirit," and his utter contempt for human sufferings and death. The eloquence and poetry of the Indians, and the dullness and want of imagination of the negroes. And yet there are few persons, who have had an opportunity of observing the Indian character, would believe the "red men" capable of the same degree of civilization as the whites; and the experience of two centuries seems to warrant this

ungenerous belief. What then are we to think of the
moral perfectibility of the negroes, who are avowedly
inferior to the Indians? The civilization of which the
negroes are reputed to be possessed, they have not acquired of their own accord; it has been forced upon
them, and is, thus far, only upheld and nourished by the
whites.

Herein consists another distinction between them and
the Indians. It is from their feebleness, and because
they have no character of their own, that they are willing
to ape the arts of civilization. The Indian is too proud
to imitate the white man; he is too ardent a lover of
liberty—the child of the American forests—to submit to
American legislation.

Hamilton observes, in his work, that he witnessed an
exhibition of negro boys at a school for black children in
New York. In his opinion, they answered questions in
geography "which would have puzzled himself." This,
I doubt not, was as the learned author says. But then
geography is a mere matter of memory, which is no distinct faculty of the mind, and of which inferior intellects
are sometimes possessed in a very superior degree. Mr.
Hamilton further states, that the teacher informed him
of the precocity of his pupils, in acquiring most elementary branches of a common school education at an earlier
period than white children. This was the assurance of
a black teacher, referring, probably, to spelling or reading. But when did we hear of negroes cultivating the
arts and sciences; though there are persons of color in
the United States, possessed of considerable property?
What is the system of schools introduced by the free,
independent negroes in St. Domingo? What progress
have they made in any of the arts? The Indians of
America had their own languages, some of which are
highly flexible and sonorous;* negro civilization has not
even a tongue for its basis, as a rallying point for the
arts. A French negro is a mutilated Frenchman; an
English, a caricature of an Englishman; the Spanish, a

---

* See Zeisberger's Grammar of the Delaware Indian Language,
translated into English by Mr. Duponceau of the Academy of Sciences
in Philadelphia.

bad copy of his indifferent original : wherever the negroes
went, they have only been copyists of the other races;
but the American negro has certainly been any thing but
a successful imitator of his shrewd, sagacious master.

And now I would ask, whether the civilised free
negroes of the United States, possessed of the same color,
the same bones, and the same hair as their African
brethren who sold their ancestors, could, by emigrating
to Africa, and preaching their science and religion, advance the cause of humanity very materially in that
unfortunate country ? I believe that the question must
be negatived ; and this is the true light in which we must
consider the natural abilities of the negroes.

The colony of Liberia has been settled by the Americans with free negroes. The establishment is now many
years old, is doing tolerably well, though it derives its
chief support from America : but have the superior arts
of the colonists made the least impression on the sur-
rounding tribes? Have they won over a single disciple
to their doctrines? or excited even a moderate share of
curiosity among their brethren of the desert? No ; the
colonists themselves require constant admonition and instruction, and the strong force of example, to retain the
civilization they have acquired. It hangs loosely on
them, like a borrowed garment, made for the use of
another man.

European civilization, though abstractedly considered
as a unit, is strongly impregnated with the peculiar spirit
of each nation, and has borne different fruits in different
countries. The arts of England, France, Germany, and
Italy, are marked by a peculiar character, and embody
the *genius* of these respective nations. The civilization
of America, though but the production of two centuries,
bears already the strongest national features, distinct
from that of Europe in general.

The Indians, when converted to Christianity, are yet
a distinct and noble race, commanding even the respect
of their enemies. But wherein consist the peculiarities
of the civilised negroes, in which may be recognised
some latent genius of their own? I must confess I remember none, save the almost total absence of independent energy of character. I have conversed with hun-

dreds of negroes, but I could not elicit from them a single original idea, capable of savoring their recitation of American phrases, or serving as an index to a mind capable of reflecting on itself. If any thing marked them as civilised beings, it was the luckless attempt to imitate the outward American, and a singular attention to fashionable manners and the toilet. It is a severe task to be employed in lowering any portion of the human family in the estimation of their fellow-creatures; but a strict adherence to truth, and impartial justice to the Americans, do not permit me to temporise, whatever offence my statement may give to individuals.

There is one fact strongly corroborative of my assertions. Most persons who have advocated the equality of the races, were theorists, drawing their inferences from general axioms; while nearly all who have had an opportunity of observing the negroes themselves, have arrived at a different conclusion. Why was there never a similar prejudice with regard to the American Indians? Some of the first families in Virginia, noted for their eminent talents as statemen and legislators, are descended, in part, from the Indians. But, instead of considering this a disgrace, they are proud of their origin; and a peculiar loftiness of mind seems to be hereditary in their families, and expressed in their manly countenances. The mulatto, on the contrary, though a shade superior to the negro, is a grovelling being, still thoroughly marked with his subjection to physical nature, the strongest characteristic of the black race.

No other human being is by nature so entirely adapted to his climate; as if to prevent him from spreading over other parts of the world. The skin of the negroes, their color, hair, and feet, are made for the African sun; and being naturally heedless of the future, they are surrounded by trees and plants which blossom and bear fruit at the same time. The negro is the slave of nature; the white man is her companion. Born in a more northern latitude, and consequently less exposed to the most powerful physical agent, the sun, his mind waxes superior to the scenes which surround him. His physical wants rouse his energy and quicken his ingenuity, and the approaching winter commands his cares of the future.

He is born to subdue and improve nature, and not to be dependent on her generosity. All that has ever improved the condition of man, every valuable principle of philosophy and religion, poetry, painting, and music, are the offsprings of the temperate zones. The universal history of all ages is but the history of that clime; the moral lever of the world was ever moved by its children.

The progress of the white race is the soul of universal history; for it is the white race which produced all the changes, and acted as the animating principle on the rest of mankind. The other nations remained stationary, bound by the limits which nature had set to their progress; the white race alone was possessed of the courage to overleap them and to traverse the ocean in quest of new land. Wherever that race has since placed its foot, there it has subdued all others, notwithstanding the inferiority of its numbers; and its march of conquest is onward, and must finish with grasping the world.

With these facts before us, is it not natural to suppose that the white race is *intrinsically* superior to every other; and, consequently *à fortiori* to the negroes? Would we not naturally come to this conclusion, even if there were no exterior distinction between them? The objection that the white race conquered by its superior arts, at a time when the others had not yet attained the same degree of civilization, avails little or nothing to the argument. Why did the other races not possess a similar degree of civilization, since it is proved that their origin is at least as remote, if not more so, than that of the white race? Are the nations of the east and their learning not older than those of Europe? Why did they not improve it as the people of Europe? What made the Europeans labor for centuries to decipher the writings of the ancients? What spirit is it, which makes them yet take an interest in the history of other nations, and descend to their remotest antiquity, when those nations evince not the least disposition to learn the history of Europe? Why is the commerce of the world yet confined to European and American vessels? Why has the principle of liberty not been born, or taken root in any other country but Europe and America? Why is Christianity yet chiefly confined to those continents, when it was

31

Asia which begot it ? Why is the white race not, like
the Chinese, satisfied with its acquired superiority but
continually improving in every department of knowledge ?
Why is the white race the only one bent on engrafting
its principles and its customs on all others ? Why does
it succeed in this enterprise, and swallow up all other
tribes ? Why is there no reaction on the part of the
other races on the whites; but, on the contrary, a gradual
yielding to its influence ? Why are the whites not
changed in contact with other races ?

But there is yet one more circumstance deserving the
attention of philosophers. In no instance have the different races shown a general disposition to amalgamate;
but rather evinced a natural dislike to one another.
When such a disposition existed, it was always on the
part of the inferior with regard to the superior race, and
never the reverse. The few individual exceptions to this
rule must rather be considered as instances of moral depravity, than a prevalent taste of the race ; or as occasioned by peculiar circumstances, which prevented a free
choice. This natural dislike was always greatest between the white and the black race, just in proportion, it
may be said, to the diversity of their color, and the great
difference in their inclinations and habits. But it existed
equally among other races, and may, therefore, be considered as something instinctive, and not produced by a
process of reasoning.

Immediately after the introduction of negro slavery
into the American colonies, the provincial assemblies
prohibited all intercourse with the negroes under the
severest penalties. The laws of Maryland of 1715
provided that any white woman, whether a servant or
free, becoming pregnant from the embrace of a negro,
whether a slave or free, should be punished with a servitude of seven years, and the children of such *"unnatural
and inordinate connections"* were doomed to servitude till
they should attain the age of thirty-one. A white man
begetting a child by a negress, was subjected to the same
penalty as a white woman committing an offence with a
negro ; and similar laws were enacted by the legislative
assembly of Virginia. Even when baptized, negroes were

not comprehended in the denomination of Christians.*
No such laws were enacted against the American aborigines ; but though the example had been set in the marriage of Captain Smith with the princess Pokahontas,
it was rarely imitated by European settlers, notwithstanding the political advantages which, at that time,
might have resulted from such unions.

The gypsies afford another striking instance of this
natural aversion between the different varieties of the
human family. They have remained a distinct race in
Scotland, France, Spain, Germany, and Hungary ; and
were they to emigrate to America, would still remain the
same. They have still their peculiar customs and manners, opposed to the laws of civilised nations. And yet,
how much more similar to the whites are they than the
negroes ! Without this mutual dislike, it is highly probable the distinctions between the races would have become
obliterated, and even the different tribes been united into
one. That the climate alone does not change the color,
is evident from the fact that the offsprings of negroes remain black, and those of the whites white, whether they
inhabit the polar region, or the vicinity of the equator.

Every race has feared the contact of the whites, in the
same manner as a weaker animal dreads to meet one
which is more powerful ; while the white race has always
sought it with the fullest conviction of its superiority.
What makes China and Japan shut their cities to Europeans, but the dread that the latter might conquer
them. They may affect to despise these " barbarians ; "
but they have seen them establish the most powerful empires in the East, and, wherever they went, take the
reins of government into their own hands. The population of China is estimated at about three hundred millions,
and that of all Europe at scarcely two hundred. China
is in possession of all the mechanic arts of Europe, and
excels the latter in the manufacture of many valuable
articles. The use of gunpowder is known to them ; and
yet they entertain doubts and suspicions as to the intentions of Europeans ! They feel that whatever be their
mechanical perfections, they are inferior to the white

* Grahame's History of the United States.

race in all the nobler qualities of the mind in enterprise and courage. No apprehensions are entertained by Europeans as to those nations ever conquering part of *their* country, or the doctrines and practices of the East undermining the Christian religion, and the principles of philosophy of Locke and Newton. China and Japan have not grown powerful by their own strength, but by the weakness of the nations which surrounded them. In contact with the whites they are aware their position would be untenable ; and it is to the race, and not to the arts of Europe, we must ascribe their puerile laws with regard to foreigners.

But to return to the negroes; who to this moment are ignorant of the mechanic arts, and even slow in acquiring dexterity when instructed and guided by the whites ; who have never prospered or improved in their own country ; on whom the light of science or religion never dawned except through the intercession of other nations ; to whom the refinements of poetry and the arts are entirely unknown; whose worship is the most hideous and barbarous on earth ; who war upon one another for the sole purpose of reducing each other to slaves ; who first sold one another, and enriched themselves with the blood of their brethren ; who, during more than three thousand years of their known existence, have not even made the first step towards civilization, by improving their soil with agriculture, and are equally unskilful in the chase, and destitute of courage or ambition ; who possess nothing of the natural skill and agility of other races ; who never dreamt of an equality with the whites, before it was discovered by European philosophers ; who never knew the definition of liberty, but are slaves in their own country ; to that race, finally, who, in whatever relation we have known them, have always shown themselves inferior beings, *and declare them equal to the whites, and inferior only in point of education ! !* There is not one point in which the equality has been established; and should we be entitled to a general conclusion ? This is not elevating the negroes, but degrading the whites, by ascribing to accident the development of those eminent qualities, which have rendered them masters of the world. Is the supposition of such an accident, which insured the permanent success of one race over all others, compatible with a belief in Divine Providence; and the moral contained in universal history?

I do not deny that the negroes are capable of *improvement;* that they may acquire the elements of many useful arts and sciences: but I do not believe that they are *capable of working out their own salvation,* or of rivalling the whites in any one branch of human knowledge or industry.

I have never heard it argued or asserted that the Malay race were naturally equal to the whites; though I certainly hold them superior to the negroes. Neither has it ever been maintained that all races have the same inclinations and capacities; and yet we should at once select the most inferior species of humanity, and declare them fit to live under the same laws, be governed by the same motives, elevated by the same hopes, and restrained by the same fears as the whites? Who would assert that the people of the East are fit to live under a republican government, similar to that of the United States? Who could doubt but that, if a majority of them were now possessed of the same liberties, their natural disposition would again lead them to monarchy? Who knows that freedom would to them be a valuable acquisition? And yet, suppose these nations, or any portion of them, placed in a republic like America; there might remain some hope of amalgamating the races—the only means by which the inferior one can be improved, though this improvement is equivalent to a gradual extinction of the race, by a continued succession of the whites. With regard to the negroes, this is entirely out of the question. There is something naturally repulsive in the physical conformation of the blacks: there are certain peculiarities of the race, which must ever prove revolting to the whites. The disparity of intellect and habit is too great to leave the least ray of hope that such an amalgamation can be effected by *marriage.*

The white man does not live, like the negro, for the present moment. His thoughts are fixed on the future; and among his fondest hopes is that of elevating his children to a prouder eminence than himself; of correcting the errors and imperfections of his own education, in the

31*

more perfect one of his children. The Americans cherish this hope in a most eminent degree. Three fourths of all the acts of legislation are intended for the benefit of the rising generation; and it is one of their chief characteristics, as I have had occasion to remark before, that their whole present lives are devoted to the welfare of their children. Neither does this feature exclusively belong to the Americans. It is a quality belonging to the race; an aspiring to immortality in this world, by perpetuating their virtues in their offsprings; and the origin of the noblest deeds recorded in the history of man. But, of all nations in the world, the Americans live the most in the future; and, should they be capable of forming marriages with the blacks, knowing full well, that, according to the laws of nature, their offsprings must be inferior to themselves, *and bear the marks of that inferiority in their countenances?* Could we suppose such a marriage based on that mutual respect and affection, which are necessary to make the union sacred and eternal? The idea is preposterous, and incompatible with that mutual disinclination—not to use a stronger term—which exists between the races. This natural dislike is so great, that a man would hardly love his offspring, if it were different from, and inferior to, himself; and the child itself would not cherish the same affection for his father.

In making a choice for life, do we not consult disposition, intellect and age, in order to secure our happiness? And why? In order that the union may be perpetual by mutual inclination; and this is considered necessary for the preservation of morality and virtue. No such happy adaptation of temper, disposition, and habit, could be thought of, in a marriage with another race; no hopes, therefore, could be entertained of promoting by it the cause of humanity. Any attempt to raise the condition of the negroes in this manner, would not only not benefit the individuals who might be selected for the experiment, but be the absolute signal for the perpetration of the most atrocious crimes against society. It would undermine every principle of morality, and destroy the very foundation of society, without advancing the cause of the negroes. I consider the doctrine of amalgamation as abominable and brutal as the first introduction of slavery; and the injury which would be sustained from it, by the white race, infinitely greater than that which was inflicted upon the Africans by exporting them from their country as slaves.

The Americans are, indeed, in a very singular predicament. Their position, opposed to the rest of the civilised world, is most perplexing and unjust. No nation proposes to take charge of the civilisation of the Africans; but the Americans are called upon, to emancipate and educate their slaves, and to raise them to an equality with themselves. Their institutions are purely democratic, and the execution of the laws entrusted to the voluntary submission of the people who enacted them ; yet several millions of another race are to be let loose amongst them, and entrusted with that voluntary submission. Their institutions, it is believed, would not be adapted to any other state of society, yet they are to invite two and a half millions of negroes to participate in its advantages. And all this they are charged to do for the sake of humanity, without inquiring whether that race is capable of enjoying those privileges, or even made happier by their acquisition. And what have the Americans done that justifies such a demand? They have continued the institution of slavery, introduced by another government, of which their forefathers availed themselves before its moral injustice was established; and which their sons have since been laboring to shake off, without finding the adequate means. In the northern states, where it could be abandoned, it was done; but the south is obliged to pause, lest, by an awful retribution of justice, they should themselves become the victims of their slaves.

> This even is the curse of evil deeds,
> That, ever propagating, they engender evil.*

The only safe means which has been proposed for the emancipation of the negro slaves, was their transportation from America to Africa. Yet, even there they require the affectionate protection of the whites, to defend themselves

---

* " Das eben ist der Fluch der bösen That
  Dass sie fortzeugend immer Böses muss gebären."
  Schiller's Bride of Messina.

against the barbarous attacks of their brethren. But, suppose the Americans willing, as they are, to support and protect such a colony, what number of negroes could be transported thither to affect at all the colored population of the United States? During twelve years the number of negroes transported to Liberia was two thousand five hundred; while those who were born in that time amounted to seven hundred thousand! The whole treasury of the United States would not suffice to purchase and convey to Africa a sufficient number of negroes to prevent the increase of the blacks in America. Neither are the negroes themselves willing to leave their masters—whom they consider as their natural protectors—and emigrate to a distant shore. They go thither as strangers, and with no other civilization than that which they have acquired in bondage. They have not the inventive genius of the whites to conquer unforeseen obstacles; and would, in all probability, perish there, but for the assistance of their former masters.

Thus, in whatever light we may consider slavery in America, we must see in it an evil which cannot be remedied without endangering the moral, political, and social relations of the United States. At the present moment the southern slaves are provided for; their sphere of action is circumscribed, and they are satisfied with their situation. To make them free is to throw them on their own resources, and force them to become competitors with their masters. All the prejudices between the two races, which are now asleep, in their state of mutual dependency, would awaken at the thought that they are rivals, and commence their work of destruction. The negroes, as I have said before, are more numerous, and increase much faster in some of the southern states, than the whites. Could we then, for one moment, believe that they would abide the issue of a moral competition with their former lords, whom they know to be superior to themselves? We might as well suppose they would be content to perish, while holding the means of preservation. What hope of success could they have, except that which is based on their numbers? The moment the contest begins, their physical force must aid them; for it is their only weapon, and the contest must become one between brutality and intelligence.

The northern states, in emancipating their negroes, shut but the doors on unprofitable servants, without fearing their entering by force. They were too strong within, and their enemies too feeble without, to give the negroes a chance of success. Their former masters may now see them die in the streets, and behold them writhing with despair, and yet not fear their revenge. It is not so with the southern planter : he cannot abandon his negroes and expose them to want, without dreading the awful consequences. He cannot with impunity make a friendly race his enemies, and mock them with the title of freemen. His negroes are protected by him ; they participate to a certain extent in his prosperity, and share even his aristocratic pretensions.* They consider themselves members of his family, and cherish a filial affection for him, which is responded to by feelings of kindness in their master. A southern gentleman, after an absence from home, will, on his return to his plantation, be received with joyful acclamations by his negroes, who will crowd round him, and shake him cordially by the hand. What negro in the northern states would dare take "such liberties with a white man ?" The prejudices against the negroes are stronger in the free states than at the south, and have reached their climax in the states which never held slaves. These may give vent to their contempt for a race, with whose fate they never have meddled : they have a clear conscience ; but the upright magistrate is not always the most lenient judge.

In the southern states the negro is comparatively happy, for his master sympathises with him, and administers to his physical wants. The southern planter does not despise the negro, who is part of his own household, but comforts him in sickness and old age. At the north, the negro is an object of scorn, and considered a natural enemy to the laboring classes, because he reduces the price of their labor. In some of the western states, which

---

* Nothing is more frequent than to see negroes, belonging to different masters, abstain from all intercourse with each other, in consequence of the different ranks of the families of which they consider themselves a part. The slave of a senator will be proud of the distinction of his master, but bow to that of the president, who considers himself above all.

were entirely settled by the whites, he is not even allowed to hold property, and his presence is considered a
nuisance.   As long as the negro is protected by his
master, he receives, as it were, an equivalent for his degraded condition ; when he is made free, his degradation
becomes more poignant and glaring, and he is left without the means of support.   He becomes more dependent
on the white race than he ever was as a slave; for he
becomes dependent *on their good will*, when, as a slave,
he had a *right* to their protection.

With such prospects before them, is it charity to emancipate the negroes ?   Is it not forcing them to take up
arms and destroy their unkind benefactors ?   The negroes
cannot love America, in which they call nothing their
own ; but they may be attached to their masters, who
enable them to live without property.   They will never
be able to compete successfully with the white race, because their judges despise them, and judge in their own
cause ; but they may hold an inferior rank of society, in
which their interests are identified with those of the
whites, and consequently sure of being protected.   They
cannot hope to change the course of legislation, as long
as there is an American capable of wielding a weapon ;
but they may make their masters relent, by a quiet submission to their will : they cannot hope to rise to honor
and distinction, but they may be happier in an humbler
situation of life, and leave ambition to the whites.   In
one word, they must prepare to be slaves of kind masters,
or face these masters as enemies, and expire in the unequal contest.

One more objection I must answer, before I dismiss
this subject.   The question has often been proposed,
whether the progress of civilization will not eventually
overcome those unfortunate prejudices which exist with
regard to the negroes, and thus open the way to a reconciliation between the two races.   The answer to this
question, I am sorry to say, will not cheer the heart of
the philanthropist.   For, according to all indications,
they will *increase in proportion as the negroes are made
free*, and terminate in feelings so perfectly hostile, as to
be totally opposed to the spirit of peace and forbearance.
The blacks return hatred for contempt, which, while im-

potent, excites still greater contempt in the whites. The Americans look upon the freedom of the negroes as a garment not fit for their use, but which has been thrown over them for want of another, to cover their disgusting nudity. Whenever they are seen dressed in this new attire, their former nakedness is remembered, and the irony excites ridicule and scorn. The contrast would have ceased to be ludicrous, had they passed through different stages of freedom. But the ascent from a negro slave, to an independent American republican, was too rapid and dangerous to make his position secure. *America is the worst place where emancipation could have been tried;* and it must fail in every other democratic republic.

Had the negroes ever evinced a love of freedom, further than is connected with physical comfort; had they ever made an effort to become free for the love of liberty, and not for personal advantages or revenge; had they, in their struggle for liberty, ever waged war against superior numbers; had they ever been known as a nation whose rise and fall might have excited our sympathies,* a different sentiment would pervade the Americans, with regard to the unhappy negroes. But whatever the negroes are, they are by the charity of the Americans; whatever they possess, they hold by that tenure; whatever right they enjoy, is by the benevolence of their masters. But the requisitions of charity give no permanent title to respect.

The Americans have fought for, and *acquired* their liberty; they have given it *gratis* to their negroes. Neither has this gift been improved by those who received it. The law has declared them free, but their sentiments are still those of slaves. Their pretensions to equality with the whites, would be esteemed as ingratitude; for where one party is the sole benefactor, and the other that which is benefited, no moral equality could exist, though it should be entered on the statutes.

* The negroes, and their kindred in Austral Asia, do not seem to have had a national fate or existence. Not the least trace of political life can be discovered, even from traditions. All other people have been united by a community of feeling and sentiment, which gave them a distinct character; but the negroes seem to have vegetated: they have neither prospered nor declined, and possess no other characteristics, except those which belong to the variety.

Neither do the negroes take the least interest in the
fate of their brethren, but rather envy the slaves of the
south. For more than two generations, the negroes in
the northern states are free; they have schools and
churches; but no appeal has ever been made by them in
favor of liberty. Some of the negroes and mulattoes of
St. Domingo have been educated in France; but few
lines have as yet been published by them in favor of
liberal institutions. The combat for and against slavery
is entirely fought by the whites; while the negroes can
hardly comprehend that their condition should depend
upon a principle. It is this inertness, this absence of
moral courage, which the Americans despise. With
great truth does *De Tocqueville* remark, that no other
account has ever been opened between the white and the
black races, except that where the white race was superior, they kept the black in subjection; but where the
blacks prevailed, they rose and murdered the whites.
The negroes have never endeavored to rival their former
masters in any moral qualification, but whenever they
felt themselves sufficiently strong, attempted to rid themselves of their formidable superiors.

But the contempt of the Americans for the Africans is
yet increased by other causes. If the civilization of
America were stationary, or progressing slowly, the free
negroes might either keep their places, or, perhaps,
gradually approximate nearer to the standard of the
whites. But this is not the case. The Americans are
progressing more rapidly than any other nation in the
world; and the free negroes, though they may be absolutely advancing, remain still, every year, further behind.
Competing with the whites only in the most menial labor,
they are reducing the price of that labor below the customary wages of native Americans; and thereby force
the latter either to emigrate to the west, or to seek some
other employment. By this means, they succeed in
monopolizing, in a measure, the situation of servants;
but, at the same time, render it more degraded in the
eyes of Americans. They continue in a state of servitude, which, as it is voluntary, excites additional contempt. The Americans are sometimes compelled, from
necessity, to hire themselves out as "helps;" but they

neither suffer the same treatment, nor are they willing to
serve at so low a rate of compensation.

Yet the greatest difference between an American and
a negro servant is this. The American looks upon service as a means of introducing himself to something better; and remains a servant only till he has acquired the
means of emigrating to the west, or commencing a small
trade. He prefers any other situation in life, with the
severest labor, to waiting on another man. The negro,
on the contrary, aspires to nothing higher. He prefers
domestic work to any other, and, in the northern states,
his physical organization disables him from laboring in
the field. He is therefore a stationary servant, one who,
in the opinions of Americans, was born to be a servant,
lives as a servant, and dies in servitude. In proportion
as negro servants become general, in that same proportion increases the contempt in which the situation is
held. The negroes work for less, or rather are paid at
a less rate, than the whites, and will therefore always
remain poor, in a country where every one prospers.
They are, by poverty, deprived of the means of instruction,* remain houseless strangers in the land which gives
them birth, and by an unavoidable succession of events,
sink every year lower in the estimation of their fellow-
creatures and their own. At last they must resign the
thought of competition in every other department of industry, and become once more what they were—hereditary bondsmen.

At present, a number of petty offices and small traffics
are resigned to the industry of the negroes, because
the general prosperity is such, that the Americans find
sufficient room for enterprise in other departments. But
in proportion as the country becomes more and more
settled, and as competition among the whites increases,
these petty channels of industry will be resorted to by the
whites themselves, and the negroes driven to a still lower
employment.†

At present they may be barbers and hair-dressers,

* There are free negro-schools in some of the cities; but there is a
degree of poverty, which obliges the parents to avail themselves of the
work of their children, instead of sending them to school.

† This gradual diminution of their means of support, together with
the exposure to a more severe climate, is undoubtedly the reason why

32

clean boots, and sell old clothes; but the time may come when they will not be able to make a living by such means; and then they will be obliged to resort to something still more humble. In this manner, the whites will chase and harass them from post to post, until misery will complete their destruction. Their fate has no parallel in history. Slavery has introduced them to life, liberty must accomplish their ruin.

I turn with pleasure from so barren a soil, incapable of maturing the seeds of philanthropy, to prospects more brightening and cheerful. I turn to the lives of the planters. They are surrounded, it is true, by slaves, and their position becomes daily more precarious. But I am willing to trust them to their genius, and to the sympathy of their northern brethren. My object here is to speak of their manners, their habits, and the large proportion of intellect and genius which is found in the southern states.

The manners of the southerners in general, but especially those of the Virginians and South Carolinians, are more highly polished than those of the industrious population of the north, and they cultivate society as indispensable to civilized life. They know and appreciate refinement and elegance; but they possess less of the enterprising spirit of the New Englanders. Having more leisure, they devote more time to study and polite reading, which render their intercourse more agreeable and attractive; and, being freed from pecuniary cares and the influence of trade and traffic, acquire that independence of mind which is necessary for science and literature. Their provisions for the education of youth are not so numerous, but they are on the most liberal scale; education and learning are not so general as in the northern states, but where they exist they are carried to a higher degree. Business talents are comparatively rare; but there is no deficiency of genius.

The north act by their masses, the south by the brilliant talents of individuals. Intelligence at the north is as much divided as property. There are no overgrown fortunes, neither is there poverty or want. In the southern states the division is more unequal. There are those

the free negro population *decreases* so rapidly in the northern states; while the slaves to the south are increasing faster than the whites.

who are "poor and lean," but the wealth of the rich is capable of concealing their poverty. The progress of intellect in the southern states resembles more that of Europe. The masses are yet in darkness, though there are beacon flames on each coast. In the northern states of America obscurity has entirely vanished. Their lights are perhaps less bright, but so contiguous as to unite in a conflagration.

But, with all the advantages of the north, the south will always command a most important influence on the deliberations of Congress. The eminent talents of her statesmen and legislators are yet unequalled in America; though there are individuals at the north who may lay just claims to a share of their fame. All the presidents of the United States but two have been born and bred in the south, and, although they held slaves, have advanced the cause of freedom. The inhabitants of the south form an aristocracy with regard to the negroes; but the principal distinction being that of color, they are on an equality with each other, and are amongst the stoutest defenders of republicanism. Democracy is a child of the south; and its early defenders were southerners. The principle of slavery operates upon them yet as it did during the revolutionary war. It instils into them even an additional love of liberty; and makes them cherish doubly those rights and privileges, without which they would sink to a level with their slaves.*

* Botta, in his first book of "The Revolutionary War of America," describes the character of the slave-owners in the most glowing colors. "In queste ancora" says he, "la schiavitù dei Neri, la quale vi era in uso quantunque sembri, a prima vista strana cosa a dirsi alletava gli uomini bianchi all'amore della libertà. Avendo questi continuamente sotto gli occhi l'esempio vivo della miserabile condizione dell' uomo ridotto in ischiavitù, dovevano sapere meglio, e più apprezzare la libertà la quale e' giovano; questa libertà riputavano non che un diritto, essere una franchigia ed un privilegio; e siccome quando si trattá dell' interesse proprio e delle passioni loro, gli uomini giudicano alla grossa e cogli occhi della mente abbacinati impazientemente sopportavano i coloni la superiorità del governo inglese, e le pretensione sue, siccome quelle che tendessero a condurgli in uno stato prossimo, o simile a quello, al quale gli schiavi loro erano ridotti, detestando eglino in se stessi ciò che escercitavano sugli altri."

CHAPTER XII.

It is an established maxim of the American government, merely to possess the elements of national defence, in order to be saved the expense of maintaining a large standing army ; and to keep from the military a power, which it is known they have at all times abused. The navy of the United States is established nearly on the same plan ; and contains but the nucleus of that maritime power, which, when called for, the Americans could direct against an enemy.

In a country like America, which commands all the materials for ship-building, and, at any time, a sufficient number of sailors, furnished by the merchants' service, the maintaining of a greater number of ships of war than is absolutely necessary to protect navigation and commerce, would prove a severe tax on the people. In proportion as the commerce of the United States increases, the means of naval attack and defence increase implicitly with it ; though the navy may not exhibit this augmentation of force in the number of its ships.

The bulwark of national defence, however, is the militia ; though their discipline and their manœuvres have been the subject of much sarcasm, both in England and America. No one can expect from free citizens the same machine-like subordination, which may be exacted from hired soldiers, whose trade is to " kill and to be killed to make a living ; " * but the citizen soldier has

* *Mon métier est tuer et être tué pour gagner ma vie.*" Voltaire.

an hundred moral advantages over the martial automaton, of which the latter is never possessed.

The militia may improve in discipline, and join military skill to superior intelligence ; but the highest mark of perfection in a mercenary is a blind obedience to his superiors, without a vestige of thought or reflection. It is this mechanical excellence of soldiers, which renders their presence dangerous in a republic, and against the evil influence of which a powerful militia is the best and only safeguard. The *ésprit du corps* is always a dangerous enemy to the *ésprit du peuple*, unless the latter be embodied in some armed force. The militia, therefore, are not only a means of defence against an external enemy, but also a preserver of peace within. They save the country the expense of a large standing army, by performing, themselves, a portion of those duties which would otherwise devolve on the soldiery. Regular standing armies were introduced by the systematic despotism of Lewis XIV.; the militia system is the daughter of liberty. The army and militia are bane and antidote of the freedom of a people. Military skill and discipline avail against one another, as a superior chess-player will beat an inferior antagonist by a better disposition of his men ; but the militia system of the present day has *changed the board;* for, instead of empty squares, the players find nothing but occupied territory.

In speaking of the American militia, as a means of national defence, I am aware I ought to confine myself, chiefly, to their capacity of resisting an armed, external force. But in order to judge of this capacity, it is necessary not only to consider the materials of which they are composed, and their numbers ; but also the circumstances which have brought them into existence, and the spirit which animates them at the present moment. The organization of society, and the *terrain* on which they are to give proof of their prowess, are important items in a computation of this kind ; without which it is impossible to obtain a result in the least approximating to truth. But before entering on this subject I will give a brief statement of the military and naval force of the United States, from the " *Army* " and " *Navy*|*Lists* " of March, 1835. These, propably, have not been materially altered

32*

since ; especially that of the navy.* If there be any thing remarkable in them, it is their exceeding shortness, and the consequently diminutive expenses of these establishments in a country comprising so large a territory, and enjoying so extensive a commerce.

Army List, March, 1835.

The head-quarters of the general-in-chief are in the district of Columbia. The head-quarters of the Western Department, are at Memphis Tennessee. The head-quarters of the Eastern Department are in the city of New York.

The Western Department comprises all west of a line drawn from the southernmost point of East Florida, to the north-west extremity of Lake Superior, taking in the whole of Tennessee and Kentucky ; the Eastern Department all east of that line, including Fort Winnebago.

The officers of the army consist of

1 major-general, commanding the army, (at present Mr. Alex. Macomb.)

1 brigadier-general, major-general by brevet, commanding the Western Department.

1 brigadier-general, major-general by brevet, commanding the Eastern Department.

1 adjutant-general. 2 inspectors-general. 1 quartermaster-general. 4 quartermasters. 1 commissary-general of subsistence. 2 commissaries. 1 surgeon-general. 12 surgeons. 55 assistant-surgeons. 1 paymaster-general. 14 paymasters. 1 commissary-general of purchase. 2 military store-keepers. 18 colonels. 13 lieutenant-colonels. 27 majors. 134 Captains. 159 first-lieutenants. 218 second-lieutenants. 5 third-lieutenants. 11 sergeant-majors. 11 quartermaster-sergeants. 428 sergeants. 454 corporals. 14 principal musicians. 212 musicians. 108 artificers. 250 enlisted for ordnance. 6059 privates.

Total. Commissioned officers, 674. Non-commissioned officers and privates, 7547. Grand Total, 8221.

* The Indian war compelled the President to accept the services of volunteers, and to increase the cavalry of the United States.

It will be observed that the number of officers is unusually large in proportion to the small number of privates. But the latter can always be obtained when wanted, whereas the officers require superior knowledge and experience. Hence it is the policy of the government of the United States merely to preserve the *cadres* of the different regiments, which may be filled up and engrossed at any time, in case of a war.

For the education of officers a national military academy was established at West Point, in the state of New York, on the plan of similar institutions in France. The same branches are taught, and the same system of discipline is introduced ; but particular attention is paid to mathematics and the modern languages. Mr. Hamilton has been very severe in his criticism on the *attitude* of the young men, styled " cadets," who are there educated at the expense of the nation ; but I believe he has not examined any of the classes in order to judge of their scientific acquirements. To supply this apparent deficiency I would state that, independent of military tactics, the pupils of that academy acquire a very comprehensive knowledge of the mathematical and physical sciences,* which enables them to serve their country in peace as well as in war. The pupils have to pass a rigorous examination on entering the academy ; and are annually examined while there, by a committee appointed by the president and senate of the United States. The cadets are considered as enlisted in the United States service, and receive about 45 dollars or £9 sterling a month. They are, moreover, subject to all the rules and regulations of regular soldiers.

The distinction between officers and citizens being less rigorously drawn in America than in Europe, the officers of the United States engineer corps are amongst the most active in promoting the internal improvements of the country. They are planning and constructing the prin-

* La Croix's Algebra and Legendre's Geometry and Trigonometry are the text books used in the elementary branches of mathematics; La Croix's Treatise on the differential and integral Calculus is studied in French; and in descriptive geometry, Professor Davis's treatise has lately been substituted for that of Monge, formerly used by the cadets.

cipal railroads; and are every where employed where
mathematical talents are required in the execution of public works.   They are thus rendering themselves useful to
the people, who have paid for their education; and become not a distinct branch of public functionaries, but,
in the true sense of the word, the servants of the people.*

The war department is divided into twelve branches;
viz., the secretary's office; the offices of bounty-lands
and of Indian affairs; the pension office, the adjutant-
general's office, the paymaster-general's office, the ordi-
nance department, the topographical bureau, the subsistence department, the surgeon-general's office, the quartermaster-general's office, and the engineer department.

The secretary's office consists of the secretary himself,
an acting chief clerk, five clerks, one messenger, and one
assistant messenger.   The bounty-lands office, of a principal and clerk; the office of Indian affairs, of a com-
missioner, a chief clerk, and nineteen other clerks; the
adjutant's office, of the adjutant-general, two officers and
three clerks; the paymaster-general's office, of the paymaster-general, one paymaster, one chief clerk, two
clerks, and one messenger; the ordnance department, of
one colonel, one captain and three clerks; the topographical bureau, of a lieutenant-colonel, (topographical
engineer,) one first lieutenant (assistant engineer,) and
one clerk; the subsistence department, of a brigadier-
general, one major (commissary of subsistence,) and three
clerks; the surgeon-general's office, of the surgeon-general, one surgeon and one clerk; the quartermaster-general's office, of the quartermaster-general, one major,
(the quartermaster,) one captain, two clerks and an assistant clerk; finally, the engineer department, of the

---

* Major M'Neill, of the United States engineers, constructed the
Boston and Lowell, Boston and Providence, Boston and Worcester,
and is now constructing the Stonington and a number of other railroads.   That between Boston and Lowell is considered the best and
most substantial in the United States, and, perhaps, in the world.   It is
built of the iron-edge rail, supported by cast-iron chairs, on stone
blocks, and iron sleepers, which rest again on stone foundations.   The
cost of this railroad is estimated at one million two hundred thousand
dollars, or two hundred and forty thousand pounds sterling, distance
only twenty-five and a half miles.   (Compare Chapter X. on internal
improvement.)

chief engineer, an assistant engineer, and three clerks. The whole expenses of the military service, including fortifications, ordnance, Indian affairs, pensions and arming the militia may be computed at thirteen millions of dollars or two millions six hundred thousand pounds sterling which is little more than half of the whole expenditure of the general government. If this sum be compared to the expenditures of European states, and if, moreover, the vastness of territory and frontier to be protected, be taken into consideration, it will appear that the expenses of the American army are, in proportion, not even the one hundredth part of those of the smaller states of Germany ; without considering the enormous indirect taxation introduced by the system of conscription.

The military service of the United States is very arduous, though the troops are better paid and provisioned than any other soldiers in the world. But then they are marched off to the forts of the western and southern states, and, during the whole period of service, not once quartered upon a town or village. This circumstance, together with the nature of the frontier posts, gives, in time of peace, rise to frequent desertions ; but on active duty I should judge the troops of the United States equal to the best soldiers in Europe, and their officers and commanders well capable of sustaining the high reputation which the arms of the young republic have already acquired. Their bravery is like the English. It is best tested in an obstinate action, and by the facility with which they recover their ranks, when by any chance they are broken. Their outward appearance is, perhaps, not quite so neat as that of European troops, as, in fact, they are never used for *parade ;* but this does not prevent their usefulness in the field, and is certainly no impediment to their courage. The United States maintain no more troops than are required to garrison the forts, and to protect the frontier against the ravages of the Indians. Their soldiers, therefore, are constantly employed, and have neither the time nor the inclination to set off their personal attractions.

The Navy List of February, 1835, contained thirty-seven captains, forty masters commandant, 357 lieutenants, forty-four surgeons, fifteen passed assistant surgeons,

forty-one assistant surgeons, forty-three pursers, nine
chaplains, 178 passed midshipmen, 274 midshipmen,
twenty-seven sailing-masters, four teachers of naval sciences, twenty boatswains, twenty-two gunners, twenty-one
carpenters, and nineteen sail-makers. The expenses of
the navy may be computed at three millions of dollars, or
six hundred thousand pounds sterling, including improvements.

The navy-department consists of the secretary, one
chief clerk, seven clerks, a clerk of the navy-pension and
hospital fund, and one messenger. Navy-commissioners
are three, with a secretary, a chief clerk, five clerks, one
draftsman, and a messenger. There is one chief naval
constructer, and one naval storekeeper.

The following is a List of the Vessels of War, (February, 1835,) with the Names and Rates of the Ships, and
their Stations.

SHIPS OF WAR.

Name of vessel.	Guns.	Where built.	When.	Where employed.
SHIPS OF THE LINE.				
Independence	74	Boston	1814	In ordinary at Boston.
Franklin	74	Philadelphia	1815	Ditto New York.
Washington	74	Portsmouth (N.H.)	1816	Ditto New York.
Columbus	74	Washington	1819	Ditto Boston.
Ohio	74	New York	1820	Ditto New York.
North Carolina	74	Philadelphia	1820	Ditto Gosport.
Delaware	74	Gosport, (Virginia)	1820	In commission in Mediterranean.
Alabama	74	- - -	-	On the stocks at Portsmouth.
Vermont	74	- - -	-	Ditto Boston.
Virginia	74	- - -	-	Ditto Boston.
Pennsylvania	74	- - -	-	Ditto Philadelphia.
New York	74	- - -	-	Ditto Norfolk.
FRIGATES OF THE FIRST CLASS.				
United States	44	Philadelphia	1797	In commission, refitting.
Constitution	44	Boston	1797	In ordinary at Boston.
Guerriere	44	Philadelphia	1814	Ditto New York.
Java	44	Baltimore	1814	Ditto Norfolk.
Potomac	44	Washington	1821	In commission, Mediterranean.
Brandywine	44	Washington	1825	Ditto Pacific Ocean.
Hudson	44	Purchased	1826	In ordinary at New York.
Santee	44	- - -	-	On the stocks at Portsmouth.
Cumberland	44	- - -	-	Ditto Boston.
Sabine	44	- - -	-	Ditto New York.
Savannah	44	- - -	-	Ditto New York.
Rariton	44	- - -	-	Ditto Philadelphia.
Columbia	44	- - -	-	Ditto Washington.
St. Lawrence	44	- - -	-	Ditto Norfolk.
FRIGATES OF THE SECOND CLASS.				
Constellation	36	Baltimore	1797	In ordinary at Norfolk.
Congress	36	Portsmouth	1799	Ditto Norfolk.
Macedonian	36	Captured	1812	On the stocks, re-building.
SLOOPS OF WAR.				
John Adams	24	Charleston, (S.C.)	1799	In commission, Mediterranean.
Cyanne	24	Captured	1815	In ordinary at Philadelphia.
Erie	18	Baltimore	1813	On the coast of Brazil.
Ontario	18	Baltimore	1813	Ditto ditto
Peacock	18	New York	1813	In ordinary at New York.
Boston	18	Boston	1825	Ditto Boston.
Lexington	18	New York	1825	Ditto Portsmouth.
Vincennes	18	New York	1826	In the Pacific.
Warren	18	Boston	1826	In ordinary at Philadelphia.
Natchez	18	Norfolk	1827	In commission, coast of Brazil.
Falmouth	18	Boston	1827	Ditto West Indies.
Fairfield	18	New York	1828	Ditto Pacific.
Vandalia	18	Philadelphia	1828	In the West Indies.
St. Louis	18	Washington	1828	Ditto ditto
Concord	18	Portsmouth	1828	In ordinary at Portsmouth.
SCHOONERS, &c.				
Dolphin	12	Philadelphia	1821	In the Pacific.
Grampus	12	Washington	1821	In the West Indies.
Shark	12	Washington	1821	In the Mediterranean.
Enterprize	12	New York	1831	On the coast of Brazil.
Boxer	12	Boston	1831	In the Pacific Ocean.
Experiment	12	Washington	1831	In commission, West Indies.
Fox	3	Purchased	1823	Receiving ship at Baltimore.
Sea-Gull (Galliot.)		Purchased	1823	Ditto at Pennsylvania.

Total:—12 ships of the line; 14 large frigates of the first class; 3 frigates of the second class; 15 sloops of war; 8 schooners and smaller vessels; of which number there were 5 ships of the line, and 7 large frigates on the stocks.

Of all the institutions of the United States, the navy is the most national and popular. It cannot, from its nature, interfere with, but only protect, the political progress of the country; and it has more than any other raised the standard of national honor. With judicious modesty have its officers abstained from all political contest, to prevent party spirit from entering their ranks. They have only known their duty towards the nation; and have fulfilled it in a manner which has reflected glory on themselves and their country. From the earliest period of the revolutionary war, to the present moment, the American navy has sustained its reputation with equal success; though surrounded by difficulties and perils, which hardly ever threatened a similar infant institution. It embodied in its ranks the enterprise and chivalry of a new-born people, and with the vigor of youth fought the unequal battle with the giant. Whatever opinions the English may entertain with regard to the naval successes obtained by the Americans in the late war, one truth must irresistibly force itself upon their minds,—that the Americans have shown no inferiority of seamanship; but evinced a familiarity with the ocean, and an habitual defiance of its dangers well worthy the offspring of the greatest maritime nation.

It was asserted that during the late war with England, the American frigates were of a larger size, and their guns of a heavier caliber. This I believe was true in some instances, but on the lakes the advantage was on the side of the English; and it was joined to a superior position. The manner, too, in which some American ships made their *escape* from whole British fleets, proved the superiority of their construction, and the seamanship of their commanders.

The navy of the United States is yet young, and comparatively small; but it possesses that which must eventually make it great, and rival the English itself—unlimited commerce, great naval genius, and the first maritime position on the globe. But in the worst case, the fame of the mother will but descend on her daughter, and the tempest be addressed in English, as in the days of Blake and Nelson.

The Americans are sensible of the debt they owe to

their navy, and of the influence of its spirit on the officers and crews of the merchants' service. Though excessively jealous of increasing the national expenditure, they have raised the pay of the naval officers, and testified their gratitude by the unanimity with which the Senate and House of Representatives supported and agreed to the measure. At the great number of public dinners, which are annually given in America, I have noticed but two toasts universally drank by all parties ; óne in dignified silence, the other with thundering applause :—" *the memory of Washington*," and " *the American navy*."

The militia system of the United States was introduced into the colonies simultaneously with their settlements, and was rendered necessary to protect the infant states against the ferocious incursions of the Indians. It was happily adapted to the feelings and sentiments of the Americans, who, at an early period of their history, were jealous of the presence of British troops in their provinces, and therefore more willing to tax themselves with the performance of a certain portion of military duties, than suffer regular soldiers to be quartered in their towns and villages. They dreaded the possibility of becoming subservient to the will and pleasure of the royal governors, and employed in subverting the liberties of the colonies. The Americans were always desirous of governing themselves ; and for that purpose required not only *moral*, but also *physical* (material) strength, which they happily discovered, was secured by arming the citizens.

At the commencement of the revolutionary war, it was but the militia, and especially the New England militia, (that of Massachusetts and Connecticut,) who were opposed to the British troops. Without their presence, and the sacrifices which they were willing to make to the cause of their country, resistance against armed force could not have been seriously contemplated, and its consequences must, unavoidably, have been ignominious or tragical. Since the conclusion of peace, the militia establishment has been improved in all the states, and a uniform system of tactics has been introduced during the administration of General Jackson.

The militia of each state assemble on particular days of the year for inspection ; when fines are inflicted on the absentees, and those whose accoutrements and arms are not in the condition prescribed by the law. This practice, it seems, is not calculated to increase the popularity of the system among the wealthier classes, who, on such occasions, are generally the sufferers; while the poorer orders, and particularly the mechanics, are always ready to shoulder their muskets, and go through the usual manœuvres. The officers, too, being generally elected by the privates, (the people,) the choice is apt to fall on those who are in a habit of associating with them; and thus it often happens that the wealthiest merchants and professional men are enlisted as privates, while the poor mechanic, in his place as officer, will summon them to appear on such a day, "armed and equipped as the law directs," at such a place, "*there to await further orders.*"

The militia system, in most states, is a tax and an annoyance to the rich; while to the people at large it is far from proving a burden, but on the contrary an additional means of asserting their sovereignty. In time of peace, when the benefits of a war establishment are never sufficiently appreciated, the annoyance occasioned by the annual exercises and manœuvres, is considered as a most uncalled for disturbance of the peace of the wealthy citizens; but the measure being a popular one, they submit to it quietly, and, by paying their annual fines, increase the good cheer of those who are ready for duty.

The young men, however, being always more or less moved by a martial spirit, escape the ignominy of obeying their tradespeople, by forming themselves into "regular uniformed companies," styled *independent;* and then elect their own officers with reference to gentility and fortune. It is to these companies English travellers frequently allude, when speaking of the American militia. They are, for the most part, equipped in an attractive style, calculated to exhibit their taste, and to set off their persons to advantage. Being generally wealthy, they give the preference to the rich uniforms of the Hungarian huzzars, or the Polish krakuzòw; so that an European, on seeing them march, would be apt to mistake them for a dismounted squadron of horse. But there are also independent companies of mechanics and other orders of society, who, being less rich, are obliged to conform a little more to the unostentatious dress and habits of soldiers, and have, therefore, a more martial appearance.

But, although the American militia have not the discipline of regular troops, but, on the contrary, evince a spirit of independence which singularly contrasts with the uniforms of soldiers, they possess, nevertheless, three great advantages over the largest standing armies which could be embarked for the shores of America. The first of these consists unquestionably in the superiority of their number, which includes the whole male population capable of bearing arms; the second, in the readiness with which they are able to supply their wants; and the last, in the universality of their genius.

It has often been remarked that the Americans never confine themselves to one trade, and on this account, become rarely as good workmen as Europeans. This objection I have already answered in the ninth chapter, when speaking of American mechanics. I will here dwell on the advantages of the system. It compels them to *think* more, and to supply the want of mechanical skill by a decided superiority of judgment. They are compelled to make themselves familiar with a variety of operations, and the principles on which they are founded, and become thus able to make themselves useful in almost every capacity. This universality of adaptation is particularly advantageous to their system of national defence. An American militia company will hardly possess the precision and military bearing of European soldiers; but, in case of necessity, they will be able to provide their own uniforms, make and mend their own shoes, and manufacture their guns, bayonets, and swords. They will understand how to construct bridges and boats, and be capable of managing a vessel. They will be used to the felling of trees, and understand how to fortify and barricade the high roads; and above all, they will not easily become fatigued, because they are all active men, and used to the hardest of labor. Their officers will require no attendance or servants; for they will, if necessary, clean and shoe their own horses, pitch their own tents, and share personally the labor of their fellow-soldiers in the construction of fortifications and new roads. It was by the indefatigable exertions of the militia that, in the war of independence, the British troops were harassed in every direction, and often surprised by the rapidity of the American marches, in the worst of seasons, and on roads of their own construction. The fortifications of Bunker's Hill (Breed's Hill) were constructed in one night; those of Dorchester Heights, which commanded the city of Boston, and caused its evacuation by the British troops, from night-fall till ten o'clock in the morning,* and with the same rapidity was the city of New Orleans fortified. Behind entrenchments, or in a *terrain coupé*, the American militia are truly formidable, for they are excellent marksmen, and possess the agility of hunters. They compose a body which may be a hundred times defeated, and will be a hundred times re-organized; for they are animated by the same spirit which gave life and power to their country, and are themselves the citizens of that country. They are, from the geographical position of the United States, only required to act on the defensive; while their enemies would have to march through a territory in which discipline would not avail, and in which they would be exposed to the merciless aim of the western rifle.

On the whole, the Americans are remarkably fond of military parade and honors. The titles of captain, major, and colonel, are flung in every direction; but being applied indiscriminately to all, no superiority is implied in the distinction. The militia system indulges their martial spirit, without the expense and danger attending a standing army, and affords sufficient scope for the reasonable ambition of individuals. As to the peculiar adaptation of Americans to the performance of military duties, my impression is, that the northern and eastern states would furnish very useful troops, the southern states the most chivalrous, and the west a peculiar, valorous species, partaking of the courage and pertinacity of the Indians.

* Botta. "*Storia della Guerra dell' Independenza degli Stati Uniti d' America.*" *Libro sesto.*

CHAPTER XIII.

POLITICAL PROSPECTS OF AMERICA.—UNIVERSAL SUFFRAGE.
—STATE OF PARTIES.—RELATIVE POSITION OF NORTH
AND SOUTH AMERICA.—OF NORTH AMERICA, WITH RE-
GARD TO ENGLAND AND THE REST OF THE WORLD.—
CONCLUSION.

As the origin and progress of the United States are
without a parallel in history, so do her political career
and prospects not admit of a comparison with the rise
and fall of the ancient republics, which were neither in
form nor substance similar to those of America. Since
those times, the condition of the civilised world has undergone a serious change, not only as regards the relation
of the governed to their rulers, but also in the position
which the different states themselves have assumed with
regard to each other. The spirit of Christianity, which
it seems is, after a lapse of eighteen hundred years, but
now beginning to unfold its true genius, the art of printing, and the establishment of posts have revolutionized
the world, and are continuing to act as reformers on
every member of the human family. The invention of
gunpowder has equalized the physical conditions; while
the periodical press is laboring to assert the power of
numbers, in opposition to the privileges of the favored
few.

The history of former ages is fraught principally with
the systematic accounts of the robberies and depreda-
tions, committed by one people upon another; in which
the masses appear and disappear, but as passive instruments in the hands of their rulers. The history of the

world was the history of a few individuals, who elevated whole nations by their prosperity, or involved them in general ruin. In this sense, the kings of the earth were truly the representatives of eternal justice, and it was but natural for the people to look upon them as immediate emanations from the Godhead.

Even the histories of Greece and Rome make no exception to this rule. For, although animated by an expansive spirit which was capable of grasping the world, the masses, which represent the natural interests of man, were still in a state of childhood—the lifeless satellites of a few radiant stars. The fate of the heroes of the ancient world excites even now greater sympathies than that of our contemporaries; because they felt and acted as the moral agents of their respective nations, and their rise or fall was the birth or funeral of a whole people. The Roman republic died with Brutus; but the martial genius of France was not crushed by the fall of Napoleon.

With the discovery of America commences a new historical era. Already had ideas been multiplied; the invention of printing had furnished a means of perpetuating them with the masses, and the latter were gradually arriving at a state of pupillarity. The mind had begun to assert its empire, and to level the conditions of men. Opposed to inert material force was the moving power of intelligence; and the people themselves had begun to assume a part in the historical drama.

In vain were weapons forged to combat liberty of conscience; in vain did ecclesiastical and political powers unite to oppose the progress of philosophy. The march of intellect cannot be impeded by physical obstacles: ideas are eternal and imperishable, and the light once dawning on the world, could not again be changed into darkness. The sun once risen, has to complete his bright career, before it can again sink below the horizon, and suffer night to reassume its empire. The interests of truth and humanity had been proclaimed paramount even to national distinctions; and instead of fighting the wars of their princes, the people had begun to reflect on their own position and safety. Arts and sciences had become the commonwealth of nations, and civilization had made them unite as members of one and the same family.

But the new empire of the mind existed only in men's ideas; it was destitute of physical power: it had no existence in time and space. The inalienable rights of men were clashing with the privileges of the favored; and the growing spirit of liberty opposed to the birthright of kings. In vain had the people struggled to obtain for it a limited territory; when a peaceful mediation presented itself—the settlement of a new continent. In this project both parties joined, one from a hope of realising the practical application of its principles; the other to rid itself of a dangerous enemy, whose existence at home filled their minds with apprehensions of dangers. That the discovery and settlement of America did not take place sooner, that the most fertile part of the American continent was settled by the *English*,—the nation which was furthest advanced in political philosophy—we must ascribe to that power which presides equally over the destinies of nations and individuals. Had the new continent been settled one century sooner, the whole feudal system and its miseries would have been entailed upon it, and instead of the intelligence of Europe, America would now reflect the melancholy picture of its suffering millions.

The settlement of the United States took place under more favorable circumstances than ever attended the birth of a nation. It was effected, in the outset, on principles the most pure and philosophical, and encountered no serious moral obstacle in its progress. The government of America was not a problem; but a proposition which had been demonstrated, and to which the declaration of independence was but a corollary.

The seed of liberty found in Europe no soil favorable to its germination; but it flourished luxuriantly in America; and has since so multiplied that there is no fear of its ever becoming extinct. The United States have assumed a rank amongst the most powerful nations on the globe; but their strength lies in the moral justice of their government. America possesses not only the elements of power, but her onward march is hailed by the sympathies of increasing civilization. Her cause is adopted by the people of all countries; and instead of exciting jealousies, her progress is identified with the success of liberal principles throughout the world. America has become the representative of freedom, and as such is destined to act as the animating principle on the rest of mankind.

If Russia had ten times the physical power of the United States, her progress would still be uncertain; for she has not the means of adapting her government to the spirit of the age. Her way is through darkness and oppression; while every new idea which quickens into life and becomes the property of thousands, is enlarging the power of America. Both countries are developing immense natural resources, and progress with a rapidity which threatens the independence of other nations; but Russia is the evil genius of history; while America is its guardian angel. The power of Russia is opposed to the interests of humanity; that of the United States is based upon wisdom and justice.

Russia, in order to preserve her power, is obliged to retain the masses in ignorance, and thereby to make her people inferior to all others. Reform, which gives new power and increases the political life of other nations, she must dread as the harbinger of death; for it would divide her ranks, and dismember her empire. She possesses a territory occupied not by one homogeneous mass of intelligence; but by some five or six dozen savage hordes, subjected to her government by a military despotism.

The power of Russia rests on her bayonets; that of America on the superiority of mind over brute force. They are to each other as darkness to light. If the power of Russia has been rapidly extending itself over a large portion of Asia, and Europe, it has created no new life in either continent; and her aggrandizement is rather the subject of statistics and political geography, than matter of universal history. The Americans have increased their territory by intelligence. Wherever they have gone they have created new life; and their country is yet in travail to give birth to powerful states.

Nor is this the only manner in which the power of America increases. The principles of liberty have been espoused by other nations, who have become her natural allies. Despotism may still claim their territory; but liberty rules in the minds of the people. In this sense the influence of America extends to the very frontiers of Russia, and penetrates even into her empire. The day of battle must come; the war of principles must ensue; but it will not be the peaceable abodes of the Americans which will be made the scenes of horror and bloodshed.

The position of America with regard to her defence against an external foe, is similar to that of China; but she possesses infinitely greater powers of attack. To her means of national defence, she joins courage and enterprise; and instead of the brutalizing despotism of the Orientals, she is animated by the spirit of liberty. From foreign enemies; therefore, America has nothing to dread: let us examine her prospects within.

Three great enemies are supposed to exist against the union of the American States:—slavery; the geographical distinctions of the north, south, and west; and last though not least in the accounts of politicians, the licentiousness of the lower classes, which, it is feared, will be the ultimate consequence of universal suffrage.

With regard to slavery I have already expressed my opinion in Chapter XI; I am therefore only to explain the manner in which its existence acts as a means of disseminating discord—or a cement, which, by rendering the two sections of the country dependent on one another, is an additional guarantee of the Union. I am inclined to believe the latter; though I am ready to admit that the north is more independent of the south, than the south of the north, and that, on this account, the slave-holding states will always be jealous of the power acquired by the north. It is true, the continuation of slavery in the southern states is connected with many dangers, some of which are almost as much to be dreaded as those which are inseparable from it sabolition; yet, as long as the Union remains, the negroes need not excite fear; for any resistance on their part would instantly be checked by the north. The south, therefore, is bound to conciliate the friendship of the northern and western states; but, in return, exchanges with them its riches. The southern states are the best customers of the northern manufacturers and merchants; and by confining themselves principally to the growing of cotton and rice, keep up the price of the western produce.

The exports of America consist chiefly of southern produce; that of cotton alone surpasses the sum total of all the rest. During the operation of the late tariff, the south contributed, in proportion, the by far greatest part to the national revenue, and the measure itself was proposed by the southern statesmen. The returns for the southern produce being principally brought to the northern ports, it is, in fact, the north which reaps all the advantages of the southern states; while the inhabitants of the latter are merely the storekeepers of its wealth. The negro slaves of America work as much for the prosperity of the northern states as for their own masters: they create the capital with which the genius of the north pursues its manufactures and commerce.

In case of a separation of the states, this source of wealth would inevitably be lost to the north; for the south itself would be compelled to establish manufactures, and to seek another channel for its exports. The north would at best be but a competitor for the southern trade; while at present it monopolizes it without a rival.

But the south is connected with the north yet by other ties. Nearly all the merchants and traders in the southern states are emigrants from the north. Through their hands, and those of their correspondents, passes nearly all the property of which the planters are possessed. Now, it is evident that, in case of a separation, this portion of the southern population would either be ejected, or obliged to take sides with their employers. In the first case they would be ruined; in the last compelled to face their own brethren.

Finally, we might suppose the north, capable of subduing the south, if the climate of those states were adapted to the constitution of the whites; but even this would not increase the wealth of the north. The inhabitants of the northern states derive, at present, greater advantages from the south, than they could hope for, from an actual possession of its soil. At present, the south is furnishing them with the materials of industry; as planters, they would have to furnish them themselves, and bear the tax of their production. Instead of advancing, they would have to recede one step, and surround themselves once more with those evils, from which they have so happily escaped. But the south and north are too well balanced to render such a conquest probable; and there is, besides, a western power, whose interests are identified with the progress of both, which would never permit such a war.

I consider the progress of the west, as I have once already observed, as one of the greatest safeguards of the union and liberties of America. It contains the most enterprising population of the United States; and is noted for its republican spirit. In case of a quarrel between the north and the south, the western interest would be appealed to; and in whose favor it would declare, on that side would be the victory. But even in this case, the union of the west with either party, would oblige the other to yield, or expose its own independence. Neither is the west more independent of the north and south, than those states of each other. One portion of its produce is exported to, and consumed in, the north; the other follows the course of the Mississippi, and passes into the southern territory. Shut the mouth of the Mississippi, and the canals and railroads of the states of New York, and Pennsylvania, and the west will be blockaded as effectually as if a *cordon* had been established on its borders.

But there is yet a fourth party in the United States, composed of elements which, though less distinguished from the rest by physical and geographical differences, are, nevertheless, strongly united by a common origin and certain moral characteristics, which mark them as a distinct people. I refer to the inhabitants of New England. The eastern states, as they are commonly termed, must become the manufacturing district of America, and will, as such, be equally interested in maintaining a good understanding with the south, which can never become their successful rival; but will furnish them the best market for their manufactures.

The presence of so many parties must evidently serve to neutralise their mutual effect on one another, and prevent any one of them from domineering over the rest. Every attempt of this kind, would be deprecated by public opinion,—the only real power which exists in the United States. But the prosperity of all parties is pledged in the continuance of peace. The money of the northern capitalists is now freely circulating throughout the Union, and is equally benefiting the west and south. The industry and success of individuals are not supported by a particular section of the country; but depend on the good will and co-operation of all. The enterprising spirit of New England would be stifled, or at least checked, if the west and south did not furnish it aliment. On the other hand, the west could not realise the value of its produce, if the north and south were unwilling to become its purchasers; and the south could not be secured the quiet possession of its slaves, if the planters could not rely on the active assistance of the north.

From the beginning of their existence, to the present hour the fate of the American Colonies was identified with their mutual friendship and good understanding. From the first moment of their existence, their interests were so intimately connected with each other that they voluntarily established that Union which has since become the means of their greatness. The same causes are still operating, with a tenfold greater force, than at the time of the revolution. Their mutual interests in the Union have increased and continue to augment every year. The mere *pecuniary* losses which would result from a separation are incalculable. Industry, commerce, and agriculture would be checked in every part of the country, and the enterprise of individuals confined to the narrow limits of single states and territories. There is no real advantage to be gained by any of the parties, at all equal to the loss it would inevitably have to sustain; and it is therefore not to be supposed that the United States, even with the most sordid view to their separate interests, will ever seriously entertain a thought of separation. But as long as the nation at large is not infected with this pest, the ambition of individuals must wreck against the firmness and good sense of the people. War and strife have ever been promoted by only a few; the masses have had nothing to gain by them. In proportion, therefore, as the latter become capable of understanding their own interests, armed opposition must cease, not only in America, but in every part of the world. The unhappy doctrine that the ruin of one country establishes the greatness of another, does not even hold of two neighboring kingdoms; much less of two sister states, united under one and the same general government.

Neither does the progress of American legislation exhibit the least symptoms of inimical feelings between the different parties. South Carolina, it is true, resisted the tariff; but the rest of the United States were willing to repeal the obnoxious law, and at the same time determined to enforce it, till it should be repealed. The southern states complained at the undue interference with their slaves; and immediately the different states of the north pass the strongest resolutions, censuring the proceedings of the abolitionists, and prohibiting their interference in the future. The same sentiments have since been espoused even by the lowest classes, while the preachers of abolition have been driven from their homes and the pulpit. The south claimed the exclusive right of legislating on the subject of slavery, a right which belongs to them by the very letter of the constitution, but which, of late, had been made the subject of serious discussion; and immediately Congress passes a vote, that the government of the United States has no right to interfere with it. Incendiary pamphlets are sent into the southern states; but the government of the Union orders the postmasters not to deliver them. Does this look like oppression on the part of the majority which now uphold the government ?* Can the south, under these circumstances, complain of the undue interference of the north? And is it not evident that, even in the case of interference, the Union has the power to protect them?

Edmund Burke, in his address to the Americans, in behalf of the minority of the House of Commons, foresaw the power which some of the American states would acquire over others; and with sagacious forecast counselled them to adhere to a government, which should have the power of protecting them against each other's aggressions. This power, though Burke applied it only to

---

* It is but justice to say that the respectable part of the opposition are as much opposed to the doctrines and practices of the abolitionists, as the supporters of the present administration; and that, in general, there is no political party in the United States, opposed to the interests of the planters.

the British king and parliament, is evidently vested in
Congress. As long as the Union lasts, the small states
will be protected; but severed from the bulk of the republic, they must be swallowed up by their more powerful
neighbors.

The small states of the German Confederation were
much more independent during the Empire than they are
now, governed by sovereign princes. Prussia and Austria have each but four votes at the Diet; but these votes
are backed by five hundred thousand bayonets; and their
propositions, therefore, meet with no opposition. Austria,
in the shape of advice, interferes more with the minor
states than she ever did, or could do, while her emperors
were emperors of Germany, and required the support of
those states.

I do not believe, that, at present, there can be found
one candidate for office in the northern states, professing
to be an abolitionist; and if he were such, the state of
public opinion is so changed within the last year, that he
would not have the least chance of being elected. The
fanaticism of a few publishers and printers of newspapers
is all that remains of the whole abolition plot; and these
cannot find an office in New York willing to insure their
property. The abolitionists were never regularly organized, and would have scarcely been able to injure the
feelings of the planters, if, in the outset, they had not
been too insignificant to attract public attention. This
evidently shows the disposition of all parties to reconcile
each other's good will, by making the utmost concessions
which are compatible with their mutual independence.

That the moral arguments in favor of the Union, to
which I have already alluded in the eleventh chapter, and
the dread of the calamities which would result from its
dissolution, are daily more engrossing the public mind, is
a fact beyond the possibility of doubt or controversy. The
Americans speak of the probability of such an event, but
still use every means to prevent its occurrence : they are
aware of the danger, and provide for an early remedy.
The conversation of southerners turns seldom on the subject; but at the north it is a common topic but too often
discussed before strangers   There are men who are so
palsied by the approach of dangers, that their very fears

accelerate the unfortunate events which they dread : but the Union of America rests on a broader basis than mere individual speculation; it is founded on the material, moral, and political interests of the people ; the people understand these interests, and are at liberty to follow their own judgment.

There is yet another peculiar feature of the American character which must have a strong influence on the stability of the Union.   No people in the world are more fond of magnitude and extension. An American would, in his own phraseology, think himself " *belittled* " if he were to be called a " citizen of New York " or " Pennsylvania." He must have room for expansion ; for, in his mind, he has already anticipated the possession of the whole continent.

The greatest pleasure of an inhabitant of the United States consists in sailing up and down the Mississippi, several thousand miles, without meeting an impediment to his progress.   How completely destructive to his dreams of greatness would be the thought of being arrested, half a dozen times, on his way to New Orleans, as he would pass from one state or territory into another, or received as a stranger in a land which he now calls his own.   The northerner would have to stop his locomotive in the same manner, on his way to business and amusement.   He would scarcely be able to accept an invitation to dine with a friend, without having a passport or a permit from the governors of the different states through which he would have to pass, on his proceeding to the place of rendezvous.

The idea of separation strikes most Americans not only as a political calamity, but also—as it ought to do— as an absolute and permanent degradation.   They know that they would forfeit the respect of the world, and that a *New Yorker* or *New Englander* would not command the same attention in Europe, which is now so liberally extended to an *American.*   They feel obliged to defend the Union, as they would their individual honors ; and behold in its continuance the surety of their happiness and power.

But in addition to all the moral and physical causes which act in favor of the Union, there exists amongst the

Americans, notwithstanding the frequent appearances to the contrary, a strong mutual attachment, and a love of country, which is always translated into *a love of the United States*. This feeling is the stronger between the different states, as it extends, in a measure, even to England. The Americans still love the country which gave them birth, and protected their early infancy, and of whose constitution and laws they have preserved so valuable a part. Whatever may have been their feelings at the time of resisting the British *Government*, they must still consider themselves as one and the same people with the British, and, as such, cherish a sincere affection for their brethren across the Atlantic. There may have existed a sectional feeling in New England, since her inhabitants have been repeatedly reproached with it; but it is now fast yielding to more enlarged and national views, and it was always connected with the strongest sympathies for their brethren of the south and west.

At the commencement of the revolutionary war, the state of Massachusetts was, with Virginia, the most enlightened and powerful province of all the British possessions of America. Her councils and her example animated the other states in the struggle for liberty, and she had, for a long time, the greatest influence on the deliberations of Congress. In proportion as the south, and especially the west, increased in population, the power and influence of New England diminished; but her intelligence remained, and created a sad disproportion between her moral and physical resources. The New England states, therefore, have, until lately, enjoyed the reputation of being the most aristocratic in the Union; because *it was their interest to increase the power of the Senate*, in which their moral superiority could avail, and to check, if possible, the rapid progress of universal suffrage, and the power vested in the House of Representatives; because their numerical force must diminish every year in proportion as the west becomes settled.

Each state, namely, sends two senators to Congress; but the number of representatives is in proportion to the population. The six New England states, Maine, New Hampshire, Vermont, Massachusetts, Connecticut, and Rhode Island, send together thirty-eight representatives;

of which Maine furnishes eight, New Hampshire five, Massachusetts twelve, Rhode Island two, and Connecticut six. The number of representatives from New York is thirty, that of Pennsylvania twenty-eight, and of Ohio nineteen. Ohio did not even exist in 1800, but has now more than fifty per cent. more influence in the Congress than the old colony of Massachusetts. The state of New York, which, during the revolutionary war, and immediately after, was much inferior to Massachusetts, has now alone as much influence as five of the New England states together; and Pennsylvania has nearly as much. But in the Senate the case is reversed. New England alone has twelve senators, while the large state of New York has but two. The New England states, therefore, when united, command, in the senate, six times the influence of the state of New York. This is sufficient to produce a sort of *"state-aristocracy"* which, indeed, has for a long time existed in the Senate. A small number of the whole population of the United States, or at least a minority, might, in the Senate, oppose the wishes of by far the majority of the people; while in the House of Representatives, the masses decide in a national manner, independent of states and local interests. In the House of Representatives the New England states must daily lose more and more of their influence, which must eventually be almost entirely absorbed by the growing west; but in the Senate, her interests will yet, for a long time, be fully and ably represented. A number of English writers have accounted for this species of state-aristocracy, by asserting that the superior education of the people of New England must naturally make them Tories; but I have never seen in the toryism of New England, any thing but a very clear perception of their own political, commercial and manufacturing interests.

But these feelings of the inhabitants of the eastern states, which may sometimes influence their political proceedings, are far from destroying their amicable relations with the south and west. The western states moreover, have been explored and settled, principally, by emigrants from New England, who will always cherish a warm affection for "the land of the pilgrims," though

34*

their political feelings may become changed with the
circumstances of their position.

Nothing, indeed, is more common in the United States,
than to hear the people of the north entertain their guests
with the severest criticism on the manners and habits of
the south. But if a foreigner join in the controversy, he
will soon be avoided, and the offence be considered as
national. In the same manner, one may hear the southerners indulge themselves in sarcasms at the north ; but
it would be exceedingly unguarded in a stranger to imitate so dangerous an example, as the interference would
always be followed by a total exclusion from society.
The Americans often quarrel with each other, but no
sooner is any portion of them attacked by a stranger,
than they are all united, and ready to oppose him as
citizens of one and the same country.

The same is the case with the different political parties. An Englishman will often be astonished with the
ultra-tory speeches of American politicians, and at their
great veneration for kings and princes, expressed sometimes, in terms of more slavish obedience than he would
be able to hear in any part of Europe ; but he is mistaken
if he believes one half of them to express their real sentiments. The Americans frequently manifest their utter
contempt for democracy, mob-government, &c.; but no
sooner will any one attack the constitution of the United
States, the wisdom of their statesmen and legislators, the
happy influence of republican institutions on the general
information and prosperity of the people, than they will
oppose him with all the vehemence and enthusiasm of
which they are capable ; and develope, in the course of
their arguments, those essential principles of radicalism,
which they pretend to despise in others.

Their contempt for democracy, it will be perceived, is
purely personal; they do not like the *men*, but they are
sincerely attached to the *principles* of a democratic government ; and their spurious respect for personal distinctions is always based on a proper regard for the superiority of their own qualifications. They may bow to
kings and nobles, and even express a wish of conjuring
them up in their own country ; but it is the moral and
physical impossibility of realising such an event, which

causes such heedless expressions. Nothing could be more *mal à propos*, than a sudden gratification of their desire; which would place them precisely in the same predicament, as the unfortunate man with the three wishes in the fairy tale.

The same I have noticed with the democrats. They will do all in their power to deprive their antagonists of political influence, and, like their opponents, will not always be particularly nice in the choice of their weapons; but if any stranger presume to join them, they are always ready to defend the character, intelligence and even patriotism of their political foes. I remember, particularly on one occasion, to have expressed an opinion with regard to the qualifications of a certain statesman, precisely the same which the gentleman whom I addressed had been in the habit of publishing for many years. I did this merely to learn his sentiments on the subject, and was therefore not a little surprised to hear him qualify and explain them entirely to the advantage of his antagonist ; whose talents, ingenuity and honor he eulogised in a manner which prevented me effectually from making any further remarks. " You are right in principle," added he, " but you do not understand the working of it. You are yet a stranger to the feelings of the community. You are a *foreigner*."

It is, in fact, very dangerous, for persons who intend residing in the United States, to attack any one of their institutions or public men, even in presence of those who oppose them. The Americans are very sensitive with regard to every thing belonging to them as a nation ; and a person excluded from society in one part of the country, will not easily obtain admission to it in another. If there be any thing really striking in the national feelings of Americans, it is their remarkable unanimity on all important questions of state, and a community of sentiments and feelings, in a country so diversified in soil and climate.

As one of the causes which must eventually destroy the government, and the Union of the states, many political writers assign the growing spirit of democracy, and the principle of universal suffrage, introduced in most of the states. I must confess I look upon democracy, as it exists in the United States, as a means of *preserving* peace and the Union ; and would sooner trust the safety of the state to the large majority of the American people, than to any faction ever so much enlightened and skilled in the art of government. The origin, manners, and habits of Americans are democratic, and nothing short of a pure democracy could have ever contented them. Under any other form of government they would necessarily approach a revolution ; but, settled into a democracy, the power is placed at its fountain, and there can be no misconstruction as to its origin or application. As long as the people, for whom government is instituted, continue to rule, no faction will dare show its head : when the people cease to rule, then will commence the intrigues of parties ; not before.

At the present moment, the majority govern with a supremacy, and a submission on the part of the minority, which inspires universal faith in the government ; by making it strong without and capable of upholding the law within. Anarchy is the bugbear with which the enlightened opposition endeavor to frighten the supporters of democracy ; but the increased facilities of credit, and the amount of banking operations and speculations in western lands, afford the clearest proof of their implicit confidence in the strength and efficiency of the government, to protect liberty, life and property. The government of the United States was, in the first instance, established on the broadest and most liberal basis. Democracy, in its widest sense, was contained in the very letter of the constitution, and in the declaration of independence. But it was not a mob which was introduced into power,—for that never existed in America ; it was the people at large, who had achieved their liberation. As the resources of the United States became more and more developed, a class of wealthy citizens sprung up, who, dreading the consequences of a democracy, or rather anarchy, as it then existed in France, intended to seize upon the government as it then was, and prevent the masses from participating in it, as an uncontrolled sovereign power. I do not mean to say that their motives were necessarily bad : they may have been actuated by patriotism, and a sincere desire of promoting the public good; yet it is but natural to suppose that the usual share of vanity, which falls to every man's lot, may have induced them to consider *themselves* as the best persons in whom to repose public trust, without that scrupulous regard for the qualifications of others, which a love of justice, and a disinterested attachment to their country might have required.

They commenced, in the first place, with the Senate, which represents the states, and not directly the people. They constantly endeavor to increase its power, and to diminish that of the representatives. I have before remarked that New England, in particular, was so situated as to have most to gain from such a measure; while, on the other hand, she had most to dread from an increase of popular power. But the democratic spirit of the people soon overthrew all the sagacious doctrines of a "strong," "concentrated," "enlightened" government, which "should have the power of acting on the people," and, in case of resistance, bring them to a proper understanding of their own interests, "of which the people themselves are never competent judges."

The unfortunate events of the French revolution seemed to offer a sufficient apology for the political zeal with which, at an early period of the history of the American republic, democratic opinions and doctrines were combatted. But the circumstances of the two countries had nothing in common with each other. The Americans in establishing a democracy, *avoided* a revolution; the French had to *create* one; at least a moral one; for the minds of the people were not prepared for it. The Americans had *accomplished* their object, and were only insuring to themselves the permanent and quiet possession of their acquired rights; the French were *fighting* for them with foreign and internal foes. The Americans had always been freemen, from the earliest establishment of their colonies; the French had been slaves previous to the revolution of 1789. In America, equality was to be *preserved* by *preventing* one class from arrogating to themselves certain exclusive privileges, which might have enabled them to domineer over the others; in France men who *possessed* power were to be divested of it, and *reduced* to an equality with the rest.

Democracy, in America, has always had justice in its favor. It was the democratic spirit of America which prevented the introduction of titled distinctions into the colonies ; it was the democratic spirit of the country, which at an early period resisted the unjust pretensions of the British government ; and it was the spirit of democracy which finally achieved the independence. The democrats, since the revolution, never deprived any party of their lawful power or property ; they did not even wish to effect a change ; but they desired to retain their public servants no longer than they chose or thought consistent with their own safety ; and appointed others in their stead who were equally men of their own choice, and the representatives of public opinion. They knew admirably well that a long exercise of power, must finally identify the power with the incumbent, and were, therefore, exceedingly anxious to remind their rulers, as often as possible, of the fact that the fee-simple is in them, and that no other party in the state possesses sovereign power. They were instinctively impressed with the truth of Livy " *Libertatis magna custodia est, si magna imperia esse non sines, et temporis modus imponatur;* " and laid it down as a maxim, that rotation in office is the only safeguard of republican institutions.

All this was contained in the very charter of the country ; and the opposers of democracy in America, if they wish to remain consequent in their arguments, must retrace their steps, and censure the first acts of the colonial assemblies, which clashed with the decrees of the royal governors. Nor would this suffice. They would have to go back to the history of Britain ; and condemn the fathers of their country, for emigrating to the shores of New England.

The present administration has, more than any previous one, carried out the principles of pure democracy. The federal (state) party was gradually dying away, when at once an opportunity presented itself, of reviving its ancient doctrines, by the forming of a new party which called itself " national republican." But this being in turn defeated by the uncompromising spirit of democracy, a new name was invented to rally its scattered fragments, and accordingly, they assumed the ingenious name of "whigs," while they stigmatised the democrats as "tories," an appellation which never sounded very grateful to American ears.

To describe the various principles embraced or professed by these parties, would be to repeat a twice-told tale. Those of the democratic party have never seriously altered, from the commencement of the revolution to the present day ; and consisted in making every power of the state immediately dependent on the people. Those of the federalists, national republicans, and modern whigs, have occasionally undergone an apparent change. The party were careful to avoid general opposition, abandoned, occasionally, some of their most obnoxious doctrines—at least for a time, until they should have an opportunity of rising once more into power—and sailed, when prudence required it, under false colors. But with all the inclinations and variations of their political compass, the point they were always endeavoring to make, was to confide power to comparatively few, and to deprive the masses of the privilege of voting. They take it as a political axiom that the people can never govern themselves ; because the people are never sufficiently enlightened for that purpose ; and yet they expect that the people, who now possess the power, will have sufficient good sense voluntarily to surrender it to them ; and to appoint them trustees of the wealth, wisdom, and progress of the nation.

The federal party deny that all men are born "free and equal,"—the very words used in the American declaration of independence,—and yet, in their arguments, will adduce the example of Greece, Rome, England and France, and maintain that one nation is exactly like another, because *human nature* is everywhere the same. They thus admit that their own does not differ from that of the rest of mankind ; but that *circumstances* have elevated them to a proud eminence over their fellow-creatures. They are, in fact, *admirably fit to govern*, and this is a sufficient reason for them to *claim* the government ; and to deride those, who from sheer ignorance, are continuing to rule themselves and their antagonists, when they might resign the irksome task to the more intelligent and learned. The federal party have studied the art of government, and reduced it to a science. They can prove

" by *a* plus *b*, divided by *z*; that the sheep must be red, and die with the small-pox," * when their ignorant opponents would never know more than that it was a sheep. The sum and substance of their argument is this. The people must be led in order to prevent them from taking a wrong direction, or from remaining too far behind. In order to lead them, it is, of course, necessary, that some citizens (always the enlightened and scientific) should be placed at the head, with sufficient power to compel the rest to follow. All this is evidently for the good of the people, which the people themselves do not know. But the people unfortunately wish to remain judges of their own good, and never like *to have the head too far removed from the body.* This is in truth all the difference of opinion which exists between the present parties in the United States, though a great deal of learning has been exhausted, by Mr. Hamilton and others, to account scientifically for the political schism.

Whoever has been an impartial observer of the Americans, will have come to the conclusion that no other form of government, save a pure democracy, could have ever insured their freedom, or satisfied their love of liberty; and that every attempt to introduce aristocratic institutions into their country, must necessarily rouse the opposition and indignation of the people. De Tocqueville observes that at the present period, the nations of Europe have no other alternative than to choose between a democracy and an absolute despotism ; but he might *à fortiori* apply the same doctrine to the Americans. Without believing with De Tocqueville that the laws of a democracy must necessarily be imperfect, but, on the contrary, convinced that they must always benefit the majority or be soon abrogated, I am fully persuaded of the correctness of the remainder of his argument, and especially of the truth of his remarks on the spirit of family.† He ap-

---

* Voltaire's *Candide.*

† " *Mais de nos jours où toutes les classes achévent de se confondre, où l'individu disparait de plus en plus dans la foule, et se perd aisément au milieu de l'obscurité commune, aujourd'hui que l'honneur monarchique ayant presque perdu son empire sans être remplacé par la vertu, rien ne soutient plus l'homme au dessus de lui-même, qui peut dire où s'arrêteraient les exigences du pouvoir et les complaisances de la faiblesse ?*

plies this part of his argument chiefly to the condition of
France ; but how much more must it hold with regard to
the United States ? If hereditary distinctions have, in a
manner, been abolished in France, where still all their
trappings and titles are left, they have never existed in
America ; and the law of primogeniture was always opposed to the manners and customs of the people. It
hardly ever takes more than two or three generations to
reduce the wealthiest families in the United States, in
point of fortune, to an equality with the industrious classes ; and in the ordinary course of nature genius is not
hereditary. The Americans, therefore, are not apt to
form attachments to certain families, who have no power
of rewarding their fidelity ; and the road to honor and
distinction being open to all, view with peculiar jealousy
any attempt at elevation resting on ancestral pretensions.

Aristocracy, in America, must first be created, before
it can exercise its influence ; but all the institutions of the
country are totally opposed to its birth.

Nothing indeed is more common, than to hear Americans themselves aver that " there is a great deal of aristocracy in their country, of which Europeans, generally,

" *Tant qu'a duré l'esprit de famille, l'homme qui luttait contre la tyran-
nie n'était jamais seul ; il trouvait autour de lui des cliens, des amis héré-
ditaires, des proches. Et cet appui lui eût-il manqué il se sentait encore
soutenu par ses aieux et animé par ses descendans. Mais quand le patri-
moine se divise, et quand en peu d'années les races se confondent, où placer
l'esprit de famille ?*"

*   *   *   *

" *Ceci ne mérite-t-il pas qu'on y songe ? Si les hommes devaient arriver,
en effet à ce point qu'il fallût les rendre tous libres ou tous esclaves, tous
égaux en droits ou tous privés de droits ? Si ceux qui gouvernent les
sociétés en étaient reduits à cette alternative d'élever graduellement la
foule jusqu' à eux, ou de laisser tomber tous les citoyens au dessous du
niveau de l'humanité n'en serait ce pas assez pour vaincre bien des doutes,
rassurer bien des consciences, et préparer chacun à faire aisément de
grands sacrifices ?*"

*   *   *   *

" *Les volontés de la démocratie sont changeantes, ses agens grossiers ;
ses lois imparfaites. Je l'accorde. Mais s'il était vrais que bientôt il ne
dût exister aucun intermédiaire entre l'empire de la démocratie et le joug
d'un seul, ne devrions nous pas plutôt tendre vers l'un que nous soumettre
volontairement à l'autre ? Et s'il fallait enfin en arriver à une complète
égalité ne voudrait-il pas mieux se laisser niveller par la liberté que par
un despote ?*"—Tocqueville de la Démocratie en Amérique.

35

are entirely unaware." Now I have remained nearly fifteen years in the United States ; but I have never been
able to discover this aristocracy, nor its trappings, power, influence, or worshippers. I have, assuredly, known
a variety of fashionable coteries, — at least, what in
America would be called fashionable,—composed of
highly respectable merchants, literary and professional
men, politicians and others, who, it was evident, considered themselves the nobility and gentry of the land;
but they never had the courage of avowing their sentiments and pretensions in public ; and have, of late, been
as much excluded from the government of the country, as
they avoided being confounded with the rest of their fellow-citizens. On the other hand, I have had an opportunity of observing a class of society, again composed of
highly respectable merchants, literary and professional
men, politicians and others, who never exhibited the least
symptoms of imaginary superiority over their countrymen, but always acknowledged themselves to be public
servants, paid and provided for by the people, and who,
in fact, possessed considerable more power and influence
than their aristocratic neighbors with the exclusive sentiments. One party was always dreaming of influence
and distinction, the other actually possessed them. This
is all the difference I have ever known between the aristocracy and democracy of America.

Universal suffrage has been decried as leading to anarchy, and thence to despotism. General Jackson had already been represented as the future dictator of the republic. How have these predictions been verified? The
democratic party have developed more union and strength
than any previous one in power. They have reconciled
the south with the north, and preserved the integrity of
the Union. They have in every instance upheld the law
and subjected states and individuals to the proper authority of Congress. They have, at the same time, abstained from any undue and unconstitutional interference
with the internal regulations of the states, and procured
justice for all that were injured. They have made the
government respected abroad, and obliged even the most
powerful nations to preserve peace and good faith with
the United States. In short, they defeated their antago-

nists at home and abroad, and inspired universal confidence in the safety and stability of American institutions.

And what has become of the dictator ? He is indeed yet the idol of the people whose interests he endeavored to protect by every act of his military and political life; but he is retiring from office, as all his predecessors, with no other personal gratification than the affections of America, and the admiration of Europe. He will leave to his successor the example of his virtue, and a government established on liberty and justice.

Democratic institutions, as they exist in America, are without a precedent in history. The ancients never dreamed of a government similar to that of the United States; and its very existence was precluded by the ignorance of the masses, and the absence of a periodical press. Never, before, have the people at large participated in, or assumed, the government of a state. All the arguments in the world in favor or against democracy must, therefore, remain conjectures till time shall have solved the problem. The question, in America, is no longer *whether democracy is to be established,* but *whether it is to be changed.* It exists there already, and cannot be abolished without a most dangerous and violent revolution. The tories are the revolutionists in America: the democrats are the conservatives, and adhere to the government. The point at issue is, whether the latter are to give up a form of government under which they have prospered, and made such immense improvements, merely because doubts are entertained as to the possibility of retaining it forever?—whether they shall surrender a power, which once departed from them will never return to its source, and to obtain which they would have to make new and additional sacrifices ?

The face of the world is changed; why should the old forms of government be the only ones adapted to its new character? The people have acquired information and power; why should they not use them in the establishment of governments, when they can do so without committing an act of injustice to others ? Democracy in America, is a *legitimate* and *historical* form of government, and does not clash with the established manners and customs of the country. The most perfect despotism—

that of China—has lasted for thousands of years; why should liberty alone be forever banished from the earth? If tyranny could find such a basis, should justice be built in the air? I much rather believe that the liberty of the ancients was not established on a basis *sufficiently large* to withstand the attacks of factions, and that the overthrow of their republics was chiefly owing to the *little* power which was vested in the majority of the people. A whole nation is seldom deceived about her true interests, and cannot be bribed by a party. The people may make faults, but they have always the power of repairing them, and where they have a share in the government, are identified with its continuance and progress. If it be true that "universal history contains the judgment of the world," [*] we must consider the downfall of Rome as the punishment of its political crimes, and may hope for the freedom of America as long as her people shall be worthy of it.

Of the greatest importance to the progress of the United States, is the present contest of the Texians with the republic of Mexico. The Americans were not bound to assist their brethren, who had quitted their country; yet the enormous sums, and the number of volunteers which, since the commencement of the war, have been sent from the United States to assist those bold adventurers, are totally incommensurate with the American interests in that province. It was the sympathy of countrymen, and of political friends, which procured money and troops for the Texians, and enabled them to repel the attacks of their enemies.

I never, from the commencement of hostilities, believed that the Mexicans would be able to reconquer their territory, and I certainly do not think so now; but I am far from considering the annexation of Texas to the United States in the light of many politicians, who view in it only the subject of future quarrels. I think it rather favorable to the continuance of the Union, than threatening to change its principles. The New England and northern states, generally, will at first lose a portion of their political influence; but they will recover it again in

[*] " Die Weltgeschichte ist das Weltgericht."—*Schiller.*

the future, enabling the south in the mean time to reassume its wonted influence in Congress. The territory of Texas may easily be divided into three or four independent states, which, for a period, would insure a majority of southern members in the Senate and House of Representatives. But I do not apprehend that the power of the south can ever be so far increased, as to endanger the safety of the north. At present, the southern states are jealous of a possible interference of the north with the institution of slavery. They are morbidly sensitive on this subject, because they feel that they are, in a measure, at the mercy of the north, who might offend them without dreading their revenge. By the accession of Texas, they will be able to defend themselves, and establish a system of equality, which cannot but be productive of greater harmony and friendship.

No passion is so destructive to a sincere attachment as fear; nothing so opposed to a mutual good understanding as a mind filled with suspicion. These obstacles to friendship can only be avoided by a greater equality of position, which shall render it impossible for one party to injure and oppress the other. Under such circumstances, an hundred concessions will be made, which the weaker would have refused from jealousy, and which, on the part of the stronger, would have had the appearance of condescension. Thus, the southern states of America may hereafter abolish slavery; but they will not do so as long as the measure appears to be forced upon them; and until they have the means of protecting themselves against the possible encroachments of the blacks. The more powerful the district is which becomes thus united by the same interests, the less will they apprehend from their slaves and the northern agitators; the more charitable therefore will they be in their treatment of their negroes, and the more ready to listen to the voice of humanity.

There is no reason to believe that the admission of Texas into the Union will create a distinct interest, opposed to that of the northern and western states. The north, and a portion of the west, (those states which increase more rapidly than all the rest,) have no material interest which could be endangered by the continuance

35*

of slavery; and the question therefore, can only be one of political eminence. But whatever additional power the south may, in this manner, acquire, must finally be overbalanced by the much more rapid increase of the white population in the western states, and can therefore only serve to re-establish, for a limited period, the position which the south held immediately after the establishment of peace. Instead of stirring up the question of slavery, with a view to excite prejudices which, in course of time, may endanger the Union, I am inclined to believe it will cause the subject to sleep—each party reposing on its own strength, until, in the natural course of events, the power of the north will have again surpassed that of the south, rendering its intentions and motives a fresh matter of suspicion. So far then from causing a separation, the annexation of Texas will be a promoter of harmony and friendship, and allay those prejudices which the ill-guided zeal of a few individuals has excited in the minds of the southerners.

Neither will the financial condition of the southern and northern states be altered by the new accumulation of territory. The soil of Texas is favorable to the cultivation of cotton, and its climate and position, in other respects, similar to those of the southern states. Texas, therefore, can only be a competitor of the south, and perhaps depress the price of cotton ; but to the north it will open an additional market for manufactures, and new means of promoting navigation and commerce. Neither will the condition of the west undergo a material change, except for the better. The inhabitants of Texas will become consumers of the western produce, without the least probability of competing with it in other markets ; and the west, enriched by its new customers, will furnish additional employment to the industry and enterprise of the north. In every direction it must increase the prosperity of the country, and enlarge the stake which the Americans have in the Union. The southern states will not be individually benefited, but their rights and privileges, *as a whole*, will receive an additional support. The northern states, on the contrary, will receive no such addition; but they are far from standing in need of it, and will be satisfied with the pecuniary advantages, which they must assuredly derive from so large an accession to their markets.

Nor will Texas be exclusively peopled by southerners. No sooner will the independence of Texas be acknowledged, and the state itself be admitted into the Union, than thousands of the most active and enterprising population of the north, and especially New Englanders, will proceed thither in quest of happiness and fortune. Texas will not represent the prejudices of a particular section, but the intelligence and industry of every part of the United States. It will derive its capital from the north ; but it must, in time, benefit every section of the country ; though its geographical position must render it an appendage to the southern and western states. In less than ten years, lines of communication will be established, from the centre of the province to all the large commercial emporiums of the United States ; and a journey from New York to Texas will be accomplished with more ease, than, twenty years ago, a trip from Washington to Boston. Every state will have a portion of its capital invested in Texas, and be united to it by ties of consanguinity and friendship. The Texians will, in every respect, be situated like the inhabitants of any other state in the Union ; but their position to Mexico will in all probability remain hostile. It is difficult to foretell to what extent the contempt for the Spanish race, and the rapid augmentation of their own strength, will finally lead the Americans; but in a further contest with Mexico the victory cannot be doubtful. The Mexicans bear to the United States very nearly the same relation as the American Indians : there is scarcely more union and discipline amongst them, though considerably less energy and bravery.

The Mexicans, it is highly probable, will have to pay the penalty of their inertness, and in course of time become subject to their more industrious and enterprising neighbors. The whole number of pure Spaniards in Meoico does not amount to one million, which, in less than ten years, will scarcely be a power sufficient to withstand the encroachments of the western settlers alone. Opposed to the United States, Mexico is but a power of the second or third rank, incapable of improving the advantages of its position, and too much divided in itself, ever to oppose an energetic force to a continental enemy. The incalculable resources of the Mexican soil, its fine climate, its inexhaustible mines, and the superiority of its geographical position, with excellent ports on the Pacific, will hold out sufficient temptations to the Americans, to venture fresh settlements on its territory, or to embroil the two nations in war ; until, finally, the United States will extend from the river St. Lawrence to the isthmus of Panamas ; and from the Atlantic to the Pacific ocean.

Neither will the progress of the Americans be arrested there. If they remain united, and the South American states do not increase in power, but, on the contrary, become more and more enfeebled by internal divisions and the growing oppositions of the Indians, the latter must, directly or indirectly, be brought to acknowledge the superiority of the United States. Already is the American influence on those countries an object of jealousy with its impotent patriots ; but the commencement being once made with Mexico, the conquest of all the remaining American states, and the final occupation of the whole continent by the Anglo-Saxon race, would be comparatively easy. Mexico is the only one of those states which has a sufficient land force to resist an enemy.

The settlements of the Portuguese in Brazil, and those of the Spaniards in Buenos Ayres, never extended into the interior of the country ; with whose wealth, resources, and facilities of navigation they are far less acquainted than the people of the United States. Their whole power is confined to the sea-coast, defended by a few frigates and minor ships of war, which, in the English or American navy, would scarcely be pronounced sea-worthy, and commanded, for the most part, in a manner equal to the fitting-out of the vessels. The whole white population of Brazil does not, probably, surpass five or six hundred thousand ; the rest are persons of color and Europeans. These, even at the present moment, could not oppose the execution of any ambitious design on the part of the United States, which could only be checked by an active interference of the European powers. The fate of these states depends chiefly on the assistance of England ; without which they may, at any time, become annexed to the United States, or reduced to

American colonies. Neither does there appear to be any other prospect for the tranquillity and welfare of those countries, than their being annexed to the United States. Florida and Louisiana have in this manner become wealthy; Texas will soon follow their example; Mexico itself will not be able to avoid its fate; and should we hope for the independence of the minor states ?

One step towards the final subjection of the whole American continent, was made by the people of the Spanish provinces themselves, in adopting the constitution of the United States, or some similar fundamental law, which they will never be able fully to carry into execution, until they shall have mixed with the American race, and acquired its customs and manners. By this means Louisiana has become reformed, and is now essentially an American state. We may even without great stretch of imagination suppose the case in which the South American republics themselves may seek the protection of the United States, and prefer being annexed to a powerful and free nation, to being exposed to the attacks of the Indians, and the cruelty and rapacity of their own military chieftains. The different powers of Europe always quarrelled for the possession of the South American continent. Brazil, especially with its diamond mines, excited their cupidity and jealousy ; why should not the descendants of those powers conclude the strife, by uniting under one and the same government ? When the United States shall have risen to that political eminence, which will enable them to make war and dictate peace, the powers of Europe may themselves be at war with each other, and be obliged to submit to such an unexpected aggrandisement.

The United States hold a position, with regard to America, somewhat similar to that which England occupies in reference to Europe. They are the first and only maritime nation of the new world ; but, at the same time, join to it the advantages of a huge continental power, occupying nearly one third of the whole continent. They are, therefore, with regard to America, what France and England, joined, would be in opposition to the rest of Europe ; only that their antagonists are less intelligent, less numerous, and by far less martially inclined than the northern powers of Europe. The only line of communication between the large settlements on the coast of Brazil is by sea ; without which the whole country would not have a single *point d'appui*. But the navy of the United States is alone more numerous than the whole naval force of the South American and Mexican states ; and the private citizens—especially the western hunters—are better soldiers than the most experienced Brazilian troops of the line. The whole remainder of the American continent does not possess such naval advantages as the United States. Three fourths of all the navigation of South America are already absorbed by United States' vessels ; and, under these circumstances, it is not probable that any of these provinces will ever become a strong maritime power. The fate of the South American republics depends on the mercy of the United States ; and unless they succeed in establishing regular governments, they may have to implore their assistance to be saved from inevitable destruction.

And is it not for the interest of the human race, that those beautiful countries should be settled and governed by a different people from those who are now vegetating in them, without advancing one step in any of the useful arts and sciences ? Is it not desirable that the interior of the South American continent should be explored, and its treasures employed in ameliorating the condition of the human family ? Are the luxuriant and healthy provinces of Brazil, and the valley of the La Plata never to yield their produce to civilised nations ; and are industry and commerce to be forever banished from one half of the American continent ? The nations who are now inhabiting those climes are scarcely capable of keeping possession of the little territory their European ancestors have conquered, and are daily degenerating in habits and principles. Their governments are insufficient to protect either life or property ; and they are equally destitute of the means of improving them. Their finances are in the most miserable condition, and their credit entirely annihilated. The number of inhabitants, too, is far from increasing in a ratio similar to that of the United States ; and their most active citizens are Indians and Mulattos. I do not wish to overcharge this picture : those who are acquainted with the situation and government of South America will readily admit the truth of my statement, to which I would only add that the condition of the Spanish and Portuguese settlements are best described, by calling them exactly the reverse of the peace and prosperity of the United States. Mexico was the only power which could have opposed the progress of America. After her humiliation and dismemberment, the United States will be left without a rival. They may now blockade the whole American continent, as England did Europe in the war against Napoleon; and the settlements being confined to the coast, reduce them with little opposition.

If Europe should ever become jealous of America, it would not be of her physical force, but of the moral energy which her citizens are wont to develope, wherever they form settlements. It is not so much the *possession* of Mexico, but what the Americans would make of it, in the course of fifty years, which would cause fears and apprehensions in Europe. When America shall once be firmly established between two oceans, commanding the Gulf of Mexico and the Pacific ocean, she will occupy the centre of the world; while Europe will act as from a corner. The historical theatre will be changed, and the centre of civilisation removed to the valley of the Mississippi.

The centre of America is giving birth to a new race of beings, more powerful and athletic than the inhabitants of the eastern coast, and more reckless of dangers than any which the world has seen. Love of liberty and adventure are their strongest passions, and they combine the intelligence of Europeans, with the physical advantages of savages. They must eventually penetrate to the borders of the Pacific, where a new life must spring up, different from that which the reflection of European civilisation has created on the shores of the Atlantic, and still more congenial with the most enlarged principle of freedom. The coast of the Pacific ocean enjoys a better and healthier climate than that of the eastern states, and is, perhaps, equally fertile. A thousand new sources of wealth will at once be opened to those settlers; and their adventurous spirit will soon make the ocean its scene of action.

From the western coast of America incursions may be made on the whole Indian archipelago, and on the coast of Asia itself. If America should ever become a conquering nation, the wealth of India would be more tempting than that of Europe, and equally near at hand. Who knows but what this hardy race of " half horse and half alligator " may renew the adventures of the Argonauts, but change the scene from Colchis to Japan and China? We have known a handful of Normans conquer all Italy and the most valuable part of France; why should not a nation like the Americans, eminently skilful and daring at sea, and possessed of the courage and energy of those western settlers, be able to make an impression on the civilised barbarians who inhabit the eastern extremities of Asia? At present, the idea is too distant to excite the least apprehensions, and it may perhaps be considered preposterous; but then no people ever had such a passion for emigration and expansion; and it is therefore not to be supposed that the sea will arrest their progress. Like every other commercial nation, the Americans will have their colonies, and revive the history of England in the new world. When the continent shall be settled, they will conquer and subdue the nearest islands, to which their naval genius will invite them; and, having succeeded in that, they may venture themselves on the neighboring continent.

As far as our knowledge of history extends, the inhabitants of our globe have, with but very few exceptions, travelled westward. It is even probable, and has lately been maintained by a number of writers, that Asia received its first population from the western shores of America. Now, why should the most enterprising nation on earth—the Anglo-Americans—arrest this general motion of the human race, and confine themselves to their own borders? And this, at an age where distances are annihilated by steam, and the terrors of the ocean disarmed by the skill of the mariner? The modern essence of European and American civilisation is *motion*, communicated by inspiring life into the masses. That of the Asiatics consists in a quiet contemplation of the past, and a calm resignation to the future. The civilisation and power of the Americans, when they shall have arrived on the shores of the Pacific, will have acquired a fearful momentum, to which the nations of the East will have nothing to oppose but inert masses.

Europe has nothing to apprehend from the Americans. Their march is westward; and they will, in their course, sooner reach China, than, by a retrograde motion, the land of their own sires. With regard to the powers of Europe, the United States will, for a long time yet, act on the defensive; but westward they will expand, and assume the air of dictators. Besides, Europe will have little to tempt the Americans, their own country being richer and more fertile, and their commercial interests opposed to a maritime war. But the East will hold out different allurements, and greater probabilities of conquest. The Americans may proceed to the very coast of China, and prevail by superior intelligence. A small naval force would be sufficient to reduce the islands, and the population of these might furnish the warriors for the continent.

As long as the Americans shall follow their favorite inclination of proceeding westward—as long as their country shall afford scope for industry and enterprise—as long as they shall be able to discover new sources of wealth and employment, either within or without their country, they will preserve the Union, which protects most effectually their own interests, and is the only means of their arriving at greatness and power. The United States are yet in their infancy; and it would be an anomaly in history, to see a young and healthful nation perish, before it has reached the climax of its power.

England must always be a natural ally of America, both nations being of the same origin, and the institutions and genius of the one, being the elements of greatness in the other. Whatever prejudices there may yet exist between them, must yield to the soothing influence of time: the injuries will be forgotten, the lasting benefits remembered, and the people of both countries—who never were opposed to each other—will look upon each other as children of one and the same family. Why should it be otherwise? Why should political and geographical limits separate two nations so intimately linked to each other by consanguinity, language, customs, manners, and laws?

Is not every new settlement in America an offspring of British genius? And are the British not invited to enjoy and partake of its benefits? Are the British excluded from America? Does British capital not find its way to the far west? And are the inhabitants of the American wilderness not consumers of British manufactures? Does the expanding greatness of America not re-act favorably on England? Is not every new village in America a new market for British productions?

An Englishman may travel all over Europe and Asia, and be a stranger in every country; but if he proceed to the west, he will recognise a whole world as his home. If he enter a private dwelling, he will behold the same domestic fireside; in the streets the hum of business will be English; at the halls of justice, he will hear the judges expound the laws of his country; at the theatres, English actors will perform English plays; and on the Sabbath, the sanctified stillness of the day will again be a picture of England. What, then, is America, but England, reflected in huge proportions, from a spherical mirror? What is England, but the vastness of American genius, concentrated and condensed to a focus?

The English must see themselves perpetuated in America; while America possesses in the mother country a sage mentor, whose political and legislative experience is still directing her progress. The only natural feeling between England and America is friendship; every other is barbarous, mean, unworthy of either nation, and destructive to the interests of both. Enmity between England and America cannot advantage either country. America, though separated from England, still lends to English influence throughout the world; Englaud, though no longer ruling over America, is still her guide and instructer; and the historian, who shall write the future history of America, will find his data in England.

The progress of America reflects but the glory of England; all the power she acquires, extends the moral empire of England: every page of American history is a valuable supplement to that of England. It is the duty of the patriots of both countries, to support and uphold each other, to the utmost extent compatible with national justice; and it is a humiliating task, either for private individuals or public men, to make the foibles of the one the subject of ridicule in the other.

The English and Americans are the only two nations which are really free, and their liberties are based on the same law. United, they are sufficient to withstand the world : why should they be envious of each other's greatness ?

There can be no more war between England and America ; for it would be detrimental to the liberties of both, and interfere with their national advancement. The most formidable power of America need not excite apprehensions in England ; for it is travelling westward —receding from Europe—and may progress for centuries, before it can come in contact with the most remote part of the British empire. In the same manner may the power of England increase without exciting suspicions in America. England can never endanger the safety of the United States ; but her political and moral influence may serve as a bulwark to American institutions.

It is a fortunate circumstance that the British sovereign should lately have been the mediator between France and America. It is the first act of royal favor extended to the Americans for many years, and will afford a proof of the disinterested attachment of England to the future welfare and prosperity of her daughter. It will serve to soothe the angry feelings, which British statesmen and British writers have often wantonly roused in their brethren beyond the Atlantic, and be hailed as the harbinger of peace and amity between the two greatest nations in the world.

May that friendship never be interrupted ; and may the Americans and the English, instead of entertaining unworthy prejudices, cherish that mutual affection to which they are invited by the ties of consanguinity, and the regard due to their mutual perfections.